Fodor's 93 Miami & the Keys

SO-AQI-425

Reprinted from *Fodor's Florida '93*

Fodor's Travel Publications, Inc.
New York • Toronto • London • Sydney • Auckland

Fodor's Miami & the Keys

Editor: Alison Hoffman
Area Editor: Herb Hiller
Editorial Contributors: Amy Hunter, Marcy Pritchard
Creative Director: Fabrizio La Rocca
Cartographer: David Lindroth
Illustrator: Karl Tanner
Cover Photograph: Morton Beebe

Design: Vignelli Associates

Special Sales

Fodor's Travel Publications are available at special discounts for bulk purchases (100 copies or more) for sales promotions or premiums. Special editions, including personalized covers, excerpts of existing guides, and corporate imprints, can be created in large quantities for special needs. For more information write to Special Marketing, Fodor's Travel Publications, 201 E. 50th St., New York, NY 10022. Inquiries from Canada should be sent to Random House of Canada, Ltd., Marketing Department, 1265 Aerowood Dr., Mississauga, Ontario L4W 1B9. Inquiries from the United Kingdom should be sent to Fodor's Travel Publications, 20 Vauxhall Bridge Rd., London, England SW1V 2SA.

Contents

Foreword *v*

Hurricane Andrew *vi*

Highlights '93 *viii*

Fodor's Choice *x*

1 Essential Information *1*

Before You Go *2*

Tourist Information *2*
Tour Groups *2*
Package Deals for Independent Travelers *3*
Tips for British Travelers *3*
When to Go *4*
Festivals and Seasonal Events *5*
What to Pack *7*
Cash Machines *7*
Traveling with Film *8*
Car Rentals *8*
Traveling with Children *9*
Hints for Disabled Travelers *11*
Hints for Older Travelers *12*
Further Reading *13*

Arriving and Departing *14*

By Plane *14*
By Car *15*
By Train *16*
By Bus *16*

Staying in Florida *16*

Tourist Information *16*
Shopping *16*
Beaches *17*
Participant Sports *18*
Parks and Nature Preserves *21*
Dining *22*
Lodging *23*
Credit Cards *25*

2 Miami and Miami Beach *26*

3 The Everglades *97*

4 Fort Lauderdale *116*

5 Palm Beach and Palm Beach County *143*

6 The Florida Keys *177*

Index *222*

Maps

The Florida Peninsula *xiii*
The United States *xiv–xv*
World Time Zones *xvi–xvii*
Downtown Miami *36*
Miami Beach *41*
Miami, Coral Gables, and Key Biscayne *46–47*
Miami Area Dining *68–69*
Miami Area Lodging *82–83*
The Everglades and Biscayne National Parks *105*
Fort Lauderdale Area *123*
Fort Lauderdale Area Dining and Lodging *133*
Palm Beach and Palm Beach County *148*
Treasure Coast *167*
The Florida Keys *186*
Key West *193*

Foreword

Florida is one of the world's most popular tourist destinations. Visitors from far and near are attracted to the state's sandy beaches, warm and sunny climate, and fine restaurants and accommodations in and around Miami to the Keys. Our Florida writers have put together information on the widest possible range of activities, and within that range present you with selections of events and places that will be safe, worthwhile, and of good value. The descriptions we provide are just enough for you to make your own informed choices from among our selections.

We wish to express our gratitude to those who have helped with this guide, including the Florida Division of Tourism, especially Rosetta Stone Land; the Florida Department of Natural Resources, especially Mary Ann Koos; the Greater Fort Lauderdale Convention and Visitors Bureau, in particular Tim Brigham, Francine Mason, and Jennifer Meriam; Mary Louise English at the Greater Miami Convention and Visitors Bureau; the Palm Beach County Convention and Visitors Bureau, especially Jennifer Clark; Warren Zeiller with the South Dade Visitors Information Center; Richard Altman at M. Silver Associates; Stuart Newman and Associates, assuredly Jean Gomez; and Delta Airlines.

While every care has been taken to assure the accuracy of the information in this guide, the passage of time will always bring change, and, consequently, the publisher cannot accept responsibility for errors that may occur.

All prices and opening times quoted here are based on information available to us at press time. Hours and admission fees may change, however, and the prudent traveler will avoid inconvenience by calling ahead.

Fodor's wants to hear about your travel experiences, both pleasant and unpleasant. When a hotel or restaurant fails to live up to its billing, let us know, and we will investigate.

Send your letters to the editors of Fodor's Travel Publications, 201 E. 50th St., New York, NY 10022.

Hurricane Andrew

What has been referred to as "the most devastating natural disaster in American history," Hurricane Andrew hit Florida hardest in the Greater Miami area, particularly South Dade County. At press time relief efforts are under way, but the extent of permanent damage is still unkown. Hundreds of homes and businesses in Kendall, Homestead, Florida City, and Cutler Ridge were demolished, but Downtown Miami, Coral Gables, Bal Harbor, Coconut Grove, and Miami Beach (Art Deco District) were mostly spared, save for some downed trees and relatively minor destruction. Don't avoid Miami because of the hurricane's damage, but plan your itinerary judiciously: The Greater Miami Convention and Visitors Bureau (tel. 305/672–1270) and local establishments will gladly answer questions. If you'd like to make a contribution that will go toward local restoration and assist the storm's victims, write to: American Red Cross Disaster Relief Fund, Box 025230, Miami 33102–5230.

Highlights'93 and Fodor's Choice

Highlights '93

Statewide Trends Severe budget shortages in 1992 jeopardized Florida's nation-leading endangered land acquisition program, and slowed environmental reform in everything from parks maintenance to trail-improvement funding. The action has shifted to the local level and is receiving a lot of attention from volunteer groups.

In 1991 and 1992, as a manatee protection measure, 13 coastal counties in Florida imposed boat speed regulations through much of their inland waters.

Also in 1992 a new smoking law went into effect that requires restaurants with a seating capacity of 50 people or more to provide a nonsmoking section for at least 35% of their seats.

Beaches South Florida's **Bahia Honda State Recreations Area** in the Lower Keys, is still enjoying kudos after being designated among the nation's top 10 beaches by the University of Maryland's Laboratory for Coastal Research in 1991.

Cuisine South Florida is developing a **Florida-Caribbean** cuisine incorporating local fruits, vegetables, and seafood. The fare differs from that found on the islands in that it is more healthful, with lighter sauces and less meat.

Environment By 1993 a pro-government compromise should be reached with the sugar industry and with cattle ranchers and dairy farmers on the issue of **cleaning up the Everglades.** Restoration of the original course of the Kissimmee River will continue so that the river will again naturally filter out nutrients that have been steadily killing life in Lake Okeechobee. The lake has become the primary source for pollutants that flow into the Everglades.

Quickening devastation of the reef off the Florida Keys is leading to last-ditch efforts to stave off demise. The region awaits the new management plan for the Florida Keys National Marine Sanctuary, to be issued early in 1993 by the National Oceanographic and Atmospheric Administration. Meanwhile, new construction moratoriums have been mandated by the Monroe County Commission to slow growth.

Politics Miami's Hispanic Community continues to play a major role in Florida's economic and political arenas. **Little Havana** is the pillar of this community and has taken root in Miami's cultural picture.

Revitalization Fort Lauderdale, once recognized as "the" spring break destination but now touted as the "Venice of America," has initiated a beautification plan, beginning with its **Ocean Drive.** The project intends to give the city's beachfront a promenade comparable with those in Rio de Janeiro and in many Mediterranean cities. Other changes for the city include the **Discovery Center Museum of Science & Technology,** scheduled to open late in 1992, and the newly opened $3-million **Esplanade educational park,** which runs along the north bank of the New River. Linking these facilities will be **Riverwalk,** which will extend a mile along the north bank and another ½-mile on the south bank. Together, the two segments will join 10 acres of public parks and facilities.

Leading a revitalization project for West Palm Beach was the 1992 debute of the $60-million **Kravis Performing Arts Center** with the **Palm Beach Opera** and **Ballet Florida.** On its heels is a massive, nearly ½-billion-dollar Downtown/Uptown redevelopment project that will include the $25-million **Palm Beach Performing Arts Public School,** due to open in 1994. By the start of 1993, the free motorized shuttle will be transporting passengers through downtown West Palm Beach as part of continuing work on West Palm's new **Inter-Modal Transfer Facility,** also scheduled to open in 1994. The system will link local, inter-county, and inter-state rail and surface transportation systems.

Meanwhile, Miami Beach's **Art Deco District**—which suffered almost no permanent damage by Hurricane Andrew, except for some downed trees—continues to attract locals and visitors as more hotels and restaurants are restored to their historic grandeur. Scheduled to reopen for the '92–'93 season is Coral Gables's presently foreclosed **Biltmore Hotel.** Other developments in Miami's future will include extensions of the north and south sections of Miami's downtown **Metromover.** The additions will tie the system to the Omni Hotel shopping area to the north and to the international banking and legal district along Brickell Avenue to the south. Also new to this exotic metropolis are the **Florida Marlins,** its National League baseball team.

Fodor's Choice

No two people will agree on what makes a perfect vacation, but it's fun, and it can be helpful, to know what others think. Here, then, is a very personal list of Fodor's Choices. We hope you'll have a chance to experience some of them yourself while visiting the Greater Miami area.

Special Moments

Sunrise on the beach at Key Biscayne

Sunset festivals at Mallory Square in Key West

Coconut Grove Arts Festival

King Orange Jamboree Parade in Downtown Miami

Fort Lauderdale's Winterfest Holiday Boat Parade

Strolling Fort Lauderdale's Riverwalk

Cycling the Palm Beach bike trail along Lake Worth

Taste Treats

Cuban fare at Islas Canarias in Miami

Chocolate concoctions at Chef Allen's in North Miami Beach

Alligator tail at Shirttail Charlie's in Fort Lauderdale

Soft-shelled crabs in Bonaventure Resort and Spa

Fresh heart-of-palm salad at Cafe Max in Pompano Beach

Tropical fruit sorbets at La Vielle Maison in Boca Raton

Off the Beaten Track

Little Haiti in Miami

Davie Rodeo Grounds

Gumbo Limbo Nature Center in Boca Raton

Loxahatchee Wildlife Refuge in Palm Beach County

Lion Country Safari in Palm Beach County

Blowing Rocks Preserve in Martin County

After Hours

Tobacco Road in Miami

Churchill's Hideaway in Little Haiti

The Island Club on Miami Beach

Biscayne Baby in Coconut Grove

Taurus Steak House in Coconut Grove

Musician Exchange Downtown Cafe in Fort Lauderdale

Pier Top Lounge at Pier 66 Hotel & Marina in Fort Lauderdale

Doherty's in Palm Beach

Hotels

Boca Raton Resort & Club, Boca Raton (*Very Expensive*)

The Breakers, Palm Beach (*Very Expensive*)

Cheeca Lodge, Islamorada (*Very Expensive*)

Doral Resort and Country Club, Miami (*Very Expensive*)

Grand Bay Hotel, Coconut Grove (*Very Expensive*)

Hyatt Regency Coral Gables (*Very Expensive*)

Hotel Inter-Continental Miami, Miami (*Very Expensive*)

Sonesta Beach Hotel and Tennis Club, Key Biscayne (*Very Expensive*)

Turnberry Isle Yacht and Country Club, North Miami Beach (*Very Expensive*)

The Curry Mansion Inn, Key West (*Very Expensive–Expensive*)

Alexander Hotel, Miami Beach (*Expensive*)

Riverside Hotel, Fort Lauderdale (*Expensive*)

Hotel Place St. Michel, Coral Gables (*Expensive*)

Carriage House Resort Motel, Fort Lauderdale (*Moderate*)

Miami River Inn, Miami (*Moderate*)

Restaurants

Grand Cafe, Coconut Grove (*Very Expensive*)

Louie's Backyard, Key West (*Very Expensive*)

The Pavillion Grill, Miami (*Very Expensive*)

Cafe Chauveron, Miami Beach (*Expensive*)

Cafe Max, Pompano Beach (*Expensive*)

Casa Juancho, Miami (*Expensive*)

Casa Rolandi, Coral Gables (*Expensive*)

Casa Vecchia, Fort Lauderdale (*Expensive*)

Chef Allen's, North Miami Beach (*Expensive*)

The Explorers, Palm Beach (*Expensive*)

La Vieille Maison, Boca Raton (*Expensive*)

Hy-Vong Vietnamese Cuisine, Miami (*Moderate*)

Marker 88, Plantation Key (*Moderate*)

Mrs. Mac's Kitchen, Key Largo (*Inexpensive*)

Richard Accursio's Capri Restaurant, Florida City (*Moderate–Inexpensive*)

The Florida Peninsula

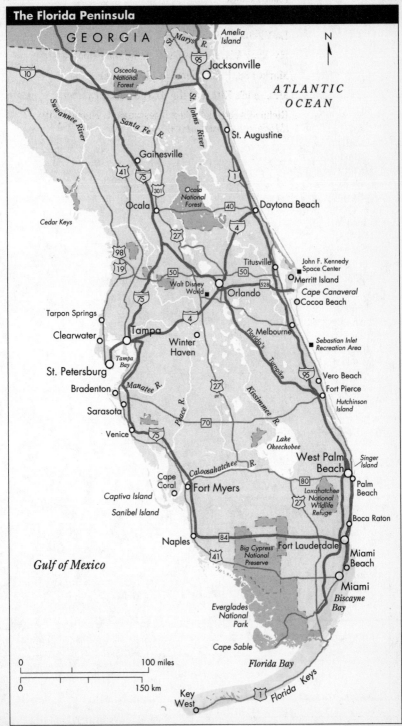

GEORGIA

ATLANTIC
OCEAN

N

Osceola
National
Forest

St. Marys R.

Amelia
Island

Jacksonville

Suwannee River

Santa Fe R.

St. Johns River

St. Augustine

Gainesville

Ocala
National
Forest

Ocala

Cedar Keys

Daytona Beach

Titusville

John F. Kennedy
Space Center

Merritt Island

Cape Canaveral

Walt Disney
World

Orlando

Cocoa Beach

Tarpon Springs

Clearwater

Tampa

Winter
Haven

Melbourne

Florida's Turnpike

Sebastian Inlet
Recreation Area

St. Petersburg

Tampa
Bay

Manatee R.

Vero Beach

Fort Pierce

Bradenton

Sarasota

Peace R.

Kissimmee R.

Hutchinson
Island

Venice

Lake
Okeechobee

West Palm
Beach

Singer
Island

Cape
Coral

Fort Myers

Captiva Island

Sanibel Island

Caloosahatchee R.

Loxahatchee
National
Wildlife
Refuge

Palm Beach

Boca Raton

Naples

Big Cypress
National
Preserve

Fort Lauderdale

Miami
Beach

Gulf of Mexico

Everglades
National
Park

Miami

Biscayne
Bay

Cape Sable

Florida Bay

0 ———— 100 miles

0 ———— 150 km

Key
West

Florida Keys

The United States

World Time Zones

MONDAY
SUNDAY

International Date Line

+12 +13   -9

-10

-11

-10

+11

+12

+11   +12 -   -11   -10   -9   -8   -7   -6   -5   -4   -3   -2

-4

-3

-4

-5   -4

-7

-5   -4

-6

-5

-5

-4   -3

-3

-3

Numbers below vertical bands relate each zone to Greenwich Mean Time (0 hrs.).
Local times frequently differ from these general indications,
as indicated by light-face numbers on map.

<table>
<tr><td>Algiers, 29</td><td>Berlin, 34</td><td>Delhi, 48</td><td>Istanbul, 40</td></tr>
<tr><td>Anchorage, 3</td><td>Bogotá, 19</td><td>Denver, 8</td><td>Jerusalem, 42</td></tr>
<tr><td>Athens, 41</td><td>Budapest, 37</td><td>Djakarta, 53</td><td>Johannesburg, 44</td></tr>
<tr><td>Auckland, 1</td><td>Buenos Aires, 24</td><td>Dublin, 26</td><td>Lima, 20</td></tr>
<tr><td>Baghdad, 46</td><td>Caracas, 22</td><td>Edmonton, 7</td><td>Lisbon, 28</td></tr>
<tr><td>Bangkok, 50</td><td>Chicago, 9</td><td>Hong Kong, 56</td><td>London (Greenwich), 27</td></tr>
<tr><td>Beijing, 54</td><td>Copenhagen, 33</td><td>Honolulu, 2</td><td>Los Angeles, 6</td></tr>
<tr><td></td><td>Dallas, 10</td><td></td><td>Madrid, 38</td></tr>
<tr><td></td><td></td><td></td><td>Manila, 57</td></tr>
</table>

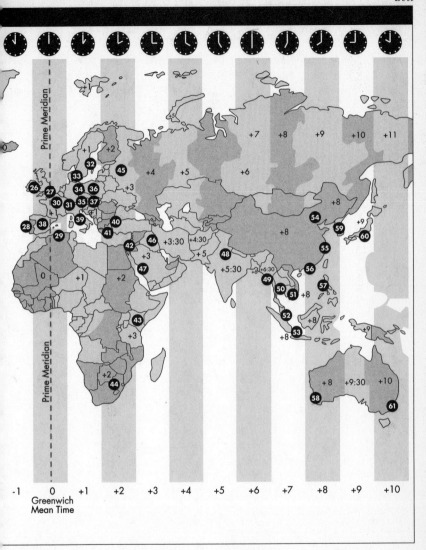

-1 0 +1 +2 +3 +4 +5 +6 +7 +8 +9 +10
Greenwich
Mean Time

Mecca, **47**	Ottawa, **14**	San Francisco, **5**	Toronto, **13**
Mexico City, **12**	Paris, **30**	Santiago, **21**	Vancouver, **4**
Miami, **18**	Perth, **58**	Seoul, **59**	Vienna, **35**
Montréal, **15**	Reykjavík, **25**	Shanghai, **55**	Warsaw, **36**
Moscow, **45**	Rio de Janeiro, **23**	Singapore, **52**	Washington, D.C., **17**
Nairobi, **43**	Rome, **39**	Stockholm, **32**	Yangon, **49**
New Orleans, **11**	Saigon (Ho Chi Minh	Sydney, **61**	Zürich, **31**
New York City, **16**	City), **51**	Tokyo, **60**	

1 Essential Information

Before You Go

Tourist Information

Contact the **Florida Division of Tourism** for information on tourist attractions and answers to questions about traveling in the state.

In Florida: 126 Van Buren St., Tallahassee 32399, tel. 904/487–1462 or 1463.

In Canada: Canadian travelers can get assistance from Travel USA in Toronto, tel. 416/595–0335.

In the United Kingdom: British travelers can get assistance from the **U.S. Travel and Tourism Administration** (USTTA–Premier House, 77 Oxford St., London W1R 1RB, tel. 071/439–4773).

For additional information, contact the regional tourist bureaus and chambers of commerce in the areas you wish to visit (*see* individual chapters for listings).

Tour Groups

If you prefer to leave the driving to someone else, consider a package tour. Although you will have to march to the beat of a tour guide's drum rather than your own, you are likely to save money on airfare, hotels, and ground transportation. For the more experienced or adventurous traveler, a variety of special-interest and independent packages are available. Listed below is a sampling of available options. Check with your travel agent or the Florida Division of Tourism (904/487–1462) for additional resources.

When considering a tour, be sure to find out exactly what expenses are included (particularly tips, taxes, side trips, additional meals, and entertainment); ratings of all hotels on the itinerary and the facilities they offer; cancellation policies for you and for the tour operator; and, if you are traveling alone, the cost for a single supplement. Most tour operators request that bookings be made through a travel agent; there is no additional charge for doing so.

General-Interest Tours **Domenico Tours** (751 Broadway, Bayonne, NJ 07002, tel. 201/823–8687 or 800/554–TOUR) offers packages to Orlando, Miami Beach, Palm Beach, St. Petersburg, Ft. Lauderdale, and Miami Beach/Bahamas/Walt Disney World. **Gadabout Tours** (700 E. Tahquitz Canyon Way, Palm Springs, CA 92262–6761, tel. 619/325–5556 or 800/952–5068) offers a nine-day tour of Florida, including a cruise to the Bahamas. **Tauck Tours** (11 Wilton Rd., Westport, CT 06881, tel. 203/226–6911 or 800/468–2825) offers tours of the resort areas of southern Florida and the Florida Keys, as well as trips to major attractions in central Florida.

Special-Interest Tours
Adventure **Sobek's International Explorers Society** (Box 1089, Angels Camp, CA 95222, tel. 209/736–4524) will take you canoeing through the Florida Everglades. **Wilderness Southeast** (711 Sandtown Rd., Savannah, GA 31410, tel. 912/897–5108) runs rugged trips through the Everglades and places like the Okefenokee Swamp in Georgia.

Nature **Capt. Vicki Impallomeni** (23 Key Haven Terr., Key West 33040, tel. 305/294–9731), a native-born Key Wester and environmental authority, operates day-long and half-day charters in the backcountry of the Florida Keys. She is especially effective with families with young children.

Package Deals for Independent Travelers

American FlyAAway Vacations (tel. 800/321–2121) offers city packages with discounts on hotels and car rentals, and a "Fly and Drive" package to the entire state. **Delta Airlines** (tel. 800/ 872–7786) offers a wide variety of packages in Florida, including trips to Ft. Lauderdale, Miami, and Key West. **American Express** (300 Pinnacle Way, Norcross, GA 30093, tel. 800/241– 1700 or, in GA, 800/421–5785) has similar city packages, with complimentary admission to certain area attractions. Also check with **Continental Airlines** (tel. 800/634–5555), **TWA Getaway Vacations** (tel. 800/GETAWAY), and **United Airlines** (tel. 800/328–6877) for packages.

Tips for British Travelers

Government
Tourist Offices
The **U.S. Travel and Tourism Administration** (Box 1EN, London W14 1EN, tel. 071/439–7433, fax 071/439–1152) will give you advice on your trip to Florida and can send brochures and an information packet.

Passports
and Visas
You will need a valid 10-year passport (£15) to enter the United States. You do not need a visa so long as you are visiting either on business or pleasure; are staying for less than 90 days; have a return ticket; are flying with a major airline (in effect, all airlines that fly to the United States); and a completed visa waiver form I–94W (supplied either at the airport of departure or on the plane and to be handed in on arrival). Otherwise you can obtain a U.S. Visitors Visa either through your travel agent or by post from the **United States Embassy** (Visa and Immigration Dept., 5 Upper Grosvenor St., London W1A 2JB, tel. 071/499– 3443). The embassy no longer accepts visa applications made by personal callers. No vaccinations are required.

Customs
Visitors age 21 or over can take in 200 cigarettes or 50 cigars or 2 kilograms of tobacco; one U.S. liter of alcohol; and duty-free gifts to a value of $100. Do not try to take in meat or meat products, seeds, plants, fruits, etc. Avoid illegal drugs like the plague.

Returning to Britain you may bring home: (1) 200 cigarettes or 100 cigarillos or 50 cigars or 250 grams of tobacco; (2) two liters of table wine with additional allowances for (a) one liter of alcohol over 22% by volume (38.8 proof, most spirits) or (b) two liters of alcohol under 22% by volume (fortified or sparkling wine) or (c) two more liters of table wine and (3) 60 milliliters of perfume and 250 milliliters of toilet water; and (4) other goods up to a value of £32, but not more than 50 liters of beer or 25 mechanical lighters.

Insurance
We recommend that you insure yourself to cover health and motoring mishaps through **Europ Assistance** (252 High St., Croydon, Surrey CRO 1NF, tel. 081/680–1234).

It is also wise to take out insurance to cover loss of luggage (though check that this isn't already covered in any existing home-owner's policy). Trip-cancellation insurance is another wise buy. **The Association of British Insurers** (51 Gresham St., London EC2V 7HQ, tel. 071/600–3333) will give comprehensive advice on all aspects of vacation insurance.

Tour Operators Numerous tour operators offer packages to Florida. Here we list just a few; contact your travel agent to find companies best suited to your needs and pocketbook.

Albany Travel (Manchester) Ltd. (Royal London House, 196 Deansgate, Manchester M3 3NF, tel. 061/833–0202) offers a 10-day "Florida Highlights" escorted coach tour that includes Orlando, the Everglades, Key West, and Miami. There are also flight/hotel/car rental packages to several Florida resorts.

British Airways Holidays (Atlantic House, Hazelwick Ave., Three Bridges, Crawley, W. Sussex RH10 1NP, tel. 0293/ 518022) has a variety of Gold Coast and Gulf Coast packages, multi-center and fly-drive holidays and flight bargains.

Cosmosair (Ground Floor, Dale House, Tiviot Dale, Stockport, Cheshire SK1 1TB, tel. 061/480–5799) offers a 15-day, escorted "Highlights of Florida" coach tour that includes Miami, Orlando, Cape Canaveral, and the Everglades. Self-drive itineraries are also available.

Jetsave Travel Ltd. (Sussex House, London Rd., East Grinstead, W. Sussex RH19 1LD, tel. 0342/312033) offers a variety of Gulf Coast and East Coast holidays in luxury homes, apartments, and hotels.

Airfares If you want to make your own way to Florida and need a reasonably priced ticket, try the small ads in the daily or Sunday newspapers or in magazines such as *Time Out*. You should be able to pick up something at rock-bottom prices. Be prepared to be flexible about your dates of travel and book as early as possible.

Also check out the APEX tickets offered by the major airlines, which are another good option. As we went to press, round-trip tickets to Orlando and Miami ranged from £508 to £559 for low and high season. Be sure to ask if there are any hidden extras, since airport taxes and supplements can increase the price dramatically.

Car Rental There are offices of the major car rental companies in most large towns, and you can either make your arrangements before you leave or when you get to your destination.

Avis (Hayes Gate House, Uxbridge Rd., Hayes, Middlesex UB4 0JN, tel. 081/848–8733) offers seven days' rental of a Chevrolet Cavalier at $105; extra days start at $26 per day.

Hertz (Radnor House, 1272 London Rd., Norbury, London SW16 4XW, tel. 081/679–1799) offers an "Affordable USA" program. Most rental offers include unlimited mileage, but don't forget to budget for the price of gas, local taxes, and collision insurance. Also check out the fly–drive offers from tour operators and airlines; some good bargains are usually available.

When to Go

Florida is a state for all seasons, although most visitors prefer October–April, particularly in southern Florida.

Winter is the height of the tourist season, when southern Florida is crowded with "snowbirds" fleeing the cold weather in the North. Hotels, bars, discos, restaurants, shops, and attractions are all crowded. Hollywood and Broadway celebrities appear in sophisticated supper clubs, and other performing artists hold the stage at ballets, operas, concerts, and theaters. In Tampa, the new multiethnic Bamboleo Festival attracts enormous crowds in midwinter.

Summer in the Greater Miami area, as smart budget-minded visitors have discovered, is often hot and humid, but the season is made bearable along the coast by ocean breezes. Besides, many hotels lower their prices considerably during summer.

For the college crowd, spring vacation is still the time to congregate in Florida, especially in Panama City Beach and the Daytona Beach area; Fort Lauderdale, where city officials, in their effort to refashion Fort Lauderdale more as a family resort, no longer indulges young revelers, so is much less popular with college students than it once was.

Climate What follows are average daily maximum and minimum temperatures for major cities in Florida.

Key West									
(The Keys)	**Jan.**	76F	24C	**May**	85F	29C	**Sept.**	90F	32C
		65	18		74	23		77	25
	Feb.	76F	24C	**June**	88F	31C	**Oct.**	83F	28C
		67	19		77	25		76	24
	Mar.	79F	26C	**July**	90F	32C	**Nov.**	79F	26C
		68	20		79	26		70	21
	Apr.	81F	27C	**Aug.**	90F	32C	**Dec.**	76F	24C
		72	22		79	26		67	19

Miami	**Jan.**	74F	23C	**May**	83F	28C	**Sept.**	86F	30C
		63	17		72	22		76	24
	Feb.	76F	24C	**June**	85F	29C	**Oct.**	83F	28C
		63	17		76	24		72	22
	Mar.	77F	25C	**July**	88F	31C	**Nov.**	79F	26C
		65	18		76	24		67	19
	Apr.	79F	26C	**Aug.**	88F	31C	**Dec.**	76F	26C
		68	20		77	25		63	17

Current weather information for foreign and domestic cities may be obtained by calling The Weather Channel Connection at 900/WEATHER from a touch-tone phone. In addition to the weather report, The Weather Channel Connection offers the local time and helpful travel tips as well as hurricane, foliage, and ski reports. The call costs 95¢ per minute.

Festivals and Seasonal Events

Top seasonal events in Florida include the Miami Film Festival in February; Florida Derby Festival from March through April; Sunfest in Palm Beach in May; and Key West's celebration of Hemingway Days in July. For exact dates and details about the following events, call the listed numbers or inquire from local chambers of commerce.

Early Jan.: Polo Season opens at the Palm Beach Polo and Country Club (13420 South Shore Blvd., West Palm Beach 33414, tel. 407/793–1440).

Mid-Jan.: Art Deco Weekend spotlights Miami Beach's historic district with an Art Deco street fair, a 1930s-style Moon Over Miami Ball, and live entertainment (1244 Ocean Dr., Miami Beach 33119, tel. 305/672–2014).

Mid-Jan.: Taste of the Grove Food and Music Festival is a popular fund-raiser put on in Coconut Grove's Peacock Park by area restaurants (tel. 305/442–2001).

Mid-Jan.: Martin Luther King, Jr., Festivals are celebrated in Miami (7225 S.W. 24th St., Miami 33155).

Late Jan.: South Florida Fair and Exposition takes place in West Palm Beach (Box 15915 West Palm Springs 33416–5915, tel. 407/793–0333).

Late Jan.: Miami River Blues Festival takes place on the south bank of the river next to Tobacco Road (626 S. Miami Ave., Miami 33130, tel. 305/374–1198).

Late Jan. or early Feb.: Key Biscayne Art Festival is an annual juried show of 175 talented artists at the entrance to Cape Florida State Park (Key Biscayne Rotary Club, Box 490174, Key Biscayne 33149, tel. 305/361–5207).

Feb.–Mar.: Winter Equestrian Festival includes more than 1,000 horses and three grand-prix equestrian events at the Palm Beach Polo and Country Club in West Palm Beach (tel. 407/798–7000).

Feb.–Mar.: Scottish Festival and Games features a variety of events in Key Biscayne (tel. 305/757–6730).

Mid-Feb.: Miami Film Festival is 10 days of international, domestic, and local films sponsored by the Film Society of America (444 Brickell Ave., Suite 229, Miami 33131, tel. 305/377–FILM).

Mid-Feb.: Islamorada Sportfishing Festival features a weekend of fishing, arts and crafts, races, and prizes (tel. 305/664–2321).

Mid-Feb.: Coconut Grove Art Festival is the state's largest (tel. 305/447–0401).

Early Mar.: Carnaval Miami is a carnival celebration staged by the Little Havana Tourist Authority (970 S.W. First St., Miami 33130, tel. 305/836–5223).

Early Apr.: Delray Affair is the biggest event in the area and features arts, crafts, and food.

Early Apr.–late May: Addison Mizner Festival in Boca Raton celebrates the 1920s in Palm Beach County (tel. 800/242–1774).

Late Apr.: River Cities Festival is a three-day event in Miami Springs and Hialeah that focuses attention on the Miami River and the need to keep it clean (tel. 305/887–1515).

Late Apr.–early May: Conch Republic Celebration in Key West honors the founding fathers of the Conch Republic, "the small island nation of Key West" (tel. 305/294–4440).

First weekend in May: Sunfest includes a wide variety of cultural and sporting events in West Palm Beach (tel. 407/659–5980).

First weekend in June: Miami-Bahamas Goombay Festival in Miami's Coconut Grove, celebrates the city's Bahamian heritage (tel. 305/443–7928).

Mid-July: Hemingway Days Festival in Key West includes plays, short-story competitions, and a Hemingway look-alike contest (tel. 305/294–4440).

Aug.: Boca Festival Days includes many educational, cultural, and recreational activities in Boca Raton (tel. 407/338–7070).

Early Sept.: Pioneer Florida Day is celebrated at the Pioneer Florida Museum in Dade City (tel. 904/567–0262).

Mid- to late Sept.: Festival Miami is three weeks of performing and visual arts sponsored by the University of Miami. (University of Miami School of Music, 6200 San Amaro Dr., Coral Gables 33124–1514, tel. 305/284–3941).

Late Oct.: Fantasy Fest in Key West is an unrestrained Halloween costume party, parade, and town fair (tel. 305/296–1817).

Late Dec.: Coconut Grove King Mango Strut is a parody of the Orange Bowl Parade (tel. 305/858–6253).

What to Pack

Pack light, because porters and luggage trolleys are hard to find. Luggage allowances on domestic flights vary slightly from airline to airline. Most allow three checked pieces and two carryons. In all cases, check-in luggage cannot weigh more than 70 pounds per bag or be larger than 62 inches (length + width + height) and carryons must fit under the seat or in the overhead luggage compartment.

The Miami area is warm year-round and often extremely humid during the summer months. Be prepared for sudden summer storms, but leave the plastic raincoats at home because they're uncomfortable in the high humidity. Although the winter months are mild, temperatures can dip into the 50s, even in the Keys, so take along a sweater or jacket, just in case.

Dress is casual throughout the state, with sundresses, jeans, or walking shorts appropriate during the day, and a pair of comfortable walking shoes or sneakers. A few of the better restaurants request that men wear jackets and ties, but most do not. Be prepared for air-conditioning bordering on freezing, especially in the Miami and Fort Lauderdale areas.

You can swim in most of peninsular Florida year-round. Be sure to take a sun hat and a good sunscreen because the sun can be fierce, even in the winter.

An extra pair of glasses, contact lenses, or prescription sunglasses is always a good idea; it is important to pack any allergy medication you may need.

Cash Machines

Virtually all U.S. banks belong to a network of ATMs (automatic teller machines), which dispense cash 24 hours a day in cities throughout the country. There are some eight major networks in the United States, the largest of which are **Cirrus**, owned by MasterCard, and **Plus**, affiliated with Visa. Some banks belong to more than one network. These cards are not automatically issued; you have to ask for them. Cards issued by American Express, Visa, and MasterCard may also be used in the ATMs, but the fees are usually higher than the fees on bank cards, and there is a daily interest charge on the "loan," even if monthly bills are paid on time. **Express Cash** allows American Express cardholders to withdraw up to $1,000 in a seven-day period (21 days overseas) from their personal checking accounts at ATMs worldwide. Gold-card members can receive up to $2,500 in a seven-day period (21 days overseas). Express Cash is not a cash advance service; only money already in the linked checking account can be withdrawn. Every transaction carries a 2% fee with a minimum charge of $2 and a maximum of $6. Apply for a

PIN (Personal Identification number) and link your accounts at least 2–3 weeks before departure.

Each network has a toll-free number you can call to locate machines in a given city. The Cirrus number is 800/424–7787; the Plus number is 800/843–7587; the Express Cash number is 800/CASH–NOW. Check with your bank for fees and for the amount of cash you can withdraw per day.

Traveling with Film

If your camera is new, shoot and develop a few rolls before leaving home. Pack some lens tissue and an extra battery for your built-in light meter. Invest about $10 in a skylight filter and screw it onto the front of your lens; it will protect the lens and also reduce haze.

Film doesn't like hot weather. If you're driving in summer, don't store film in the glove compartment or on the shelf under the rear window. Put it behind the front seat on the floor, on the side opposite the exhaust pipe.

On a plane trip, never pack unprocessed film in check-in luggage; if your bags get X-rayed, say goodbye to your pictures. Always carry undeveloped film with you through security and ask to have it inspected by hand. (It helps to isolate your film in a plastic bag, ready for quick inspection.) Inspectors at American airports are required by law to honor requests for hand inspection.

The newer airport scanning machines used in all U.S. airports are safe for anything from five to 500 scans, depending on the speed of your film. The effects are cumulative; you can put the same roll of film through several scans without worry. After five scans, though, you're asking for trouble.

If your film gets fogged and you want an explanation, send it to the National Association of Photographic Manufacturers (550 Mamaroneck Ave., Harrison, NY 10528). It will try to determine what went wrong. The service is free.

Car Rentals

Florida is a car renter's bazaar, with more discount companies offering more bargains—and more fine print—than anywhere else in the nation. If you're planning to rent a car in Florida, shop around for the best combination rate for car and airfare. Jacksonville, for example, is often somewhat cheaper to fly into than Miami, but Miami's car-rental rates are usually lower than Jacksonville's. In major Florida cities, peak-season rates for a subcompact average around $110 a week, often with unlimited mileage. Some companies advertise peak-season promotional rates as low as $69 a week with unlimited mileage, but only a few cars are available at this rate, and you may have to pay twice as much if you keep the car less than seven days! Some of these companies require you to keep the car in the state and are quick to charge for an extra day when you return a vehicle late.

Avis (tel. 800/331–1212), **Budget** (tel. 800/527–0700), **Dollar** (tel. 800/800–4000), **Hertz** (tel. 800/654–3131), **National** (tel. 800/227–7368), **Sears** (tel. 800/527–0770), and **Thrifty** (tel. 800/

367–2277) maintain airport and city locations throughout Florida. So do **Alamo** (tel. 800/327–9633) and **General** (tel. 800/327–7607), which offer some of the state's lowest rates. **Rent-A-Wreck** (tel. 800/535–1391) and **Ugly Duckling** (tel. 800/843–3825) rent used cars throughout the state, usually with more stringent mileage restrictions. Neither operation, however, has locations in Orlando.

Besides the national rental companies, several regional and local firms offer good deals in major Florida cities. These include **Auto Host** (tel. 800/448–4678), **Payless** (tel. 800/237–2804), **Superior** (tel. 800/237–8106), **USA** (tel. 800/872–2277), and **Value** (tel. 800/327–2501). In Fort Lauderdale, local companies include **Aapex Thompson** (tel. 305/566–8663) and **Air and Sea** (tel. 305/764–1008). In Miami, **Superior Rent-A-Car** (tel. 305/649–7012) is a local budget company, as are **Pass** (tel. 305/444–3923) and **InterAmerican Car Rental** (tel. 305/871–3030). Down in Key West, try **Tropical Rent-a-Car** (tel. 305/294–8136).

It's always best to know a few essentials *before* you arrive at the car-rental counter. Find out what the collision damage waiver (CDW), usually an $8–$12 daily surcharge, covers and whether your corporate or personal insurance already covers damage to a rental car (if so, bring a photocopy of the benefits section along). More and more companies are now holding renters responsible for theft and vandalism damages if they don't buy the CDW; in response, some credit card and insurance companies are extending *their* coverage to rental cars. These include **Chase Manhattan Bank Visa Cards** (tel. 800/645–7352), and **Dreyfus Consumer Bank Gold and Silver MasterCards** (tel. 800/847–9700). Find out, too, if you must pay for a full tank of gas whether you use it or not, and make sure you get a reservation number.

Traveling with Children

Grandtravel (600 Wisconsin Ave., Suite 706, Chevy Chase, MD 20815, tel. 301/986–0790 or 800/247–7651) offers dozens of domestic (and international) tours that are appropriate for both the grandparent and grandchild.

Publications *Family Travel Times* is an 8- to 12-page newsletter published 10 times a year by **Travel with Your Children** (TWYCH: 45 W. 18th St., 7th Floor Tower, New York, NY 10011, tel. 212/206–0688). The $35 subscription includes access to back issues and twice-weekly opportunities to call in for specific advice. Send $1 for a sample issue.

Great Vacations with Your Kids: The Complete Guide to Family Vacations in the U.S., second edition, by Dorothy Ann Jordon and Marjorie Adoff Cohen (E. P. Dutton, 375 Hudson St., New York, NY 10014, tel. 212/366–2000) details everything from city vacations to adventure vacations to child-care resources.

Traveling with Children–and Enjoying It (The Globe Pequot Press, Box Q, Chester CT 06412) offers tips on how to cut costs, keep children occupied, reduce jet lag, and pack properly. It costs $11.95.

Periodicals for parents that are filled with listings of events, resources, and advice are available free at such places as libraries, supermarkets, and museums; *Florida Parent* (Box 2321,

Boca Raton 33427, tel. 305/776–3305), a monthly, covers Palm Beach, Broward, and Dade counties.

Hotels Florida may have the highest concentration of hotels with organized children's programs in the United States. The following list gives examples of the kinds of services and activities offered by some of the major chains. It is by no means exhaustive. Be sure to ask about children's programs when you make a reservation.

Club Med (40 W. 57th St., New York, NY 10019, tel. 800/CLUB–MED) opened its new Sandpiper resort village in Port St. Lucie, including a "Baby Club" (4–23 months), "Mini Club" (2 years and up), and "Kids Club" (8 years and up). **Guest Quarters Suite Hotels** (Fort Lauderdale, tel. 800/424–2900) offers the luxury of two-room suites with kitchen facilities and children's menus in the restaurant. It also allows children under 18 to stay free in the same suite with their parents. The **Sonesta International Hotels** (tel. 800/766–3782), including Sonesta Beach Hotel Key Biscayne, have children's programs. Also look for children's programs at **Marriott's Harbor Beach Resort** (3030 Holiday Dr., Fort Lauderdale 33316, tel. 305/525–4000 or 800/228–9290) and at **La Concha Holiday Inn** (430 Duval St., Key West 33040, tel. 305/296–2991 or 800/227–6151). Most **Days Inn** hotels (tel. 800/325–2525) charge only a nominal fee for children under 18 and allow kids 12 and under to eat free (many offer efficiency-type apartments, too).

Condo Rentals See *The Condo Lux Vacationer's Guide to Condominium Rentals in the Southeast* by Jill Little (Vintage Books/Random House, New York; $9.95).

Home Exchange Exchanging homes is a surprisingly low-cost way to enjoy a vacation in another part of the country. A good choice for home exchange in the United States is the **Vacation Exchange Club, Inc.** (Box 820, Haleiwa, HI 96712, tel. 800/638–3841). The club publishes four directories a year, in January, March, July, and September, and updated, late listings throughout the year. Annual membership, which includes your listing in one book, a newsletter, and copies of all publications (mailed first class) is $50.

Getting There On domestic flights, children under 2 who do not occupy a seat travel free. Various discounts apply to children 2–12. Reserve a seat behind the bulkhead of the plane, which offers more legroom and can usually fit a bassinet (supplied by the airline). At the same time, inquire about children's meals, snacks, or special dietary needs, which are addressed by most airlines. (See "TWYCH's Airline Guide," in the February 1990 and 1992 issues of *Family Travel Times,* for a rundown of the services offered by 46 airlines.) Regulations about infant travel on airplanes are in the process of changing. Until they do, however, if you want to be sure your infant is secure, you must bring your own car seat and buy your baby a separate ticket. The booklet *Child Infant Safety Seats Acceptable for Use in Aircraft* is available from the Federal Aviation Administration (APA–200, 800 Independence Ave., SW, Washington, DC 20591, tel. 202/267–3479). If you opt to hold your baby on your lap, do so with the infant outside the seat belt rather than inside it so he or she doesn't get crushed in case of a sudden stop.

Hints for Disabled Travelers

Visitors may request the "Florida Services Directory for the Physically Challenged Traveler" from the Florida Department of Commerce, Division of Tourism (126 W. Van Buren St. Tallahassee 32399-2000, tel. 904/487–1462).

The Information Center for Individuals with Disabilities (Fort Point Place, 1st floor, 27–43 Wormwood St., Boston, MA 02210, tel. 617/727–5540—voice and TDD) offers useful problem-solving assistance, including lists of travel agents that specialize in tours for the disabled.

Moss Rehabilitation Hospital Travel Information Service (1200 W. Tabor Rd., Philadelphia, PA 19141–3099, tel. 215/456–9600; TDD 215/456–9602) provides information on tourist sights, transportation, and accommodations in destinations around the world. There is a small fee.

Mobility International USA (Box 3551, Eugene, OR 97403, tel. 503/343–1284) is a membership organization with a $20 annual fee offering information on accommodations, organized study, and so forth.

The Society for the Advancement of Travel for the Handicapped (SATH, 347 5th Ave., Suite 610, New York, NY 10016, tel. 212/447–7284, fax 212/725–8253) offers access information. Annual membership costs $45, or $25 for senior travelers and students. Send $1 and a self-addressed envelope.

The **National Park Service** provides a **Golden Access Passport** free of charge to those who are medically blind or have a permanent disability; the passport covers the entry fee for the holder and anyone accompanying the holder in the same private, non-commercial vehicle and a 50% discount on camping, boat launching, and parking. All charges are covered except lodging. Apply for the passport in person at any national recreation facility that charges an entrance fee; proof of disability is required. For additional information, write to the National Park Service (Box 37127, Washington, DC 20013–7127).

Greyhound/Trailways (tel. 800/752–4841) will carry a disabled person and companion for the price of a single fare.

Amtrak (tel. 800/USA–RAIL; TDD 800/523–6590) requests 72 hours' notice to provide redcap service, special seats, or wheelchair assistance at stations equipped to provide this service. All disabled and elderly passengers are entitled to a 15% discount on the lowest available fare. Reduced-price fares are also available for children. For a free copy of *Access Amtrak,* a guide to its services for elderly and disabled travelers, write to Amtrak (National Railroad Corporation Passenger Services, 60 Massachusetts Ave., NE, Washington, DC 20002).

Publications Twin Peaks Press (Box 129, Vancover, WA 98666, tel. 206/694–2462; 800/637–2256 for orders only) specializes in books for the disabled. Add $2 postage for the first book; $1 each additional book. *Travel for the Disabled* ($9.95) offers a comprehensive list of guidebooks and facilities geared to the disabled. *Directory of Travel Agencies for the Disabled* ($12.95) lists more than 350 agencies throughout the world. *Wheelchair Vagabond* ($9.95) helps independent travelers plan for extended trips in cars, vans, or campers. Twin Peaks also offers a "Traveling Nurse's Network," which provides registered nurses trained in all medical areas to accompany and assist disabled travelers.

Access America: An Atlas and Guide to the National Parks for Visitors with Disabilities (published by Northern Cartograph-

ic, Box 133, Burlington, VT 05402, tel. 802/860–2886) contains
detailed information about access for the 37 largest and most
visited national parks in the United States. This award-
winning book costs $44.95 plus $5 shipping directly from the
publisher.

Hints for Older Travelers

The **American Association of Retired Persons** (AARP, 601 E.
St., NW, Washington, DC 20049, tel. 202/434–2277) has two
programs for independent travelers: (1) the Purchase Privilege
Program, which offers discounts on hotels, airfare, car rentals,
RV rentals, and sightseeing, and (2) the AARP Motoring Plan,
provided by Amoco, which offers emergency aid (road service)
and trip-routing information for an annual fee of $39.95 per per-
son or per married couple. The AARP also arranges group
tours, cruises, and apartment living all over the world through
"AARP Travel Experience from American Express" (400 Pinnacle Way, Suite 450, Norcross, GA 30071, tel. 800/659–5678).
AARP members must be 50 or older. Annual dues are $8 per
person or per married couple.

If you're planning to use an AARP or other senior-citizen identification card to obtain a reduced hotel rate, mention it at the
time you make your reservation, not when you check out. At
participating restaurants, show your card to the maître d' before you're seated, because discounts may be limited to certain
set menus, days, or hours. When renting a car, be sure to ask
about special promotional rates which might offer greater sav-
ings than the available discount.

Travel Industry and Disabled Exchange (TIDE, 5435 Donna
Ave., Tarzana, CA 91356, tel. 818/368–5648) is an industry-
based organization with a $15-per-person annual membership
fee. Members receive a quarterly newsletter and a directory of
travel agents for the disabled.

National Council of Senior Citizens (1331 F St., NW, Washington, DC 20004, tel. 202/347–8800) is a nonprofit advocacy group
with some 5,000 local clubs across the country. Annual membership is $12 per person or couple. Members receive a monthly
newspaper with travel information and an ID for reduced rates
on hotels and car rentals.

Mature Outlook (6001 N. Clark St., Chicago, IL 60660, tel. 800/
336–6330), a subsidiary of Sears Roebuck & Co., is a travel club
for people over 50, offering discounts at Holiday Inns and a bi-
monthly newsletter. Annual membership is $9.95 per person or
per married couple. Instant membership is available at Sears
stores and participating Holiday Inns.

Golden Age Passport is a free lifetime pass to all parks, monuments, and recreation areas run by the federal government.
People 62 and over should pick one up in person at any national
park that charges admission. A driver's license or other proof of
age is required.

September Days Club (tel. 800/241–5050) is run by the moder-
ately priced Days Inns of America. The $12 annual membership
fee for individuals or couples over 50 entitles them to reduced
car rental rates and reductions of 15%–50% at 95% of the
chain's more than 350 motels. Members also receive *Travel*

Holiday Magazine Quarterly for updated information and travel articles.

Elderhostel (75 Federal St., 3rd floor, Boston, MA 02110–1941, tel. 617/426–7788) is an innovative, low-cost educational program for people aged 60 or over (only one member of a traveling couple needs to qualify). Participants live in dorms on 1,600 campuses in the United States and around the world. Mornings are devoted to lectures and seminars, afternoons to sightseeing and field trips. The fee includes room, board, tuition (in the United States and Canada), and round-trip transportation (overseas). Special scholarships are available for those who qualify financially.

Saga International Holidays (120 Boylston St., Boston, MA 02116, tel. 800/343–0273) specializes in group travel for people over age 60. A selection of variously priced tours allows you to choose the package that best meets your needs.

Publications **_The Senior Citizen's Guide to Budget Travel in the United States and Canada_** is available for $5.95 (including shipping) from Pilot Books (103 Cooper St., Babylon, NY 11702, tel. 516/422–2225).

Although Florida probably attracts more elderly people than any other state, the state publishes no booklet addressed directly to senior citizens.

Senior-citizen discounts are common throughout Florida, but there are no set standards. Some discounts, like those for prescriptions at the Eckerd Drug chain, require that you fill out a card and register. The best bet is simply to ask whether there is a senior-citizen discount available on your purchase, meal, or hotel stay.

Further Reading

Look for *Princess of the Everglades*, a novel about the 1926 hurricane by Charles Mink. Pat Booth's novel *Palm Beach* describes the glitzy Palm Beach scene. *The Tourist Season* is Carl Hiaasen's immensely funny declaration of war against the state's environment-despoiling hordes. His latest is *Native Tongue*. New—from sexy hot to mystic cool—are Pat Booth's *Miami*, and Sam Harrison's *Birdsong Ascending*. T.D. Allman's *Miami* is the best of a recent flock of titles about the city. Other recommended novels include *Florida Straits*, by Laurence Shames; *No Enemy But Time*, by Evelyn Mayerson; *To Have and Have Not*, by Ernest Hemingway; and *The Day of the Dolphin*, by Robert Merle.

Among the recommended nonfiction books are *Key West Writers and Their Homes*, Lynn Kaufelt's tour of homes of Hemingway, Wallace Stevens, Tennessee Williams, and others; *The Everglades: River of Grass*, by Marjory S. Douglas; *Florida*, by Gloria Jahoda, published as part of the Bicentennial observance; *Miami Alive*, by Ethel Blum; and *Florida's Sandy Beaches*, University Press of Florida. Mark Derr's *Some Kind of Paradise* is an excellent review of the state's environmental follies; John Rothchild's *Up for Grabs*, equally good, is about Florida's commercial lunacy. Good anthologies include *The Florida Reader: Visions of Paradise* (Maurice O'Sullivan and Jack Lane, eds.); *The Rivers of Florida* (Del and Marty Marth, eds.), and *Subtropical Speculations: An Anthology of Florida Science Fiction* (Richard Mathews and Rick Wilber, eds.).

Arriving and Departing

By Plane

Most major U.S. airlines schedule regular flights into Florida, and some, such as Delta and United Airlines, serve the Florida airports extensively.

Delta and USAir all have regular service into West Palm Beach, Fort Lauderdale, Miami, and Key West. Delta also flies into Fort Pierce.

Other major airlines that serve the Florida airports include Continental, American, American Trans Air, Northwest, United, and TWA. Many foreign airlines also fly into some of the major airports in Florida; the smaller, out-of-the-way airports are usually accessible through the commuter flights of major domestic carriers.

Packages that combine airfare and vacation activities at special rates are often available through the airlines. For example, Delta (tel. 800/872–7786) offers travel packages to Ft. Lauderdale, Miami, and Key West (*see* Package Deals for Independent Travelers).

When booking reservations, keep in mind the distinction between nonstop flights (no stops and no changes), direct flights (no changes of aircraft, but one or more stops), and connecting flights (one or more changes of planes at one or more stops). Connecting flights are often the least expensive, but they are the most time-consuming, and the biggest nuisance.

Smoking　Smoking regulations prohibit smoking on all domestic flights under six hours. This rule applies to both domestic and foreign carriers.

Carry-on Luggage　Passengers are usually limited to two carry-on bags. For bags stored under your seat, the maximum dimensions are 9″ × 14″ × 22″. For bags that can be hung in a closet, the maximum dimensions are 4″ × 23″ × 45″. For bags stored in an overhead bin, the maximum dimensions are 10″ × 14″ × 36″. Any item that exceeds the specified dimensions will generally be rejected as a carryon and handled as checked baggage. Keep in mind that an airline can adapt these rules to circumstances; on an especially crowded flight, don't be surprised if you are allowed only one carry-on bag.

In addition to the two carryons, passengers may also bring aboard: a handbag (pocketbook or purse), an overcoat or wrap, an umbrella, a camera, a reasonable amount of reading material, an infant bag, and crutches, a cane, braces, or other prosthetic device upon which the passenger is dependent. Infant/child safety seats can also be brought aboard if parents have purchased a ticket for the child or if there is space in the cabin.

Note that these regulations are for U.S. airlines only. Foreign airlines generally allow one piece of carry-on luggage in tourist class, in addition to handbags and bags filled with duty-free goods. Passengers in first and business class may also be

allowed to carry on one garment bag. It is best to check with
your airline ahead of time to find out what its exact rules are
regarding carry-on luggage.

Checked Luggage Luggage allowances vary slightly from airline to airline. Many
carriers allow three checked pieces; some allow only two. It is
best to consult with the airline before you go. In all cases,
check-in luggage cannot weigh more than 70 pounds per piece
or be larger than 62 inches (length + width + height).

Lost Luggage On domestic flights, airlines are responsible for lost or damaged property only up to $1,250 per passenger. If you're carry-
ing valuables, either take them with you on the airplane or
purchase additional insurance for lost luggage. Some airlines
will issue additional luggage insurance when you check in, but
many do not. Insurance for lost, damaged, or stolen luggage is
available through travel agents or directly through various insurance companies. Two that issue luggage insurance are **Tele-
Trip** (Box 31685, 3201 Farnam St., Omaha, NE 68131–0618, tel.
800/228–9792), a subsidiary of Mutual of Omaha, and **The Travelers Insurance Corporation** (Ticket and Travel Dept., 1 Tower
Sq., Hartford, CT 06183–5040, tel. 203/277–0111 or 800/243–
3174). Tele-Trip operates sales booths at airports, and it also
issues insurance through travel agents. Tele-Trip will insure
checked or hand luggage through its travel insurance packages. Rates vary according to the length of the trip. The Travelers will insure checked or hand luggage at $500–$2,000
valuation per person, for a maximum of 180 days. Rates for 1–5
days for $500 valuation are $10; for 180 days, $85.

Other companies with comprehensive policies include **Access
America, Inc.,** a subsidiary of Blue Cross–Blue Shield (Box
11188, Richmond, VA 23230, tel. 800/334–7525 or 800/284–
8300) and **Near Services** (450 Prairie Ave., Suite 101, Calumet
City, IL 60409, tel. 708/868–6700 or 800/654–6700).

Before you go, itemize the contents of each bag in case you need
to file an insurance claim. Be certain to put your home address
on each piece of luggage, including carry-on bags. If your luggage is stolen and later recovered, the airline will deliver the
luggage to your home free of charge.

By Car

Three major interstates lead to Florida from various parts of
the country. I–95 begins in Maine, runs south through New
England and the Mid-Atlantic states, and enters Florida just
north of Jacksonville. It continues south past Daytona Beach,
the Space Coast, Vero Beach, Palm Beach, and Fort Lauderdale, eventually ending in Miami.

I–75 begins at the Canadian border in Michigan and runs south
through Ohio, Kentucky, Tennessee, and Georgia before enter-
ing Florida. The interstate moves through the center of the
state before veering west into Tampa. It follows the west coast
south to Naples, then crosses the state and ends in Miami.

Travelers heading from the Midwest or other points west for
the lower east coast of Florida will want to use Florida's Turnpike from Wildwood, which crosses the state for 321 miles and
goes as far as Florida City. In 1990 and 1991 toll cards were replaced at many locations with coin-drops. Eight service plazas

were all attractively rebuilt in 1989 at a cost of $28 million and feature a mix of fast-food restaurants. For current information on tolls and other services, call the Florida Turnpike public information number (tel. 800/447–1781).

Speed Limits In Florida the speed limits are 55 mph on the state highways, 30 mph within city limits and residential areas, and 55–65 mph on the interstates and on Florida's Turnpike. These limits may vary, so be sure to watch road signs for any changes.

By Train

Amtrak (tel. 800/USA-RAIL) provides service to Miami and several other major cities in Florida.

By Bus

Greyhound/Trailways passes through practically every major city in Florida, including West Palm Beach, Fort Lauderdale, Miami, and Key West. For information about bus schedules and fares, contact your local Greyhound Information Center.

Staying in Florida

Tourist Information

The **Florida Division of Tourism** operates **welcome centers** on I–10, I–75, I–95, U.S. 231 (near Graceville), and in the lobby of the new Capitol in Tallahassee (Department of Commerce, 126 Van Buren St., Tallahassee 32399, tel. 904/487–1462).

Shopping

Malls in Florida are full of nationally franchised shops, major department-store chains, and one-of-a-kind shops catering to a mass audience. Small shops in out-of-the-way places, however, often have the best souvenirs and most special gift items.

Indian Artifacts Native American crafts are abundant, particularly in the southern part of the state, where you'll find billowing dresses and shirts, hand-sewn in striking colors and designs. At the Miccosukee Indian Village, 25 miles west of Miami on the Tamiami Trail (U.S. 41), as well as at the Seminole and Miccosukee reservations in the Everglades, you can also find handcrafted dolls and beaded belts.

Seashells Shell shops, selling mostly kitsch items, abound throughout Florida.

Citrus Fruit Fresh citrus is available most of the year, except in summer. Two kinds of citrus grow in Florida: the sweeter and more costly Indian River fruit from a thin ribbon of groves along the east coast, and the less-costly fruit from the interior. After killer freezes in 1984, 1985, and 1989 ruined many groves in the Orlando area, the interior growers began planting in warmer areas south and west of Lake Okeechobee.

Citrus is sold in ¼, ½, ¾, and full bushels. Many shippers offer special gift packages with several varieties of fruit, jellies, and other food items. Some prices include U.S. postage, others may not. Shipping may exceed the cost of the fruit. If you have a choice of citrus packaged in boxes or bags, take the boxes. They are easier to label, are harder to squash, and travel better than the bags.

Malls and Boutiques The Greater Miami area has many look-alike shopping strips and malls with the same retail and discount shops. You'll find finer boutiques in specialty malls such as Cocowalk in Coconut Grove (*see* Exploring Coral Gables/Coconut Grove/South Miami in Chapter 2) and the Bal Harbour Shops (9700 Collins Ave., Bal Harbour 33154, tel. 305/866–0311). For ½ mile, Flagler Street, in the heart of downtown Miami, is the nation's most important import–export center, where bargain items for international travelers include cameras, electronics, and jewelry (*see* Exploring Downtown Miami in Chapter 2). Bayside Marketplace provides entertainment along with boutiques. The Caribbean Marketplace offers good Haitian imports.

Fort Lauderdale's finest shops cluster along six blocks of Las Olas Boulevard (*see* Exploring Fort Lauderdale in Chapter 4) and at the 150-store Galleria At Fort Lauderdale (2414 E. Sunrise Blvd., tel. 305/564–1015).

For the ultimate Florida shopping experience, stroll Palm Beach's Worth Avenue (*see* Shopping in Chapter 5). Here you'll find shops like Brooks Brothers and Tiffany's tucked between galleries selling ancient Chinese art or Oriental rugs, gourmet restaurants, one-of-a-kind jewelry stores, and chocolatiers.

Antiques lovers should explore S.W. 28th Lane and Unity Boulevard in Miami (near the Coconut Grove Metrorail station).

Beaches

No point in Florida is more than 60 miles from saltwater. This long, lean peninsula is bordered by a 526-mile Atlantic coast from Fernandina Beach to Key West and a 792-mile coast along the Gulf of Mexico and Florida Bay from Pensacola to Key West. If you were to stretch Florida's convoluted coast in a straight line, it would extend for about 1,800 miles. What's more, if you add in the perimeter of every island surrounded by saltwater, Florida has about 8,500 miles of tidal shoreline— more than any other state except Alaska. Florida's coastline comprises about 1,016 miles of sand beaches.

Visitors unaccustomed to strong subtropical sun run a risk of sunburn and heat prostration on Florida beaches, even in winter. The natives go to the beach early in the day or in the late afternoon. If they must be out in direct sun at midday, they limit their sun exposure and strenuous exercise, drink plenty of liquids, and wear hats. Wherever you plan to swim, ask if the water has a dangerous undertow.

The state owns all beaches below the mean high-tide line, even in front of hotels and private resorts, but gaining access to the public beach can be a problem along much of Florida's coastline. You must pay to enter and/or park at most state, county, and local beachfront parks. Where hotels dominate the beach frontage, public parking may be limited or nonexistent.

From the Treasure Coast south, erosion has affected the beaches. Major beach rehabilitation projects have been completed in Fort Lauderdale, the Sunny Isles area of north Dade County, Miami Beach, and Key Biscayne.

In the Florida Keys, coral reefs and prevailing currents prevent sand from building up to form beaches. The few Keys beaches are small, narrow, and generally have little or no sandy bottom.

Participant Sports

The Governor's Council on Physical Fitness and Sports (1330 N.W. 6th St., Gainesville 32601, tel. 904/336–2120) puts on the annual **Sunshine State Games** in July each year in a different part of the state, and promotes the business of sports. Call for information on events.

Bicycling   Bicycling is popular throughout Florida. The terrain is flat in the south and gently rolling along the central ridge and in much of the Panhandle. Most cities of any size have bike-rental shops, which are good sources of information on local bike paths.

Florida's Department of Natural Resources (Div. of Recreation and Parks, Mail Station 585, 3900 Commonwealth Blvd., Tallahassee 32399–3000, tel. 904/487–4784) is developing three overnight bicycle tours of different areas of the state. The tours will vary in length between 100 and 450 miles (for 2–6 days of cycling), and will use state parks for rest stops and overnight camping.

Florida's Department of Transportation (DOT) publishes free bicycle trail guides, which you can request from the state bicycle–pedestrian coordinator (605 Suwannee St., Mail Station 19, Tallahassee 32399-0450, tel. 904/487–1200). DOT also sells 7 maps for bicycle trips of 35 to 300 miles. Write to Maps and Publications, 605 Suwannee St., Mail Station 12, Tallahassee 32399–0450, tel. 904/488–9220. Cost: $1 plus 6% sales tax per map.

For information on local biking events and clubs, contact **Florida Bicycle Association** (Box 16652, Tampa 33687–6652, tel. 800/ FOR BIKE or 210 Lake Hollingsworth #1707, Lakeland 33803, tel. 813/985–4326). In Greater Miami, contact Dade County's bicycle–pedestrian coordinator (Office of the County Manager, Metro-Dade Government Center, 111 N.W. 1st St., Suite 910, Miami 33128, tel. 305/375–4507).

For specific information about Florida's rails-to-trails network contact the Department of Natural Resources (*see* above).

Canoeing   The best time to canoe in Florida is winter, the dry season, when you're less likely to get caught in a torrential downpour or be eaten alive by mosquitoes.

The Everglades has areas suitable for flat-water wilderness canoeing that are comparable to spots in the Boundary Waters region of Minnesota. Other popular canoeing rivers include the Blackwater, Juniper, Loxahatchee, Peace, Oklawaha, Suwannee, St. Marys, and Santa Fe. A free guide issued by the Florida Department of Natural Resources (DNR), *Florida Recreational Trails System Canoe Trails,* describes nearly 950 miles of designated canoe trails and support services along 36 Florida creeks, rivers, and springs (Div. of Recreation and Parks, Bureau of Operational Services, MS 535, 3900 Commonwealth Blvd., Tallahassee 32399–3000, tel. 904/488–7896). Contact individual national forests, parks, monuments, reserves, and seashores for information on their canoe trails. Local chambers of commerce have information on canoe trails in county parks.

Two Florida canoe-outfitter organizations publish free lists of canoe outfitters who organize canoe trips, rent canoes and canoeing equipment, and help shuttle canoeists' boats and cars. *Canoe Outpost System* is a brochure listing six independent outfitters serving 11 Florida rivers (Rte. 7, Box 301, Arcadia 33821, tel. 813/494–1215). The **Florida Association of Canoe Liveries and Outfitters (FACLO)** publishes a free list of 33 canoe outfitters who organize trips on 28 creeks and rivers (Box 1764, Arcadia 33821).

Fishing In Atlantic and Gulf waters, fishing seasons and other regulations vary by location, and by the number and size of fish of various species that you may catch and retain. For a free copy of the annual *Florida Fishing Handbook,* write to the Florida Game and Fresh Water Fish Commission (620 S. Meridian St., Tallahassee 32399–1600, tel. 904/488–1960).

Opportunities for saltwater fishing abound from the Keys all the way up the Atlantic Coast to Georgia and up the Gulf Coast to Alabama. Many seaside communities have fishing piers that charge admission to anglers (and usually a lower rate to watchers). These piers usually have a bait-and-tackle shop. Write the **Florida Sea Grant Extension Program** for a free list of Florida fishing piers (Rm. G-022, McCarty Hall, University of Florida, Gainesville 32611, tel. 904/392–1771).

It's easy to find a boat-charter service that will take you out into deep water. The Keys are dotted with charter services, and Key West has a sportfishing and shrimping fleet as extensive as what you would expect to find in large cities. Depending on your taste, budget, and needs, you can charter anything from an old wooden craft to a luxurious, waterborne palace with state-of-the-art amenities.

Licenses are required for both freshwater and saltwater fishing. The fees for a saltwater fishing license are $30 for nonresidents and $12 for residents. A nonresident seven-day saltwater license is $15. Nonresidents can purchase freshwater fishing licenses good for 10 days ($15) or for one year ($30); residents pay $12 for an annual license. Combined annual freshwater fishing and hunting licenses are also available at $22 for residents.

Golf Except in the heart of the Everglades, you'll never be far from one of Florida's more than 1,050 golf courses. Palm Beach County, the state's leading golf locale with 130 golf courses, also houses the home offices of the National Golf Foundation and the Professional Golfers Association of America. Many of the best golf courses in Florida allow visitors to play without being members or hotel guests.

Especially in winter, you should reserve tee-off times in advance. Ask about golf reservations when you make your lodging reservations.

Horseback Riding Trail and endurance riding are popular throughout the state, with seven state parks providing overnight camping with stables, facilities, and 14 parks with trails and campgrounds for horses. Spring and fall meetings for riders are held. For more information, contact **AHOOF** (Affiliated Horse Organization of Florida, Box 448, Laurel 34272, tel. 813/484–6449).

Hunting Hunters in Florida stalk a wide variety of resident game animals and birds, including deer, wild hog, wild turkey, bobwhite quail, ducks, and coots. A plain hunting license costs $11 for Florida residents, $150 for nonresidents, except nonresidents from Alabama who pay $100. Nonresidents can get a 10-day hunting license for $25, except for nonresidents from Georgia, who pay $121.

Each year in June, the **Florida Game and Fresh Water Fish Commission** announces the dates and hours of the fall hunting seasons for public and private wildlife-management areas. Hunting seasons vary across the state. Where hunting is allowed, you need the landowner's written permission—and you must carry that letter with your hunting license in the field. Trespassing with a weapon is a felony. For a free copy of the annual *Florida Hunting Handbook,* contact the game commission (620 Meridian St., Tallahassee 32399–1600, tel. 904/488–4676).

Jogging, Running, and Walking All over Florida, you'll find joggers, runners, and walkers on bike paths and city streets—primarily in the early morning and after working hours in the evening. Some Florida hotels have set up their own running trails; others provide guests with information on measured trails in the vicinity. The first time you run in Florida, be prepared to go a shorter distance than normal because of higher heat and humidity.

Two major Florida festivals include important running races. Each year in December the **Capital Bank Orange Bowl 10K,** one of the state's best-known running events, brings world-class runners to Miami. In April, as part of the Florida Keys annual Conch Republic Days, runners congregate near Marathon on one of the world's most spectacular courses for the **Seven Mile Bridge Run.**

Local running clubs all over the state sponsor weekly public events for joggers, runners, and walkers. For a list of local clubs and events throughout the state, call or send a self-addressed stamped envelope to the **Florida Athletics Congress** (1330 N.W. 6th St., Gainesville 32601, tel. 904/378–6805). For information about events in south Florida contact the 1,500-member **Miami Runners Club** (7900 S.W. 40th St., Miami 33155, tel. 305/227–1500).

Scuba Diving and Snorkeling South Florida and the Keys attract most of the divers and snorkelers, but the more than 300 dive shops throughout the state schedule drift-, reef-, and wreck-diving trips for scuba divers all along Florida's Atlantic and Gulf coasts. The low-tech pleasures of snorkeling can be enjoyed all along the Overseas Highway in the Keys and elsewhere where shallow reefs hug the shore.

Contact the **Dive Industry Association** for lists of advertisers who provide services for boaters, divers, and fisherfolk. The Keys packet is $6.95, and the all-inclusive Florida state packet, $14.95 (Teall's Inc., 111 Saguaro La., Marathon 33050, tel. 305/743–3942).

Tennis Many Florida hotels have a resident tennis pro and offer special tennis packages with lessons. Many local park and recreation departments throughout Florida operate modern tennis centers like those at country clubs, and most such centers welcome nonresidents, for a fee. For general information and schedules for amateur tournaments, contact the **Florida Tennis Association** (801 N.E. 167th St., Suite 301, North Miami Beach 33162, tel. 305/652–2866).

Trails Trails for biking, canoeing, sea-kayaking, hiking, horseback riding, and jogging are getting new attention in Florida. Contact the **State Trails Coordinator** in the Bureau of Park Planning, Department of Natural Resources (3900 Commonwealth Blvd., Tallahassee 32399-3000, tel. 904/487–4784). Impetus stems from the **Florida Trail Association** (Box 13708, Gainesville, FL 32604, tel. 800/343–1882 in FL, 904/378–8823 outside FL), which since 1964 has developed more than 1,000 miles of trail through the state, including more than 300 miles of certified Florida National Scenic Trail; and from the Florida Chapter of the **Rails-to-Trails Conservancy** (2545 Blairstone Pines Dr., Tallahassee, FL 32301, tel. 904/942–2379).

Parks and Nature Preserves

Although Florida is the fourth-most-populous state in the nation, there are 9,711,043 acres of public and private recreation facilities set aside in national forests, parks, monuments, reserves, and seashores; state forests and parks; county parks; and nature preserves owned and managed by private conservation groups.

On holidays and weekends, crowds flock to Florida's most popular parks—even to some on islands that are accessible only by boat. Come early or risk being turned away. In winter, northern migratory birds descend on the state. Many resident species breed in the warm summer months, but others (such as the wood stork) time their breeding cycle to the winter dry season. In summer, mosquitoes are voracious and daily afternoon thundershowers add to the state's humidity, but this is when the sea turtles come ashore to lay their eggs and when you're most likely to see frigate birds and other tropical species.

National Parks The federal government maintains no centralized information service for its natural and historic sites in Florida. You must contact each site directly for information on current recreational facilities and hours. To obtain a copy of **Guide and Map of National Parks of U.S.**, which provides park addresses and facilities lists, write to U.S. Government Printing Office, Washington, DC 20402. GPO No. 024005008527. Cost: $1.25 (no tax or postage).

In 1908 the federal government declared the keys around what is now **Fort Jefferson National Monument** in the Dry Tortugas a wildlife sanctuary to protect the sooty tern. **Everglades National Park** was established in 1947. Other natural and historic sites in the Miami area under federal management include **Big Cypress National Preserve** and **Biscayne National Park** in the Everglades, and **Canaveral National Seashore** in central Florida.

The federal government operates three national forests in Florida: the two in the Miami area are the 336,000-acre **Ocala**

National Forest, including the sandhills of the Big Scrub, and the 157,000-acre **Osceola National Forest,** dotted with cypress swamps and numerous sinkhole lakes.

National wildlife refuges in the region include the **Great White Heron National Wildlife Refuge** and **National Key Deer Refuge** (in the Keys) and **Loxahatchee National Wildlife Refuge** near Palm Beach. The federal government also operates the **Key Largo National Marine Sanctuary, Looe Key National Marine Sanctuary,** and the **Florida Keys National Marine Sanctuary,** largest in the national system, established in 1990.

State Parks
The **Florida Department of Natural Resources** is responsible for hundreds of historic buildings, landmarks, nature preserves, and an expanding state park system. When you request a free copy of the *Florida State Park Guide,* mention which parts of the state you plan to visit. For information on camping facilities at the state parks, ask for the free *Florida State Parks, Fees and Facilities* and *Florida State Parks Camping Reservation Procedures* brochures (Marjory Stoneman Douglas Bldg., MS 535, 3900 Commonwealth Blvd., Tallahassee 32399–3000, tel. 904/488–7896).

Private Nature Preserves
In 1905, Audubon Society warden Guy Bradley died while protecting the egrets nesting at Cuthbert Rookery, in what is now Everglades National Park. Private efforts to preserve Florida's fragile ecosystems continue today, as the **National Audubon Society** and the **Nature Conservancy** acquire and manage sensitive natural areas.

On Big Pine Key, Audubon has leased acreage without charge to the U.S. Fish and Wildlife Service in the **National Key Deer Refuge.** Audubon also controls more than 65 other Florida properties, including islands, prairies, forests, and swamps. Visitation at these sites is limited. For information, contact National Audubon Society, Sanctuary Director (Miles Wildlife Sanctuary, RR 1, Box 294, W. Cornwall Rd., Sharon, CT 06069, tel. 203/364–0048).

For access to these tracts, information on self-guided tour information, and a guide to the Conservancy's holdings contact the Florida Chapter of the Nature Conservancy (2699 Lee Rd., Suite 500, Winter Park 32789, tel. 407/628–5887). Visitors are welcome at the offices in Miami, Key West, and West Palm Beach. *Rivergate Plaza Bldg., 444 Brickell Ave., Ste. 224, Miami 33131, tel. 305/530–8585; 201 Front St., Bldg. 21, Key West 33040, tel. 305/296–3880; Comeau Bldg., 319 Clematis St., Ste. 611, West Palm Beach 33401, tel. 407/833–4226. Open weekdays 9–5.*

Dining

The state's restaurateurs are developing a Florida–Caribbean cuisine in which local vegetables, seafood, and fruits are used. The fare changes, however, as you move from region to region, based on who settled the area and who now operates the restaurants. But always you can expect seafood to be a staple on nearly every menu. Look for traditional Miccosukee and Seminole Indian fried bread, catfish, and frogs' legs at tribe-owned restaurants in the Everglades. South Florida's diverse assortment of Latin American restaurants offers the distinctive national fare of Argentina, Brazil, Colombia, Cuba, El Salvador, Mexico, Nicaragua, and Puerto Rico as well as West Indian delicacies from the Bahamas, Haiti, and Jamaica, and an acclaimed new tropical-Continental-nouvelle fusion that originated in Miami.

The influence of earlier Hispanic settlements remains in Key West and Tampa's Ybor City.

All over Florida, Asian cuisine no longer means just Chinese. Indian, Japanese, Pakistani, Thai, and Vietnamese specialties are now available. Continental cuisine (French, German, Italian, Spanish, and Swiss) is also well represented all over Florida. Many of these restaurants have excellent wine lists.

Every Florida restaurant claims to make the best Key lime pie. Pastry chefs and restaurant managers take the matter very seriously—they discuss the problems of getting good lime juice and maintaining top quality every day. Traditional Key lime pie is yellow, not green, with an old-fashioned Graham cracker crust and meringue top. The filling should be tart, and chilled but not frozen. Some restaurants serve their Key lime pie with a pastry crust; most substitute whipped cream for the more temperamental meringue. Each pie will be a little different. Try several, and make your own choice.

Ratings

Category	Cost*: Major Cities	Cost*: Other Areas
Very Expensive	over $50	over $40
Expensive	$30–$50	$25–$40
Moderate	$15–$30	$10–$25
Inexpensive	under $15	under $10

per person, excluding drinks, service, and 6% sales tax

Lodging

Hotels and Motels All the major hotel and motel chains are represented in Florida. Holiday Inn, Marriott, and Quality Inns operate under a variety of brand names offering varying levels of amenities and prices.

Although many hotels in Florida have affiliated with a chain to get business from its central reservation system, some fine hotels and resorts still remain independent. They include The Breakers in Palm Beach and Pier House in Key West.

The Florida Hotel & Motel Association (FH&MA) publishes an *Annual Travel Directory* which you can obtain without charge from the **Florida Division of Tourism** (Department of Commerce, 126 Van Buren St., Tallahassee 32399, tel. 904/487-1462). You can also order it from the FH&MA if you send a stamped, addressed No. 10 envelope and $1 for handling (117 W. College Ave., Box 1529, Tallahassee 32301–1529, tel. 904/224-2888).

Ratings	Category	Cost*: Major Cities	Cost*: Other Areas
	Very Expensive	$150 peak season $100 off-peak	$100
	Expensive	$120–$150 peak season $80–$100 off-peak	$70–$100
	Moderate	$80–$120 peak season $50–$80 off-peak	$40–$70
	Inexpensive	under $80 peak season under $50 off-peak	under $40

All prices are for a standard double room, excluding 6% state sales tax (some counties also have a local sales tax), and nominal (1%–4%) tourist tax.

Alternative Lodgings Small inns and guest houses are becoming increasingly numerous and popular in Florida. Many offer the convenience of bed-and-breakfast accommodations in a homelike setting; many, in fact, are in private homes, and the owners treat you almost like a member of the family. **Inn Route, Inc.** (525 Simonton St., Key West 33040, tel. 305/294–6712), a statewide association of small, architecturally distinctive historic inns, will send you a free brochure newly published in 1992. You can also order the award-winning *Guide to the Small and Historic Lodgings of Florida*, a paperback book updated every two years, the latest one in 1993 (Pineapple Press Inc., Drawer 16008, Sarasota 34239, tel. 813/952–1085. Cost: $14.95 plus 6% sales tax).

Bed-and-breakfast referral and reservation agencies in Florida include: **Bed & Breakfast Co., Tropical Florida** (Box 262, Miami 33243, tel. 305/661–3270), **Bed & Breakfast East Coast** (Box 1373, Marathon 33050, tel. 305/743–4118), **Open House Bed & Breakfast,** (Box 3025, Palm Beach 33480, tel. 407/842–5190), **Southern Comfort Reservation & Referral Service** (8021 S.E. Helen Terr., Hobe Sound 33455, tel. 407/546–6743), and **Suncoast Accommodations of Florida** (8690 Gulf Blvd., St. Petersburg Beach 33706, tel. 813/360–1753).

Camping and RV Facilities Contact the national parks and forests you plan to visit directly for information on camping facilities (*see* National Parks, above). For information on camping facilities in state parks, contact the Florida Department of Natural Resources (*see* State Parks, above).

The free annual *Florida Camping Directory* lists 200 commercial campgrounds in Florida with 50,000 sites. It's available at Florida welcome centers, from the Florida Division of Tourism, and from the **Florida Campground Association** (1638 N. Plaza Dr., Tallahassee 32308–5364, tel. 904/656–8878).

Vacation Ownership Resorts Vacation ownership resorts sell hotel rooms, condominium apartments, or villas in weekly, monthly, or quarterly increments. The weekly arrangement is most popular; it's often referred to as "interval ownership" or "time sharing." Of more than 2,500 vacation ownership resorts around the world, some 400 are in Florida, with the heaviest concentration in the Disney World/Orlando area. Most vacation ownership resorts are affiliated with one of two major exchange organizations—**Interval International** (6262 Sunset Dr., Penthouse One, S. Miami

33143, tel. 305/666–1861 or 800/828–8200) or **Resort Condominiums International** (3502 Woodview Trace, Indianapolis, IN 46268–3131, tel. 317/876–8899 or 800/338–7777). As an owner, you can join your resort's exchange organization and swap your interval for another someplace else in any year when you want a change of scene. Even if you don't own an interval, you can rent at many vacation ownership resorts where unsold intervals remain and/or owners have placed their intervals in a rental program. For rental information, contact the exchange organizations (Worldex, tel. 800/722–1861; Resort Condominiums International, tel. 800/654–5000), the individual resort, or a local real estate broker in the area where you want to rent.

Credit Cards

The following credit card abbreviations are used: AE, American Express; CB, Carte Blanche; D, Discover; DC, Diners Club; MC, MasterCard; V, Visa. It's always a good idea to call ahead to confirm current credit card policies.

2 Miami and Miami Beach

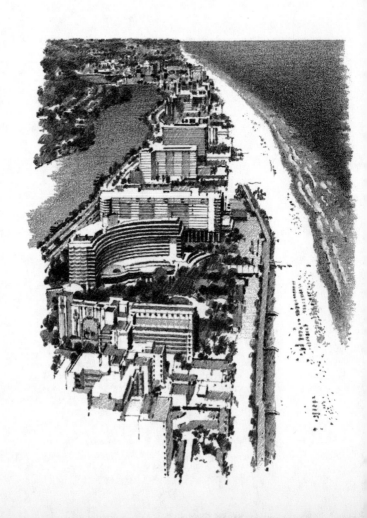

By George and Rosalie Leposky

Updated by Herb Hiller

Editor of the Ecotourism Society Newsletter, *Herb Hiller is also a freelance writer whose pieces often focus on backroads travel and cycling.*

What they say about Miami is true. The city *is* different. Miami is different from what it once was and it's different from other cities. Once a sleepy southern resort town, Miami today is a burgeoning giant of international commerce and finance as well as a place to find pleasure and relaxation. Like all big cities, Miami inspires the first-time visitor with hopes and dreams. Also as in other cities, many of these hopes and dreams can be side-tracked by crime and violence.

Miami's natural difference can be detected when you fly into the city. Clinging to a thin ribbon of dry land between the marshy Everglades and the Atlantic Ocean, Miami remains vulnerable to its perennial mosquitoes, periodic flooding, and worst of all, to torrential storms such as Hurricane Andrew that, in late summer 1992, destroyed parts of Greater Miami's South Dade County. Thousands of residents in Kendall, Florida City, Homestead, and Cutler Ridge lost homes and businesses, many of which will never be rebuilt. Andrew, which has been called "the most devastating natural disaster in American history," mercilessly ripped through the communities in its path, leaving few relics except the remains of trees and buildings brought to the ground by its fury. If there is any consolation here, however, it is that Andrew's route only braised Downtown Miami, Coral Gables, Coconut Grove, Bal Harbour, and Miami Beach (Art Deco District), where the city's history is still preserved in the historic buildings and parks. Except for minor damage, the much-touristed cosmopolitan area was spared. So don't avoid Miami: It's pulse beats ever stronger for having weathered the storm. If you have any questions concerning your itinerary the Greater Miami Convention and Visitors Bureau (tel. 305/672–1270) can advise you.

Miami may be the wrong place for a city, but it's the right place for a crossroads. Long before Spain's gold-laden treasure ships passed offshore in the Gulf Stream, the Calusa Indians who lived here had begun to trade with their mainland neighbors to the north and their island brethren to the south. Repeating this prehistoric pattern, many U.S. and multinational companies now locate their Latin American headquarters in Greater Miami because no other city can match its airline connections to the Western Hemisphere.

That same ease of access, coupled with a congenial climate, attracts hordes of Latin tourists. Access and climate also explain why Miami has become what *Newsweek* calls "America's Casablanca." Whenever a Latin American or Caribbean government erupts in revolution and economic chaos, the inevitable refugees flock to Miami (where they open restaurants).

Today, almost half of Greater Miami's population is Hispanic— the majority from Cuba, with significant populations from Colombia, El Salvador, Nicaragua, Panama, Puerto Rico, and Venezuela. About 150,000 French- and Creole-speaking Haitians also live in Greater Miami, as do Brazilians, Chinese, Germans, Greeks, Iranians, Israelis, Italians, Jamaicans, Lebanese, Malaysians, Russians, Swedes, and more—a veritable Babel of tongues.

Try not to think of Miami as a melting pot. Where ethnic and cultural diversity are the norm, there's less pressure to conform. Miamians practice matter-of-factly the customs they brought here—much to the consternation of other Miamians whose customs differ. The community wrestles constantly with these tensions and sensitivities.

As a big city, Miami has its share of crime, violence, and drug trafficking. And though the city dubiously led the nation in car thefts in 1992, you probably won't find the city's seamy underside unless you go looking for it. Still, just to make sure, and reflecting a new maturity, the Greater Miami Chamber of Commerce in 1991 began issuing a bilingual pamphlet with tips for avoiding crime while vacationing in the city. The hope is that more than ever visitors will find in Miami a multicultural metropolis that works and plays with vigor and that welcomes you to share its celebration of diversity.

Essential Information

Arriving and Departing by Plane

Airport **Miami International Airport (MIA),** 6 miles west of downtown Miami, is Greater Miami's only commercial airport. MIA has the nation's second-largest volume of international passenger and cargo traffic, and in 1991 was 10th busiest passenger airport in the world, ahead of New York's Kennedy International. MIA's busiest hours, when flight delays may occur, are 11 AM–8 PM. MIA contains 118 aircraft gates along seven concourses. Road improvements speed access into the departure area southbound from S.R. 112.

The airport has undertaken a $2 billion expansion program that will require much of the decade to complete; passengers will mainly notice expanded gates for American (concourses D and part of E) and United Airlines (concourse F, where Pan Am used to operate). A new 18-gate arrival/departure concourse A will go into construction by 1993, and will probably be completed in 1995. Improvements will help reduce congestion at concourses C, H, and F, all to be rebuilt; work on F is set for completion by 1993, and on C and H, by 1994. A largely underused convenience for passengers who have to get from one concourse to another in this long, linear terminal is the moving, cushioned Skywalk, one level up from the departure level, with access points at every concourse.

When you fly out of MIA, plan to check in 55 minutes before departure for a domestic flight and 90 minutes before departure for an international flight. Services for international travelers include 24-hour multilingual information and paging phones and foreign currency conversion booths throughout the terminal. An information booth with multilingual staff and 24-hour currency exchange are at Concourse E.

Between the Airport and Center City *By Bus* **Metrobus.** The county's Metrobus system has one benefit—its modest cost—if you're willing to put up with the inconveniences of infrequent service, scruffy equipment, and the circuitous path that many routes follow. Some routes from the airport are #7 to downtown (operates every 40 minutes from 6 AM to 10 PM; 9–5 on weekends); #37 South to Coral Gables and South Miami (operates every 30 minutes from 6 AM to 10 PM); #37 North to Hialeah (operates every 30 minutes from 5:30 AM to 11:30 PM); "J" to Coral Gables (operates every 30 minutes from 6 AM to 12:30 AM); #42 to Coconut Grove (operates hourly from 5:40 AM to 6:30 PM); and "J" east to Miami Beach (operates every 30 minutes from 4:30 AM to 11:30 PM). *Tel. 305/638–6700. Fare: $1.25 (exact change), transfer 25¢; 60¢ with 10¢ transfer for senior citizens and students.*

By Taxi   For trips originating at MIA or the Port of Miami, a $1 toll is added to the meter fare—except for the flat-fare trips described below. You'll pay a $14 flat fare between MIA and the Port of Miami, in either direction.

For taxi service from the airport to destinations in the immediate vicinity, ask a uniformed county taxi dispatcher to call an **ARTS (Airport Region Taxi Service)** cab for you. These special blue cabs will offer you a short-haul flat fare in two zones: an inner-city ride is $5; an outer-city fare is $8. Maps are posted in cab windows on both sides.

SuperShuttle vans transport passengers between MIA and local hotels, the Port of Miami, and even individual residences on a 24-hour basis. The company's service area extends from Palm Beach to Monroe County (including the Lower Keys). Drivers provide narration en route. It's best to make reservations 24 hours before departure, although the firm will try to arrange pickups within Dade County on as little as four hours' notice. *For information and reservations from inside MIA, tel. 305/ 871–8488. Reservations outside MIA, tel. 305/871–2000 (Dade and Monroe counties) or 305/674–1700 (Broward and Palm Beach counties). Pet transport fee: $5. Lower rate for 2nd passenger in same party for many destinations. Children 3 and under ride free with parents. AE, DC, MC, V.*

By Limousine   **Bayshore Limousine** has chauffeur-driven four-door town cars and stretch limousines available through the 24-hour reservation service. It serves Miami, Fort Lauderdale, Palm Beach, and the Keys. *11485 S.W. 87th Ave., Miami, tel. 305/253–9046, 235–3851, or 858–5888. AE, MC, V.*

Arriving and Departing by Car, Train, and Bus

By Car   The main highways into Greater Miami from the north are Florida's Turnpike (toll) and I–95. From the northwest, take I–75 or U.S. 27 into town. From the Everglades to the west, use the Tamiami Trail (U.S. 41). From the south, use U.S. 1 and the Homestead Extension of Florida's Turnpike. In 1993 and 1994 the Brickell Avenue (U.S. 1) bridge—a major north–south artery into downtown—will be closed. Drivers will have to use I–95. Construction will begin in late 1993/early 1994 on flyover ramps in the Golden Glades interchange, while by 1994 construction is scheduled for completion on upgrades between N.W. 58th and 95th streets, on new ramps where I–95 and S.R. 836 meet, and on a new off-ramp southbound onto N.W. 8th Street. Widening the six lanes of the MacArthur Causeway and accompanying installation of safety shoulders along this road (bordered on both sides by water) is expected to be completed in the summer of 1993.

Rental Cars   Five rental-car firms—**Avis Rent-a-Car** (tel. 800/331–1212), **Dollar Rent-a-Car** (tel. 800/800–4000), **Hertz Rent-a-Car** (tel. 800/654–3131), **National Rent-a-Car** (tel. 800/328–4567), and **Value Rent-a-Car** (tel. 800/327–2501)—have booths near the baggage claim area on MIA's lower level—a convenience when you arrive.

By Train **Amtrak's** two trains between Miami and New York City, the
Silver Meteor and *Silver Star*, make different stops along the
way. Each has a daily Miami arrival and departure.

Amtrak's "All Aboard" fare is the most economical way to travel to Florida, if you have time to meet the length-of-stay requirements. Trains run full all year, except in October and
May. For the best fare, contact Amtrak as soon as you decide to
take a trip. Ask for Amtrak's 1992 travel planner. *Amtrak Station, 8303 N.W. 37th Ave., Miami 33147. For recorded arrival/
departure information, tel. 305/835-1200; package and express service, tel. 305/835-1225. Advance reservations required. Reservations: Amtrak Customer Relations, 400 N.
Capitol St., NW, Washington, DC 20001, tel. 800/USA-RAIL
in the U.S., 800/4AMTRAK in Canada.*

The 4-year old **Tri-Rail** commuter train system connects Miami
with Broward and Palm Beach Monday-Saturday. Call for
schedule and details on weekly and monthly passes. *Suite 200, 1
River Plaza, 305 S. Andrews Ave., Fort Lauderdale, FL 33301,
tel. 305/728-8445 or 800/TRI-RAIL.*

By Bus **Greyhound/Trailways** buses stop at five bus terminals in Greater Miami. *700 Biscayne Blvd., Miami, tel. 305/379-7403 (fares
and schedules only). No reservations.*

Getting Around Miami

Greater Miami resembles Los Angeles in its urban sprawl and
traffic congestion. You'll need a car to visit many of the attractions and points of interest listed in this book. Some are accessible via public transportation.

A department of county government, the Metro-Dade Transit
Agency, runs the public transportation system. It consists of
more than 450 Metrobuses on 74 routes, the 21-mile Metrorail
elevated rapid transit system, and the 1.9-mile Metromover in
downtown Miami. Free maps, schedules, and a First-Time Rid-
er's Kit are available. *6601 N.W. 72nd Ave., Miami 33166.
Maps by Mail, tel. 305/638-6137. For route information, tel.
305/638-6700 daily 6 AM-11 PM. Fare $1.25, transfer 25¢, exact
change only.*

By Train Metrorail runs from downtown Miami north to Hialeah and
south along U.S. 1 to Dadeland. *Service every 7½ minutes in
peak hours, every 15-30 minutes other times. Weekdays 6 AM-
midnight, weekends 6:30 AM-6:30 PM. Runs until midnight on
weekends for special events such as the Orange Bowl parade.
Fare: $1.25.*

Metromover's two loops circle downtown Miami, linking major
hotels, office buildings, and shopping areas (*see* Exploring
Downtown Miami, below). An extension of Metromover (north
to the Omni district and south to Brickell Ave. at Coral Way)
began in 1991 and is expected to be completed by 1994. *Service
every 90 seconds. Weekdays 6:30 AM-midnight, weekends 8:30
AM-midnight. Later for special events. Fare 25¢.*

By Bus Metrobus stops are marked by blue-and-green signs with a bus
logo and route information. The frequency of service varies
widely. Obtain specific schedule information in advance for the
routes you want to ride. *Tel. 305/638-6700.*

By Taxicab There are some 2,000 taxicabs in Dade County. Fares are $1.10 for the first ⅓ mile, 20¢ for each additional ⅓ mile; waiting time 20¢ for each ⅖ minute. No additional charge for extra passengers, luggage, or road and bridge tolls. Taxi companies with dispatch service are **All American Taxi** (tel. 305/947–3333), **Central Taxicab Service** (tel. 305/534–0694), **Diamond Cab Company** (tel. 305/545–7575), **Dolphin Cab** (tel. 305/948–6666), **Magic City Cab Company** (tel. 305/757–5523), **Metro Taxicab Company** (tel. 305/888–8888), **Miami-Dade Yellow Cab** (tel. 305/633–0503), **Miami Springs Taxi** (tel. 305/888–8541), **Society Cab Company** (tel. 305/757–5523), **Speedy Cab** (tel. 305/861–9999), **Super Yellow Cab Company** (tel. 305/888–7777), **Tropical Taxicab Company** (tel. 305/945–1025), and **Yellow Cab Company** (tel. 305/444–4444). Many now accept credit cards. Inquire when you call.

It is recommended that you be on your guard when traveling by cab in Miami, as some drivers are rude and unhelpful, and have even been known to take advantage of visitors who are unfamiliar with their destinations or the layout of the city. If it's possible, avoid taking a cab; if you must, try to be familiar with your route and destination.

By Car Finding your way around Greater Miami is easy if you know how the numbering system works. Miami is laid out on a grid with four quadrants—northeast, northwest, southeast, and southwest—which meet at Miami Avenue and Flagler Street. Miami Avenue separates east from west and Flagler Street separates north from south. *Avenues* and *courts* run north-south; *streets*, *terraces*, and *ways* run east-west. *Roads* run diagonally, northwest-southeast.

Many named streets also bear numbers. For example, Unity Boulevard is N.W. and S.W. 27th Avenue, LeJeune Road is N.W. and S.W. 42nd Avenue. However, named streets that depart markedly from the grid, such as Biscayne Boulevard and Brickell Avenue, have no corresponding numerical designations. Dade County and most other municipalities follow the Miami numbering system.

In Miami Beach, *avenues* run north-south; *streets*, east-west. Numbers rise along the beach from south to north and from the Atlantic Ocean in the east to Biscayne Bay in the west.

In Coral Gables, all streets bear names. Coral Gables uses the Miami numbering system for north-south addresses but begins counting east-west addresses westward from Douglas Road (S.W. 37th Ave.).

Hialeah has its own grid. Palm Avenue separates east from west; Hialeah Drive separates north from south. *Avenues* run north-south and *streets* east-west. Numbered streets and avenues are designated west, east, or southeast.

Important Addresses and Numbers

Tourist Information The Greater Miami Convention and Visitors Bureau has opened satellite tourist information centers in Miami Beach (Miami Beach Chamber of Commerce, 1920 Meridian Ave., 33139, tel. 305/672–1270), and in Homestead–Florida City (South Dade Visitors Information Center, 1160 U.S. 1, Florida City 33034, tel. 305/245–9180 or 800/852–8675). Additional satellite centers were to open in 1992 at Bayside downtown and in

Miami Beach and at the corner of Lincoln Road and Washington Avenue. Contact the bureau for locations and hours or to request information by mail.

Visitor Services, Greater Miami Convention and Visitors Bureau (701 Brickell Ave., Suite 2700, Miami 33131, tel. 305/539–3063 or 800/283–2707); Surfside Tourist Board (9301 Collins Ave., Surfside 33154, tel. 305/864–0722).

Chambers of Commerce
Greater Miami has a central chamber—the **Greater Miami Chamber of Commerce** (1601 Biscayne Blvd., Miami 33132, tel. 305/350–7700)—as well as more than 20 local chambers of commerce, each promoting its individual community. Most maintain racks of brochures on tourist information in their offices and will send you information about their community.

Coconut Grove Chamber of Commerce (2820 McFarlane Rd., Coconut Grove 33133, tel. 305/444–7270).
Coral Gables Chamber of Commerce (50 Aragon Ave., Coral Gables 33134, tel. 305/446–1657).
Gold Coast Chamber of Commerce (1100 Kane Concourse, Suite 210, Bay Harbor Islands 33154, tel. 305/866–6020). Serves the beach communities of Bal Harbour, Bay Harbor Islands, Golden Beach, North Bay Village, Sunny Isles, and Surfside.
Key Biscayne Chamber of Commerce (Key Biscayne Bank Bldg., 95 W. McIntyre St., Key Biscayne 33149, tel. 305/361–5207).
Miami Beach Chamber of Commerce (1920 Meridian Ave., Miami Beach 33139, tel. 305/672–1270).
North Miami Chamber of Commerce (13100 W. Dixie Hwy., North Miami 33181, tel. 305/891–7811).
Greater South Dade/South Miami Chamber of Commerce (6410 S.W. 80th St., South Miami 33143–4602, tel. 305/661–1621).

Emergencies
Dial 911 for **police** and **ambulance.** You can dial free from pay phones.

Telecommunication lines for the hearing impaired are used by hearing-impaired travelers with telecommunication devices (TDD) to reach TDD-equipped public services:

Fire/Police/Medical/Rescue (tel. 305/595–4749 TDD)
Operator and Directory Assistance (tel. 800/855–1155 TDD)
Deaf Services of Miami (5455 SW 8th St., Room 255, Miami, tel. 305/444–2211 TDD or voice 305/444–2266). Operates 24 hours.

Ambulance
Randle Eastern Ambulance Service Inc. Serves Greater Miami. Meets air ambulances and takes patients to hospitals. Services include advanced life-support systems. *35 S.W. 27th Ave., Miami 33135, tel. 305/642–6400. Open 24 hrs. AE, MC, V.*

Hospitals
The following hospitals have 24-hour emergency rooms:

Miami Beach: *Mt. Sinai Medical Center* (4300 Alton Rd., Miami Beach, tel. 305/674–2200; physician referral, tel. 674–2273). Just off Julia Tuttle Causeway (I–195).

St. Francis Hospital (250 W. 63rd St., Miami Beach, tel. 305/868–2770; physician referral, tel. 305/868–2728). Near Collins Ave. and north end of Alton Rd.

Central: *University of Miami/Jackson Memorial Medical Center.* Includes Jackson Memorial Hospital, a county hospital with Greater Miami's only trauma center. Near Dolphin Expressway. Metrorail stops a block away. *1611 N.W. 12th Ave., Miami, tel. 305/325–7429. Emergency room, tel. 305/585–6901. Interpreter service, tel. 305/549–6316. Patient relations, tel. 305/549–7341. Physician referral, tel. 305/547–5757.*

Mercy Hospital (3663 S. Miami Ave., Coconut Grove, tel. 305/285–2171; physician referral, tel. 305/285–2929). Greater Miami's only hospital with an emergency boat dock.

Miami Children's Hospital (6125 S.W. 31st St., tel. 305/662–8280; physician referral, ext. 2563).

South: *Baptist Hospital of Miami* (8900 N. Kendall Dr., Miami, tel. 305/596–6556; physician referral, tel. 305/596–6557).

24-Hour Pharmacies Of some 300 pharmacies in Greater Miami, only five are open 24 hours a day. Most pharmacies open at 8 or 9 AM and close between 9 PM and midnight. Many pharmacies offer local delivery service.

Eckerd Drugs. 1825 Miami Gardens Dr. N.E. (185th St.), North Miami Beach, tel. 305/932–5740 and 9031 S.W. 107th Ave., Miami, tel. 305/274–6776.

Walgreens. 500–B W. 49th St. (Palm Springs Mall), Hialeah, tel. 305/557–5468; 12245 Biscayne Blvd., Miami, tel. 305/893–6860; 5731 Bird Rd., Miami, tel. 305/666–0757.

Physician Referral Services **Dade County Medical Association** (1501 N.W. N. River Dr., Miami, tel. 305/324–8717). Office open weekdays 9–5 for medical referral.

East Coast District Dental Society (420 S. Dixie Hwy., Suite 2E, Coral Gables, tel. 305/667–3647). Office open weekdays 9 AM–4:30 PM for dental referral. Services include general dentistry, endodontics, periodontics, and oral surgery.

Guided Tours

Orientation Tours **Old Town Trolley of Miami.** Ninety-minute narrated tours of Miami and 90-minute tours of Miami Beach leave Bayside Marketplace every half hour between 10 and 4. *Box 12985, Miami 33101, tel. 305/374–8687. Miami and Miami Beach tours: $14 adults, $5 children 3–12. No credit cards.*

Special-Interest Tours *Air Tours* **Air Tours of Miami** offers 1-hour sightseeing tours of Miami, the Everglades, and nearby waters in a Piper Seneca II six-seater. *1470 N.E. 123rd St., Ste. 602, Miami, tel. 305/893–5874. Tours depart from Opa-locka Airport; inquire for directions. Cost: $75 adults, $50 children, minimum of 3 adults, maximum of 5. Reservations required. Other tours to Key West, Orlando, Southeast Florida, and Caribbean are offered. AE, MC, V.*

Gold Coast Helicopters. This family business offers Bell-47 helicopter rides that last eight minutes or longer. *15101 Biscayne Blvd., N. Miami, tel. 305/940–1009. Cost: $60 for 1 or 2, for 8 min. Longer rides cost more. Reservations advised.*

Boat Tours ***Heritage of Miami II.*** Miami's official tall ship, an 85-foot steel sailing schooner, docks at Bayside Marina. Carries up to 49 passengers for day sailing, sleeps 16; children and cameras welcome. Ice and ice chest on board, soft drinks for sale; bring your own food. Standard Biscayne Bay day trip lasts two hours. Reservations recommended. *3145 Virginia St., Coconut Grove*

33133, tel. 305/442–9697. Cost: $10 adults, $5 children under 12. Sails daily, weather permitting.

Island Queen and **Good Times Too** are a pair of 150-passenger double-decker tour boats that dock at Bayside Marketplace (401 Biscayne Blvd.) and offer 90-minute narrated tours of Port of Miami and Millionaires' Row. *Cost: $10 adults, $5 children. Tel. 305/379–5119. Tours daily.*

Nikko Gold Coast Cruises. Two 150-passenger boats based at Haulover Park Marina specialize in water tours to major Greater Miami attractions. *10800 Collins Ave., Miami Beach, tel. 305/945–5461. Tours include Bayside Marketplace ($9.59 adults, $5.33 children under 13); Seaquarium ($27.64/$18.06, including admission); Vizcaya ($18.11/$9.59, including admission); and 2-hr sightseeing trips at 10 AM and 2 PM ($7.95/ $4.19). (Second price is for children under 13.)*

History Tours   **Art Deco District Tour.** Meet your guide at 10:30 AM Saturday and Sunday, 5 PM Wednesday at the Leslie Hotel (1244 Ocean Dr., Miami Beach), the **Miami Design Preservation League's** welcome center, for a 90-minute tour. Wear comfortable shoes. Also available is the League's *Art Deco District Guide*, a book with six detailed walking or driving tours of the square-mile Art Deco District on Miami Beach. *Bin L, Miami Beach 33119, tel. 305/672–2014. Cost: $6 for tour, $10 for book.*

Prof. Paul George. Explore Miami's history with a professional historian on a 3-hour walking tour of downtown. Paul George is a history professor at Miami-Dade Community College and the past-president of the Florida Historical Society. His tour begins either on the north bank of the Miami River behind the Hyatt Regency Hotel, 400 S.E. 2nd Ave., or at Bayside Marketplace (*see* Exploring Downtown Miami, below). Wear comfortable walking shoes and a hat. Tours are usually held Saturdays, 9 AM–1 PM, and by appointment. George also gives 2½-hour walking tours of Brickell Avenue, Buena Vista, Coconut Grove, Coral Gables, Little Havana, Miami's old City Cemetery, the Miami Beach Art Deco District, historic Morningside, Southside, and Fort Lauderdale and Fort Lauderdale Beach. *1345 S.W. 14th St., Miami, tel. 305/858–6021, $10 adults, $7 children 7–14, under 7 free.*

Rickshaw Tours   **Majestic Rickshaw.** Look for rickshaws along Main Highway in Coconut Grove's Village Center (75 N.E. 156 St., Biscayne Gardens, tel. 305/256–8833) nightly 8 PM–2 AM in Coconut Grove. Rickshaw holds two adults. $3 per person for 10-minute ride through Coconut Grove, $6 per person for 20-minute lovers' moonlight ride down to Biscayne Bay. No credit cards.

Self-Guided Tours   **The Junior League of Miami** publishes five excellent self-guiding tours to architectural and historical landmarks in Coconut Grove, Coral Gables, downtown Miami, the northeast, and south Dade. *2325 Salzedo, Coral Gables 33134, tel. 305/ 443–0160. Cost: $3 each.*

Exploring Miami

Exploring Downtown Miami

Numbers in the margin correspond to points of interest on the Downtown Miami map.

Orientation From a distance you see downtown Miami's future—a 21st-century skyline already stroking the clouds with sleek fingers of steel and glass. By day, this icon of commerce and technology sparkles in the strong subtropical sun; at night, it basks in the man-made glow of floodlights.

Staid, suited lawyers and bankers share the sidewalks with Hispanic merchants wearing open-neck, intricately embroidered shirts called *guayaberas.* Fruit merchants sell their wares from pushcarts. European youths with backpacks stroll the streets. Foreign businessmen haggle over prices in import–export shops. You hear Arabic, Chinese, Creole, French, German, Hebrew, Hindi, Japanese, Portuguese, Spanish, Swedish, Yiddish, and even a little English now and then.

With effort, you can find remnants of downtown Miami's past, though still less this year than last, when two venerable hotels, the McAlister and the Columbus, were demolished. Most of the city's "old" downtown buildings date from only the 1920s and 1930s—an incongruity if you're from someplace that counts its past in centuries. Remember that Miami is a young city, incorporated in 1896 with just 3,000 residents. A Junior League book, *Historic Downtown Miami,* locates and describes 27 older structures in and near downtown, including 21 you can see in a two-hour self-guided walking tour of slightly more than a mile.

Touring Downtown Miami Parking downtown is inconvenient and expensive. If you're staying elsewhere in the area, leave your car at an outlying Metrorail station and take the train downtown. Metromover, a separate light-rail mass-transit system, circles the heart of the city on twin elevated loops. No part of the downtown tour is more than 2 blocks from one of Metromover's nine stations. We've organized the tour around those stations, so you can ride Metromover directly to the downtown attractions that interest you most.

❶❷ When you get off the Metrorail train at **Government Center Station,** notice the **Dade County Courthouse** (73 W. Flagler St.). It's the building to the east with a pyramid at its peak, where turkey vultures roost in winter. Built in 1928, it was once the tallest building south of Washington, D.C.

❸ As you leave the Metrorail station, you'll enter **Metro-Dade Center,** the county government's 30-story office building. Designed by architect Hugh Stubbins, it opened in 1985.

❹ Across N.W. 1st Street from Metro-Dade Center stands the **Metro-Dade Cultural Center** (101 W. Flagler St.), opened in 1983. The 3.3-acre complex is a Mediterranean expression of architect Philip Johnson's postmodern style. An elevated plaza provides a serene haven from the city's pulsations and a superb setting for festivals and outdoor performances.

The Center for the Fine Arts, an art museum in the tradition of the European *kunsthalle* (exhibition gallery), has no permanent collection but it organizes and borrows temporary exhibitions on many artistic themes. Shows scheduled for early 1993 include "Florida Collects" and "Portrait Drawings from the Portrait Gallery of London." *Tel. 305/375–1700. Admission: $5 adults, $2 children 6–12, under 6 free. Donations Tues. Open Tues.–Sat. 10–5, Thurs. 10–9, Sun. noon–5.*

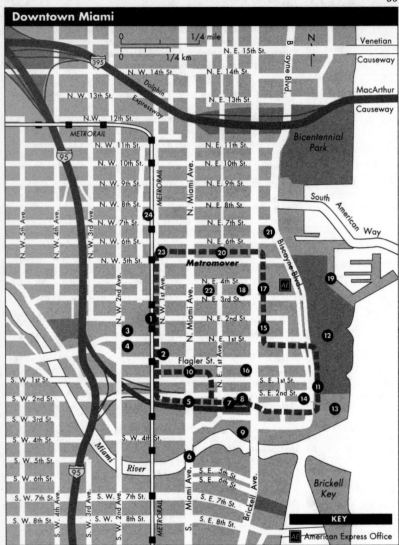

Downtown Miami

Bayfront Park, **12**
Bayfront Park
Station, **11**
Bayside
Marketplace, **19**
College Bayside
Station, **17**

Dade County
Courthouse, **2**
Edcom Station, **20**
First St. Station, **15**
Ft. Dallas Park
Station, **5**
Freedom Tower, **21**
Government Center
Station, **1**
Gusman Center, **16**

Hotel Inter-
Continental Miami, **13**
International Place, **8**
James L. Knight
International Center, **9**
Knight Center
Station, **7**
Metro-Dade Center, **3**
Metro-Dade Cultural
Center, **4**

Miami Arena, **24**
Miami Ave. Bridge, **6**
Miami Ave. Station, **10**
Miami-Dade
Community
College, **18**
Southeast Financial
Center, **14**
State Plaza/Arena
Station, **23**
U.S. Courthouse, **22**

The Historical Museum of Southern Florida is a regional museum that interprets the human experience in southern Florida from prehistory to the present. Artifacts on permanent display include Tequesta and Seminole Indian ceramics, clothing, and tools; a 1920 streetcar; and an original edition of Audubon's *Birds of America*. *Tel. 305/375–1492. Admission: $4 adults, $2 children 6–12, under 6 free. Donations Mon. Open Mon.–Sat. 10–5, Thurs. 10–9, Sun. noon–5.*

The Main Public Library has 3,231,306 holdings as of late 1991 and a computerized card catalog. Inside the entrance, look up at the rotunda mural, where artist Edward Ruscha interpreted a quotation from Shakespeare: "Words without thought never to heaven go." You'll find art exhibits in the auditorium and second-floor lobby. *Tel. 305/375–BOOK. Open Mon.–Sat. 9–6, Thurs. 9–9, Sun. 1–5. Closed Sun. May–mid-Oct.*

At Government Center Station, you can also transfer to Metromover's inner and outer loops through downtown. We've listed the stations and their attractions in sequence along the outer loop.

⑤ **⑥** The first stop is **Ft. Dallas Park Station.** If you disembark here, you're a block from the **Miami Ave. Bridge,** one of 11 bridges on the river that open to let ships pass. From the bridge approach, watch freighters, tugboats, research vessels, and luxury yachts ply this busy 5-mile waterway.

Time Out Stroll across the bridge to **Tobacco Road** for a drink, snack, or meal. Built in 1912, this friendly neighborhood pub was a speakeasy during Prohibition. *626 S. Miami Ave., tel. 305/374–1198. Open weekdays 11:30 AM–5 AM, weekends 12:30 PM–5 AM. Lunch weekdays 11:30–2:30. Dinner nightly. AE, DC, MC, V.*

⑦ **⑧** The next Metromover stop, **Knight Center Station,** nestles inside the **International Place** (100 S.E. 1st St.), a wedge-shape 47-story skyscraper designed by I. M. Pei & Partners. The building is brilliantly illuminated at night. Inside the Tower, **⑨** follow signs to the **James L. Knight International Center** (400 S.E. 2nd Ave., tel. 305/372–0929), a convention and concert hall adjoining the Hyatt Regency Hotel.

At the Knight Center Station, you can transfer to the inner **⑩** loop and ride one stop to the **Miami Avenue Station,** a block south of **Flagler Street,** downtown Miami's commercial spine. Like most such thoroughfares, Flagler Street lost business in recent years to suburban malls—but unlike most, it found a new lease on life. Today, the ½-mile of Flagler Street from Biscayne Boulevard to the Dade County Courthouse is the most important import-export center in the United States. Its stores and arcades supply much of the world with bargain automotive parts, audio and video equipment, medical equipment and supplies, photographic equipment, clothing, and jewelry.

Time Out Walk about 2½ blocks north of Flagler Street to **The Eating Place,** an open-air Jamaican restaurant as authentic as any in Kingston. The jukebox pours reggae onto Miami Avenue while waitresses pour the native beer, Red Stripe, which goes well with the oxtail stew or curried goat. *240 N. Miami Ave., tel. 305/375–0156. Open daily 8–6:30. No credit cards.*

⑪ ⑫ If you stay on the outer loop, you'll come next to **Bayfront Park Station,** opposite **Claude and Mildred Pepper Bayfront Park,** which extends from Biscayne Boulevard east to the edge of the bay. Japanese sculptor Isamu Noguchi redesigned the park just before his death in 1989; it now includes a memorial to the *Challenger* astronauts, an amphitheater, and a fountain honoring the late Florida congressman Claude Pepper and his wife.

⑬ Just south of Bayfront Park, the lobby of the **Hotel Inter-Continental Miami** (100 Chopin Plaza) contains *The Spindle,* a huge sculpture by Henry Moore.

⑭ West of Bayfront Park Station stands the tallest building in Florida, the 55-story **Southeast Financial Center** (200 S. Biscayne Blvd.), with towering royal palms in its 1-acre Palm Court plaza beneath a steel-and-glass space frame. Just north on the boulevard is where a 2-mile beautification is to begin in fall 1992 of Biscayne Boulevard. The new mosaic tile sidewalks will follow a design of Brazilian landscape architect Roberto Burle Marx.

⑮ ⑯ The next Metromover stop, **First Street Station,** places you a block north of Flagler Street and the landmark **Gusman Center for the Performing Arts,** an ornate former movie palace restored as a concert hall. Gusman Center resembles a Moorish courtyard with twinkling stars in the sky. Performances here include the Miami City Ballet, directed by Edward Villella, and the New World Symphony, a unique, advanced-training orchestra led by Michael Tilson Thomas. Gusman Center: *174 E. Flagler St., Miami 33131. Box office tel. 305/372–0925;* ballet: *905 Lincoln Rd., Miami Beach 33139, tel. 305/532–4880;* symphony: *555 Lincoln Rd., Miami Beach 33139, tel. 305/673–3330.*

⑰ ⑱ The **College/Bayside Station** Metromover stop serves the downtown campus of **Miami-Dade Community College,** where, in building 1, you can browse through two fine galleries: the Centre Gallery on the third floor, and the Frances Wolfson Art Gallery on the fifth floor, which houses traveling exhibitions of contemporary art. *300 N.E. 2nd Ave., tel. 305/237–3278. Admission free. Open weekdays 9–5:30.*

⑲ College/Bayside Station is also the most convenient Metromover stop for **Bayside Marketplace,** a waterside entertainment and shopping center built by the Rouse Company, between Bayfront Park and the entrance to the Port of Miami. Bayside's 235,000 square feet of retail space include 150 specialty shops, pushcarts in the center's Pier 5 area, outdoor cafés, and an international food court. The center adjoins the 145-slip Miamarina, where you can see luxurious yachts moored; you can also ride in an authentic 36-foot-long Venetian gondola. Pier 5 extends to a fisherman's wharf, where you can buy fresh seafood or sign on for a deep-sea or bay-fishing charter with any of 35 boats. Street performers entertain free throughout the day and evening, and live bands perform on the marina stage daily. *401 Biscayne Blvd., tel. 305/577–3344, for gondola rides 305/529–7178. Open Mon.–Sat. 10–10, Sun. noon–8; extended hours for restaurants and outdoor cafés.*

Just north of Bayside a twin-span bridge with five traffic lanes, completed in 1991, gives new access to the Port of Miami.

⑳ ㉑ As Metromover rounds the curve between College/Bayside Station and **Edcom Station,** look northeast to see **Freedom Tow-**

er (600 Biscayne Blvd.), where the Cuban Refugee Center pro-
cessed more than 500,000 Cubans who entered the United
States to flee Fidel Castro's regime in the 1960s. Built in 1925
for the *Miami Daily News*, this imposing Spanish-baroque
structure was inspired by the Giralda, an 800-year-old bell tower in Seville, Spain. After years in derelict condition, Freedom
Tower was renovated in 1988 and opened for office use in 1990,
though oddly, it has remained untenanted. To see it up close,
walk north from Edcom Station to N.E. 6th Street, then 2
blocks east to Biscayne Boulevard.

(22) A 2-block walk south from Edcom Station will bring you to the
U.S. Courthouse, a handsome keystone building erected in 1931
as Miami's main post office. On the second-floor central courtroom is *Law Guides Florida Progress*, a huge depression-era
mural by artist Denman Fink. *300 N.E. 1st Ave. Building open
weekdays 8:30–5; during those hours, security guards will
open courtroom on request. No cameras or tape recorders
allowed in building.*

(23)
(24) From **State Plaza/Arena Station,** walk two blocks north on
N.W. 1st Avenue to the new **Miami Arena** (721 N.W. 1st Ave.,
tel. 305/530–4444), home of the Miami Heat, a National Basketball Association team. Other sports and entertainment events
take place at the arena, which is also one block east of the
Overtown Metrorail Station.

Just across the Miami River from downtown, a canyon of tall
buildings lines **Brickell Avenue,** a southward extension of S.E.
2nd Avenue that begins in front of the Hyatt Regency Hotel
(400 S.E. 2nd Ave.). For the best views, drive Brickell Avenue
from north to south. You'll pass the largest concentration of international banking offices in the United States.

South of S.E. 15th Street several architecturally interesting
condominiums rise between Brickell Avenue and Biscayne
Bay. Israeli artist Yacov Agam painted the rainbow-hued exterior of **Villa Regina** (1581 Brickell Ave.). Arquitectonica, a nationally prominent architectural firm based in Miami, designed
three of these buildings: **The Palace** (1541 Brickell Ave.), **The
Imperial** (1627 Brickell Ave.), and **The Atlantis** (2025 Brickell
Ave.).

At S.E. 25th Road, turn right, follow signs to **I–95,** and return
to downtown Miami on one of the world's most scenic urban
highways. Paralleling Brickell Avenue and soaring 75 feet
above the Miami River, I–95 offers a superb view of the downtown skyline. At night, International Place is awash with light,
and, on the adjoining Metrorail bridge, a neon rainbow glows—
Rockne Krebs's 3,600-foot-long light sculpture, *The Miami
Line*. Just beyond the river, take the Biscayne Boulevard exit
back to S.E. 2nd Avenue in front of the Hyatt Regency Hotel.

Miami Beach

*Numbers in the margin correspond to points of interest on the
Miami Beach map.*

Orientation   Most visitors to the Greater Miami area don't realize that Miami and Miami Beach are separate cities. Miami, on the main-
land, is south Florida's commercial hub. Miami Beach, on 17
islands offshore in Biscayne Bay, is sometimes considered Am-

erica's Riviera, luring refugees from winter to its warm sunshine, sandy beaches, and graceful palms.

In 1912, what would become Miami Beach was little more than a sandspit in the bay. Then Carl Graham Fisher, a millionaire promoter who built the Indianapolis Speedway, began to pour much of his fortune into developing the island city.

Ever since, Miami Beach has experienced successive waves of boom and bust—thriving in the early 1920s and the years just after World War II, but also enduring the devastating 1926 hurricane, the Great Depression, travel restrictions during World War II, and an invasion of criminals released from Cuba during the 1980 Mariel boatlift.

Today, a renaissance is under way as Miami Beach revels in the architectural heritage of its mile-square Art Deco District. About 650 significant buildings in the district are listed on the National Register of Historic Places.

The term Art Deco describes the modern architecture that emerged in the 1920s and 1930s. Its forms are eclectic, drawn from nature (including birds, butterflies, and flowers); from ancient Aztec, Mayan, Babylonian, Chaldean, Egyptian, and Hebrew designs; and from the streamlined, aerodynamic shapes of modern transportation and industrial machinery. For detailed information on touring the Art Deco District, contact the Miami Design Preservation League (*see* Guided Tours, above).

Driving Tour of Miami Beach In our exploration, we direct you from the mainland to Miami Beach and through a cross section of the Art Deco District and the elegant residential neighborhood surrounding the La Gorce Country Club.

From the mainland, cross the **MacArthur Causeway** (Rte. 41) to Miami Beach. To reach the causeway from downtown Miami, turn east off Biscayne Boulevard north of N.E. 11th Street. From I–95, turn east onto I–395. The eastbound Dolphin Expressway (Rte. 836) becomes I–395 east of the I–95 interchange. As you approach the MacArthur Causeway bridge across the Intracoastal Waterway, *The Miami Herald* building looms above Biscayne Bay on your left.

❶ Cross the bridge to **Watson Island,** created by dredging in 1931. To your right is **Chalk's International Airlines** seaplane base (Watson Island, tel. 305/371–8628), the oldest scheduled international air carrier; it was bought in 1991 by Atwood Enterprises. Chalk's added seaplane service to Key West in 1991, and future plans include service to Havana. To your left across the causeway drive is the **Japanese Garden,** which has stone lanterns, a rock garden, and an eight-ton, eight-foot-tall statue of Hotei, Japanese god of prosperity. Industrialist Kiyoshi Ichimura gave the one-acre garden to the City of Miami in 1961 as an expression of friendship.

East of Watson Island, the causeway leaves Miami and enters Miami Beach. On the left, you'll pass the bridge to **Palm** and **Hibiscus islands** and then the bridge to **Star Island.** Celebrities who have lived on these islands include Al Capone (93 Palm Ave., Palm Island), author Damon Runyon (271 Hibiscus Island), and actor Don Johnson (8 Star Island).

East of Star Island, the causeway mounts a high bridge. Look **❹** left to see an island with an obelisk, the **Flagler Memorial Mon-**

Art Deco District, 8
Bass Museum
of Art, 15
Espanola Way, 9
Flagler Memorial
Monument, 4
Fontainebleau
Hilton Resort, 16
Hibiscus Island, 3
Hotel National, 14
Jackie Gleason
Theater of the
Performing Arts, 13
La Gorce Country
Club, 17
Lincoln Road Arts
District, 10
Miami Beach City
Hall, 11
Miami Beach
Convention Center, 12
Miami Beach
Marina, 5
Palm Island, 2
Penrod's Beach
Club, 7
South Pointe Park, 6
Watson Island, 1

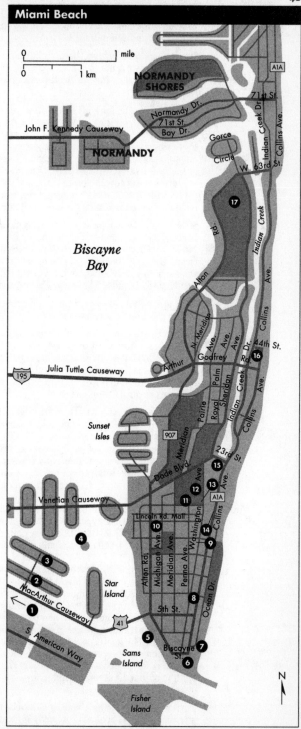

Miami Beach

ument. The memorial honors Henry M. Flagler, who built the Florida East Coast Railroad to Miami, opening south Florida to tourism and commerce.

⑤ Just beyond the bridge, turn right onto Alton Road past the **Miami Beach Marina** (300 Alton Rd., tel. 305/673–6000), where dive boats depart for artificial reefs offshore in the Atlantic Ocean.

⑥ Continue to the foot of Alton Road, turn left on Biscayne Street, then go right at Washington Avenue to enter **South Pointe Park** (1 Washington Ave.). From the 50-yard Sunshine Pier, which adjoins the mile-long jetty at the mouth of Government Cut, you can fish while watching huge ships pass. No bait or tackle is available in the park. Other facilities include two observation towers, volleyball courts, and a Crawdaddy's Restaurant and Lounge (1 Washington Ave., tel. 305/673–1708) with inside and outside dining for lunch (dinner, inside only).

⑦ When you leave the park, continue right to the foot of Biscayne Street at Ocean Drive. The sea here offers the best surfing in Miami Beach. **Penrod's Beach Club and South Beach Raw Bar** (1 Ocean Dr., tel. 305/538–1117) is noted for its food, drink, game tables, volleyball courts, and late-night dancing, weekends to 5 AM; May–December, Thursday, Friday, and Saturday.

Turn around on Biscayne Street, going back the way you came, and go right on Collins Avenue.

⑧ Return to 5th Street, go a block east to Ocean Drive, and turn left. A block north at 6th Street, the **Art Deco District** begins. Take Ocean Drive north past a line of pastel-hued Art Deco hotels on your left and palm-fringed Lummus Park and the beach on your right. Turn left on 15th Street, and left again at the next corner onto Collins Avenue.

Now drive along the Art Deco District's two main commercial streets. Take Collins Avenue south, turn right at 5th Street, and right again at the next corner onto **Washington Avenue,** an interesting mixture of delicatessens, produce markets, and stores selling Jewish, Cuban, and Haitian religious books and artifacts. Most intriguing on the avenue is the eclectic **Botánica La Caridad** (651 Washington Ave., tel. 305/538–7961).

Time Out Turn right on 12th Street to **Muff'n Man** (234 12th St., tel. 305/538–6833). Multiberry, apple, and cinnamon-raisin muffins and brownies and cookies are baked here daily. The interior is filled with Deco District photos and silk pillows.

⑨ Back on Washington Avenue, go past 14th Street to **Espanola Way,** a narrow street of Mediterranean-revival buildings constructed in 1925 and frequented through the years by artists and writers. In the 1930s, Cuban bandleader Desi Arnaz performed in the Village Tavern, now part of the **Clay Hotel & AYH International Youth Hostel** (1438 Washington Ave., tel. 305/534–2988). The hostel caters to young visitors from all over the world who seek secure, inexpensive lodgings within walking distance of the beach. On both sides of the revived street a collection of imaginative clothing, jewelry, and art shops has opened.

Turn left onto Espanola Way, go 3 blocks to Meridian Avenue, and turn right. Three blocks north of Espanola Way is **Lincoln**

Road Mall, a landscaped shopping thoroughfare known during its heyday in the 1950s as "Fifth Avenue of the South." Trams shuttle shoppers along the mall, which is closed to all other vehicular traffic between Washington Avenue and Alton Road.

⑩ Park in the municipal lot ½-block north of the mall to stroll through the **Lincoln Road Arts District,** where 5 blocks of storefronts on Lincoln Road from Pennsylvania Avenue to Lenox Avenue have been transformed into galleries, studios, classrooms, and art-related boutiques and cafés.

The arts district also includes the 500-seat **Colony Theater** (1040 Lincoln Rd., tel. 305/674–1026), a former movie house. Now it's a city-owned performing arts center featuring dance, drama, music, and experimental cinema. At 541–545 Lincoln Road, the **New World Symphony,** a national advanced training orchestra, rehearses and performs in a classical Art Deco theater (tel. 305/673–3331).

From the parking lot, go to the first main street north of Lincoln Road Mall and turn right. You're on 17th Street, named **Hank Meyer Boulevard** for the local publicist who persuaded the late comedian Jackie Gleason to broadcast his TV show from Miami Beach in the 1950s. Two blocks east on your left,
⑪ beside the entrance to **Miami Beach City Hall** (1700 Convention Center Dr., tel. 305/673–7030), stands *Red Sea Road*, a huge red sculpture by Barbara Neijna.

⑫ Also to your left is the **Miami Beach Convention Center** (1901 Convention Center Dr., tel. 305/673–7311), doubled in size in 1988 to 1.1 million square feet of exhibit space.

Behind the Convention Center, at the northwest end of the parking lot near Meridian Avenue, is the **Holocaust Memorial** (1933–45 Meridian Ave., tel. 305/538–1663 or 305/538–1673), a monumental sculpture and graphic record in memory of the 6 million Jewish victims of the Holocaust. A garden conservatory (2000 Convention Center Dr., tel. 305/673–7256) next door is worth a visit but has limited public hours.

⑬ Continuing 2 more blocks east, you'll see another large sculpture, *Mermaid*, by Roy Lichtenstein, in front of **Jackie Gleason Theater of the Performing Arts** (1700 Washington Ave., tel. 305/673–7300), where Gleason's TV show originated. Now the 3,000-seat theater hosts touring Broadway shows and classical music concerts. Near the sculpture, stars appearing in the theater since 1984 have left their footprints and signatures in concrete. This **Walk of the Stars** includes George Abbott, Julie Andrews, Leslie Caron, Carol Channing, and Edward Villella. For information about the Broadway show series, which each year presents five or six major productions (or other performances), contact the box office (505 17th St., tel. 305/673–8300) around the corner.

Return to Ocean Drive, turn right to the Leslie Hotel and the **Art Deco District Welcome Center** (1244 Ocean Dr., tel. 305/672–2014), open weekdays 10–6, Saturdays 10–5.

⑭ Go 1 block west to Collins Avenue, turn right (north) toward three of the largest Art Deco hotels, built in the 1940s with streamlined tower forms reflecting the 20th century's transportation revolution: The round dome atop the tower of the 11-story **Hotel National** (1677 Collins Ave., tel. 305/532–2311) resembles a balloon. The tower at the 12-story **Delano Hotel** (1685

Collins Ave., tel. 305/538–7881) sports fins suggesting the
wings of an airplane or a Buck Rogers spaceship. The 11-story
Ritz Plaza (1701 Collins Ave., tel. 305/534–3500) rises to a cy-
lindrical tower resembling a submarine periscope.

Turn left on Collins Avenue. At 21st Street, turn left beside the
Miami Beach Public Library in Collins Park, go 2 blocks to Park
🟢 Avenue, and turn right. You're approaching the **Bass Museum
of Art,** which houses a diverse collection of European art, including *The Holy Family,* a painting by Peter Paul Rubens; *The
Tournament,* a 16th-century Flemish tapestry; and works by
Albrecht Dürer and Henri de Toulouse-Lautrec. Park behind
the museum and walk around to the entrance past massive
tropical baobab trees. *2121 Park Ave., tel. 305/673–7530. Admission: $2 adults, $1 students with ID, children 16 and under
free. Some exhibitions may be more expensive. Donations
Tues. Open Tues.–Sat. 10–5, Sun. 1–5.*

Return on 21st Street or 22nd Street to Collins Avenue and
turn left. As you drive north, a triumphal archway looms
ahead, framing a majestic white building set in lush vegetation
beside a waterfall and tropical lagoon. This vista is an illu-
sion—a 13,000-square-foot outdoor mural on an exterior wall of
🟢 the **Fontainebleau Hilton Resort and Spa** (4441 Collins Ave.,
tel. 305/538–2000). Artist Richard Haas designed the mural to
illustrate how the hotel and its rock-grotto swimming pool
would look behind the wall. Locals call the 1,206-room hotel
"Big Blue." It's the giant of Miami Beach, with 190,000 square
feet of meeting and exhibit space.

Go left on 65th Street, turn left again at the next corner onto
Indian Creek Drive, and right at 63rd Street, which leads into
Alton Road, a winding, landscaped boulevard of gracious
🟢 homes styled along Art Deco lines. You'll pass the **La Gorce
Country Club** (5685 Alton Rd., tel. 305/866–4421), which devel-
oper Carl Fisher built and named for his friend Oliver La
Gorce, then president of the National Geographic Society.

To return to the mainland on the MacArthur Causeway, stay on
Alton Road south to 5th Street, then turn right.

Little Havana

*Numbers in the margin correspond to points of interest on the
Miami, Coral Gables, and Key Biscayne map.*

Orientation   More than thirty years ago, the tidal wave of Cubans fleeing
the Castro regime flooded an older neighborhood just west of
downtown Miami with refugees. This area became known as
Little Havana. Today, with a half-million Cubans widely dispersed throughout Greater Miami, Little Havana remains a
magnet for Cubans and Anglos alike. They come to experience
the flavor of traditional Cuban culture.

That culture, of course, functions in Spanish. Many Little Havana residents and shopkeepers speak almost no English. If
you don't speak Spanish, point and smile to communicate.

Touring Little   Begin this tour in downtown Miami, westbound on Flagler
Havana   Street. Cross the Miami River to Little Havana, and park near
Flagler Street and Ronald Reagan Avenue (S.W. 12th Ave.) to
explore a thriving commercial district.

❶ Continue west on Flagler Street to Teddy Roosevelt Avenue (S.W. 17th Ave.) and pause at **Plaza de la Cubanidad,** on the southwest corner. Redbrick sidewalks surround a fountain and monument with a quotation from José Martí, a leader in Cuba's struggle for independence from Spain: *"Las palmas son novias que esperan."* (The palm trees are girlfriends who will wait.)

❷ Turn left at Douglas Road (S.W. 37th Ave.), drive south to **Calle Ocho** (S.W. 8th St.), and turn left again. You are now on the main commercial thoroughfare of Little Havana.

Time Out For a total sensory experience, have a snack or meal at **Versailles,** a popular Cuban restaurant. Etched-glass mirrors lining its walls amplify bright lights, and there's the roar of rapid-fire Spanish. Most of the servers don't speak English; you order by pointing to a number on the menu (choice of English or Spanish menus). Specialties include *palomilla,* a flat beefsteak; *ropa vieja* (literally, old clothes), a shredded-beef dish in tomato sauce; and *arroz con pollo,* chicken and yellow rice. *3555 S.W. 8th St., tel. 305/445-7614. AE, DC, MC, V. Open Sun.–Thurs. 8 AM–2 AM, Fri. 8 AM–3:30 AM, Sat. 8 AM–4:30 AM.*

East of Unity Boulevard (S.W. 27th Ave.), Calle Ocho becomes a one-way street eastbound through the heart of Little Havana, where every block deserves exploration. If your time is limited, we suggest the 3-block stretch from S.W. 14th Avenue to S.W. 11th Avenue. Parking is more ample west of Ronald Reagan Avenue (S.W. 12th Ave.).

❸ At Calle Ocho and Memorial Boulevard (S.W. 13th Ave.) stands the **Brigade 2506 Memorial,** commemorating the victims of the unsuccessful 1961 Bay of Pigs invasion of Cuba by an exile force. An eternal flame burns atop a simple stone monument with the inscription: *"Cuba—A Los Martires de La Brigada de Asalto Abril 17 de 1961."* The monument also bears a shield with the Brigade 2506 emblem, a Cuban flag superimposed on a cross. Walk a block south on Memorial Boulevard from the Brigade 2506 Memorial to see other monuments relevant to Cuban history, including a statue of José Martí.

❹ When you return to your car, drive 5 blocks south on Ronald Reagan Avenue to the **Cuban Museum of Art and Culture.** Created by Cuban exiles to preserve and interpret the cultural heritage of their homeland, the museum has expanded its focus to embrace the entire Hispanic art community. In 1989, some artists who had previously exhibited in Havana were invited to show here. Because of political conditions concerning U.S./ Cuba relations, this event has caused controversy for the museum. Albeit controversial, the museum survives and mounts temporary exhibitions and shows works from its small permanent collection. *1300 S.W. 12th Ave., tel. 305/858-8006. Donation requested. Open Wed.–Sun. 1–5.*

To return to downtown Miami, take Ronald Reagan Avenue back north to S.W. 8th Street, turn right, go east to Miami Avenue or Brickell Avenue, turn left, and go north across the Miami River.

Coral Gables/Coconut Grove/South Miami

Orientation This tour directs you through three separate communities, each unique in character. Two of them, Coral Gables and South

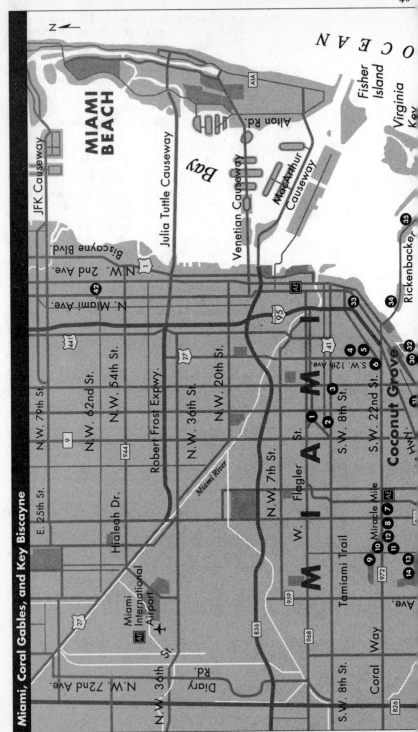

Miami, Coral Gables, and Key Biscayne

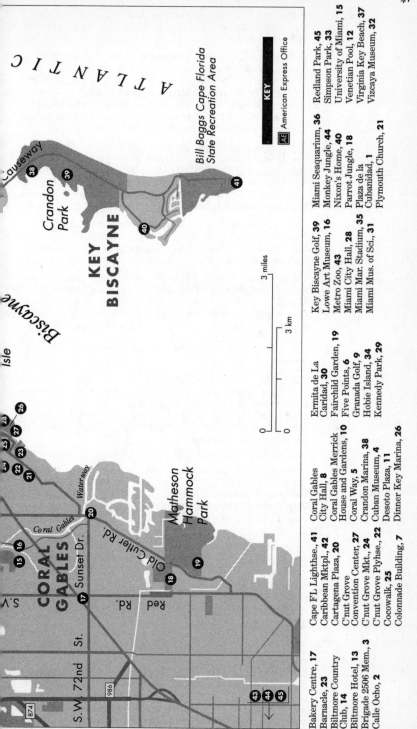

Miami, are independent suburbs. The third, Coconut Grove, was annexed to the City of Miami in 1925 but still retains a distinctive personality.

Coral Gables, a planned community of broad boulevards and Spanish Mediterranean architecture, justifiably calls itself "The City Beautiful." Developer George E. Merrick began selling Coral Gables lots in 1921 and incorporated the city in 1925. He named most of the streets for Spanish explorers, cities, and provinces. Street names are at ground level beside each intersection on whitewashed concrete cornerstones.

The 1926 hurricane and the Great Depression prevented Merrick from fulfilling many aspects of his plan. The city languished until after World War II but then grew rapidly. Today, Coral Gables has a population of about 41,000. In its bustling downtown, more than 100 multinational companies maintain headquarters or regional offices.

A pioneer farming community that grew into a suburb, **South Miami** today retains small-town charm, despite a failed, oversized shopping mall called The Bakery Centre, constructed on the former site of Holsum Bakery.

Coconut Grove is south Florida's oldest settlement, inhabited as early as 1834 and established by 1873, two decades before Miami. Its early settlers included Bahamian blacks, "conchs" from Key West, and New England intellectuals. They built a community that attracted artists, writers, and scientists to establish winter homes. By the end of World War I, more people listed in *Who's Who* gave addresses in Coconut Grove than anyplace else.

To this day, Coconut Grove reflects the pioneers' eclectic origins. Posh estates mingle with rustic cottages, modest frame homes, and starkly modern dwellings—often on the same block. To keep Coconut Grove a village in a jungle, residents lavish affection on exotic plantings while battling to protect remaining native vegetation.

The historic center of the Village of Coconut Grove went through a hippie period in the 1960s, laid-back funkiness in the 1970s, and a teenybopper invasion in the early 1980s. Today, the tone is upscale, and urban, with a mix of galleries, boutiques, restaurants, and bars and sidewalk cafés. On the weekends it's particularly trendy and congested.

Driving Tour This tour begins in downtown Miami. Go south on S.E. 2nd Avenue, which becomes Brickell Avenue and crosses the Miami River. Half a mile south of the river, turn right onto **Coral Way,** which at this point is S.W. 13th Street. Within ½ mile, Coral Way doglegs left under I–95 and becomes S.W. 3rd Avenue. It continues another mile to a complex intersection, **Five Points,** and doglegs right to become S.W. 22nd Avenue.

Along the S.W. 3rd Avenue and S.W. 22nd Avenue segments of Coral Way, banyan trees planted in the median strip in 1929 arch over the roadway. The banyans end at the Miami/Coral Gables boundary, where **Miracle Mile** begins. This 4-block stretch of Coral Way, from Douglas Road (37th Ave.) to Le Jeune Road (42nd Ave.) in the heart of downtown Coral Gables, is really ½-mile long. To stroll the full mile, walk up one side and down the other. Miracle Mile's 160 shops range from chain restaurants and shoe stores to posh boutiques and beauty sa-

lons. The stores are numbered from 1 to 399. As you go west,
numbers and quality both increase. Request a complete directory from the Miracle Mile Association (220 Miracle Mile, Suite
218, Coral Gables 33134, tel. 305/445–0591).

7 **The Colonnade Building** (133–169 Miracle Mile, Coral Gables)
on Miracle Mile once housed George Merrick's sales office. Its
rotunda bears an ornamental frieze and a Spanish-tile roof 75
feet above street level. The Colonnade Building has been restored and connected to the new 13-story Colonnade Hotel and
an office building that echoes the rotunda's roofline.

The ornate Spanish Renaissance structure facing Miracle Mile
8 just west of Le Jeune Road is **Coral Gables City Hall**, opened in
1928. It has a three-tier tower topped with a clock and a 500-
pound bell. Inside the domed ceiling, a mural by artist Denman
Fink depicting the four seasons can be seen from the second
floor. *405 Biltmore Way, Coral Gables, tel. 305/446–6800. Open
weekdays 7:30–5.*

Proceed west to the corner of Segovia Avenue, turn right, then
9 left onto Coral Way. You'll pass the **Granada Golf Course** (2001
Granada Blvd., Coral Gables, tel. 305/460–5367), one of two
public courses in the midst of the largest historic district of
Coral Gables.

One block west of the golf course, turn right on Toledo Street to
10 park behind **Coral Gables Merrick House and Gardens,** George
Merrick's boyhood home. The city acquired the dwelling in
1976 and restored it to its 1920s appearance. It contains Merrick family furnishings and artifacts. *907 Coral Way, Coral Gables, tel. 305/460–5361. Admission: $2 adults, $1 children.
Open Sun. and Wed. 1–4.*

Return to Coral Way, turn right, then left at the first stoplight.
Now you're southbound on Granada Boulevard, approaching
11 **DeSoto Plaza and Fountain,** a classical column on a pedestal
with water flowing from the mouths of four sculpted faces. The
closed eyes of the face looking west symbolize the day's end.
Denman Fink designed the fountain in the early 1920s.

Follow the traffic circle almost completely around the fountain
to northeast-bound DeSoto Boulevard. On your right in the
12 next block is **Venetian Pool,** a unique municipal swimming pool
transformed from a rock quarry. *2701 DeSoto Blvd., Coral Gables, tel. 305/460–5356. Admission (nonresident): $4 adults,
$3.50 teens, $1.60 children under 12. Free parking across
DeSoto Blvd. Summer hours: weekdays 11–7:30, weekends 10–
4:30; winter hours: Tues.–Fri. 11–4:30, weekends 10–4:30.*

From the pool, go around the block with right turns onto Almeria Avenue, Toledo Street, and Sevilla Avenue. You'll return to
the DeSoto Fountain and take DeSoto Boulevard southeast to
13 emerge in front of **The Biltmore Hotel** (1200 Anastasia Ave.,
Coral Gables, tel. 305/445–1926). Like the Freedom Tower in
downtown Miami, the Biltmore's 26-story tower is a replica of
the Giralda Tower in Seville, Spain. Unfortunately, after extensive renovations the hotel closed and plans for its future are
still unclear. However, open to the public is the Biltmore Golf
Course, known for its scenic and competitive layout, and for
having the largest hotel pool in the United States, with a capacity of 1.25 million gallons. In 1992 a $1.4-million renovation re-
stored the course to its original Donald Ross design.

Just west of The Biltmore Hotel stands a separate building,
⓮ **The Biltmore Country Club,** which the city restored in the late
1970s. It's a richly ornamented Beaux Arts–style structure
with a superb colonnade and courtyard. On its ground floor are
facilities for golfers. In the former club lounge, meeting rooms
include one lofty space paneled with veneer from 60 species of
trees. In 1989 the structure was reincorporated into The
Biltmore Hotel, of which it was an original part.

From the hotel, turn right on Anastasia Avenue, go east to
Granada Boulevard, and turn right. Continue south on Granada Boulevard over a bridge across the **Coral Gables Waterway,**
which connects the grounds of The Biltmore Hotel with Biscayne Bay. In the hotel's heyday, Venetian gondolas plied the
waterway, bringing guests to a bayside beach.

At Ponce de León Boulevard, turn right. On your left is
Metrorail's Stonehenge-like concrete structure, and on your
⓯ right, the **University of Miami**'s 260-acre main campus. With
about 13,000 full-time, part-time, and noncredit students, UM
is the largest private research university in the Southeast.

Turn right at the first stoplight to enter the campus and park in
⓰ the lot on your right designated for visitors to UM's **Lowe Art
Museum.** The Lowe's permanent collection of 8,000 works includes Renaissance and Baroque art, American paintings, Latin American art, and Navajo and Pueblo Indian textiles and
baskets. The museum also hosts traveling exhibitions. *1301
Stanford Dr., Coral Gables, tel. 305/284–3535 for recorded information, 305/284–3536 for museum office. Admission: $4
adults, $3 senior citizens, $2 students, children under 6 free.
Open Sun. 12–5, Tues.–Sat. 10–5.*

Now exit the UM campus on Stanford Drive, pass under
Metrorail, and cross Dixie Highway. Just beyond the Burger
King on your right, bear right onto Maynada Street. Turn
right at the next stoplight onto **Sunset Drive.** Fine old homes
and mature trees line this officially designated "historic and
scenic road" that leads to and through downtown South Miami.

On the northwest corner of Sunset Drive and Red Road (57th
Ave.), note the pink building with a mural in which an alligator
seems ready to devour a horrified man. This trompe l'oeil fantasy, *South Florida Cascade,* by illusionary artist Richard Haas,
⓱ highlights the main entrance to **The Bakery Centre** (5701 Sunset Dr., South Miami, tel. 305/662–4155).

On the third level of The Bakery Centre, the **Miami Youth Museum** features cultural arts exhibits, hands-on displays, and activities to enhance a child's creativity and inspire interest in
artistic careers. At press time there is talk that the museum
may move to another location. Call ahead. *5701 Sunset Dr., S.
Miami, tel. 305/661–ARTS. Admission: $3 adults, senior citi-
zens and children under 1 free. Open weekdays 10–5, weekends
11–5; closed holidays.*

Go south on Red Road and turn right just before Killian Drive
⓲ (S.W. 112th St.) into the grounds of **Parrot Jungle,** where more
than 1,100 exotic birds are on display. Many of the parrots, macaws, and cockatoos fly free, but they'll come to you for seeds,
which you can purchase from old-fashioned gumball machines.
Attend a trained-bird show, watch baby birds in training, and
pose for photos with colorful macaws perched on your arms.

The "jungle" is a natural hammock surrounding a sinkhole. Stroll among orchids and other flowering plants nestled among ferns, bald-cypress trees, and massive live oaks. Other highlights include a primate show, small-wildlife shows, a children's playground, and a petting zoo. Also see the cactus garden and Flamingo Lake, with a breeding population of 75 Caribbean flamingos. Opened in 1936, Parrot Jungle is one of Greater Miami's oldest and most popular commercial tourist attractions. *11000 S.W. 57th Ave., Miami, tel. 305/666–7834. Admission: $10.50 adults, $6 children 3–12. Open daily 9:30–6. Café opens 8 AM.*

From Parrot Jungle, take Red Road ⅛ mile south and turn left at Old Cutler Road, which curves north along the uplands of south Florida's coastal ridge. Visit 83-acre **Fairchild Tropical Garden,** the largest tropical botanical garden in the continental United States. *10901 Old Cutler Rd., Coral Gables, tel. 305/667–1651. Admission: $5 adults, children under 13 free with parents. Hourly tram rides, $1 adults; 50¢ children under 13. Open daily except Christmas 9:30–4:30.*

North of the garden, Old Cutler Road traverses Dade County's oldest and most scenic park, **Matheson Hammock Park.** The Civilian Conservation Corps developed the 100-acre tract of upland and mangrove swamp in the 1930s on land donated by a local pioneer, Commodore J. W. Matheson. The park's most popular feature is a bathing beach, where the tide flushes a saltwater "atoll" pool through four gates. *9610 Old Cutler Rd., Coral Gables, tel. 305/666–6979. Parking fee for beach and marina $3 per car, $5 per car with trailer. Limited upland parking free. Park open 6 AM–sundown. Pool lifeguards on duty winter 8:30 AM–6 PM, summer 7:30 AM–7 PM.*

Continue north on Old Cutler Road to **Cartagena Plaza,** cross the Le Jeune Road bridge over the waterway, and turn right at the first stoplight onto Ingraham Highway. Four blocks later, you're back in the City of Miami, at the south end of Coconut Grove. Follow Ingraham Highway to Douglas Road and turn right at the next stoplight onto Main Highway. You're following old pioneer trails that today remain narrow roads shaded by a canopy of towering trees.

One block past the stoplight at Royal Palm Avenue, turn left onto Devon Road in front of **Plymouth Congregational Church.** Opened in 1917, this handsome coral-rock structure resembles a Mexican mission church. The front door, of hand-carved walnut and oak with original wrought-iron fittings, came from an early-17th-century monastery in the Pyrenees. *3400 Devon Rd., Coconut Grove, tel. 305/444–6521. Ask at the office to go inside the church, weekdays 9–4:30. Service Sun. 10 AM.*

When you leave the church, go around the block opposite the church. Turn left from Devon Road onto Hibiscus Street, left again onto Royal Palm Avenue, and left at the stoplight onto Main Highway.

You're now headed for the historic **Village of Coconut Grove,** a trendy commercial district with redbrick sidewalks and more than 300 restaurants, stores, and art galleries.

Parking can be a problem in the village—especially on weekend evenings, when police direct traffic and prohibit turns at some intersections to prevent gridlock. Be prepared to walk several blocks from the periphery into the heart of the Grove.

As you enter the village center, note the apricot-hued Spanish rococo **Coconut Grove Playhouse** to your left. Built in 1926 as a movie theater, it became a legitimate theater in 1956 and is now owned by the State of Florida. The playhouse presents Broadway-bound plays and musical revues and experimental productions in its 1,100-seat main theater and 100-seat cabaret-style Encore Room. *3500 Main Hwy., Coconut Grove, tel. 305/442–4000, box office; tel. 305/442–2662, administrative office. Parking lot: $2 daytime; $4 evenings.*

Benches and a shelter opposite the playhouse mark the entrance to **The Barnacle,** a pioneer residence that is now a state historic site. Commodore Ralph Munroe built The Barnacle in 1891. Its broad, sloping roof and deeply recessed verandas channel sea breezes into the house. A central stairwell and rooftop vent allow hot air to escape. Many furnishings are original. While living at the Barnacle, Munroe built shoal-draft sailboats. One such craft, the ketch *Micco,* is on display. *3485 Main Hwy., Coconut Grove, tel. 305/448–9445. Admission: $2. Reservations required for groups of 8 or more; others meet ranger on porch of Barnacle house. Open Thurs.–Mon. 9–4; tours 10, 11:30, 1, and 2:30; closed Tues. and Wed.*

Time Out Turn left at the next street, Commodore Plaza, and pause. Cafés at both corners overflow the brick sidewalks. Try the **Green Streets Café** on the south side; this French gourmet café features—among other fare—16 kinds of muffins and a superb Greek-style salad bulging with brine-soaked olives and feta cheese. *3110 Commodore Plaza, Coconut Grove, tel. 305/444–0244. Inside and outdoor service and carryouts available. MC, V. Open 6:30–3.*

If your timing is right, visit the **Coconut Grove Farmers Market,** a laid-back, Brigadoon-like happening that appears as if by magic each Saturday on a vacant lot. To get there from Commodore Plaza, go north to Grand Avenue, cross McDonald Avenue (S.W. 32nd Ave.), and go a block west to Margaret Street. Vendors set up outdoor stands to offer home-grown tropical fruits and vegetables (including organic produce); honey, seafoods, macrobiotic foods; and ethnic fare from the Caribbean, the Middle East, and Southeast Asia. Nonfood items for sale include plants, handicrafts, candles, jewelry, and homemade clothing. A masseur plies his trade, musicians play, and the Hare Krishnas come to chant. People-watching is half the fun. *Open Sat. 8–3.*

Now return to the village center. On your left is **Cocowalk,** a multilevel open mall of Mediterranean-style brick courtyards and terraces overflowing with people. Opened early in 1991, Cocowalk has revitalized Coconut Grove's nightlife. The mix of shops, restaurants, and theaters has renewed the Grove by creating a new circuit for promenading between these attractions and the historic heart of the Grove along Commodore Plaza. The area now teems with Manhattan-like crowds, especially on weekend evenings. Across Virginia Street is **Mayfair,** an artistic but aloof mall originally built for the extravagant, free-spending South Americans who no longer come.

Leaving the village center, take McFarlane Road east from its intersection with Grand Avenue and Main Highway. Peacock Park, site of the first hotel in southeast Florida, is on your right. Ahead, seabirds soar and sailboats ride at anchor in

26 **Dinner Key Marina** (3400 Pan American Dr., Coconut Grove, tel. 305/579–6980), named for a small island where early settlers held picnics. With 580 moorings at eight piers, all renovated in 1990, it's Greater Miami's largest marina.

McFarlane Road turns left onto South Bayshore Drive. Turn right at the first stoplight onto Unity Boulevard (S.W. 27th Ave.), and go east into a parking lot that serves the marina and

27 the 105,000-square-foot **Coconut Grove Convention Center** (2700 S. Bayshore Dr., Coconut Grove, tel. 305/579–3310), where antique, boat, and home-furnishings shows are held.

28 At the northeast corner of the lot is **Miami City Hall,** which was built in 1934 as the terminal for the Pan American Airways seaplane base at Dinner Key. The building retains its nautical-style art deco trim. *3500 Pan American Dr., Coconut Grove, tel. 305/250–5400. Open weekdays 8–5.*

From City Hall, drive west on Pan American Drive toward South Bayshore Drive, with its pyramidlike Grand Bay Hotel. Turn right on South Bayshore Drive, and go north past

29 **Kennedy Park.** Leave your car in the park's lot north of Kirk Street and walk toward the water. From a footbridge over the mouth of a small tidal creek, you'll enjoy an unobstructed view across Biscayne Bay to Key Biscayne. Film crews use the park often to make commercials and Italian westerns.

From South Bayshore Drive, turn right, and go north past the entrance to Mercy Hospital, where South Bayshore Drive becomes South Miami Avenue. At the next stoplight beyond the hospital, turn right on a private road that goes past St.

30 Kieran's Church to **Ermita de La Caridad**—Our Lady of Charity Shrine—a conical building 90 feet high and 80 feet wide overlooking the bay so worshipers face toward Cuba. A mural above the shrine's altar depicts Cuba's history. *3609 S. Miami Ave., Coconut Grove, tel. 305/854–2405. Open daily 9–9.*

Return to South Miami Avenue, turn right, go about ³⁄₁₀ of a

31 mile, and turn left to the **Miami Museum of Science and Space Transit Planetarium,** where in 1991 the museum added 3,200 square feet of new exhibition spaces, new classrooms, 90 more parking spaces, and a new Mediterranean facade. This is a participatory museum, chock-full of sound, gravity, and electricity displays for children and adults alike to manipulate and marvel at. A wildlife center houses native Florida snakes, turtles and tortoises, birds of prey, and large wading birds. *3280 S. Miami Ave., Miami, tel. 305/854–4247; 24-hour Cosmic Hotline for planetarium show times and prices, 305/854–2222. Admission to museum: $6 adults, $4 children 3–12; to planetarium shows $5 adults, $2.50 children and senior citizens; to laser light shows $6 adults, $2.50 children and senior citizens. Open daily 10–6.*

32 Across South Miami Avenue is the entrance to **Vizcaya Museum and Gardens,** an estate with an Italian Renaissance–style villa built in 1912–16 as the winter residence of Chicago industrialist James Deering. The house and gardens overlook Biscayne Bay on a 30-acre tract that includes a native hammock and more than 10 acres of formal gardens and fountains. You can leave your car in the Museum of Science lot and walk across the street or drive across and park in Vizcaya's own lot.

The house contains a total of 70 rooms, with 34 rooms of antique furniture, paintings, sculpture, and other decorative arts, open to the public. These objects date from the 15th through the 19th centuries, representing the Renaissance, Baroque, Rococo, and Neoclassic styles. *3251 S. Miami Ave., Miami, tel. 305/579–2813. Admission: $8 adults, $4 children 6–12. Guided 45-min tours available, group tours by appointment. House open 9:30–4:30; ticket booth open until 4:30, garden until 5:30. Closed Christmas.*

As you leave Vizcaya, turn north (left from the Museum of Science lot, right from the Vizcaya lot) onto South Miami Avenue.

㉝ Continue to 17th Road and turn left to **Simpson Park.** Enjoy a fragment of the dense tropical jungle—large gumbo-limbo trees, marlberry, banyans, and black calabash—that once covered the entire five miles from downtown Miami to Coconut Grove. You'll get a rare glimpse of how things were before the high-rises towered. Avoid the park during summer when mosquitoes whine as incessantly today as they did 100 years ago. You may follow South Miami Avenue the rest of the way downtown or go back two stoplights and turn left to the entrance to the Rickenbacker Causeway and Key Biscayne.

Virginia Key and Key Biscayne

Hurricane Andrew struck this area hard, causing some attractions on this tour to close temporarily. With the exception of Bill Baggs Cape Florida State Recreation Area and the Cape Florida Lighthouse—whose reopening dates were uncertain— all the sights listed below plan to be operational in 1993. Still, we advise you to call ahead before planning your day's itinerary.

Government Cut and the Port of Miami separate Miami Beach from Virginia Key and Key Biscayne. Parks occupy much of both keys, providing facilities for basking on the beach, golf, tennis, softball, and picnicking—plus uninviting but ecologically valuable stretches of mangrove swamp.

Driving Tour To reach Virginia Key and Key Biscayne, take the **Rickenbacker Causeway** across Biscayne Bay from the mainland at Brickell Avenue and S.W. 26th Road, about 2 miles south of downtown Miami. A fitness pathway for biking and jogging parallels the causeway. In 1990 a new bike lane was added in each direction of the causeway from the new high bridge to the village of Key Biscayne. An older and somewhat uprooted path still meanders as a scenic alternative through pine forests and marsh, and here and there through parking lots. *Toll: $1 per car, bicycles and pedestrians free.*

About 200 feet east of the tollgate (just across the first low

㉞ bridge), you can rent windsurfing equipment on **Hobie Island.** *Sailboards Miami, Box 16, Key Biscayne 33149, tel. 305/361–SAIL. Cost: $17 per hour for 10 hours, $9.50 for each hour thereafter; $39 for a 2-hour windsurfing lesson. Open daily 9:30–dusk.*

The **Old Rickenbacker Causeway Bridge,** built in 1947, is now a fishing pier. The west stub begins about a mile from the tollgate. Park near its entrance and walk past fishermen tending their lines to the gap where the center draw span across the Intracoastal Waterway was removed. There you can watch boat traffic pass through the channel, pelicans and other seabirds soar and dive, and porpoises cavort in the bay.

The new high-level **William M. Powell Bridge** rises 75 feet above the water to eliminate the need for a draw span. The panoramic view from the top encompasses the bay, keys, port, and downtown skyscrapers, with Miami Beach and the Atlantic Ocean in the distance. The speed limit is 45 mph, and you can't stop on the bridge, so park in the fishing pier lot and walk up.

35 Next along the causeway stands the 6,536-seat **Miami Marine Stadium** (3601 Rickenbacker Causeway, Miami, tel. 305/361–6732), where summer pop concerts take place and name entertainers occasionally perform. You can join the audience on land in the stadium or on a boat anchored just offshore. Fourth of July concertgoers enjoy a spectacular fireworks display that is visible for miles up and down the bay.

36 Down the causeway from Marine Stadium at the **Miami Seaquarium,** Lolita, a killer whale, cavorts in a huge tank. She performs two or three times a day, as do sea lions and dolphins in separate shows. Exhibits include a shark pool, 235,000-gallon tropical reef aquarium, and manatees. *4400 Rickenbacker Causeway, Miami, tel. 305/361–5705; Admission: $16.95 adults, $13.95 senior citizens, $11.95 children 3–12. Open daily 9:30–6.*

37 Opposite the causeway from the Seaquarium, a road leads north to **Virginia Key Beach,** a City of Miami park, with a 2-mile stretch of oceanfront, shelters, barbecue grills, ball fields, nature trails, and a fishing area. Ask for directions at the entrance gate. *Cost: $2 per car.*

In 1992, a 400-acre portion on the west side of this mangrove-edged island was dedicated as the **Virginia Key Critical Wildlife Area.** Birds to be seen here include reddish egrets, black-bellied plovers, black skimmers, and roseate spoonbills—but only May through July. Undisturbed the other nine months, the area will be more amenable to migratory shorebirds.

38 From Virginia Key, the causeway crosses **Bear Cut** to the north end of Key Biscayne, where it becomes Crandon Boulevard. The **Crandon Park Marina,** behind Sundays on the Bay restaurant, sells bait and tackle. *4000 Crandon Blvd., Key Biscayne, tel. 305/361–1161. Open 7–5 weekdays, 7–6 weekends.*

Beyond the marina, Crandon Boulevard bisects 1,211-acre **Crandon Park.** Turnouts on your left lead to four parking lots, adjacent picnic areas, ball fields, and 3.3 miles of beach. *Parking: $2 per car. Open daily 8 AM–sunset.*

39 On your right are entrances to the **Key Biscayne Golf Course** and the **International Tennis Center,** where in 1992 a $16.5-million, 7,500-seat tennis stadium was being constructed in preparation for the March 1993 Lipton International Players Championships.

40 From the circle at the south end of Crandon Park, Crandon Boulevard continues for two miles through the developed portion of Key Biscayne. You'll come back that way, but first detour to the site of former **President Nixon's home** (485 W. Matheson Dr.). Turn right at the first light onto Harbor

Drive, go about a mile, and turn right at Matheson Drive. A later owner enlarged and totally changed Nixon's home.

Emerging from West Matheson Drive, turn right onto Harbor Drive and go about a mile south to Mashta Drive; follow Mashta Drive east past Harbor Drive to Crandon Boulevard, and turn right.

You are approaching the entrance to **Bill Baggs Cape Florida State Recreation Area,** named for a crusading newspaper editor whose efforts prompted the state to create this 406-acre park. The park includes 1¼ miles of beach and a seawall along Biscayne Bay where anglers catch bonefish, grouper, jack, snapper, and snook. There is a nature trail with native plants now rare on Key Biscayne.

●41 Also in the park is the oldest structure in south Florida, the **Cape Florida Lighthouse,** erected in 1825 to help ships avoid the shallows and reefs offshore. In 1836 a band of Seminole Indians attacked the lighthouse and killed the keeper's helper. You can no longer climb the 122 steps to the top of the 95-foot-tall lighthouse because the structure awaits about $1 million in repairs—a sum that Dade Heritage Trust, the local preservation society, is endeavoring to raise. *1200 S. Crandon Blvd., Key Biscayne, tel. 305/361–5811. Admission to park: $3.25 per vehicle; to lighthouse and keeper's residence: $1 per person, under age 6 free. Park open all year 8–sunset. Lighthouse tours daily except Tues. at 1, 2:30, and 3:30.*

When you leave Cape Florida, follow Crandon Boulevard back to Crandon Park through Key Biscayne's commercial center, a mixture of posh shops and stores catering to the needs of the neighborhood. On your way back to the mainland, pause as you approach the Powell Bridge to admire the downtown Miami skyline. At night, the brightly lit International Place looks from this angle like a clipper ship running under full sail before the breeze.

Little Haiti

Of the more than 150,000 Haitians who have settled in Greater Miami, some 60,000 live in Little Haiti, a 200-block area on Miami's northeast side. More than 400 small Haitian businesses operate in Little Haiti.

For many Haitians, English is a third language. French is Haiti's official language, but much day-to-day conversation takes place in Creole, a French-based patois. Smiling and pointing will bridge any language barrier you may encounter.

This tour takes you through the Miami Design District on the margin of Little Haiti, then along two main thoroughfares that form the spine of the Haitian community. The tour begins in downtown Miami. Take Biscayne Boulevard north to N.E. 36th Street, turn left, go about ⁴⁄₁₀ of a mile west to North Miami Avenue. Turn right, and go north through the **Miami Design District,** where about 225 wholesale stores, showrooms, and galleries feature interior furnishings and decorative arts.

Little Haiti begins immediately north of the Design District in an area with some of Miami's oldest dwellings, dating from the dawn of the 20th century through the 1920s land-boom era.

Drive the side streets to see elegant Mediterranean-style homes, and bungalows with distinctive coral-rock trim.

Return to North Miami Avenue and go north. A half-block east on 54th Street is the tiny storefront office of the **Haitian Refugee Center** (119 N.E. 54th St., tel. 305/757–8538), a focal point of activity in the Haitian community.

Continue north on North Miami Avenue past the former Cuban consulate, a pretentious Caribbean-Colonial mansion that is now the clinic of Haitian physician Lucien Albert (5811 N. Miami Ave., tel. 305/758–2700).

North of 85th Street, cross the Little River Canal into **El Portal,** a tiny suburban village of modest homes where more than a quarter of the property is now Haitian-owned. Turn right on N.E. 87th Street and right again on N.E. 2nd Avenue. You are now southbound on Little Haiti's main commercial street.

Time Out   Stop for Haitian breads and cakes made with coconut and other tropical ingredients at **Baptiste Bakery.** *7488 N.E. 2nd Ave., tel. 305/756–1119. Open 7–7, sometimes later.*

Along N.E. 2nd Avenue between 79th Street and 45th Street, rows of storefronts in faded pastels reflect a first effort by area merchants to dress up their neighborhood and attract outsiders.

42   More successful—aesthetically, if not yet commercially—is the **Caribbean Marketplace,** which the Haitian Task Force (an economic development organization) opened in 1990. Its 10 or so merchants sell handmade baskets, Caribbean art and craft items, books, videos, and ice cream. *Tel. 305/758–8708, 5927 N.E. 2nd Ave., Miami.*

This concludes the Little Haiti tour. To return to downtown Miami, take N.E. 2nd Avenue south to N.E. 35th Street, turn left, go east one block to Biscayne Boulevard, and turn right to go south.

South Dade

South Dade County suffered severe damage when Hurricane Andrew hit. Although most of the attractions were closed at press time, those that have remained in the tour below plan to be open in 1993. Before planning your visit, however, call the individual sights or the Greater Miami Convention and Visitors Bureau (tel. 305/672–1270).

This tour directs you to major attractions in the suburbs southwest of Dade County's urban core. A Junior League book, *Historic South Dade,* locates and describes 40 historic structures and attractions in a South Dade County driving tour. You can contact the Junior League (2325 Salzedo Dr., Coral Gables, tel. 305/443–0160) for additional information.

From downtown Miami, take the Dolphin Expressway (Rte. 836) west to the Palmetto Expressway (Rte. 826) southbound. Bear left south of Bird Road (S.W. 40th St.) onto the Don Shula Expressway (Rte. 874). Exit westbound onto Killian Drive (S.W. 104th St.) and go south on Lindgren Road to Coral Reef

43 Drive (S.W. 152nd St.). Turn left and go east to **Metro Zoo.** The Metro Zoo was nearly devastated by Hurricane Andrew, but its staff hopes it will be at least partially open in 1993. If you'd like to make a donation toward repairs, write to the Metro Zoo Crisis Fund (c/o Ron Magill, 12400 S.W. 152 St., Miami 33177).

In its fully operational state the Metro Zoo covers 290 acres and is cageless; animals roam free on islands surrounded by moats. In "Wings of Asia," a 1.5-acre aviary, hundreds of exotic birds from southeast Asia fly through a rain forest beneath a protective net enclosure. The zoo has 3 miles of walkways, a monorail with four stations, and an open-air amphitheater for concerts. Paws, a petting zoo for children, opened in 1989 and features three shows daily. *12400 Coral Reef Dr. (S.W. 152nd St.), tel. 305/251-0400 for recorded information; 305/251-0401 for other information. Admission: $8.79 adults, $4.53 children 3-12. Admission for Florida residents with proof of citizenship (Mon.-Sat. 9:30-11 AM) $5.33 adults, $2.66 children. Admission includes monorail tickets. AE, MC, V. No credit cards at snack bar. Gates open daily 9:30-4. Park closes at 5:30.*

Return to Coral Reef Drive, turn right (east) to the Homestead Extension of Florida's Turnpike, take the turnpike south, exit at Hainlin Mill Drive (S.W. 216th St.), and turn right. Cross South Dixie Highway (U.S. 1), go 3 miles west, and turn right **44** into **Monkey Jungle,** home to more than 400 monkeys representing 35 species—including orangutans from Borneo and Sumatra, golden lion tamarins from Brazil, and brown lemurs from Madagascar. Performing monkey shows begin at 10 AM and run continuously at 45-minute intervals. The walkways of this 30-acre attraction are caged; the monkeys roam free. *14805 Hainlin Mill Dr. (S.W. 216 St.), tel. 305/235-1611. Admission: $9.85 adults, $8.85 senior citizens, $5.35 children 4-12. AE, D, MC, V. Open daily 9:30-5.*

Continue west on Hainlin Mill Drive to Krome Avenue (S.W. 177th Ave.). Cross Krome to Redland Road (S.W. 187th Ave.). Turn left to Coconut Palm Drive (S.W. 248th St.). You are at **45** the **Redland Fruit & Spice Park,** a Dade County treasure since 1944, when it was established as a 20-acre showcase of tropical fruits and vegetables. More than 500 varieties of exotic fruits, herbs, spices, and nuts from throughout the world grow here, including poisonous plants. There are 50 varieties of bananas, 40 varieties of grapes, and 100 varieties of citrus. A gourmet and fruit shop offers many varieties of tropical fruit products, jellies, seeds, aromatic teas, and reference books. *24801 S.W. 187th Ave. (Redland Rd.), tel. 305/247-5727. Admission: $1 adults, 50¢ children; fee for guided weekend tours (1 and 3 PM): park admission plus $1.50 adults, $1 children. MC, V. Open daily 10-5.*

Drive east on Coconut Palm Drive (S.W. 248th St.) to Newton Road (S.W. 157th Ave.). Turn right and go south to **Orchid Jungle,** where you can stroll under live-oak trees to see orchids, ferns, bromeliads, and anthuriums, and peer through the win-

dows of an orchid-cloning laboratory. *26715 S.W. 157th Ave.,
Homestead, tel. 305/247–4824 or 800/344–2457. Admission: $5
adults, $4 senior citizens and children 13–17, $1.50 children 6–
12. Open daily 8:30–5:30.*

Continue south on Newton Road to South Dixie Highway (U.S.
1), and turn left. Almost immediately, you'll find **Coral Castle
of Florida** on your right. It was built by Edward Leedskalnin, a
Latvian immigrant, between 1920 and 1940. The 3-acre castle
has a 9-ton gate a child can open, an accurate working sundial,
and a telescope of coral rock aimed at the North Star. *28655
South Dixie Hwy., Homestead, tel. 305/248–6344. Admission:
$7.75 adults, $4.50 children 6–12. MC, V. Open daily 9–9.*

To return to downtown Miami after leaving Coral Castle, take
South Dixie Highway to Biscayne Drive (S.W. 288th St.) and
go east to the turnpike. Take the turnpike back to the Don
Shula Expressway (Rte. 874), which leads to the Palmetto Expressway (Rte. 826), which leads in turn to the Dolphin Expressway (Rte. 836).

Miami for Free

Concerts **PACE** (Performing Arts for Community and Education, tel.
305/681–1470; 305/237–1718 for recorded information on up-
coming events) supports free concerts in parks and cultural and
religious institutions throughout the Greater Miami area.

University of Miami School of Music (1314 Miller Dr., tel. 305/
284–6477) offers many free concerts at the Coral Gables campus.

Museums Some museums are free all the time. Others have donation
days, when you may pay as much or as little as you wish.

Parks There are 28 national, state, and county parks in metro Miami
with a variety of beaches, picnic shelters, barbecue grills,
playgrounds, trails, athletic fields, and other facilities. Most
are open free to the public. For a list and for information about
hours of use, contact the **Greater Miami Convention & Visitors
Bureau** (*see* Important Numbers and Addresses, above).

What to See and Do with Children

Greater Miami is a family-oriented vacation destination. Most
of the major hotels can provide access to baby-sitting for young
children.

American Police Hall of Fame and Museum. Here you can view
more than 10,000 law enforcement–related items, including
weapons, a jail cell, and an electric chair, as well as a 400-ton
marble memorial listing the names of more than 3,000 police officers killed in the line of duty since 1960. *3801 Biscayne Blvd.,
tel. 305/891–1700. Open daily 10–5:30. Admission: $3 adults,
$1.50 senior citizens and children 6–12.*

Ancient Spanish Monastery. This is the oldest building in the
western hemisphere, dating from 1141 in Segovia, Spain.
Newspaper magnate William Randolph Hearst had it removed
in pieces and stored it in California for 25 years. In 1954 Miami
developers rebuilt it at its present site. *16711 W. Dixie Hwy.,
N. Miami Beach, tel. 305/945–1461. Open Mon.–Sat. 10–5,*

Sun. noon–5. Admission: $4 adults, $2.50 senior citizens, $1.50 students (12–18), $1 children (7–12).

Ice Castle Skating Arena. This state-of-the-art ice skating arena includes a complete blade shop, skate rentals, snack bar, and video arcade. *255 N.E. 2nd Dr., Homestead, tel. 305/255–4144 (recording) or 305/245–2020. Reservations advised. Admission: $3.50–$7.50, depending on activity and time of day; skate rental $1.*

Shopping

Except in the heart of the Everglades, visitors to the Greater Miami area are never more than 15 minutes away from a major shopping area. Downtown Miami long ago ceased to be the community's central shopping hub. Today Dade County has more than a dozen major malls, an international free zone, and hundreds of miles of commercial streets lined with storefronts and small neighborhood shopping centers. Many of these local shopping areas have an ethnic flavor, catering primarily to one of Greater Miami's immigrant cultures.

In the Latin neighborhoods, children's stores sell *vestidos de fiesta* (party dresses) made of organza and lace. Men's stores sell the *guayabera,* a pleated, embroidered shirt that replaces the tie and jacket in much of the tropics. Traditional bridal shops display formal dresses that Latin families buy or rent for a daughter's *quince,* a lavish 15th-birthday celebration.

No standard store hours exist in Greater Miami. Phone ahead. When you shop, expect to pay Florida's 6% sales tax unless you have the store ship your goods out of Florida.

Shopping Districts
Fashion District Greater Miami is the fashion marketplace for the southeastern United States, the Caribbean, and Latin America. Many of the 500 garment manufacturers in Miami and Hialeah sell their clothing locally, in more than 30 factory outlets and discount fashion stores in the Miami Fashion District, east of I-95 along 5th Avenue from 29th Street to 25th Street. Most stores in the district are open Monday–Saturday 9–5, and accept credit cards.

Miami Free Zone The Miami Free Zone (MFZ) is an international wholesale trade center where the U.S. Customs Service supervises the exhibition and sales space. You can buy goods duty-free for export or pay duty on goods released for domestic use. More than 140 companies sell products from 75 countries, including aviation equipment, chemicals, clothing, computers, cosmetics, electronics, liquor, and perfumes. The 51-acre MFZ is five minutes west of Miami International Airport off the Dolphin Expressway (Rte. 836), and about 20 minutes from the Port of Miami. *Miami Free Zone, 2305 N.W. 107th Ave., tel. 305/591–4300. Open weekdays 9–5.*

Cauley Square A tearoom and craft, antiques, and clothing shops now occupy this complex of clapboard, coral-rock, and stucco buildings erected 1907–20 for railroad workers who built and maintained the line to Key West. Three festivals are held each year—the first Saturday in March, the last Saturday in July, and first Saturday in November—when 10 acres of booths are set up for the sale of crafts. Turn right off U.S. 1 at S.W. 224th Street.

*22400 Old Dixie Hwy., Goulds, tel. 305/258–3543. Open Mon.–
Sat. 10–4:30, Sun. from Thanksgiving to Christmas Eve 12–5.*

Books Greater Miami's best English-language bookstore, **Books &
Books, Inc.,** specializes in books on the arts, architecture,
Floridiana, and contemporary and classical literature. Collec-
tors enjoy the rare-book room upstairs, which doubles as a photography gallery. *296 Aragon Ave., Coral Gables, tel. 305/442–
4408, and 933 Lincoln Rd. (Sterling Bldg.), Miami Beach, tel.
305/532–3222. AE, MC, V. Coral Gables store open weekdays
10–8, Sat. 10–7, Sun. noon–5. Miami Beach store open Mon.–
Thurs. 10–9, Fri. and Sat. 10–midnight, Sun. noon–5.*

**Children's
Books and Toys** The friendly staff at **A Likely Story** will help you choose books
and educational toys that are appropriate to your child's inter-
ests and stage of development. *5740 Sunset Dr., South Miami,
tel. 305/667–3730. MC, V. Open Mon.–Sat. 10–6.*

A good choice north in the city is **A Kid's Book Shoppe.** (1849
N.E. Miami Gardens Dr., No. Miami Beach, tel 305/937–2665).

Beaches

*At press time all Dade County beaches were closed in order to
clean up the debris that washed onto the shores in the wake of
Hurricane Andrew. Fortunately, the beaches have not eroded
and there has been no permanent damage. Beaches will be open
in 1993.*

Miami Beach From Haulover Cut to Government Cut, a broad beach extends
for 10 continuous miles. Amazingly, it's a man-made beach—a
marvel of engineering to repair the ravages of nature.

Along this stretch, erosion had all but eliminated the beach by
the mid-1970s. Waves threatened to undermine the seawalls of
hotels and apartment towers. From 1977 to 1981, the U.S.
Army Corps of Engineers spent $51.5 million to pump tons of
sand from offshore, restoring the beach to a 300-foot width. Between 21st and 46th streets, Miami Beach built boardwalks and
protective walk-overs atop a sand dune landscaped with sea
oats, sea grape, and other native plants whose roots keep the
sand from blowing away.

The new beach lures residents and visitors alike to swim and
stroll. More than 7 million people visit the 7.1 miles of beaches
within the Miami Beach city limits annually. The other 2.9
miles are in Surfside and Bal Harbour. Here's a guide to where
kindred spirits gather:

The best windsurfing on Miami Beach occurs at First Street,
just north of the Government Cut jetty, and at 21st Street. You
can also windsurf at Lummus Park at 10th Street and in the vicinity of 3rd, 14th, and 21st streets. Lifeguards discourage
windsurfing from 79th Street to 87th Street. The best area is
south of town at Hobie Island/Virginia Key.

*City of Miami Beach beaches are open daily with lifeguards,
winter 8–5, summer 9–sunset. Bal Harbour and Surfside have
no lifeguards; beaches open daily 24 hours. Beaches free in all
three communities; metered parking nearby.*

**County Park
Beaches** Metropolitan Dade County operates beaches at several of its
major parks. Each county park operates on its own schedule

that varies from day to day and season to season. Phone the park you want to visit for current hours and information on special events.

Crandon Park. Atlantic Ocean beach, popular with young Hispanics and with family groups of all ethnic backgrounds. *4000 Crandon Park Blvd., Key Biscayne, tel. 305/361–5421. Admission: $3 per car. Open daily 8:30–5.*

Haulover Beach Park. Atlantic Ocean beach. A good place to avoid crowds. Lightly used compared to other public beaches, except on weekends and in the peak tourist season, when it attracts a diverse crowd. *10800 Collins Ave., Miami, tel. 305/ 947–3525. Admission: $3 per car. Open daily 8–sunset.*

Cape Florida **Bill Baggs Cape Florida State Recreation Area** (*see* Exploring Virginia Key and Key Biscayne, above).

Participant Sports

Unfortunately, Hurricane Andrew damaged some Dade County golf courses, marinas, and hiking and cycling trails, though most were being cleaned up at press time. Call before planning your itinerary.

Bicycling Dade County has about 100 miles of off-road bicycling trails. In 1992 the county issued a color-coded map outlining Dade's 4,000 miles of roads suitable for bike travel. The map is available for $3.50 from area bike shops or from the Dade County Bicycle Coordinator, Metropolitan Planning Organization (111 N.W. 1st St., Ste. 910, Miami 33128, tel. 305/375–4507). Also, for information on dozens of monthly group rides contact the **Everglades Bicycle Club** (Box 430282, S. Miami 33243–0282, tel. 305/598–3998). Among the best shops for renting bicycles is **Dade Cycle** (3216 Grand Ave., Coconut Grove, tel. 305/444–5997).

Golf From the famed "Blue Monster" at the Doral Resort & Country Club to the scenic Key Biscayne Golf Course overlooking Biscayne Bay, Greater Miami has more than 30 private and public courses. For information, contact the appropriate Parks and Recreation Department: Metro-Dade County (tel. 305/579–2968), City of Miami (tel. 305/575–5256), and City of Miami Beach (tel. 305/673–7730).

Spa The **Doral Saturnia International Spa Resort** opened in 1987 on the grounds of the Doral Resort and Country Club. Formal Italian gardens contain the spa pool and a special waterfall under which guests can enjoy natural hydromassage from the gentle pounding of falling water. The spa's 100-foot-high atrium accommodates a 5,000-pound bronze staircase railing created in 1920 by French architect Alexandre Gustave Eiffel and fabricated by artist Edgar Brandt for Paris's Bon Marché department store. The spa combines mud baths and other European pampering techniques with state-of-the-art American fitness and exercise programs. A one-day sampler is available. *8755 N.W. 36th St., Miami 33178, tel. 305/593–6030. 48 suites. Facilities: 4 exercise studios (2 with spring-loaded floors), 2 outdoor heated pools, indoor heated pool, David fitness equipment, beauty salon, 2 restaurants. AE, DC, MC, V.*

Water Sports Listed below are the major marinas in Greater Miami. The dock
Marinas masters at these marinas can provide information on other ma-

rine services you may need. Also ask the dock masters for *Teall's Tides and Guides*, *Miami-Dade County*, and other local nautical publications.

The U.S. Customs Service requires boats of less than five tons that enter the country along Florida's Atlantic Coast south of Sebastian Inlet to report to designated marinas and call U.S. Customs on a direct phone line. The phones, located outside marina buildings, are accessible 24 hours a day. U.S. Customs phones in Greater Miami are at Haulover Marina and Watson Island Marina (both listed below).

Dinner Key Marina. Operated by City of Miami. Facilities include dockage with space for transients and a boat ramp. *3400 Pan American Dr., Coconut Grove, tel. 305/579–6980. Open daily 7 AM–11 PM.*

Haulover Park Marina. Operated by county lessee. Facilities include a bait-and-tackle shop, marine gas station, and boat launch. *15000 Collins Ave., Miami Beach, tel. 305/945–3934. Open weekdays 7 AM–5 PM, weekends 7 AM–6 PM.*

Miami Beach Marina. Facilities include dockage, boat ramp, fueling station, bait and tackle, and bathrooms with showers. This is one of five locations for renting Club Nautico power boats (Pier E, 300 Alton Rd., Miami Beach, tel. 305/673–2502). *300 Alton Rd., Miami Beach, tel. 305/673–6000. Open daily 8–6; 24-hr guard with communications capability.*

Watson Island Marina. City of Miami marina. Facilities include bait and tackle, boat ramp, and fuel. When the marina is busy, it stays open until all boaters are helped. *1050 MacArthur Causeway, Miami, tel. 305/371–2378. Open Mon.–Thurs. 7:30 AM–8 PM, Fri. 7:30–10, Sat. and Sun. 6:30–10, and often open later.*

Sailing Dinner Key and the Coconut Grove waterfront remain the center of sailing in Greater Miami, although sailboat moorings and rentals are located along other parts of the bay and up the Miami River. For instruction and rentals, Easy Sailing offers a fleet ranging from 19 to 127 feet for rent by the hour or for the day. Services include sailboat lessons, scuba diving lessons and certification, and on-board catering. *Dinner Key Marina, 3400 Pan American Dr., tel. 305/858–4001 or 800/780–4001. Reservation and advance deposit required. Open daily 9–sunset.*

Windsurfing **Beach Sports International.** You can rent windsurfers and hobie cats, and arrange parasailing at this shop just north of the Art Deco District. *2401 Collins Ave., Miami Beach 33140, tel. 305/538–0752. AE, MC, V. Open daily 8:30–6.*

Sailboards Miami (tel. 305/361–SAIL).

Diving Summer diving conditions in greater Miami have been compared to those in the Caribbean. Winter diving can be adversely affected when cold fronts come through. Dive-boat schedules vary with the season and with local weather conditions.

Fowey, Triumph, Long, and Emerald Reefs all are shallow 10- to 15-foot dives that are good for snorkelers and beginning divers. These reefs are on the edge of the continental shelf, a quarter of a mile from depths greater than 100 feet. You can also paddle around the tangled prop roots of the mangrove trees that line Florida's coastline, peering at the fish, crabs, and other on-shore creatures that hide there.

Dive Boats and Instruction. Look for instructors who are affiliated with PADI (Professional Association of Dive Instructors) or NAUI (National Association of Underwater Instructors).

Divers Paradise Corp (4000 Crandon Blvd., Key Biscayne, tel. 305/361–DIVE). Complete dive shop and diving charter service, including equipment rental and scuba instruction. PADI affiliation. *AE, DC, MC, V. Open weekdays 10–6, weekends 7:30–6.*

Omega Diving International. Private instruction throughout Greater Miami. Equipment consultation and specialty courses, including instructor training and underwater photography. PADI affiliation. *13885 S.W. 70th Ave., Miami, tel. 305/238–3039 or 800/255–1966. Open daily 8–6.*

Bubbles Dive Center. This all-purpose dive shop is located right at the Miami Beach marina. PADI affiliation. *2671 S.W. 27th Ave., Miami, 33133, tel. 305/856–0565. AE, MC, V. Open Mon.–Sat. 10 AM–6 PM. Closed Sun.*

Tennis Greater Miami has more than 60 private and public tennis centers, of which 11 are open to the public. All public tennis courts charge nonresidents an hourly fee.

Coral Gables **Biltmore Tennis Center.** Ten well-maintained hard courts. Site of annual Orange Bowl Junior International Tennis Tournament for children 14 and under in December. *1150 Anastasia Ave., tel. 305/460–5360. Nonresident day rate $4.30, night rate $5 per person per hour. Open weekdays 8 AM–10 PM, weekends 8–8.*

Miami Beach **Flamingo Tennis Center.** Has 19 well-maintained clay courts. Site of the Rolex–Orange Bowl Junior International Tennis Tournament for teenagers 12–18. *1000 12th St., tel. 305/673–7761. Cost: day $2.13, night $2.65 per person per hour. Open weekdays 8 AM–9 PM, weekends 8–7.*

Metropolitan Dade County **International Tennis Center.** Has 17 Laykold Cushion Plus hard courts, six lighted. Reservations necessary for night play. Closed to public play for about two weeks before and after the annual Lipton International Players Championship in March. *7300 Crandon Blvd., Key Biscayne, tel. 305/361–8633. Open daily 8 AM–10 PM. Cost: days $2, nights $3 per person per hour. Rental rackets $5 per hour.*

Spectator Sports

Greater Miami offers a broad variety of spectator sports events, including such popular pastimes as football and baseball, and more specialized events, such as boat racing and rugby. Major stadium and arena diagrams appear in the Community Interest Pages of the telephone directory. However, the community lacks a central clearinghouse for sports information and ticket sales.

Generally you can find daily listings of local sports events on the last page of the sports section in *The Miami Herald*. The weekend section on Friday carries detailed schedules and coverage of spectator sports.

Orange Bowl Festival. The activities of the annual Orange Bowl and Junior Orange Festival take place early November–late February. Best-known for its **King Orange Jamboree Parade**

and the **Federal Express/Orange Bowl Football Classic,** the festival also includes two tennis tournaments: the **Rolex–Orange Bowl International Tennis Championships** for top amateur national and international tennis players 18 and under, and an international tournament for players 14 and under.

Auto Racing **Hialeah Speedway.** The Greater Miami area's only independent raceway holds stock-car races on a ⅓-mile asphalt speedway in a 5,000-seat stadium. Five divisions of stock cars run weekly. The Marion Edwards, Jr., Memorial Race for late-model stock cars is in November. Located on U.S. 27, ¼ mile east of Palmetto Expressway (Rte. 826). *3300 W. Okeechobee Rd., Hialeah, tel. 305/821–6644. Admission: $10 adults, under 12 free. Open every Sat. late Jan.–early Dec. Gates open 6* PM, *racing 7:30–11.*

Grand Prix of Miami. Currently held in February or April each year for the Camel GT Championship on a 1.9-mile, E-shape track in downtown Miami, south of MacArthur Causeway and east of Biscayne Boulevard. Drivers race three hours; the one completing the most laps wins. Sanctioned by International Motor Sports Association (IMSA). At press time the site of the 1993 Grand Prix was in question. *Miami Motor Sports, Inc., 7254 S.W. 48th St., Miami 33155, tel. 305/662–5660. Tickets available from Miami Motor Sports, Inc., tel. 305/665–RACE or Ticketmaster (see* Important Addresses and Numbers, *above).*

Baseball **Florida Marlins.** The Marlins—members of the Eastern Division of the National League—will play all home games at the beautiful Joe Robbie Stadium where the Miami Dolphins established major league sports in Florida in 1966. For transportation information, *see* Football, below.

Basketball **Miami Heat.** Fifth 41 home-game season November–April for Miami's National Basketball Association team. *Tickets: Miami Arena, Miami 33136–4102, tel. 305/577–HEAT or Ticketmaster (see* Important Addresses and Numbers, above).

Dog Racing The Biscayne Kennel Club and the Flagler Dog Track in Greater Miami divide the annual racing calendar. Check with the individual tracks for dates.

Biscayne Kennel Club. Greyhounds chase a mechanical rabbit around illuminated fountains in the track's infield. Near I–95 at N.W. 115th Street. *320 N.W. 115th St., Miami Shores, tel. 305/ 754–3484. Admission: table seats $1, grandstand $1, clubhouse $2, sports room $3. Parking 50¢–$2. Season: late Apr. into July and Oct.–Dec.*

Flagler Dog Track. Inner-city track in the middle of Little Havana, five minutes east of Miami International Airport off Dolphin Expressway (Rte. 836) and Douglas Road (corner of N.W. 37th Ave. and 7th St.). *401 N.W. 38th Ct., Miami, tel. 305/649–3000. General admission $1, clubhouse $3, parking 50¢–$2. Open Apr.–July and Sept.–Oct. Dates may fluctuate; call ahead for exact times.*

Football **Miami Dolphins.** President Tim Robbie took over for his dad in late 1989 after the curmudgeonly Joe Robbie passed away. Miami has the elder Robbie to thank for a state-of-the-art football arena—Joe Robbie Stadium—that the late president named for himself.

JRS, as the stadium is called, has 73,000 seats and a grass play-ing-field surface with built-in drainage under the sod to carry off rainwater. It's on a 160-acre site, 16 miles northwest of downtown Miami, one mile south of the Dade-Broward county line, accessible from I–95 and Florida's Turnpike. On game days, the Metro-Dade Transit Authority runs buses to the sta-dium. Bus information, tel. 305/638–6700.

Dolphins tickets: *Miami Dolphins, Joe Robbie Stadium, 2269 N.W. 199th St., Miami 33056, tel. 305/620–2578. Open week-days 10–6, Sat. during season. Also available through Ticketmaster (see Important Addresses and Numbers, above).*

Horse Racing   **Calder Race Course.** Opened in 1971, Calder is Florida's largest glass-enclosed, air-conditioned sports facility. This means that Calder actually has two racing seasons, one in fall or winter, another in spring or summer. Contact the track for this year's dates. In May, Calder holds the Tropical Park Derby for three-year-olds, the last major race in Florida before the Kentucky Derby. On the Dade-Broward county line near I–95 and the Hallandale Beach Boulevard exit, ¾ mile from Joe Robbie Sta-dium. *21001 N.W. 27th Ave., Miami, tel. 305/625–1311. Gener-al admission $2, clubhouse $4, programs 75¢, parking $1–$3. Gates open 10:30 AM, post time 12:30 PM, races end about 5:30.*

Hialeah Park. A superb setting for thoroughbred racing, Hialeah's 228 acres of meticulously landscaped grounds sur-round paddocks and a clubhouse built in a classic French-Medi-terranean style. Since it opened in 1925, Hialeah Park has survived hurricanes and now seems likely to survive even changing demographics as the racetrack crowd has steadily moved north and east, away from Hialeah. This grand old park has a dismal 1989 season, and no racing took place the next two seasons. However, the track saw racing again in 1991–92, and dates for the 1992–93 season are likely to be between Novem-ber and January. Even if you're not a race fan, during racing season you can take advantage of the early gate opening Satur-day and Sunday mornings and breakfast at Hialeah Park. You can watch the horses work out, explore Hialeah's gardens, munch on breakfast fare of tolerable palatability, and admire the park's breeding flock of 600 Cuban flamingos. Hialeah Park opens daily for free tours 9–5. Metrorail's Hialeah Station is on the grounds of Hialeah Park. *2200 E. 4th Ave., Hialeah, tel. 305/885–8000. Gates open during race season at 10:30, post time 12:30 or 1. Races end 5:30. Other times of year, park open Mon.–Sat. 10–5. Admission $2 grandstand, $4 clubhouse. Parking $1–$3.*

Jai Alai   **Miami Jai-Alai Fronton.** This game, invented in the Basque re-gion of northern Spain, is the world's fastest. Jai-alai balls, called *pelotas,* have been clocked at speeds exceeding 170 mph. The game is played in a 176-foot-long court called a *fronton.* Players climb the walls to catch the ball in a *cesta*—a woven basket—with an attached glove. You bet on a team to win or on the order in which teams will finish. Built in 1926, Miami Jai-Alai is the oldest fronton in America. Each evening, it presents 13 games—14 on Friday and Saturday—some singles, some doubles. Located a mile east of Miami International Airport. *3500 N.W. 37th Ave., Miami, tel. 305/633–6400. Admission: $1, clubhouse $5. Dinner available. AE, D, DC, MC, V. Open nightly early Nov.–late Apr. and May–late Sept., 7:10–mid-*

night; closed Sun. year-round and Tues. and Wed. Mar.–Apr. Matinees Mon., Wed., and Sat. noon–5.

Soccer **Miami Freedom.** Miami's entry in the newly consolidated American Professional Soccer League typically plays a seven-game exhibition season followed by an eight-game home season at the Orange Bowl (1400 N.W. 4th St.). Day games start at 2 PM. *1801 Coral Way, Miami, tel. 305/446–3136. Tickets: $5 adults, $3 children 14 and under and senior citizens (admission subject to change).*

Tennis **Lipton International Players Championship (LIPC).** This 10-day spring tournament at the 64-acre International Tennis Center of Key Biscayne is one of the largest in the world in terms of attendance. The two main professional tennis organizations—Association of Tennis Professionals and Women's International Tennis Association—helped create this tournament and own part of it. *7300 Crandon Blvd., Key Biscayne, tel. for tickets 305/361–5252 or Ticketmaster (see* Important Addresses and Numbers, above).

Dining

By Rosalie Leposky

Updated by Herb Hiller

You can eat your way around the world in Greater Miami, enjoying just about any kind of cuisine imaginable, and in every price category. The rich mix of nationalities here encourages individual restaurateurs and chefs to retain their culinary roots. Thus, Miami offers not just Latin fare but dishes distinctive to Spain, Cuba, Nicaragua, and other Hispanic countries; not just Oriental fare but specialties of China, India, Thailand, Vietnam, and other Asian cultures. And don't neglect American fare just because it's not "foreign." In recent years the city has gained eminence for the distinctive cuisine introduced by chefs who have migrated north from the tropics, and here combine fresh, natural foods—especially seafoods—with classically inspired dedication. Dining is definitely one of the signs of Miami's coming of age.

Highly recommended restaurants are indicated by a star ★.

Category	Cost*
Very Expensive	over $55
Expensive	$35–$55
Moderate	$15–$35
Inexpensive	under $15

per person, excluding drinks, service, and 6% sales tax

American **The Pavillon Grill.** The mahogany, jade marble, and leather ap-
Downtown Miami pointments of the restaurant's salon and dining room exude the
★ conservative bias of an English private club. A harpist plays, and the attentive staff serves regional American fare, including items that are low in calories, cholesterol, and sodium for diners who are on restricted diets. Specialties include tournedos of Pacific salmon in a light cream-herb sauce and duck in two acts: duck breast with caramelized apples, and grilled leg on greens. For dessert, the restaurant features a gratin of berries perfumed with Cointreau in an almond cream sauce. The menu changes often, but there's always an extensive wine list. *100*

Miami Area Dining

Miami Gdns. Dr.
Palmetto Expwy.
N. Miami Beach Blvd.
NORTH MIAMI BEACH
N.E. 135th St.
N.W. 135th St.
NORTH MIAMI
Gratigny Rd.
Broad Causeway
Biscayne Blvd.
N.E. 6th Ave.
27th Ave.
7th Ave.
8th Ave.
N.W. 57th Ave.
Okeechobee Rd.
Florida's Turnpike (W. Dade Expwy.)
W. 49th St.
E. 49th St.
N.W. 103rd St.
N.E. 103rd St.
N.W. 95th St.
N.E. 95th St.
Red Rd.
E. 25th St.
N.W. 79th St.
JFK Causeway
N. Miami Ave.
N.W. 2nd Ave.
N.W. 62nd St.
N.W. 58th St.
N.W. 72nd Ave.
Hialeah Dr.
N.W. 54th St.
MIAMI BEACH
Collins Ave.
OCEAN
N.W. 36th St.
Robert Frost Expwy.
Julia Tuttle Causeway
N.W. 87th Ave.
Diary Rd.
N.W. 20th St.
Venetian Causeway
Dolphin Expwy.
N.W. 7th St.
W. Flagler St.
MIAMI
MacArthur Causeway
S.W. 8th St.
Tamiami Trail
Bay
S.W. 24th St.
Coral Way
Miracle Mile

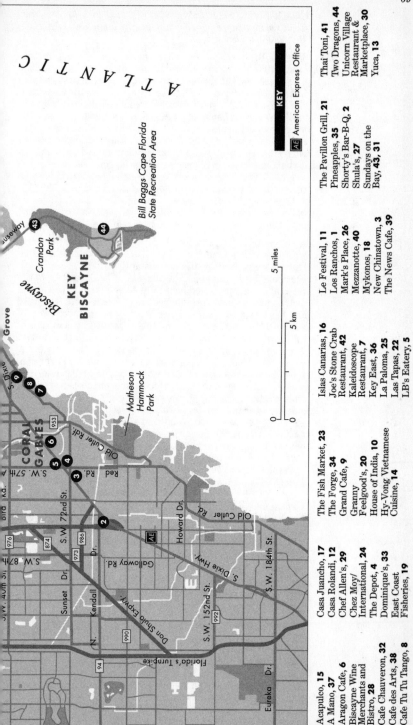

69

KEY

AE American Express Office

Acapulco, **15**
A Mano, **37**
Aragon Cafe, **6**
Biscayne Wine
Merchants and
Bistro, **28**
Cafe Chauveron, **32**
Cafe des Arts, **38**
Cafe Tu Tu Tango, **8**

Casa Juancho, **17**
Casa Rolandi, **12**
Chef Allen's, **29**
Chez Moy/
International, **24**
The Depot, **4**
Dominique's, **33**
East Coast
Fisheries, **19**

The Fish Market, **23**
The Forge, **34**
Grand Cafe, **9**
Granny
Feelgood's, **20**
House of India, **10**
Hy-Vong Vietnamese
Cuisine, **14**

Islas Canarias, **16**
Joe's Stone Crab
Restaurant, **42**
Kaleidoscope
Restaurant, **7**
Key East, **36**
La Paloma, **25**
Las Tapas, **22**
LB's Eatery, **5**

Le Festival, **11**
Los Ranchos, **1**
Mark's Place, **26**
Mezzanotte, **40**
Mykonos, **18**
New Chinatown, **3**
The News Cafe, **39**

The Pavillon Grill, **21**
Pineapples, **35**
Shorty's Bar-B-Q, **2**
Shula's, **27**
Sundays on the
Bay, **43, 31**

Thai Toni, **41**
Two Dragons, **44**
Unicorn Village
Restaurant &
Marketplace, **30**
Yuca, **13**

Chopin Plaza, tel. 305/577–1000, ext. 4494 or 4462. Reserva-
tions recommended. Jacket required. Closed Sun. AE, DC,
MC, V. Very Expensive.

Kendall
(S.W. Suburb)

Shorty's Bar-B-Q. Shorty Allen opened his barbecue restaurant in 1951 in a log cabin, and this restaurant has since become
a tradition. Parents bring their teenage children to show them
where mom and dad ate on their honeymoon. Huge fans circulate fresh air through the single screened dining room, where
meals are served family-style at long picnic tables. On the walls
hang an assortment of cowboy hats, horns, saddles, an ox yoke,
and heads of boar and caribou. Specialties include barbecued
pork ribs, chicken, and pork steak slow-cooked over hickory
logs and drenched in Shorty's own warm, spicy sauce, and side
orders of tangy baked beans with big chunks of pork, corn on
the cob, and coleslaw. *9200 South Dixie Hwy., tel. 305/665–*
5732. A second location opened in 1989 at 5989 South Universi-
ty Dr., Davie, tel. 305/680–9900. No reservations. Dress: infor-
mal. Closed Thanksgiving, Christmas. MC, V. Inexpensive.

Miami Beach

A Mano. Acclaimed Florida chef Norman Van Aken (formerly
with Key West's Louie's Backyard) opened this intimate Deco
District restaurant in 1991 and instantly made it one of South
Florida's finest dining establishments. When speaking of the
tropical cuisine prepared here, Van Aken says it's "Old World
methods with New World ingredients." Terra-cotta floor tiles
and black-trimmed aqua chairs accent a mottled orange wall
with black panels, contributing to the interesting contrasts of
the interior design. *A mano* means "by hand, reflecting the tradition and philosophy of the food preparation at the restaurant,
where everything is lovingly prepared. For an appetizer consider the triple-decker blue corn tortilla with grilled duck and
accoutrements such as smoky chipotle mayonnaise and tropical
fruit chutney. On any given evening the menu may include
spiny lobster tail stir-fry with wasabi, soba noodles, and ginger–lemon grass–tamari vinaigrette, among other inspired offerings. A separate dessert menu boasts such delectables as
berry trifle, pecan caramel tart, and "fallen" chocolate-cognac
cake with passion fruit chantilly. There's an extensive wine list
with some expensive choices. *1140 Ocean Dr. (in the Betsy Ross*
Hotel), Miami Beach, tel. 305/531–6266. Reservations recom-
mended. Dress: casual but neat. Closed Mon. AE, DC, MC, V.
Expensive.

Key East. This is a favorite hangout for the art, theater, and
bookish crowd who get their kicks from the natural foods and
naturally good-natured ways of a fast-moving staff. Because of
its location near a number of theaters the waiters are experts at
filling orders before curtain time. Dine outside where you can
watch Rollerbladers brake for the bluesy sounds or other musical offerings. Big salads and fresh homemade pastas go well
with the crusty sourdough rolls that keep coming. There's
nothing deep-fried, and no salt is used in preparation. Try a
crispy baked fruit dessert. *647 Lincoln Rd. Mall, tel. 305/672–*
3606. Closed Sun., Thanksgiving, Christmas, New Year's Day.
No reservations. Casual but neat. AE, MC, V. Moderate.

The News Cafe. Owners Mark Soyka, who trained on the cosmopolitan beach scene in Tel Aviv, and Jeffrey Dispenzieri from
New York, are right on the money here with quick, friendly
waiters and waitresses who don't hurry the guests who have
come to shmooze or the intellects who are deep in a Tolstoi novel
picked out of the book rack. A raw bar has been added in back

with 15 stools, but most visitors prefer seating outside to feel the salt breeze and look at the beach. This is the hippest joint on Ocean Drive. Offering a little of this, and a little of that—bagels, pâtés, chocolate fondue—The News Cafe attracts people who come here for a snack, light meal, or aperitif, and invariably, to indulge in the people parade. *800 Ocean Dr., tel. 305/538–6397. No reservations. Dress: casual. AE, DC, MC, V. Open 24 hours. Inexpensive.*

North Miami Beach ★ **Chef Allen's.** Thirty more seats have been added, thus reducing the waiting time for this top-of-the-line restaurant. Also new is the bar and full-liquor service. In this Art Deco world of glass block, neon trim, and fresh flowers, your gaze nonetheless remains riveted on the kitchen. Chef Allen Susser designed it with a picture window, 25 feet wide, so you can watch him create new American masterpieces almost too pretty to eat. Specialties include mesquite-grilled rare tuna with glazed onions and cranberry chutney, and lamb medallions with pinenuts and wilted spinach garnished with goat cheese. Among the dessert choices are white-chocolate macadamia nut torte, chocolate pizza, and a sugar junkie's delight—scoops of chocolate, raspberry, caramel, and pistachio ice cream floating in caramel sauce. Fine wines by the glass from a wine bar. *19088 N.E. 29th Ave., tel. 305/935–2900. Reservations accepted. Dress: informal. AE, MC, V. Expensive.*

★ **Mark's Place.** Since 1986, owner/chef Mark Militello has cooked regional Florida fare in a special oak-burning oven imported from Genoa. The menu changes nightly, based on the availability of fresh ingredients, but typical selections include appetizers of rock shrimp hash with cayenne mustard sauce and red pepper aioli, grilled shrimp with curried infused oil, and ginger and tropical fruit paella; for salad, try calamari with spinach, mint, sweet mango, and red bell pepper (many of the vegetables are organically grown by staffers). Entrees may include porcini-crusted cobia with fricassee of lobster, mango, and colorful pepper; grilled swordfish with rosemary, pinenuts, and vegetable couscous; and duck with chayote, plantains, green apple, and red onion confit. For dessert, the chocolate espresso torte with a hazelnut crust and a warm apple tart with homemade vanilla and caramel sauce receive high ratings. *2286 N.E. 123rd St., North Miami 33181, tel. 305/893–6888. Reservations advised. Dress: neat but casual. AE, DC, MC, V. Closed Thanksgiving, Christmas. No lunch weekends. Expensive.*

South Miami **The Depot.** Aptly named, this restaurant is situated across the highway from where trains to Key West once ran and near the site of the old Larkins depot (in what was once the town of South Miami). Lit with oil font chandeliers and wall lamps and as long as a Pullman car, The Depot is decorated with mahogany paneling and stained-glass transoms. Glass-topped tables are placed over dimly lit model railroad layouts that operate on 90-second timers. As pleasing as the ambience is the menu, which, in addition to featuring some of the finest beef in town, also includes snapper *fruits de mer* (sauteed fillet of snapper topped with scallops and shrimp in a white wine garlic butter suace); black pepper fettucini tossed with smoked salmon and bell peppers in a light cream sauce, and grilled sea scallops and shiitake mushrooms with tropical fruit coulis. *5830 S. Dixie Hwy., tel. 305/665–6261. Reservations advised. Dress: neat but casual. AE, DC, MC, V. Moderate.*

West Dade **Shula's.** Surrounded by memorabilia of coach Don Shula's perfect 1972 season with the Miami Dolphins, you can drink or dine in this shrine for the NFL-obsessed. The certified black angus beef is almost an afterthought to the icons that include quarterback Earl Morall's rocking chair, assistant coach Howard Schnellenberger's pipe, and the autographed playbook from President Nixon to coach Shula. The Sports Ticker fills in for any gaps in conversation, ditto—in season—the weekly stat sheets of all NFL games. The ladies room mirrors the Orange Bowl locker room from where the magic took place, with pictures of the beefy perfect-season squad. Otherwise it's steaks, prime rib, and fish (including dolphinfish) in a woody, fireplace-cheered and cedar-shingled setting—not to mention its location on the grounds of Miami Lakes. *15400 N.W. 77th Ave., tel. 305/821–1150. Reservations advised. Dress: neat but casual. AE, DC, MC, V. Expensive–Moderate.*

Chinese **Two Dragons.** Run like a small family restaurant, the ingredients served in this Chinese restaurant are all fresh and entrees are prepared to order. Specialties include a Cantonese seafood nest (shrimp, scallops, and crabmeat with Chinese vegetables in a nest of crisp noodles), an orange beef Mandarin, and Szechuan eggplant with a spicy garlic-mustard sauce guaranteed to clear the sinuses. Dine in an intimate pagodalike booth behind hanging curtains of wooden beads or at an open table overlooking an outdoor Oriental garden. A Japanese steak house—the "second dragon"—serves Teppanyaki-style cuisine at six cooking tables in a separate room. *Sonesta Beach Hotel, 350 Ocean Dr., tel. 305/361–2021. Reservations advised. Dress: neat but casual. AE, D, DC, MC, V. Dinner only. Closed 2 weeks in Sept. Moderate.*

South Miami **New Chinatown.** This spacious 200-seat restaurant offers bright and busy family dining. The big menu features Cantonese, Mandarin, Szechuan, and sizzling Teppan regional choices, as well as chow mein, chop suey, and moo goo gai pan. Vegetarians can find steamed Chinese vegetables among five special entrées or order any of the more than 60 dishes without meat. Entrées include hot and spicy *mo-po-to-fu* (bean curd sautéed with fresh scallions) with or without ground pork; orange chicken; and lotus prawns in a garlic and Hoisin sauce. New Chinatown will reduce but not eliminate the MSG in dishes, insisting the taste suffers. *5958 S. Dixie Hwy., tel. 305/662–5649 or 662–5650. No reservations. Dress: casual. AE, MC, V. Closed Thanksgiving. Moderate.*

Continental **Grand Cafe.** Understated elegance at all hours is the hallmark—a bilevel room with pink tablecloths and floral bouquets, sunbathed by day, dim and intimate after dark. Japanese-born, French-trained executive chef Katsuo Sugiura creates "international" cuisine (the menu theme changes every six weeks—look for special Brazilian, Caribbean, Cajun, and Oriental specialties), combining ingredients from all over the world in pleasing presentations that intrigue the palate. Specialties include black linguini (colored with squid ink); fresh smoked salmon; a superbly rich she-crab soup with roe, sherry, and cayenne pepper; "boned" Maine lobster presented in the shape of a lobster, with artichokes and a cream sauce of vermouth and saffron. Dessert specialties include a white-chocolate and pistachio mousse with blackberry sauce and Beaujolais essence. *2669 S. Bayshore Dr., tel. 305/858–9600.*

Coconut Grove ★

Reservations advised. Jacket preferred. AE, DC, MC, V. Very Expensive.

Kaleidoscope Restaurant. The tropical ambience here extends to a choice of indoor or outdoor seating—all in air-conditioned comfort, because fans blow cold air around a glass-roofed terrace overlooking a landscaped courtyard. Specialties include pastas and seafood. *3112 Commodore Plaza, tel. 305/446–5010. Reservations advised. Dress: casual. AE, DC, MC, V. Moderate.*

Coral Gables **Aragon Cafe.** If George Merrick, the founder of Coral Gables, entered the bar of Aragon Cafe, he would see on display some of his mother's hand-painted china and silver. In this restaurant designed to look old and classy, subdued lighting emanates from gaslight-style chandeliers and etched-glass wall lights. The menu emphasizes fresh Florida seafoods, and reflects Merrick's desire to re-create the best of the Mediterranean in a Florida setting. Specialties include seafood minestrone made with shrimp, scallops, clams, new potatoes, carrots, and kidney and green beans; grilled goat cheese in banana leaves; grilled Florida dolphinfish with native starfruit sauce; and tuna steak au poivre in a mushroom-based sauce of peppercorns and cream. Dessert offerings include a white-chocolate terrine with pistachio sauce. *180 Aragon Ave. in the Colonnade Hotel, Coral Gables 33134, tel. 305/448–9966. Reservations advised. Jacket required. Free valet parking. AE, DC, MC, V. No lunch Sat. Closed Sun. Expensive.*

Miami Beach **The Forge.** Miraculously reopened in late 1991 after a devastating fire, The Forge has in fact gained something: improved intimacy. Seats have been reduced by 300 to 175 through the loss of several rooms, which may reopen in time. Otherwise, this landmark (often compared to a museum) still stands behind a facade of 19th-century Parisian mansions, where an authentic forge once stood. Dinner is served in intimate dining salons, each with its own historical artifacts, including a 250-year-old chandelier that hung in James Madison's White House. A fully stocked wine cellar contains an inventory of 380,000 bottles—including more than 500 dating from 1822 (and costing as much as $35,000) and recorked in 1989 by experts from Domaines Barons de Rothschild. Specialties include veal chop with mushrooms and grapes and pear-scented breast of chicken beaujolais. Desserts are extravagant; try the famous blacksmith pie. *432 Arthur Godfrey Rd., tel. 305/538–8533. Reservations advised. Dress: casual but neat. AE, DC, MC, V. Dinner only. Expensive.*

North Miami **La Paloma.** This fine Swiss Continental restaurant offers a total sensory experience: fine food, impeccable service, and the ambience of an art museum. In sideboards and cases throughout, owners Werner and Maria Staub display ornate European antiques that they have spent decades collecting. The treasures include Baccarat crystal, Limoges china, Meissen porcelains, and Sevres clocks. The staff speaks Spanish, French, German, Portuguese, or Arabic. Specialties include fresh local fish and seafood; Norwegian salmon Caroline (poached, served on a bed of spinach with hollandaise sauce); Wiener schnitzel; lamb chops à la *diable* (coated with bread crumbs, mustard, garlic, and herbs), veal chop with morrel sauce, chateaubriand; and for dessert, passion-fruit sorbet and kiwi soufflé with raspberry sauce. *10999 Biscayne Blvd., tel. 305/891–0505. Reser-*

vations advised. Jacket preferred. AE, MC, V. No lunch. Closed Mon., July, and part of Aug. Expensive.

Biscayne Wine Merchants and Bistro. In this 35-seat retail beer and wine store with a deli counter, strangers often become friends while sharing tables and sampling the merchandise. Owners Jan Sitko and Esther Flores stock about 300 wines (sold by the glass or bottle) and 92 brands of beer. The menu changes daily but always includes bean and cream soups. Typical fare may include chicken Crustaces (a chicken breast stuffed with leeks, dill, and crab with a light dill sauce) and daily fresh fish specials such as dolphin, shark, snapper, swordtail, wahoo, and salmon. Sitko and Flores like to create new dishes with fresh herbs, spices, fruits, and vegetables. One favorite is a tangy-sweet sauce with jalapeño and citrus. *12953 Biscayne Blvd., North Miami, tel. 305/899-1997. No reservations. Dress: informal. AE, MC, V. No lunch Sat., Sun. Closed Thanksgiving, Christmas, New Year's Day, sometimes other holidays. Moderate.*

Cuban
Coral Gables
★

Yuca. This high-style Cuban eatery is chicly designed with track lighting, blond woods, tiles, and art prints. The cuisine is presented colorfully also, by chef Douglas Rodriguez, who takes good advantage of the tropical foods available in Miami. Entrées include meat-filled empanadas with a pickled garlic rémoulade arranged with watercress and lime. Also featured are homemade gnocchi of malanga and sweet potato served with picadillo; and grilled loin pork chops with roasted cumin seed and carmelized onion butter served with moros and avocado. Owner Efrain Veiga relocated to expanded quarters in 1991. *177 Giralda Ave., tel. 305/444-4448. Dress: neat but casual. No lunch weekends. Reservations required. AE, DC, MC, V. Closed Thanksgiving, Christmas, New Year's Day. Expensive.*

Little Havana

Islas Canarias. A gathering place for Cuban poets, pop music stars, and media personalities. Wall murals depict a Canary Islands street scene and an indigenous dragon tree (*Dracaena draco*). The menu includes such Canary Islands dishes as baked lamb, ham hocks with boiled potatoes, and *tortilla Española* (a Spanish omelet with onions and chorizo, a spicy sausage), as well as Cuban standards, including palomilla steak, and fried kingfish. Don't miss the three superb varieties of homemade chips—potato, malanga, and plantain. Islas Canarias has another location in Westchester at Coral Way and S.W. 137th Ave. *285 N.W. Unity Blvd. (N.W. 27th Ave.), tel. 305/649-0440. No reservations. Dress: informal. No credit cards. Open Christmas Eve and New Year's Eve to 6 PM. Inexpensive.*

Family Style
Coral Gables

LB's Eatery. Town and gown meet at this sprout-laden haven a ½-block from the University of Miami's baseball stadium. Kitschy food-related posters plaster the walls of this relaxed restaurant with low prices. Since there are no waiters, you order at the counter and pick up your food when called. Vegetarians thrive on LB's salads and daily meatless entrées, such as lasagna and moussaka. Famous for Saturday night lobster. (If you plan to come after 8, call ahead to reserve a lobster.) Other specialties include barbecued baby-back ribs, lime chicken, croissant sandwiches, and carrot cake. *5813 Ponce de León Blvd., tel. 305/661-7091. No reservations. Dress: informal. MC, V. Closed Sun., all major holidays. Inexpensive.*

French
Coral Gables

Le Festival. The modest canopied entrance to this classical French restaurant understates the elegance within. Decor includes etched-glass filigree mirrors and light pink walls. Appetizers of salmon mousse, baked oysters with garlic butter, and lobster in champagne sauce en croute lead the way for special entrées such as rack of lamb (for two), and medallions of veal with two sauces—a pungent, creamy lime sauce and a dark port-wine sauce with mushrooms. Dinners come with real french-fried potatoes. Don't pass up dessert here; the mousses and soufflés are positively decadent. *2120 Salzedo St., tel. 305/442–8545. Reservations required for dinner and for lunch parties of 5 or more. Dress: neat but casual. AE, DC, MC, V. No lunch weekends. Closed Sat. noon, all day Sun., and Sept.–Oct. Expensive.*

Miami Beach **Dominique's.** Woodwork and mirrors from a Vanderbilt home
★ and other demolished New York mansions create an intimate setting for a unique nouvelle cuisine dining experience. Specialties include exotic appetizers, such as buffalo sausage, sautéed alligator tail, and rattlesnake-meat salad; rack of lamb (which accounts for 35% of the restaurant's total sales) and fresh seafood; and an extensive wine list. The restaurant also serves brunch on Sunday. *Alexander Hotel, 5225 Collins Ave., tel. 305/865–6500 or 800/327–6121. Reservations advised. Jacket recommended. AE, DC, MC, V. Very Expensive.*

★ **Cafe Chauveron.** After a lapse of service, this café again reigns as doyen of traditional French cuisine in Miami. The international clientele is personally looked after by an attentive, multilingual staff. Stellar Chef Jean-Claude Plihon offers Escoffier cookery with a nouvelle presentation in a setting that overlooks Indian Creek. Consider as appetizer the crab cake with chives, cayenne, saffron, and a touch of garlic in lobster sauce. A *feuillete* of lobster is elegant in its pastry shell. The broiled pheasant with truffle and goose liver pâté is flambéed with cognac and served with fried potato slivers filled with inoke and chanterelle mushrooms. The bouillabaise is suffused with saffron in an herbed fish stock and includes mussels, scallops, lobster, clams, and shrimp. For dessert, indulge in a Grand Marnier soufflé served with raspberry, chocolate, and custard sauce. *9561 E. Bay Harbor Dr., tel. 305/866–8779. Jacket required. Reservations advised. Closed June–Sept. AE, DC, MC, V. Expensive.*

Cafe des Arts. Enjoy French-provincial cuisine in an Art Deco setting amid tropical plants, antiques, and an art gallery that changes every six to eight weeks. Indoor and outdoor seating. Specialties include smoked-salmon pasta with artichokes, mushrooms, and brie sauce; braised duck in grape sauce; and seafood salad. *918 Ocean Dr., tel. 305/534–6267. Reservations advised. Dress: casual. AE, MC, V. No lunch. Moderate.*

Greek **Mykonos.** A family restaurant serving typical Greek fare since
Southwest Miami 1974 in a Spartan setting—a single 74-seat room adorned with Greek travel posters. Specialties include gyro; moussaka; marinated lamb and chicken; calamari (squid) and octopus sautéed in wine and onions; and sumptuous Greek salads thick with feta cheese and briny olives. *1201 Coral Way, tel. 305/856–3140. Reservations accepted for dinner. Dress: informal. AE, MC, V. Open Sun. at 5 PM. Closed July 4, Thanksgiving, Christmas Eve, New Year's Eve, New Year's Day. Inexpensive.*

Haitian **Chez Moy International.** Seating is outside on a shaded patio or
Little Haiti in a pleasant room with oak tables and high-backed chairs. Specialties include *grillot* (pork boiled, then fried with spices);

fried or boiled fish; stewed goat; and conch with garlic and hot pepper. Try a tropical fruit drink such as sweet sop (also called *anon* or *cachiman*) or sour sop (also called *guanabana* or *corrosol*) blended with milk and sugar, and sweet potato pie for dessert. *1 N.W. 54th St., tel. 305/756–7540. Reservations accepted. Dress: casual. No smoking. No credit cards. Inexpensive.*

Indian
Coral Gables

House of India. The haunting strains of sitar music lull diners at this popular spot in Coral Gables. Vegetarian and nonvegetarian specialties include hot coconut soup with cardamom, milk, rose water, and sugar; curried goat; and authentic chicken tandoori, cooked in a clay oven. The weekday luncheon buffet is a good bargain. Another location is in Fort Lauderdale at 3060 N. Andrews Avenue (tel. 305/566–5666). *22 Merrick Way, tel. 305/444–2348. Weekend reservations accepted. Dress: casual. AE, MC, V. Closed Labor Day, Thanksgiving, Christmas. Moderate.*

Italian
Coral Gables
★

Casa Rolandi. Italian art and two working brick ovens add a warm feeling here. Among the tasty entrées you'll find *agnolotti Fiorentina* (spinach pasta stuffed with ricotta cheese and topped with tomato sauce and sage); *fusilli al pesto* with pine nuts, parsley, basil and olive oil, parmesan cheese, and a touch of cream; and *tortelloni de fonduta al sugo d'arrosto di vitello e tartufi* (homemade cheese tortelloni served with a veal juice demiglaze and pared white truffles). The snapper *livornesa*—a special—comes with compote of green and yellow squash, radicchio, and parslied potato arranged artfully on a plate shaped like a scallop shell. All meals come with a pita-style house bread baked with virgin olive oil. For dessert, the *tiramisù* is a winner. *1930 Ponce de León Blvd., tel. 305/444–2187. Reservations required. Dress: neat but casual. AE, DC, MC, V. No lunch Fri.–Sun. Closed Thanksgiving, Christmas, New Year's Day. Expensive.*

Miami Beach

Mezzanotte. Chic, but not intimate, this restaurant is noted for fine food at moderate prices. Among the entrées is *zuppe nettuno*, with fish, octopus, squid, and crab served with angel hair pasta. The *spiedano Romano* includes sautéed porcini mushrooms under melted fontina cheese in a white wine sauce, and capers with mustard and garlic served over bread. Mezzanotte is known for its pastas, especially the *capellini primavera*, and for its veal dishes, including *piccata* (lemon butter sauce and roasted peppers), *lombata* (lightly breaded with radicchio, endive, tomatoes, and onions), and six scaloppines. Desserts are decadent. *1200 Washington Ave., tel. 305/673–4343. Reservations accepted for parties of 5 or more. Dress: neat but casual. AE, DC, MC, V. No lunch. Moderate.*

Latin
Coconut Grove

Cafe Tu Tu Tango. Brilliant artists such as local William DeLaVega set up their easels in the rococo-modern arcades of this eclectic, imaginative café-lounge on the second story of the highly popular Cocowalk. All the while, throngs of people frequent this place to savor the frittatas, *cosas frías*, and empanadas. Hot recorded jazz sets the mood and you can sit indoors or out; the latter offers some of the best people-watching in the entire South. Between the oak floors and the paddle-fans on the ceiling, guests at the more than 250 seats graze on chips, dips, breads, and spreads. House specials include crusted tempura-like "fritangas" of ham and crabmeat, and *boniato relleno* (white sweet tubers stuffed with picadillo). A few wines are available, but nothing that costs too much. Don't miss out on this place. *3015 Grand Ave. (Cocowalk), tel. 305/529–2222. Open Mon.–Wed. and Sun. 11:30 AM–midnight, Thurs. 11:30 AM–1 AM, Fri. and Sat. 11:30 AM–2 AM. No reservations. Dress: casual but neat. AE, DC, MC, V. Closed Christmas. Moderate.*

Mexican
Little Havana

Acapulco. Authentic Mexican cuisine is served in an intimate 70-seat room with adobe walls, wooden beams, tabletops of Mexican tiles, and sombreros and serapes on the walls. As soon as you sit down, a waiter descends on you with a free, ample supply of *totopos*, homemade corn chips served hot and crunchy, salt free, with a fiery *pico de gallo* sauce. Specialties include a rich, chunky guacamole; *carnitas asadas* (marinated pork chunks in lemon and butter sauce); *mole poblano* (chicken in chocolate sauce); shrimp and rice in a cherry wine sauce; and combination platters of tacos, burritos, and enchiladas. *727 N.W. Unity Blvd. (N.W. 27th Ave.), tel. 305/642–6961. Weekend reservations recommended. Dress: informal. AE, DC, MC, V. Moderate.*

Natural
Downtown Miami

Granny Feelgood's. "Granny" is a shrewd gentleman named Irving Field, who caters to health-conscious lawyers, office workers, and cruise-ship crews at five locations. Since 1989 Jack Osman has owned the original Granny's, and with Field plans to franchise locations outside Miami. Specialties include chicken salad with raisins, apples, and cinnamon; spinach fettucini with pinenuts; grilled tofu; apple crumb cake; and carrot cake. *190 S.E. 1st Ave., tel. 305/358–6233. No reservations. Dress: casual. No smoking. AE, MC, V. Closed Sun. Inexpensive.*

Miami Beach

Pineapples. Art Deco pink pervades this health-food store and restaurant. Specialties include Chinese egg rolls; lasagna filled with tofu and mushrooms; spinach fettucini with feta cheese, fresh garlic, walnuts, and cream sauce; and salads with a full-flavored Italian-style dressing. *530 Arthur Godfrey Rd., tel. 305/532–9731. No reservations. Dress: casual. No smoking. AE, MC, V. Closed Rosh Hashanah, Yom Kippur. Moderate.*

North Miami Beach
★

Unicorn Village Restaurant & Marketplace. Ten years after opening a 1960s-style health food store and restaurant, Terry Dalton relocated his top-notch natural foods restaurant to the Shoppes at the Waterways in 1990. Now with 300 seats (up from the original 80), the restaurant caters to vegetarian and nonvegetarian diners. In an outdoor setting of free-form ponds and fountains by a bayfront dock, or in a plant-filled, natural-woods interior under three-story-high wood-beamed ceilings sun-bright with skylights, guests enjoy spinach lasagna, a Tuscan vegetable sauté with Italian seasonings, grilled honey-mustard chicken, wok-barbecued shrimp, spicy seafood cakes; fresh fish, poultry, and Coleman natural beef; and the Unicorn's spring roll of uncooked veggies wrapped in a thin rice paper with cellophane noodles. The 16,000-square-foot food market is the largest natural foods source in Florida and features desserts all baked on premises. *3565 N.E. 207th St., tel. 305/933–8829. No reservations. Dress: casual. No smoking. MC, V. Moderate.*

Nicaraguan
Little Managua

Los Ranchos. Julio Somoza, owner of this busy establishment and nephew of Nicaragua's late president, Anastasio Somoza, fled to south Florida in 1979. Somoza sustains a tradition begun 30 years ago in Managua, when the original Los Ranchos

instilled in Nicaraguan palates a love of Argentine-style beef—
lean, grass-fed tenderloin with *chimichurri*, a green sauce of
chopped parsley, garlic, oil, vinegar, and other spices. Nicaragua's own sauces are a tomato-based marinara and the fiery
cebollitas encurtidas, with slices of jalapeño pepper and onion
pickled in vinegar. Specialties include *chorizo* (sausage);
cuajada con maduro (skim cheese with fried bananas); and
shrimp sautéed in butter and topped with a creamy jalapeño
sauce. *125 S.W. 107th Ave., tel. 305/221–9367. Also at Bayside
Marketplace, tel. 305/375–8188. Reservations advised, especially on weekends. Dress: casual. Nightly entertainment.
AE, DC, MC, V. Closed Good Friday, Christmas Eve, New
Year's Day. Moderate.*

Seafood
Downtown Miami

The Fish Market. Tucked away in a corner of the Omni International Hotel's lobby, this fine restaurant boasts a kitchen staff
fluent in seafood's complexities. The menu changes with availability of fresh fish, fruits, and vegetables, but typical menu
items may include sautéed dolphin in a basil-perfumed olive oil;
fillet of pompano; pan-baked red snapper; and Florida lobster
tail. Daily seafood specials might include bluefish, dolphin,
lemon sole, marlin, pompano, redfish, sea bass, sea trout, tuna,
and a whole, peppery yellowtail. The chocolate pecan tart and
pistachio chocolate terrine with orange cream sauce are just
two of the featured desserts. *Biscayne Blvd. at 16th St., 33132,
tel. 305/374–0000. Jacket recommended. Reservations advised. Free valet parking. AE, DC, MC, V. No lunch Sat.;
closed Sun. Expensive.*

East Coast Fisheries. This family-owned restaurant and retail
fish market on the Miami River features fresh Florida seafood
from its own 38-boat fleet in the Keys. From tables along the
second-floor balcony railing, watch the cooks prepare your dinner in the open kitchen below. Specialties include a complimentary fish-pâté appetizer, blackened pompano with owner David
Swartz's personal herb-and-spice recipe, lightly breaded fried
grouper, and a homemade Key lime pie so rich it tastes like ice
cream. *360 W. Flagler St., tel. 305/373–5515. Dress: casual.
Beer and wine only. AE, MC, V. Moderate.*

Key Biscayne

Sundays on the Bay. Two locations overlook the water: the
Crandon Park Marina at Key Biscayne and Salty's, as it's now
called, on the Intracoastal Waterway at Haulover. Both have
inside dining and outdoor decks, bars, live bands playing island
music and top-40 hits nightly, and an energetic young serving
staff. Specialties from an extensive seafood menu include conch
fritters, conch chowder (tomato-based, served with sherry and
Tabasco sauce), and baked grouper topped with crabmeat and
shrimp scampi. *Key Biscayne: 5420 Crandon Blvd., tel. 305/
361–6777; Haulover Beach Park: 10880 Collins Ave., tel. 305/
945–5115. Reservations advised for Sun. brunch. Dress: casual. AE, D, DC, MC, V. Moderate.*

Miami Beach

Joe's Stone Crab Restaurant. A south Florida tradition since
1913, Joe's is a family restaurant in its fourth generation. You
go to wait, people watch, and finally settle down to an ample à
la carte menu. About a ton of stone crab claws are served daily,
with drawn butter, lemon wedges, and a piquant mustard
sauce (recipe available). Popular side orders include a vinegary
coleslaw, salad with a brisk vinaigrette house dressing,
creamed garlic spinach, french-fried onion rings and eggplant,
and hash brown potatoes. Save room for dessert—a slice of

Key-lime pie with graham cracker crust and real whipped cream or apple pie with a crumb-pecan topping. *227 Biscayne St., tel. 305/673–0365; 800/780–CRAB (for carry out orders or overnight shipping). No reservations. Dress: casual, but no T-shirts or tank tops. To minimize wait, come for lunch at 11:30, for dinner at 5 or after 9. AE, DC, MC, V. Closed May 15–Oct. 15. Moderate.*

Spanish
Downtown Miami

Las Tapas. Overhung with dried meats and enormous show breads, this popular spot offers a lot of imaginative creations. *Tapas*—"little dishes"—come in appetizer-size portions to give you a variety of tastes during a single meal. Specialties include *la tostada* (smoked salmon on melba toast, topped with a dollop of sour cream, across which are laid baby eels, black caviar, capers, and chopped onion) and *pincho de pollo a la plancha* (grilled chicken brochette marinated in brandy and onions). Also available are soups, salads, sandwiches, and standard-size dinners. *Bayside Marketplace, 401 Biscayne Blvd., tel. 305/372–2737. Reservations for large parties only. Dress: casual. AE, DC, MC, V. Moderate.*

Little Havana
★

Casa Juancho. A meeting place for the movers and shakers of Miami's Cuban community, Casa Juancho serves a cross section of Spanish regional cuisines. The interior recalls old Castile: brown brick, rough-hewn dark timbers, and walls adorned with colorful Talavera platters. Strolling Spanish balladeers will serenade you. Specialties include *cochinillo Segoviano* (roast suckling pig), and *parrillada de mariscos* (fish, shrimps, squid, and scallops grilled in a light garlic sauce) from the Pontevedra region of northwest Spain. For dessert, the *crema Catalana* has a delectable crust of burnt caramel atop a rich pastry custard. The wine list includes fine labels from Spain's Rioja region. *2436 S.W. 8th St., tel. 305/642–2452. Reservations advised; not accepted after 8 PM Fri. and Sat. Dress: casual but neat. AE, DC, MC, V. Closed Christmas Eve. Expensive.*

Thai
Miami Beach

Thai Toni. Thai silks, bronze Buddhas, ceiling drapes, and two raised platforms for guests who want to dine seated on cushions highlight this fine eatery. The mellow, Thai Singha beer sets you up for the spicy grilled squid appetizer or the vegetarian or pork *pad Thai* (rice noodles tossed with shrimp, egg, bean sprouts, and peanuts). Traditional entrées include a hot-and-spicy deep-fried whole snapper garnished with basil leaves and mixed vegetables. Try the homemade lemonade. *890 Washington Ave., tel. 305/538–THAI. Dress: neat but casual. AE, MC, V. Dinner only. Moderate.*

Vietnamese
Little Havana
★

Hy-Vong Vietnamese Cuisine. Under new ownership since 1989, the magic continues to pour forth from the tiny kitchen of this 36-seat restaurant as it has since 1980. Now the word is out, so come before 7 PM to avoid a wait. Specialties include spring rolls, a Vietnamese version of an egg roll, with ground pork, cellophane noodles, and black mushrooms wrapped in homemade rice paper; a whole fish panfried with *nuoc man* (a garlic-lime fish sauce); and thinly sliced pork, barbecued with sesame seeds and fish sauce, served with bean sprouts, rice noodles, and slivers of carrots, almonds, and peanuts. *3458 S.W. 8th St., tel. 305/446–3674. Reservations accepted for 5 or more. Dress: casual. No smoking. No credit cards. Closed lunch and Mon., American and Vietnamese/Chinese New Years, and 2 weeks in Aug. Moderate.*

Lodging

Few urban areas can match Greater Miami's diversity of hotel accommodations. The area has hundreds of hotels and motels with lodgings in all price categories, from $8 for a night in a dormitory-style hostel bed to $2,000 for a night in the luxurious presidential suite atop a posh downtown hotel.

As recently as the 1960s, many hotels in Greater Miami opened only in the winter to accommodate Yankee "snowbirds." Now all stay open all year. In summer, they cater to European and Latin American vacationers who find Miami quite congenial despite the heat, humidity, and intense thunderstorms almost every afternoon.

Although some hotels (especially on the mainland) have adopted year-round rates, many still adjust their rates to reflect the ebb and flow of seasonal demand. The peak occurs in winter, with only a slight dip in summer when families with schoolchildren take vacations. You'll find the best values between Easter and Memorial Day (a delightful time in Miami but a difficult time for many people to travel), and in September and October (the height of hurricane season).

The list that follows is a representative selection of the best hotels and motels, organized geographically.

The rate categories in the list are based on the all-year or peak-season price; off-peak rates may be a category or two lower.

Highly recommended places are indicated by a star ★.

Category	Cost*
Very Expensive	over $120
Expensive	$90–$120
Moderate	$50–$90
Inexpensive	under $50

All prices are for a standard double room, excluding 6% state sales tax and nominal tourist tax.

Coconut Grove

★ **Grand Bay Hotel.** This modern high rise overlooking Biscayne Bay features rooms with traditional furnishings and original art. The building's stairstep facade, like a Mayan pyramid, gives each room facing the bay a private terrace, but the best views come from rooms at the northeast corner that look out on downtown Miami. Only slightly more special than most rooms is 814, Luciano Pavarotti's two-level suite with a baby-grand piano, circular staircase, and canopied king-size bed. You can rent it when he's not there. Most remarkable, however, is the meticulous attention the staff pays to guests' desires. *2669 S. Bayshore Dr., Coconut Grove 33133, tel. 305/858–9600. 181 rooms with bath, including 49 suites, 20 nonsmoker rooms. Facilities: outdoor pool, hot tub, health club, saunas, masseur, afternoon tea in lobby, gourmet restaurant, lounge, poolside bar. AE, DC, MC, V. Very Expensive.*

Grove Isle. This luxurious mid-rise urban resort sits on a 26-acre island and adjoins the equally posh condominium apartment towers and private club. Developer Martin Margulies displays selections from his extensive private art collection on the premises (*see* Exploring Coconut Grove, above). The over-sized rooms have patios, bay views, ceiling fans, and tropical decor with area rugs and Spanish tiles; rooms with the most light and best bay view are 201–205. *4 Grove Isle Dr., Coconut Grove 33133, tel. 305/858–8300. 49 rooms with bath, including 9 suites. Facilities: outdoor freshwater pool and whirlpool; 12 tennis courts; 85-slip marina; running track around the island; in-room refreshment bar and coffee maker; free cable TV; restaurant with indoor and outdoor seating. AE, DC, MC, V. Very Expensive.*

Mayfair House. This European-style luxury hotel sits within an exclusive open-air shopping mall (*see* Exploring Coconut Grove, above). Public areas have Tiffany windows, polished mahogany, marble walls and floors, and imported ceramics and crystal. Also impressive is the glassed-in elevator that whisks you to the corridor on your floor; a balcony overlooks the mall's central fountains and walkways. In all suites, outdoor terraces face the street, screened from view by vegetation and wood latticework. Each has a Japanese hot tub on the balcony or a Roman tub in the suites. Otherwise, each suite is unique in size and furnishings. Sunset (Room 505) is one of 48 suites with antique pianos. Some aspects of the building's design are quirky; you can get lost looking for the ballroom or restaurant, and, in many rooms, you must stand in the bathtub to turn on the water. The worst suite for sleeping is Featherfern (Room 356), from which you can hear the band one floor below in the club. *3000 Florida Ave., Coconut Grove 33133, tel. 305/441–0000 or 800/433–4555. 181 suites, including 22 nonsmoker suites. Facilities: rooftop recreation area with sauna in a barrel, small outdoor freshwater swimming pool; snack bar. AE, DC, MC, V. Very Expensive.*

Doubletree Hotel at Coconut Grove. This high rise with a bay view was built in 1970 and renovated in 1988. Large rooms—most with balconies—have comfortable chairs, armoires, original artwork, and either a mauve or turquoise color scheme. Best rooms are on upper floors with bay views. Homemade chocolate-chip cookies are offered to arriving guests. *2649 S. Bayshore Dr., Coconut Grove 33133, tel. 305/858–2500 or 800/ 528–0444. 190 rooms with bath, including 32 nonsmoker rooms, and 3 rooms for handicapped guests. Facilities: outdoor freshwater pool, 2 tennis courts, restaurant, bar. Casablanca, a private club, is on the top floor. AE, DC, MC, V. Expensive.*

Coral Gables **The Biltmore Hotel.** A historic high rise built in 1926, the Biltmore was restored and renovated in 1986 and reopened as a luxury hotel. Upper-floor rooms facing north and east toward the airport, downtown Miami, and Biscayne Bay have the most spectacular views. The hotel has been in foreclosure but is expected to reopen in 1993. *1200 Anastasia Ave., Coral Gables 33134, tel. 305/445–1926 or 800/445–2586. 275 rooms with bath, including 45 suites. Facilities: 18-hole championship golf course, 10 lighted tennis courts, health spa with sauna, pool, restaurant, coffee shop, lounge. AE, DC, MC, V. Very Expensive.*

★ **The Colonnade Hotel.** The twin 13-story towers of this $65-million hotel, office, and shopping complex dominate the heart of Coral Gables. Architectural details echo the adjoining two-story Corinthian-style rotunda on Miracle Mile from which 1920s developer George Merrick sold lots in his fledgling city.

Miami Area Lodging

OCEAN

MIAMI BEACH

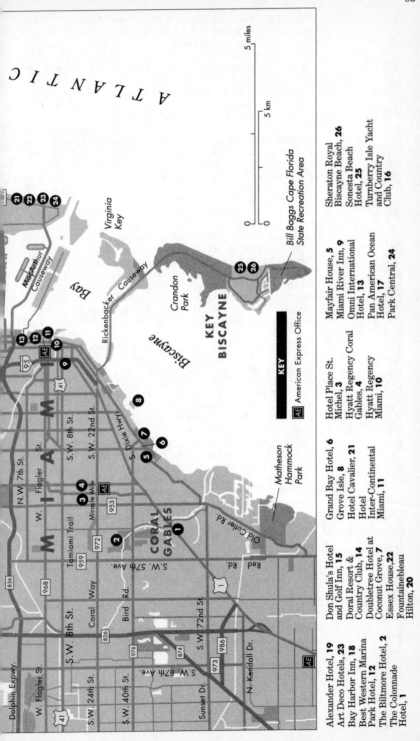

Merrick's family provided old photos, paintings, and other heirlooms that are on display throughout the hotel. The over-size rooms come in 26 different floor plans, each with a sitting area, built-in armoires, and traditional furnishings of mahogany. The hospitality bars feature marble counters and gold-plated faucets with 1920s-style ceramic handles. The pool on a 10th-floor terrace offers a magnificent view south toward Biscayne Bay. *180 Aragon Ave., Coral Gables 33134, tel. 305/441–2600 or 800/533–1337. 157 rooms, including 17 bi-level suites, 18 nonsmoker rooms, and 4 rooms for handicapped guests. Amenities include terry-cloth bathrobes, minibar, champagne and orange juice at check-in, complimentary coffee and news-paper with wake-up call, and complimentary shoeshine. Facilities: outdoor heated pool and Jacuzzi with 2 saunas, Nautilus exercise equipment, 24-hr room service, 2 restaurants. AE, DC, MC, V. Very Expensive.*

★ **Hyatt Regency Coral Gables.** Opened in 1987, this highrise hotel, patronized by business travelers, is part of a mega-structure that includes two office towers. The entire complex reflects Spanish Mediterranean architecture, with tile roofs, white-frame casement windows, and pink-stucco exterior. The hotel's interior decor of pastel hues and antique-style furnishings gives a comfortable, residential feel to the rooms and public areas. Rooms facing the pool are best; the worst face north toward the airport. *50 Alhambra Plaza, Coral Gables 33134, tel. 305/441–1234. 242 rooms with bath, including 50 suites, 45 nonsmoker rooms. Facilities: two ballrooms, 1 with restaurant, lounge, fifth-floor pool, outdoor whirlpool, health club with Nautilus equipment, Life Cycles, sauna, and steam rooms. AE, DC, MC, V. Very Expensive.*

★ **Hotel Place St. Michel.** Art Nouveau chandeliers suspended from vaulted ceilings grace the public areas of this intimate jewel in the heart of downtown Coral Gables. The historic low-rise hotel, built in 1926 and restored 1981–86 is filled with the scent of fresh flowers that's circulated by the paddle fans hanging from the ceilings. Each room has its own dimension, personality, and imported antiques from England, Scotland, and France. *162 Alcazar Ave., Coral Gables 33134, tel. 305/444–1666 or 800/247–8526. 28 rooms with bath, including 3 suites. Facilities: welcome basket of fruit and cheese in every room, morning newspaper, Continental breakfast, restaurant, lounge, French snack shop. AE, DC, MC, V. Expensive.*

Downtown Miami **Hotel Inter-Continental Miami.** Stand on the fifth-floor recreation plaza and gaze up at this 34-story granite monolith that appears to be arching over you. The grain in the lobby's marble floor matches that in *The Spindle*, a massive centerpiece sculpture by Henry Moore. With all that marble, the lobby could easily look like a mausoleum—and did before the addition of palm trees, colorful umbrellas, and oversize wicker chairs and tables. Atop a five-story atrium, a skylight lets the afternoon sun pour in. The triangular hotel tower offers bay, port, and city views that improve with height. *100 Chopin Plaza, Miami 33131, tel. 305/577–1000 or 800/327–3005. 644 rooms with bath, including 34 suites, 48 nonsmoker rooms; corner rooms have extra-wide doors for handicapped guests. Facilities: outdoor heated freshwater pool beside the bay, ¼-mile jogging track with rubber surface, in-room minibar, restaurants, lounge. AE, DC, MC, V. Very Expensive.*

Hyatt Regency Miami. This centrally located, 24-story convention hotel adjoins the James L. Knight International Center (*see* Exploring Downtown Miami, above). Nestled beside the Brickell Avenue Bridge on the north bank of the Miami River, the Hyatt offers views of tugboats, freighters, and pleasure craft from its lower lobby. The best rooms are on the upper floors, facing east toward Biscayne Bay. A $7-million room renovation began in 1991. *400 S.E. 2nd Ave., Miami 33131, tel. 305/358-1234 or 800/233-1234. 615 rooms with bath, 25 suites, 43 nonsmoker rooms, 17 rooms for handicapped guests. Facilities: outdoor freshwater pool, $10 admission to nearby Downtown Athletic Club, in-room safe, in-house pay-TV movies, 2 restaurants, lounge. AE, DC, MC, V. Very Expensive.*

Omni International Hotel. A 20-story hotel built in 1977, the Omni stands atop a 10.5-acre shopping and entertainment complex that includes J. C. Penney, a number of specialty shops, the Children's Workshop child-care center, and a hand-made Italian wood carousel. The lowest hotel floor is five stories up; rooms on upper floors have spectacular views of downtown Miami and Biscayne Bay. Many rooms feature a blue-and-tan color scheme and mahogany furniture. *1601 Biscayne Blvd., Miami 33132, tel. 305/374-0000 or 800/THE-OMNI. 535 rooms, including 50 suites, 25 nonsmoker rooms, and 2 rooms for handicapped guests. Facilities: outdoor heated pool on a terrace 5 stories above street, lobby bar, terrace café, restaurant (The Fish Market), access to nearby health club and spa. AE, DC, MC, V. Very Expensive.*

Best Western Marina Park Hotel. Centrally located, this midrise hotel, owned by a French chain, has an inviting tiled lobby filled with wicker furnishings. Pastel-color rooms, also with rattan amenities, provide soft mattresses and trilingual TV. The best views are from east rooms that overlook Bayside and the Port of Miami. *340 Biscayne Blvd., Miami 33132, tel. 305/371-4400 or 800/327-6565. 200 rooms with bath, including 25 suites. Facilities: pool, restaurant, bar. AE, D, DC, MC, V. Expensive-Moderate.*

★ **Miami River Inn.** Preservationist Sallye Jude has restored this landmark property (the oldest continuously operating inn south of St. Augustine) as an oasis of country hospitality at the edge of downtown. It is a 10-minute walk across the 1st Street Bridge to the heart of the city, and a few hundred feet from José Martí Park (one of the city's prettiest). The inn—dating to 1904—consists of five antiques-filled clapboard buildings that are the only concentration of houses remaining from that period. The best rooms are second- and third-story river-views with stunning vistas of the city. Avoid the tiny rooms in building "D" that overlook the stark condo to the west. *118 S.W. S. River Dr., Miami 33130, tel. 305/325-0045. 40 rooms (39 with bath, some with tub only). Facilities: freshwater outdoor pool and heated Jacuzzi, use of refrigerator, AC, heat, phones, small meeting room. Rate includes Continental breakfast. Moderate.*

Key Biscayne **Sheraton Royal Biscayne Beach Resort and Racquet Club.** The Sheraton was hit very hard by Hurricane Andrew and is in the process of rebuilding the devastated portions of the hotel. The staff was uncertain of a reopening date at press time. In its fully operational state, the Art Deco pinks, wicker furniture, and chattering macaws and cockatoos in the lobby set the tone for this three-story beachfront resort set amid the waving fronds of coconut palms. Built in

1952 and restored in 1985, this laid-back hotel maintains a casual demeanor. All rooms have garden and bay views; most have terraces. *555 Ocean Dr., Key Biscayne 33149, tel. 305/361–5775. 192 rooms with bath, including 4 oceanfront suites, 17 junior suites with kitchenette, 15 nonsmoker rooms. Facilities: ¼-mi of ocean beach, 2 outdoor freshwater heated pools, children's wading pool, 10 tennis courts (4 lighted), sailboats, windsurfers, Hobie Cats, aquabikes, snorkeling kits, rental bicycles, pay-TV movies, unisex beauty salon, restaurant, lounge. AE, DC, MC, V. Very Expensive.*

★ **Sonesta Beach Hotel & Tennis Club.** Among the features of this eight-story beachfront resort are the displays of museum-quality modern art pieces by prominent painters and sculptors. Don't miss Andy Warhol's three drawings of rock star Mick Jagger in the hotel's disco bar, Desires. The best rooms, on the eighth floor, face the ocean. All guest rooms were completely renewed in 1991 and 1992. *350 Ocean Dr., Key Biscayne 33149, tel. 305/361–2021 or 800/SONESTA. 290 rooms with bath, including 12 suites and 11 villas (3-, 4-, and 5-bedroom homes with full kitchens and screened-in pools). Facilities: 750-ft ocean beach, outdoor freshwater heated Olympic-size pool and whirlpool, water sports including sailboarding, 10 tennis courts (3 lighted); health center with Jacuzzi, steam rooms, aerobic dance floor, weight room, massage room, and tanning room; gift shops; restaurants, snack bar, deli, lounge with live entertainment. AE, DC, MC, V. Very Expensive.*

Miami Beach **Fontainebleau Hilton Resort and Spa.** The Miami area's foremost convention hotel boasts an opulent lobby with massive chandeliers, a sweeping staircase, and new meeting rooms in Art Deco hues. There are always some rooms in the hotel that are under renovation; most recently completed in mid-1992, as part of a $10 million program, are 375 rooms in the north tower building, which have been redone in a tropical theme and have new bathroom fixtures. Decor is varied; you can request a '50s look or one that's contemporary. Upper-floor rooms in the Chateau Building have the best views. *4441 Collins Ave., Miami Beach 33140, tel. 305/538–2000. 1,206 rooms with bath, including 60 suites, 120 nonsmoker and handicapped rooms. Facilities: ocean beach with 30 cabanas, 2 outdoor pools (one fresh, one salt), marina, windsurfing, parasailing, Hobie Cats, volleyball, 3 whirlpool baths, 7 lighted tennis courts, health club with exercise classes, saunas, free children's activities, 12 restaurants and lounges, Tropigala nightclub. AE, DC, MC, V. Very Expensive.*

★ **Pan American Ocean Hotel, A Radisson Resort.** This beach hotel—built in 1954—sits back from Collins Avenue behind a refreshing garden of coconut palms and seasonal flowers. In 1992 all guest rooms received a facelift. The best view is from rooms 330, 332, and 333 on the third floor of the north wing, which overlooks the ocean. Direct north- and south-facing rooms have only a sliver view of ocean or bay. *17875 Collins Ave., Miami Beach 33160, tel. 305/932–1100 or 800/327–5678. 146 rooms, including 4 suites and handicapped rooms. Facilities: 400 ft of ocean beach, outdoor heated pool, 4 hard-surface tennis courts, tennis pro and pro shop, 2 shuffleboard courts, 9-hole putting green, exercise room, volleyball, beauty salon, coffee shop, pool gazebo bar, terrace lounge and oceanfront restaurant, ping-pong room, video game room, card room, free shuttle service to Bal Harbour and Aventura shopping malls, coin* *laundry, minibar in all rooms. AE, D, DC, MC, V. Very Expensive.*

Park Central. Across the street from the glorious beach, this seven-story mauve, turquoise, and white deco hotel—with wraparound corner windows—makes all the right moves to stay in front of the deco revival. Most of the high-fashioned models visiting town come to this property, which dates back to 1937. Black-and-white photos of old beach scenes, hurricanes, and familiar faces attest to the hotel's longevity. Stylishly, rooms are decorated with Philippine mahogany furnishings— originals that have been restored. An Italian theme prevails, with the Barocco Beach restaurant and espresso served in the lobby. *640 Ocean Dr., 33139, tel. 305/538–1611, fax 305/534– 7520. 80 rooms with bath. Facilities: restaurant, bar, espresso bar. AE, DC, MC, V. Very Expensive–Expensive.*

★ **Alexander Hotel.** A spa and diet center was added in 1990 to this 16-story hotel that offers ocean and bay views from every suite, all of which have antique furnishings or reproductions and original art. Suites facing south have the best views. A computer keeps track of the mattresses, so you can request the degree of firmness you prefer. *5225 Collins Ave., Miami Beach 33140, tel. 305/865–6500. 212 suites, each with 2 baths, 2 phones, kitchen, minibar, free cable movies, daily newspaper. Facilities: ocean beach, 2 outdoor heated freshwater pools, 4 poolside Jacuzzis, cabanas, Sunfishes and catamarans for rent, Dominique's gourmet restaurant, and coffee shop. AE, DC, MC, V. Expensive.*

Bay Harbor Inn. Here you'll find down-home hospitality in the most affluent zip code in the county. Retired Washington lawyer Sandy Lankler and his wife Celeste operate this 35-room lodging in two sections—two moods. The buildings are modern, but townside furnishings are antiques. Townside is the oldest building in Bay Harbor Islands, vaguely Georgian in style but dating from 1940. Behind triple sets of French doors under fan windows, the lobby is full of oak desks, handmills, grandfather clocks, historical maps, and potted plants. Rooms are antiques-filled and no two are alike. Along Indian Creek the inn incorporates the former Albert Pick Hotella, a shipshape tropical-style set of rooms on two floors off loggias surrounded by palms with all rooms facing the water. Mid-century modern here, and chintz. The popular The Palms restaurant is located both townside and creekside. *9660 East Bay Harbor Dr., Bay Harbor Islands 33154, tel. 305/868–4141. 36 rooms with bath, including 12 suites and penthouse. Facilities: outdoor freshwater pool, 2 restaurants, lounge. Complimentary Continental breakfast and champagne tea. AE, DC, MC, V. Expensive.*

Essex House. From the beginning, this has been one of the premiere lodgings of the Art Deco era. It was all here to start: designed by architect Henry Hohauser, Everglades mural by Earl LaPan. Here are the ziggurat arches, the hieroglyph-style ironwork, etched glass panels of flamingos under the palms, five-foot rose medallion Chinese urns. Hallways have recessed showcases with original deco sculptures. The original 66 rooms from 1938 are now 41, plus two petite suites, six grand. Amenities include complete turndown service with clothes hung and shoes polished, designer linens and towels, all feather-and-down pillows and sofa rolls, and individually controlled air conditioning and central heat plus ceiling fans. The rooms are soundproofed from within (otherwise unheard of in beach properties of the thirties), and rooms to the east have ex-

tra thick windows to reduce the band noise from a nearby hotel.
Smallest rooms are yellow-themed and face north. Best are the
two-room oceanview suites: 305 and 308, and 205 and 208. Continental breakfast is free. *1001 Collins Ave., Miami Beach
33139, tel. 305/534–2700, 800/55–ESSEX. 64 rooms and suites
with bath. Facilities: breakfast room. AE, MC, V. Expensive.*

Hotel Cavalier. Rooms in this three-story beachfront hotel have
period maple furnishings, new baths, and air conditioning. The
Cavalier is popular with the film and fashion industry; many
guests are artists, models, photographers, and writers. The
best rooms face the ocean; the worst are on the ground floor,
rear south, where the garbage truck goes by in the morning.
*1320 Ocean Dr., Miami Beach 33139, tel. 305/534–2135 or 800/
338–9076. 44 rooms with bath, including 2 suites. Amenities
include Evian water and flowers in all rooms, Continental
breakfast in lobby of adjacent Cardozo Hotel. AE, D, DC, MC,
V. Expensive.*

Art Deco Hotels. Four hotels, which kicked off revival of the
Deco District a decade ago, as well as the **Hotel Cavalier,** were
bought at auction in 1992 by local developers who have excellent reputations in South Beach revival. These include the **Hotel Cardozo,** which dates from 1939, the **Hotel Leslie** from 1937,
the **Hotel Carlyle** from 1941, and the **Victor Hotel** from the same
period (the last two recently closed). All are attractively decorated in Art Deco pinks, whites, and grays. Many contain original walnut furniture, restored and refinished. Rooms are
comfortable but small; inspect your room before registering to
assure that it meets your needs; all have air conditioning, but
most of the time you won't need it—especially if you're in one
that faces the water, where a sea breeze usually blows. *1244
Ocean Dr., Miami Beach 33139, tel. 305/534–2135 or 800/338–
9076. 220 rooms with bath, including suites. Facilities: restaurants, bar with live entertainment in the Carlyle. AE, DC,
MC, V. Expensive–Moderate.*

North Dade **Turnberry Isle Yacht and Country Club.** In 1991, a two-year,
★ $80-million redevelopment project was completed, adding a
271-room, three-wing Mediterranean-style resort and club,
new restaurants, and the *Ms. Turnberry* (a custom-built yacht)
to this upscale condominium community on a 300-acre bayfront
site. Guests can also choose from the European-style Marina
Hotel, the Yacht Club, or the Mizner-style Country Club Hotel
beside the golf course—340 rooms in all. Interiors of the over-
size rooms feature light woods and earth-tone colors, a nauti-
cal-blue motif at the hotel, large curving terraces, Jacuzzis,
honor bar, and in-room safes. *1999 W. Country Club Dr.,
Aventura 33180, tel. 305/932–6200, 800/327–7028, 340 rooms
with bath, including 40 suites. Facilities: Ocean Club with 250
feet of private beach frontage, diving gear, Windsurfers and
Hobie Cats for rent, and complimentary shuttle service to the
hotel; 4 outdoor freshwater pools; 24 tennis courts (18 lighted);
2 Robert Trent Jones–designed 18-hole golf courses; helipad;
marina with moorings for 117 boats up to 150 ft; full-service
spa with physician, nutritionist, saunas, steam rooms, whirlpools, facials, herbal wraps, Nautilus exercise equipment, indoor racquetball courts, and outdoor jogging course; 5 private
restaurants, lounge, nightly entertainment. AE, DC, MC, V.
Very Expensive.*

West Dade **Don Shula's Hotel and Golf Inn.** This low-rise suburban resort
is part of a planned town developed by Florida Senator Bob

Graham's family about 14 miles northwest of downtown Miami. The golf resort opened in 1962 and added two wings in 1978. Its decor is English-traditional throughout, rich in leather and wood. All rooms have balconies. The inn opened in 1983 with a typically Florida-tropic look—light pastel hues and furniture of wicker and light wood. In both locations, the best rooms are near the lobby for convenient access; the worst are near the elevators. *Main St., Miami Lakes 33014, tel. 305/821–1150. 301 rooms with bath, including 32 suites. Facilities: 2 outdoor freshwater heated pools; 9 lighted tennis courts; golf (18-hole par-72 championship course, lighted 18-hole par-54 executive course, golf school); saunas, steam rooms, and whirlpools; 8 indoor racquetball courts; Shula's Athletic Club with Nautilus fitness center; full-size gym for volleyball and basketball; aerobics classes; restaurants and lounges; shopping discount at Main St. shops. AE, DC, MC, V. Very Expensive.*

★ **Doral Resort & Country Club.** Millions of airline passengers annually peer down upon this 2,400-acre jewel of an inland golf and tennis resort while fastening their seat belts. It's 4 miles west of Miami International Airport and consists of eight separate three- and four-story lodges nestled beside the golf links. The resort follows a tropical theme, with light pastels, wicker, and teak furniture. All guest rooms have minibars; most have private balconies or terraces with views of the golf courses or tennis courts. This is the site of the Doral Ryder Open Tournament, played on the Doral "Blue Monster" golf course. *4400 N.W. 87th Ave., Miami 33178, tel. 305/592–2000. 650 rooms with bath, including 58 suites. Facilities: five 18-hole golf courses, and a 9-hole, par-3 executive course; pro shop and boutique; 15 tennis courts (4 lighted), Olympic-size heated outdoor freshwater pool; 3-mi jogging and bike path; bicycle rentals; lake fishing; restaurants and lounges; transportation to beach. AE, DC, MC, V. Very Expensive.*

The Arts

Performing arts aficionados in Greater Miami will tell you they survive quite nicely despite the area's historic inability to support a professional symphony orchestra. In recent years, this community has begun to write a new chapter in its performing arts history.

The New World Symphony, a unique advanced-training orchestra, marks its sixth season in 1993. The Miami City Ballet has risen rapidly to international prominence in its seven-year existence. The opera company ranks with the nation's best, and a venerable chamber music series brings renowned ensembles to perform here. Several churches and synagogues also run classical music series with international performers.

In theater, Miami offers English-speaking audiences an assortment of professional, collegiate, and amateur productions of musicals, comedy, and drama. Spanish theater also is active. High hopes and funding have lately buoyed prospects that the nonprofit regional repertory theater **Miami's Skyline** (tel. 305/358–7529) may present productions by 1993. Call for information.

In the cinema world, the Miami Film Festival attracts more than 45,000 people annually to screenings of new films from all over the world—including some made here.

Arts Information. Strongest on reviews, also with comprehensive listings, is Greater Miami's English-language daily newspaper, *The Miami Herald*, which publishes information on the performing arts in its Weekend Section on Friday and the Lively Arts Section on Sunday. Phone ahead to confirm details before you go.

If you read Spanish, check *El Nuevo Herald* (a Spanish version of *The Miami Herald*) or *Diario Las Américas* (the area's largest independent Spanish-language paper) for information on the Spanish theater and a smattering of general performing arts news.

Another good source of information on the performing arts is the calendar in *Miami Today*, a free weekly newspaper available each Thursday in downtown Miami, Coconut Grove, and Coral Gables. The best, most complete source is the *New Times*, a free weekly distributed throughout Dade County each Wednesday.

The free *Greater Miami Calendar of Events* is published twice a year by the Dade County Cultural Affairs Council (111 N.W. 1st St., Ste. 625, Miami, tel. 305/375–4634).

Guide to the Arts/South Florida is a pocket-size monthly publication covering all the cultural arts in Greater Miami, Broward, and Palm Beach. *Kage Publications, 2340 N.E. 171st St., North Miami Beach, tel. 305/956–7801. Annual subscription $15; individual copy $2. No credit cards.*

Real Talk/WTMI (93.1 FM) provides concert information on its Cultural Arts Line (tel. 305/358–8000, ext. 9398).

Ticketmaster. You can use this service to order tickets for performing arts and sports events by telephone. A service fee is added to the price of the ticket. *Tel. 305/358–5885 (Dade), 305/523–3309 (Broward), or 407/839–3900 (Palm Beach). AE, MC, V.*

Art In addition to museums described in the self-guided tours, other museums of interest include:

Black Heritage Museum: In 1991 the dispersed collections of the museum found a permanent home on the first level of the Miracle Center, a vertical shopping mall. Rotating exhibits add to permanent collections that include carvings from Africa, artifacts of Black Americana, and vestiges and arts of local history. *Miracle Center, 3301 Coral Way, Miami, tel. 305/446–7304. Admission free. Open weekdays 11–4, weekends 1–4.*
North Miami Center of Contemporary Art: Rotating exhibits feature contemporary paintings, photographs, and Florida artworks. Avant-garde films are also screened. *12340 N.E. 8th Ave., N. Miami, tel. 305/893–6211. Admission free. Open weekdays 10–4, Sat. 1–4.*
South Florida Art Center: The center houses the workrooms of emerging and established visual artists of the Lincoln Road Arts District. The artists open their studios and showrooms to the public. The center and studios hold an open house the third Friday of each month from 7–10 PM. *924 Lincoln Rd., Miami Beach, tel. 305/674–8278. Admission free. Open Mon.–Fri. 12–7, Sat. 12–5, closed Sun.*
Bacardi Art Gallery: This unusual, tiled Bacardi Imports building exhibits works by local and international artists in its not-for-profit art gallery. Tours are available in English and Span-

ish if requested in advance. *2100 Biscayne Blvd., tel. 305/573–8511. Admission free. Open weekdays 9–5.*

Bakehouse Art Complex: Built as the Flowers Bakery in the 1920s, this two-story masonry building was revived in 1987 as a gallery and studios for area artists. The best time to visit is for the monthly Second Sunday, when, from 1 to 5 PM, artists meet with visitors. New to the complex are the **Miami Jewelry Institute** and **Threshold Gallery of Art,** showing ceramics, basketry, fiber, and glass. *561 N.W. 32nd St., tel. 305/576–2828. Admission free. Open Tues.–Fri. 10–4.*

Ballet **Miami City Ballet.** Florida's first major fully professional resident ballet company. Edward Villella, the artistic director, was principal dancer of the New York City Ballet under George Balanchine. Now the Miami City Ballet re-creates the Balanchine repertoire and introduces new works of its own. Miami City Ballet performances are at the Dade County Auditorium; the Broward Center for the Performing Arts; Bailey Concert Hall, also in Broward County; at the Raymond F. Kravis Center for the Performing Arts; and at the Naples Philharmonic Center for the Arts. Demonstrations of works in progress are at the 800-seat Lincoln Theater in Miami Beach. Villella narrates the children's and works-in-progress programs. *905 Lincoln Rd., Miami Beach 33139, tel. 305/532–7713. Ticketmaster (see* Important Addresses and Numbers, above*). Season: Sept.–Mar. AE, MC, V.*

Cinema **The Alliance Film/Video Project.** Cutting-edge cinema from around the world is featured, with special midnight shows. *927 Lincoln Rd. Mall, suite 119, Sterling Building, Miami Beach 33139, tel. 305/531–8504.*

The Miami Film Festival. During 10 days in February, new films from all over the world are screened in the Gusman Center for the Performing Arts. Tickets and schedule: *444 Brickell Ave., Ste. 229, Miami 33131, tel. 305/377–3456. AE, MC, V. Ticketmaster (see* Important Addresses and Numbers, above*).*

Concerts **Concert Association of Florida.** A not-for-profit organization, directed by Judith Drucker, this is the South's largest presenter of classical artists. Ticket and program information: *555 Hank Meyer Blvd. (17th St.), Miami Beach 33139, tel. 305/532–3491. AE, MC, V.*

Friends of Chamber Music (44 W. Flagler St., Miami 33130, tel. 305/372–2975) presents an annual series of chamber concerts by internationally known guest ensembles, such as the Beaux Arts Trio, I Musici, and the Juilliard String Quartet.

Drama Check *Guide to the Arts/South Florida* for a complete English-language theater schedule. Traveling companies come and go; amateur groups form, perform, and disband. Listed below are the more enduring groups of Greater Miami's drama scene.

Acme Acting Company. Thought provoking, on-the-edge theater by new playwrights is presented during winter and summer seasons at the Colony Theater (1040 Lincoln Rd. Mall, Miami Beach, tel. 305/674–1026). *174 E. Flagler St., Miami, tel. 305/372–1718.*

Actor's Playhouse. This six-year-old professional equity company, based in Kendall, performs adults' and children's productions year-round. *8851 S.W. 107th Ave., Miami 33176, tel. 305/595–0010.*

Area Stage. This company emphasizes new works. *645 Lincoln Rd., Miami Beach, tel. 305/673–8002.*

Coconut Grove Playhouse. Arnold Mittelman, artistic director, stages Broadway-bound plays and musical reviews and experimental productions. *3500 Main Hwy., Coconut Grove 33133, tel. 305/442–4000. AE, D, MC, V.*

Minorca Playhouse. The playhouse is the long-established home of several theater companies, including the Florida Shakespeare Theatre and the Hispanic Theatre Festival. *323 Minorca Ave., Coral Gables, tel. 305/446–1116.*

New Theatre. Productions here showcase contemporary and classical plays. *65 Almeria St., Coral Gables 33134, tel. 305/443–5909.*

Ring Theater. The University of Miami's Department of Theatre Arts presents eight complete plays a year, two each season, in this 311-seat hall. *University of Miami, 1380 Miller Dr., Coral Gables 33124, tel. 305/284–3355. AE, MC, V.*

Opera   **Greater Miami Opera.** Miami's resident opera company presents two complete casts for four or five operas in the Dade County Auditorium. The International Series brings such luminaries as Placido Domingo and Luciano Pavarotti; the National Series features rising young singers in the principal roles, with the same sets and chorus, but with more modest ticket prices. All operas are sung in their original language, with titles in English projected onto a screen above the stage. *1200 Coral Way, Miami 33145, tel. 305/854–7890. AE, D, MC, V. Ticketmaster (see Important Addresses and Numbers, above). Box office open weekdays 9–4.*

Symphony   **New World Symphony.** Although Greater Miami still has no resident symphony orchestra, the New World Symphony, conducted by Michael Tilson Thomas, helps to fill the void. Musicians aged 22–30 who have finished their academic studies perform here before moving on. *541 Lincoln Rd., Miami Beach 33139, box office tel. 305/673–3331, main office 305/673–3330. AE, MC, V. Ticketmaster (see Important Addresses and Numbers, above). Season: Oct.–Apr.*

Theaters   **Dade County Auditorium** (2901 W. Flagler St., Miami 33135, tel. 305/545–3395) satisfies patrons with 2,498 comfortable seats, good sight lines, and acceptable acoustics.

Jackie Gleason Theater of the Performing Arts (TOPA, 1700 Washington Ave., Miami Beach 33139, tel. 305/673–7700 for information; 305/673–8300 for ticket sales for the Broadway Series). In 1990 TOPA completed a $23-million, three-year series of improvements that have finally provided adequate acoustics and good visibility for all 2,750 seats.

Gusman Center for the Performing Arts (174 E. Flagler St., Miami 33131, tel. 305/372–0925). Located in downtown Miami, the center has 1,739 seats made for sardines—and the best acoustics in town. An ornate former movie palace, the hall resembles a Moorish courtyard. Lights twinkle, starlike, from the ceiling.

Gusman Concert Hall (1314 Miller Dr., Coral Gables 33124, tel. 305/284–2438). This 600-seat hall on the University of Miami's Coral Gables campus has good acoustics, and plenty of room. Parking is a problem when school is in session.

Jan McArt's International Room (Marco Polo Hotel, 19201 Collins Ave., Miami Beach 33180, tel. 305/932–7880) is the new Miami-area venue for musicals, which are performed year-round in the 270-seat hotel theater.

Spanish Theater Spanish theater prospers, although many companies have short lives. About 20 Spanish companies perform light comedy, puppetry, vaudeville, and political satire. To locate them, read the Spanish newspapers. When you phone, be prepared for a conversation in Spanish. Most of the box-office personnel don't speak English.

Teatro Avante. Three to six productions are staged annually at El Carrosel (235 Alcazar Ave., tel. 305/445–8877). A Hispanic theater festival is held each May. *Box 453005, Miami 33245–3005, tel. 305/858–4155.*

Prometeo. This theater has produced three to four bilingual Spanish-English plays a year for 19 years. *Miami-Dade Community College, New World Center Campus, 300 N.E. 2nd Ave., Miami, tel. 305/237–3263. Admission free. Call for invitation.*

Teatro de Bellas Artes. A 255-seat theater on Calle Ocho, Little Havana's main commercial street, Teatro de Bellas Artes presents eight Spanish plays and musicals a year. *2173 S.W. 8th St., Miami, tel. 305/325–0515. No credit cards. Dramas Fri.–Sat. 9 PM and Sun. 3 PM. Musical comedy Sat. midnight and Sun. 9 PM. Recitals Sun. 6 PM.*

Nightlife

Greater Miami has no concentration of night spots like Bourbon Street in New Orleans or Rush Street in Chicago, but nightlife thrives throughout the Miami area in scattered locations, including Miami Beach, Little Haiti, Little Havana, Coconut Grove, the fringes of downtown Miami, and south-suburban Kendall. Individual clubs offer jazz, reggae, salsa, various forms of rock-and-roll, and top-40 sounds on different nights of the week. Some clubs refuse entrance to anyone under 21; others set the age limit at 25.

For current information, see the Weekend Section in the Friday edition of *The Miami Herald;* the calendar in *Miami Today*, a free weekly newspaper available each Thursday in downtown Miami, Coconut Grove, and Coral Gables; and *New Times*, a free weekly distributed throughout Dade County each Wednesday.

Love 94 (WLVE, 93.9 FM) sponsors an entertainment line with information on touring groups of all kinds, except classical (tel. 305/654–9436). Blues Hot Line lists local blues clubs and bars (tel. 305/666–6656). Jazz Hot Line lists local jazz programs (tel. 305/382–3938).

On Miami Beach, where the sounds of jazz and reggae spill into the streets, fashion models and photographers frequent the lobby bars of small Art Deco hotels.

Throughout the Greater Miami area, bars and cocktail lounges in larger hotels operate discos nightly, with live entertainment on weekends. Many hotels extend their bars into open-air courtyards, where patrons dine and dance under the stars throughout the year.

Bars **Cactus Cantina.** An unpretentious local hangout, this presents live music every night but Thursday—comedy night. The food and beer selections are tops. *630 6th St., Miami Beach, tel. 305/*

532–5095. Open weekdays, 5–5, weekends 5–7. Cover on weekends.

Churchill's Hideaway. This enclave of Anglicism in Little Haiti is popular with cruise-line employees and international sports fans. Its satellite dish picks up BBC news programs, and a Sharp Six System VHS plays foreign-format tapes of international soccer and rugby games. Not for the unadventurous. Live music Tuesday and Thursday through Saturday. *5501 N.E. 2nd Ave., Miami, tel. 305/757–1807. No credit cards. Open Mon.–Thurs. 11 AM–1 AM, Fri. 11 AM–3 AM, Sat. 9:30 AM–3 AM, Sun. noon–2 AM, but sometimes it opens earlier and closes later. Call ahead.*

Hungry Sailor. This small English-style pub is decorated with nautical charts, marine flags, and flotsam and jetsam. It's Coconut Grove's answer to *the pub* with six English/Irish ales and beers on tap plus 18 varieties of bottled brews. The "Sailor" serves, in addition to English-American food, traditional Caribbean clam chowder and other island tidbits. Reggae and calypso nightly. *3064½ Grand Ave., Coconut Grove, tel. 305/444–9359. AE, DC, MC, V. Open 11:30 AM–2:30 AM.*

Mac's Club Deuce. This South Miami Beach gem shows off top international models who pop in to have a drink, shoot some pool. All you get late at night are minipizzas, but the pizzazz lasts, akin to that of the bar scene in *Star Wars*, they'll tell you. One of the best. *222 14th St., Miami Beach, tel. 305/673–9537. No credit cards. Open daily 8 AM–5 AM.*

Stuart's Bar-Lounge. *Esquire* called Stuart's (built 1926) one of the best new bars of 1987. Six years later locals still favor it. It is decorated with beveled mirrors, mahogany paneling, French posters, pictures of old Coral Gables, and art nouveau lighting. *162 Alcazar Ave., Coral Gables, tel. 305/444–1666. Open Mon.–Sat. 5 PM–12:30 AM. AE, DC, MC, V. Closed Sun.*

Taurus Steak House. The bar, built in 1922 of native cypress, nightly draws an over-30 singles crowd that drifts outside to a patio. A band plays on weekends. *3540 Main Hwy., Coconut Grove, tel. 305/448–0633. AE, DC, MC, V. Open weekdays 11:30 AM–midnight, Fri.–Sun. 11:30 AM–3. Dinner nightly.*

Tobacco Road. This bar, opened in 1912, holds Miami's oldest liquor license. Upstairs, in space occupied by a speakeasy during Prohibition, local and national blues bands perform Friday and Saturday and in scheduled weeknight concerts. Excellent bar food. *626 S. Miami Ave., Miami, tel. 305/374–1198. AE, DC, MC, V. Open weekdays 11:30 AM–5 AM, weekends 1 PM–5 AM. Lunch served weekdays. Dinner served Sun.–Thurs.*

Tropics International Restaurant. Music from right-on jazz to rhythm-and-blues, and no cover charge, make Tropics worth popping into. This Memphis-style bar was created by Victor Farinas, one of Miami's top nouveau designers. And if the heat's up, bring your suit and take a dip in the pool where there's live music Thursday through Saturday nights. International menu. *960 Ocean Dr., Miami Beach, tel. 305/531–5335. AE, D, DC, MC, V. Open Mon.–Thurs. 11 AM–2 AM, Fri. 11 AM–4 AM, Sat. 8:30 AM–4 AM, Sun. 8:30 AM–2 AM.*

Comedy Clubs

Coconut Grove. Three comedy clubs make the scene in this popular part of town: **Coconuts Comedy Club** at the Peacock Cafe (2977 McFarlane Rd., tel. 305/446–2582) and at the Howard Johnson Motor Lodge (Golden Glades Interchange, 16500 N.W. 2nd Ave., tel. 305/940–7371); the **Improv** (3015 Grand Ave., tel. 305/441–8200) in the new Cocowalk indoor/out mall;

and the long-standing and outrageous **Mental Floss** (3138 Commodore Plaza, tel. 305/448–1011).

Uncle Funny's Comedy Club. This 1990s version of vaudeville comedy thrives with humor that's adult, but not obscene. Two acts per show; new performers each week. *Mark Twain's Riverboat Playhouse, 13700 N. Kendall Dr., Miami, tel. 305/388–1992. MC, V. $6 cover Fri., $7 Sat., both nights have 2-drink-minimum policy. Shows weekends 9:30 and 11:30.*

Disco/Jazz/ Rock Clubs

Baja Beach Club. Waiters and waitresses dress in beach attire as they cater to the 6,000 or so people who go through here on the weekends. You'll find three bars under one roof and a very popular balcony where customers hang out to watch the goings-on in the heart of Coconut Grove, below. There's live entertainment, lots of sports events, dancing, and good food. *3015 Grand Ave., Cocowalk in Coconut Grove, tel. 305/445–0278. AE, MC, V. All rooms open until 5 AM. Sports Bar opens 11 AM; Baja Beach Club 5 PM; Music Room 8 or 9 PM.*

Copacabana Supper Club. In 1992, a gala new South American revue with up to 40 cast members was introduced Friday through Sunday nights, complete with chorus line, song and dance, and individual performers. During the week expect theme nights. Complete restaurant service. *3600 S.W. 8th St., Miami, tel. 305/443–7020. AE, MC, V. Open Wed.–Sun. 5:30 PM–4 AM. Reservations advised.*

Stringfellows. Opened in May 1989, Peter Stringfellow's Coconut Grove club has been attracting guests from international artistic, business, and social circles, many of whom are already familiar with Stringfellow's other clubs in London and New York. Guests enter through green glass doors decorated with an etched-glass butterfly crest and ascend to the club's second-floor restaurant and nightclub. The restaurant, decorated with art-deco furnishings, pink tablecloths, and fresh orchids, features well-prepared international cuisine. The nightclub, which opens at 11:30, features rock music pumped through a state-of-the-art sound system and a sophisticated light system capable of producing hundreds of variations. *3390 Mary St., Miami 33133, tel. 305/446–7555. Reservations advised. Club cover charge: $10 Tues.–Thurs., $15 Sat. AE, DC, MC, V. Closed Sun., Mon., Christmas. À la carte menu served 8 PM–2:30 AM, late-night supper from 2:30–4 AM. Club open 11 PM–5 AM.*

Stefano's of Key Biscayne. Live band performs nightly, 7–11 PM. Then this northern Italian restaurant becomes a disco, complete with wood dance floor. *24 Crandon Blvd., Key Biscayne, tel. 305/361–7007. AE, DC, MC, V. Open 5 PM–5 AM nightly.*

Nightclubs

Three trendy new clubs that have opened in South Beach include the **Paragon** (1235 Washington Ave., Miami Beach 33139, tel. 305/534–1235; $10 cover, open Thurs.–Sat.) that draws a gay crowd, **Van Dome** (1532 Washington Ave., Miami Beach 33139, tel. 305/534–4288; cover $10 Saturday, variable Fri.), in a former synagogue, and **The Whiskey** (1250 Ocean Dr., Miami Beach 33139, tel. 305/531–0713; cover $5 Fri. and Sat. only, open nightly), a spinoff of Manhattan's pop Paramount Plaza Hotel bar.

Mako's Bay Club. This new Top-40 club on the north side of town, close by Bay Vista Campus of Florida International University, has been a quick hit among the younger set since its late 1991 opening. *17290 Biscayne Blvd., No. Miami Beach,* *tel. 305/944–7805. Cover: $3 to $5. AE, DC, MC, V. Open nightly 9 PM–6 AM, from 6 PM Sat.*

Les Violins Supper Club. This standby has been owned for 26 years by the Cachaidora-Currais family, who ran a club and restaurant in Havana. Live dance band. Wood dance floor. Dinner. *1751 Biscayne Blvd., Miami, tel. 305/371–8668. Open 7 PM. Closes Tues.–Thurs. and Sun. 1 AM, Fri. 2 AM, Sat. 3 AM. Reservations advised. AE, D, DC, MC, V. Closed Mon.*

Club Tropigala at La Ronde in the Fontainebleau Hilton Hotel. A seven-level round room decorated with orchids, banana leaves, and philodendrons to resemble a tropical jungle, this club is operated by owners of Les Violins. Two bands play Latin music for dancing on the wood floor. One live costumed show Wednesday, Thursday, and Friday; two Wednesday, Thursday, Sunday, some Friday, and Saturday. Dinner. Long wait for valet parking. *4441 Collins Ave., Miami Beach, tel. 305/672–7469. Reservations advised. AE, DC, MC, V. Open Wed.–Sun. 7 PM, or later.*

Performance Art Club

Miami Arts Asylum. Arty Bohemianism flourishes here in painting, sculpture, performance, music. Attire and attitudes make it eclectic and electric. *1445 Washington Ave., Miami Beach, tel. 305/532–0922. Call for nights, hours, admission.*

3 The Everglades

Introduction

By George and Rosalie Leposky

Updated by Herb Hiller

Greater Miami is the only metropolitan area in the United States with two national parks in its backyard: Everglades and Biscayne. Even before Hurricane Andrew ripped through the area in late summer 1992, the long-term survival of both parks was threatened by pollution and other serious environmental problems. The hurricane further devastated the already precarious ecosystem by causing extensive damage to the tree population, which includes royal palms, hardwood hammocks, Florida pines, and mangroves. At press time, the estimated cost of damage to the two parks was around $27 million.

Although it's still too early to know how the hurricane has impacted the wildlife that inhabits the parks, scientists have begun extensive research, studying crocodile hatchlings, the endangered Florida panthers (23 of the 50 that live in the Everglades have radio collars so they can be easily tracked), manatees, and other animals. Among the primary concerns immediately following the storm was the conditioning of the coral reefs, but marine biologists report minimal damage. On an up note, fish in the Everglades are proliferating, because an abundance of plankton and other food that the storm stirred up from the river's floor. The long-term survival of both parks is threatened by environmental problems.

Everglades National Park, created in 1947, was meant to preserve the slow-flowing "river of grass" that was under stress from channelizing and from weirs installed for flood control. But the water has been steadily more polluted by pesticide runoff from dairy, sugar cane, and vegetable growers and, in turn, the disrupted flow has caused further subtle but steady changes in Everglades wildlife habitat and the quickening demise of Florida Bay. Visitors to the park over the years note diminished numbers of birds; the black bear has been eliminated and the Florida panther reduced to near extinction. In 1992 the nonprofit group American Rivers declared the Everglades the fourth most endangered river in North America.

Biscayne National Park, established as a national monument in 1968, and 12 years later expanded and upgraded to park status, is mostly underwater. The park includes the northernmost sections of Florida's tropical reef, which is under assault from the polluted and massive freshwater outflow of the canals that drain the Everglades, as well as from direct damage to corals by boat anchors and from commercial shipping that runs off course and onto the reefs.

Biscayne National Park encompasses almost 274 square miles, of which 96% are under water. Biscayne includes 18 miles of inhospitable mangrove shoreline on the mainland and 45 mangrove-fringed barrier islands seven miles to the east across Biscayne Bay. The bay is a lobster sanctuary and a nursery for fish, sponges, and crabs. Manatees and sea turtles also frequent its warm, shallow waters.

The islands (called keys) are fossilized coral reefs that emerged from the sea when glaciers trapped much of the world's water supply during the Ice Age. Today a tropical hardwood forest grows in the crevices of these rocky keys.

East of the keys, coral reefs 3 miles seaward attract divers and snorkelers (*see* Participant Sports and Outdoor Activities, below). Biscayne is the only national park in the continental United States with living coral reefs and is the nation's largest marine park. The park boundary encompasses the continental shelf to a depth of 60 feet. East of that boundary, the shelf falls rapidly away to a depth of 400 feet at the edge of the Gulf Stream.

At press time residences and businesses within Everglades and Biscayne parks reported severe damage, but most commercial businesses planned to rebuild. Many properties could still not be reached by the time of publication, but local tourist offices suggested that the majority would be operational in 1993. We urge you to call ahead, before you plan any itineraries involving the Everglades.

Essential Information

Getting Around

By Plane
Commercial Flights

Miami International Airport (MIA) is the closest commercial airport to Everglades National Park and Biscayne National Park. It's 34 miles from Homestead and 83 miles from the Flamingo resort in Everglades National Park.

By Car

From the north, the main highways to Homestead-Florida City are U.S. 1, the Homestead Extension of the Florida Turnpike, and Krome Avenue (Rte. 997/old U.S. 27).

From Miami to Biscayne National Park, take the turnpike extension to the Tallahassee Road (S.W. 137th Ave.) exit, turn left, and go south. Turn left at North Canal Drive (S.W. 328th St.), go east, and follow signs to park headquarters at Convoy Point. The park is about 30 miles from downtown Miami.

From Homestead to Biscayne National Park, take U.S. 1 or Krome Avenue (Rte. 997) to Lucy Street (S.E. 8th St.). Turn east. Lucy Street becomes North Canal Drive (S.W. 328th St.). Follow signs about 8 miles to the park headquarters.

From Homestead to Everglades National Park's Main Visitor Center and Flamingo, take U.S. 1 or Krome Avenue (Rte. 997/ Old U.S. 27) south to Florida City. Turn right (west) onto Rte. 9336. Follow signs to the park entrance. The Main Visitor Center is 11 miles from Homestead; Flamingo is 49 miles from Homestead.

To reach the western gateway to Everglades National Park, take U.S. 41 (the Tamiami Trail) west from Miami. It's 40 miles to the Shark Valley Information Center and 83 miles to the Gulf Coast Ranger Station at Everglades City.

To reach the south end of Everglades National Park in the Florida Keys, take U.S. 1 south from Homestead. It's 27 miles to the Key Largo Ranger Station (between MM 98 and 99 on the Overseas Hwy.).

Rental Cars

American Eagle Rent-A-Car, (28400 S. Dixie Hwy., Homestead, 33033, tel. 305/245–0300; 305/247–0873), **Enterprise Rent-a-Car** (30428 S. Fed. Hwy., Homestead 33030, tel. 305/246–2056). Rental cars also available at MIA.

By Van   **Super Shuttle.** 11-passenger air-conditioned vans operate between MIA and Homestead. Service on demand from MIA; go to Super Shuttle booth outside most luggage areas on lower level. 24-hour advance reservation requested returning to MIA. *Tel. 305/871–2000. 24-hr daily service. $26–$35 per person depending on zip code in Homestead, $5 each additional person traveling together. 10% discount for round-trips anyplace in Dade County. AE, DC, MC, V.*

The Airporter. Five shuttle bus services a day run between the Holiday Inn, Homestead (with a stop at the Holiday Inn, Cutler Ridge), and the airport. Service from Homestead is between 8 AM and 6:20 PM; from the airport between 9:15 AM and 7:30 PM. Trips take approximately one hour. The airport station is in the bus loop in front of Concourse E. *One-way fares $15. Reservations required. Tel. 305/247–8874, 305/247–8877.*

By Bus   **Metrobus.** Route 1A runs from Homestead to MIA only during peak weekday hours: 6:30–9 AM and 4–6:30 PM.

Greyhound/Trailways operates three trips daily north to near Miami International Airport, but the trip is not direct. The Greyhound/Trailways depot (4111 N.W. 27th St.) is about a $5 cab ride from the airport. Coming from the airport to connect with one of Greyhound's three daily buses south to Homestead, you can take an ARTS (Airport Region Taxi Service) car for about $5 (including the normal $1 surcharge on cab service from MIA),stopping at the Homestead Bus Station (5 N.E. 3rd Rd., tel. 305/247–2040).

By Taxi   **Homestead Yellow Cab Company.** Service in Homestead-Florida City area. Full service to and from Flamingo and the tour boats in Biscayne National Park. Service from Homestead to MIA. *416 N.E. 1st Rd., Homestead, tel. 305/247–7777. No credit cards.*

By Boat   **U.S. Customs.** The nearest U.S. Customs phones to the two national parks are at **Watson Island Marina** (1050 MacArthur Causeway, Miami, tel. 305/371–2378), about 25 nautical miles to Biscayne National Park headquarters, 50 nautical miles to Flamingo; and **Tavernier Creek Marina** (MM 90.5, U.S. 1, Tavernier, tel. 305/252–0194 from Miami, 305/852–5854 from the Keys), about 48 nautical miles to Biscayne National Park headquarters, 25 nautical miles to Flamingo.

Scenic Drives   **Main road to Flamingo in Everglades National Park.** It's 38 road miles from the Main Visitor Center to Flamingo, across six distinct ecosystems (with access from the road to two others). Highlights of the trip include a dwarf cypress forest, the ecotone (transition zone) between saw grass and mangrove forest, and a wealth of wading birds at Mrazek and Coot Bay ponds. Boardwalks and trails along the main road and several short spurs allow you to see the Everglades without getting your feet wet. Well-written interpretive signs en route will help you understand this diverse wilderness.

Tamiami Trail. U.S. 41 from Miami to the Gulf Coast crosses the Everglades and the Big Cypress National Preserve. Highlights of the trip include sweeping views across the saw grass to the Shark River Slough, a visit to the Miccosukee Indian Reservation, and the Big Cypress National Preserve's variegated pattern of wet prairies, ponds, marshes, sloughs, and strands.

It's 83 miles to the Gulf Coast Ranger Station at Everglades City.

Guided Tours

Tours of Everglades National Park and Biscayne National Park typically focus on native wildlife, plants, and park history. Concessionaires operate the Everglades tram tours and the boat cruises in both parks. In addition, the National Park Service organizes a variety of free programs at Everglades National Park. Ask a ranger for the daily schedule.

Orientation Tours Since 1980 **All Florida Adventure Tours** has operated from one-day to two-week tours that emphasize nature, history, and ecology. Custom tours also arranged upon request. *8263–B S.W. 107th Ave., Miami 33173–3729, tel. 305/270–0219. MC, V.*

Special-Interest Tours
Agricultural Tour **Agricultural Guided Tour.** Seasonal 2½-hour narrated bus tour leaves from the State Farmers Market in Florida City and visits among 2,400 nurseries and 90,000 acres of groves and farmed land that produces such unusual fruit crops as mamey sapote, mangos, papayas, plantains, and popular tropical root crops that include calabaza, malanga, and yucca. *300 N. Krome Ave., Florida City 33034, tel. 305/248–6798. Cost: $10 adults, $8 youths 12–17, children under 12 free. No credit cards. Tours Dec. 1–Apr. 1, weekdays 9 and 1:30.*

Air Tours **Air Tours of South Florida.** Three 50-minute narrated tours cover either the Everglades, Florida Keys, or Miami and Miami Beach; an 80-minute Grand Circle Tour covers all. *Homestead General Aviation Airport, 28720 S.W. 217th Ave., Homestead 33030, tel. 305/248–1100 or 800/628–3610. Cost: $59 per person for 50-min tour, $110 for 80-min, minimum 2 people. Reservations recommended. AE, MC, V. Open daily 9 AM–4 PM.*

Airboat Rides **Buffalo Tiger's Florida Everglades Airboat Ride.** The former chairman of the Miccosukee tribe will take you on a 35-minute airboat ride through the Everglades, with a stop at an old Indian camp. Opportunities to watch birds, turtles, and alligators. *Tour location: 12 mi west of Krome Ave., 20 mi west of the Miami city limits (Rte. 997), tel. 305/559–5250. Cost: $8 adults, $5 children under 10. No credit cards. Open daily 10–5 winter, 10–6 summer. Closed Fri. Sept. and Oct.*

Coopertown Airboat Ride. This 30-minute airboat ride through the Everglades saw grass takes you to two hammocks (subtropical hardwood forests) and alligator holes. Bird-watching opportunities. *Tamiami Trail, 5 mi west of Krome Ave., 15 mi west of Miami city limits, tel. 305/226–6048. Cost: $7 per person for 3 or more; minimum $18 for the boat. No credit cards. Open daily 8 AM–dusk.*

Everglades Alligator Farm. A 4-mile, 30-minute tour of the River of Grass leaves at least every half hour and includes free tour of an alligator farm. Big improvements have been made at this site since 1991, with new fencing, new landscaping, and a new gift shop. *40351 S.W. 192nd Ave., tel. 305/AIRBOAT. Cost: $9 adults, $8 senior citizens, $4.50 children 4–12, under 4 free. AE, D, MC, V. Open daily 9–5.*

Boat Tours **Biscayne National Park Tour Boats.** You'll ride to Biscayne National Park's living coral reefs 10 miles offshore on a 53-foot glass-bottom boat. A separate tour to Elliott Key visitor center, on a barrier island 7 miles offshore across Biscayne Bay, is conducted only in winter, based on demand, when mosquitoes are less active. *East end of North Canal Dr. (S.W. 328th St.), Homestead, tel. 305/247–2400. Glass-bottom boat cost: $16.50 adults, $8.50 children, $24.50 snorkelers. Elliott Key tour Sun. only at 10 AM, if demand warrants, prices same as for glass-bottom-boat tour. Reservations required. MC, V. Office open daily 8:30–6. Phone for daily schedule.*

Back Country Tour. A two-hour cruise from Flamingo Lodge Marina & Outpost Resort aboard a 40-passenger pontoon boat covers 12–15 miles through tropical estuaries fringed with impenetrable mangrove forests. You may see manatees, dolphins, sharks, alligators, and many species of bird life, including bald eagles. *Flamingo Marina, Flamingo, tel. 305/253–2241 or 813/695–3101; fax 813/695–3921. Cruises daily. Tours Nov.–Apr. Phone for schedule. Reservations accepted. Cost: $10.50 adults, $5 children 6–12, under 6 free. AE, DC, MC, V.*

Everglades National Park Boat Tours. Sammy Hamilton operates three separate 14-mile tours through the Ten Thousand Islands region along the Gulf of Mexico on the western margin of the park. *Everglades National Park's Gulf Coast Ranger Station on Rte. 29, about 3 mi south of U.S. 41 (Tamiami Trail), tel. 813/695–2591 or in FL 800/445–7724. Phone for schedule. Cost: $10 adults, $5 children 6–12, under 6 free. MC, V. Office open daily 8:30–5.*

Florida Bay Cruise. A 90-minute tour of Florida Bay from Flamingo Lodge Marina & Outpost Resort aboard *Bald Eagle*, a 90-passenger pontoon boat. The tour offers a close look at bird life on rookery islands in the bay and on sandbars during low tide. In winter, you're likely to see white pelicans; in summer, magnificent frigatebirds. Also offers backcountry and sunset tours. *Flamingo Marina, Flamingo, tel. 305/253–2241 or 813/695–3101. Phone for schedule. Reservations accepted. Cost: $7.75 adults, $3.75 children 6–12. AE, DC, MC, V. Cruises daily.*

Florida Boat Tours. Back-country tours outside Everglades National Park in Everglades City area. Runs three 24-passenger airboats for 30-minute rides, 48-passenger pontoon boat and airboat for one-hour cruise, which includes visit to Indian Village; departure is from Everglades City. Boats are Coast Guard approved. *Tel. 813/695–4400 or in FL 800/282–9194. Phone for schedule. Cost: $12 adults, $6 children 4–12. MC, V.*

Tram Tours **Wilderness Tram Tour.** Snake Bight is an indentation in the Florida Bay shoreline near Flamingo. You can go there aboard a 48-passenger screened tram on this two-hour tour through a mangrove forest and a coastal prairie to a 100-yard boardwalk over the mud flats at the edge of the bight. It's a good birding spot. Tram operates subject to mosquito, weather, and trail conditions. Driver has insect repellent on board. *Departs from Flamingo Lodge gift shop 10:30 AM, 1:30 and 3:30, tel. 305/253–2241 or 813/695–3101. Reservations accepted. Cost: $7 adults, $3.50 children 6–12. AE, DC, MC, V.*

Shark Valley Tram Tours. The trams take a new 15-mile loop road, which is elevated, has 200 culverts, and is considerably less flood prone when the summer rains come. Propane- and gas-powered trams travel into the interior, stopping at a 50-foot observation tower on the site of an oil well drilled in the 1940s. From atop the tower, you'll view the Everglades' vast "river of grass" sweeping south toward the Gulf of Mexico. The trams are covered but have open sides, so carry rain gear. (Plastic raincoats are sold for $1.) *Shark Valley entrance to Everglades National Park, 40 mi west of Miami off U.S. 41 (Tamiami Trail), tel. 305/221–8455. Cost: $7 adults, $3.50 12 and under, $6.25 senior citizens. No credit cards. Open daily all year 9–4. Reservations recommended Dec.–Mar.*

Personal Guides **Swampland Airboat Tours.** Collier County native and licensed guide Donald McDowell will take up to six people on day or night tours of the Big Cypress National Preserve. Pick-ups arranged at any of six landings. *Box 619, Everglades City 33929, tel. 813/695–2740. Cost: 1–2 persons $60/hr., $10 each additional person up to 6. Reservations required.*

Flamingo Lodge Marina & Outpost Resort. Captains of charter fishing boats are available to give individual tours out of Flamingo. Make reservations several weeks in advance through the marina store. *TW Services Inc., Everglades National Park, Box 428, Flamingo 33030, tel. 305/253–2241 or 813/695–3101. Cost: $265 a day (for up to 3 persons), $165 a half day. Additional persons $20 each. AE, DC, MC, V. Available year-round.*

Historical **Florida Pioneer Museum.** This down-home collection of articles
Attraction from daily life evokes the homestead period on the last frontier of mainland America. Housed in three yellow structures from the early 20th century—the relocated Homestead East Coast Railway Station, railway agent's house, and a caboose—the collections recall a time when Henry Flagler's railroad vaulted the Florida Keys on its epic extension to Key West, and when Homestead and Florida City were briefly the take-charge supply outposts. The agent's house was moved to the museum grounds in 1964, the station in 1976. *826 N. Krome Ave., Florida City 33034, tel. 305/246–9531. Donation: $3 adults, $1 children. Open daily 1–5. Closed major holidays.*

Important Addresses and Numbers

Tourist **South Dade Visitors Information Center.** *160 U.S. 1, Florida*
Information *City 33034, tel. 305/245–9180 or 800/388–9669. Open daily 8–6.*

Greater Homestead-Florida City Chamber of Commerce. (43 N. Krome Ave., Homestead 33030, tel. 305/247–2332).

Emergencies Homestead, Florida City, and unincorporated Dade County use the same emergency number, 911. You can dial free from pay phones.

In the national parks, the rangers perform police, fire, and medical-emergency functions. Look for the rangers at park visitor centers and information stations, or phone the park switchboards: Biscayne (tel. 305/247–2044); Everglades (tel. 305/247–6211).

Hospitals **South Miami Hospital of Homestead.** 24-hour emergency room. *160 N.W. 13th St., Homestead, tel. 305/248–3232. Physician referral service, tel. 305/248–DOCS.*

Marine Phone **Biscayne National Park** (tel. 305/247–2044). Rangers staff Elli-
Numbers ott Key Visitor Center and Adams Key Information Center

around the clock and can call the mainland on ship-to-shore radio. Park headquarters on Convoy Point open daily 8:30–6 winter, 9–5 summer. Park open 8–sunset year-round.

Florida Marine Patrol. Law-enforcement arm of the Florida Department of Natural Resources. Boating emergencies: 24-hour tel. 305/325–3346. Natural resource violations, including marine fishery laws, mangrove cuttings, manatee reports, filling of wetlands. *Tel. 305/325–3346.*

National Weather Service. National Hurricane Center office in Coral Gables supplies local forecasts. *Open weekdays 7:30–5, tel. 305/665–0429. For 24-hr weather recording, tel. 305/661–5065.*

U.S. Coast Guard **Miami Beach Coast Guard Base** (tel. 305/535–4314 or 305/535–4315, VHF-FM Channel 16). Local marine emergencies, search-and-rescue, and reporting of navigation hazards.

Exploring the Everglades

Biscayne National Park

Numbers in the margin correspond to points of interest on the Everglades and Biscayne National Parks map.

Because 96% of Biscayne National Park's acreage is under water, you must take a boat ride to visit most of it and snorkel or scuba dive to appreciate it fully. If you don't have your own boat, a concessionaire will take you to the coral reefs 10 miles offshore. These dome-shape patch reefs—some the size of a student's desk, others as broad as a large parking lot—rely on the delicate balance of temperature, depth, light, and water quality that the park was created to maintain.

A diverse population of colorful fish flits through the reefs: angelfish, gobies, grunts, parrot fish, pork fish, wrasses, and many more.

From December through April, when the mosquito population is relatively quiescent, you can comfortably explore several of the mangrove-fringed barrier islands 7 miles offshore. Tropical hardwood forests cloak the upper reaches of these fossilized coral reefs.

The list below describes the facilities at each of Biscayne National Park's visitor service areas, and also at the Metro-Dade County parks within the national park's boundaries.

1 **Adams Key Information Station.** Boat dock, picnic area, rest rooms, short nature trail. Ranger station has ship-to-shore radio contact with mainland. Day use only.

2 **Boca Chita Key.** Mark C. Honeywell, former president of Minneapolis's Honeywell Co., bought this island in 1937 and built the ornamental lighthouse, rainwater catchment cisterns, a wall, and other buildings of coral rock. There is a boat dock, picnic area, and rest rooms. Lighthouse open on occasion; ask rangers.

3 **Convoy Point Information Station.** Park headquarters. New $8 million administration and visitor center with exhibits, docks, and boardwalk is scheduled to open by 1993. Currently small visitor center and outdoor kiosk with bulletin boards. Launch-

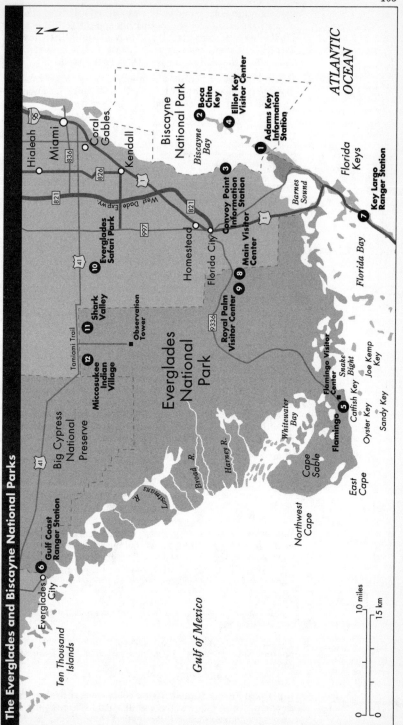

The Everglades and Biscayne National Parks

ATLANTIC OCEAN

Biscayne National Park

2 Boca Chita Key

4 Elliot Key Visitor Center

1 Adams Key Information Station

Biscayne Bay

3 Convoy Point Information Station

Coral Gables

Kendall

Hialeah

Miami

Barnes Sound

Florida Keys

7 Key Largo Ranger Station

West Dade Expwy.

Everglades Safari Park **10**

Homestead

Florida City

8 Main Visitor Center

9 Royal Palm Visitor Center

Florida Bay

11 Shark Valley

Observation Tower

12 Miccosukee Indian Village

Tamiami Trail

Everglades National Park

Big Cypress National Preserve

Snake Bight

Flamingo Visitor Center

5 Flamingo

Catfish Key

Oyster Key

Joe Kemp Key

Sandy Key

Whitewater Bay

Cape Sable

East Cape

Shark R.

Harney R.

Broad R.

Lostmans R.

Northwest Cape

Gulf of Mexico

6 Gulf Coast Ranger Station

Everglades City

Ten Thousand Islands

10 miles

15 km

ing ramp for canoes and sailboards. Boardwalk over shallow water near shore to jetty and path along jetty. Picnic area. Dock where you board tour boats to reefs and Elliott Key. *At east end of North Canal Dr. (S.W. 328th St.), Homestead, tel. 305/247–PARK. Admission free. Open year-round.*

❹ Elliott Key Visitor Center. Indoor exhibit area on second floor displays coral, sponges, and sea-turtle shells on a "touching table" that children especially enjoy. A screened enclosure under the exhibit area houses picnic tables, bulletin boards, and a slide show. *Tel. 305/247–PARK. Open most weekends and holidays 10–4.*

The Everglades

Winter is the best time to visit Everglades National Park. Temperatures and mosquito activity are moderate. Low water levels concentrate the resident wildlife around sloughs that retain water all year. Migratory birds swell the avian population. Winter is also the busiest time in the park. Make reservations and expect crowds at Flamingo, the main visitor center, and Royal Palm—the most popular visitor service areas.

In spring the weather turns increasingly hot and dry. After Easter, fewer visitors come, and tours and facilities are less crowded. Migratory birds depart, and you must look harder to see wildlife. Be especially careful with campfires and matches; this is when the wildfire-prone saw-grass prairies and pinelands are most vulnerable.

Summer brings intense sun and billowing clouds that unleash torrents of rain on the Everglades. Thunderstorms roll in almost every afternoon, bringing the park 90% of its annual 60-inch rainfall from June through October. Water levels rise. Wildlife disperses. Mosquitoes hatch, swarm, and descend on you in voracious clouds. It's a good time to stay away, although some brave souls do come to explore. Europeans constitute 80% of the summer visitors.

Summer in south Florida lingers until mid-October, when the first cold front sweeps through. The rains cease, water levels start to fall, and the ground begins to dry out. Wildlife moves toward the sloughs. Flocks of migratory birds and tourists swoop in, as the cycle of seasons builds once more to the winter peak activity.

Whenever you come, we urge you to experience the real Everglades by getting your feet wet—but most people who visit the park won't do that. Boat tours at Everglades City and Flamingo, a tram ride at Shark Valley, and boardwalks at several locations along the main park road allow you to see the Everglades with dry feet.

The list below describes the facilities at each of the park's visitor service areas.

❺ Flamingo. Museum, lodge, restaurant, lounge, gift shop, marina, and campground. *Mailing address: Box 279, Homestead 33030, tel. 305/247–6211 (Park Service), tel. 305/253–2241 (Everglades Lodge). Visitor center open daily 8–5.*

❻ Gulf Coast Ranger Station. Visitor center, where back-country campers pick up required free permits; exhibits; gift shop. *Follow Everglades National Park signs from Tamiami Trail*

(U.S. 41) south on Rte. 29, tel. 813/695–3311. Admission free. Open daily in winter 7–4:30, reduced hours in summer.

❼ Key Largo Ranger Station. No exhibits, no docks, chiefly for canoers. *98710 Overseas Hwy., Key Largo, tel. 305/852–5119. Not always staffed; phone ahead. Admission free.*

❽ Main Visitor Center. Exhibits, film, bookstore, park headquarters. *11 mi west of Homestead on Rte. 9336, tel. 305/242–7700. Visitor center open 8–5. Admission: $5 per car (good for 7 days); $2 per person on foot, bicycle, or motorcycle; U.S. senior citizens over 62 free. Park open 24 hrs.*

❾ Royal Palm Visitor Center. Anhinga Trail boardwalk, Gumbo Limbo Trail through hammock, museum, bookstore, vending machines. *Tel. 305/242–7700. Open 8–4:30, with ½ hour off for lunch.*

❿ Everglades Safari Park. This commercial attraction includes an airboat ride, jungle trail, observation platform, alligator wrestling, wildlife museum, gift shop, and restaurant. *9 mi west of Krome Ave., 17 mi west of Miami city limits, on Tamiami Trail (U.S. 41), tel. 305/226–6923 or 305/223–3804. Admission: $10 adults, $5 children under 12. No credit cards. Open daily 8:30–5.*

⓫ Shark Valley. Tram tour, ¼-mile boardwalk, hiking trails, rotating exhibits, bookstore. *Box 42, Ochopee 33943, tel. 305/221–8776. Open daily 8:30–5. Admission: $3 per car, $1 per person on foot, bicycle, or motorcycle (good for 7 days); U.S. senior citizens over 62 free. 2-hr. tram tours: $7 adult, $3.50 12 and under. Departures every hour between 9 and 4 in winter, less frequently in summer. Reservations recommended Dec.–Mar. No credit cards. Show Shark Valley admission receipt at Main Visitor Center and pay only the difference there.*

⓬ Miccosukee Indian Village. Near the Shark Valley entrance to Everglades National Park, the Miccosukee tribe operates an Indian village as a tourist attraction. You can watch Indian families cooking and making clothes, dolls, beadwork, and baskets. You'll also see an alligator-wrestling demonstration. The village has a boardwalk and a museum. *On Tamiami Trail (U.S. 41) 25 mi west of Miami. Mailing address: Box 440021, Miami 33144, tel. 305/223–8380. Admission: $5 adults, $3.50 children. Airboat rides: $7 for 30-min trip to another Indian camp on an island in the heart of the Everglades. Open daily 9–5.*

Shopping

Biscayne National Park **Biscayne National Park Tour Boats.** T-shirts, snorkeling and diving gear, snacks, and information on Biscayne National Park are available at park headquarters north of the canal. A dive shop van with air compressor is parked south of the canal at Homestead Bayfront Park. *Tel. 305/247–2400. MC, V. Open daily. Office open 8–6.*

Everglades National Park **Flamingo Lodge Marina & Outpost Resort** (*see* Participant Sports, below). The gift shop sells mosquito repellent, Everglades guides, popular novels, T-shirts, souvenirs, and artwork. *Tel. 305/253–2241 or 813/695–3101. AE, DC, MC, V. Open Nov.–Mar. 9–8, though hours are extended during high season.*

Homestead Homestead's main shopping streets are Homestead Boulevard (U.S. 1), Krome Avenue (Rte. 997), where the heart of old Homestead has been historically themed with brick sidewalks, now attracting many antique stores, and Campbell Drive (S.W. 312th St., N.E. 8th St.). Shopping centers with major department stores are 10–20 miles north of Homestead along South Dixie Highway (U.S. 1).

Participant Sports and Outdoor Activities

Most of the sports and recreational opportunities in Everglades National Park and Biscayne National Park are related in some way to water or nature study, or both. Even on land, be prepared to get your feet wet on the region's marshy hiking trails. In summer, save your outdoor activities for early or late in the day to avoid the sun's strongest rays and use a sunscreen. Carry mosquito repellent at any time of year.

Water Sports
Boating Carry aboard the proper *NOAA Nautical Charts* before you cast off to explore the waters of the parks. The charts cost $15.95 each and are sold at many marine stores in south Florida, at the Convoy Point Visitor Center in Biscayne National Park, and in Flamingo Marina.

Waterway Guide (southern regional edition) is an annual publication, which many boaters use as a guide to these waters. Bookstores all over south Florida sell it, or you can order it directly from the publisher. *Communications Channels, Book Department, 6255 Barfield Rd., Atlanta, GA 30328, tel. 800/ 233–3359. Cost: $32.95 plus $3 shipping and handling.*

Canoeing The subtropical wilderness of southern Florida is a mecca for flat-water paddlers. In winter, you'll find the best canoeing that the two parks can offer. Temperatures are moderate, rainfall is minimal, and the mosquitoes are tolerable.

Before you paddle into the back country and camp overnight, get a required free permit from the rangers in the park where you plan to canoe (at Convoy Point, Elliott Key, and Adams Key for Biscayne; at Everglades City or Flamingo for Everglades. The Biscayne permit isn't valid for Everglades, and vice versa).

You don't need a permit for day trips, but tell someone where you're going and when you expect to return. Getting lost out here is easy, and spending the night without proper gear can be unpleasant, if not dangerous.

At Biscayne, you can explore five creeks through the mangrove wilderness within 1½ miles of park headquarters at Convoy Point.

Everglades has six well-marked canoe trails in the Flamingo area, including the southern end of the 100-mile Wilderness Waterway from Flamingo to Everglades City. North American Canoe Tours in Everglades City runs a three-hour shuttle service to haul people, cars, and canoes 151 road-miles between Everglades City and Flamingo.

The vendors listed below all rent aluminum canoes. Most have 17-foot Grummans. Bring your own cushions.

Biscayne National Park Tour Boats. At Convoy Point in Biscayne National Park. *Tel. 305/247–2400. Cost: $5 per hr., $17.50 for 4 hrs, $22.50 per day. No launch fee. MC, V. Office open daily 8:30–6.*

Everglades National Park Boat Tours. Gulf Coast Ranger Station in Everglades City. *Tel. 813/695–2591, in FL 800/445–7724. Cost: $15 per half day, $20 per day; Flamingo–Everglades City shuttle costs $100 round-trip with two canoes. MC, V. Open daily 8:30–4:30.*

North America Canoe Tours at Glades Haven. This outfitter rents canoes and runs guided Everglades trips approved by the National Park Service. *800 S.E. Copeland Ave., Box 5038, Everglades City 33929, tel. 813/695–4666. Canoes $20 the first day, $18 per day thereafter. Outfitter in 1990 opened a bed-and-breakfast in Everglades City called The Ivey House. Inquire for rates. No children under age 8 on guided tours. No pets in park campsites. Reservations required. MC, V. Open daily 7 AM–9 PM; guided trips Nov. 1–Mar. 31.*

Marinas Listed below are the major marinas serving the two parks. The dock masters at these marinas can provide information on other marine services you may need.

Black Point Marina. Facilities at this 155-acre Metro-Dade County Park with a hurricane-safe harbor basin, 5 miles north of Homestead Bayfront Park, include storage racks for 300 boats, 178 wet slips, 10 ramps, fuel, a bait-and-tackle shop, canoe-launching ramp, power-boat rentals, police station, and outside grill serving lunch and dinner, with bar. Shrimp fleet docks at the park. At east end of Coconut Palm Drive (S.W. 248th St.). From Florida's Turnpike, exit at S.W. 112th Avenue, go 2 blocks north, and turn east on Coconut Palm Drive. *24775 S.W. 87th Ave., Naranja, tel. 305/258–4092. AE, MC, V (restaurant only). Office open daily 8:30–5; park open 6 AM–sundown; restaurant open Thurs.–Sun. 11 AM–midnight. AE, MC, V.*

Marine Management. At Black Point Marina. Rents 15- to 20-foot open fishermen boats and bow riders. *Tel. 305/258–3500. MC, V. Open winter, weekdays 8–5, weekends 7–5; summer, weekdays until 6, weekends 7:30. Opening and closing times may vary. Closed Christmas.*

Pirate's Spa Marina. Just west of Black Point Park entrance. Shrimp boats dock along canal. Facilities include boat hoist, wet and dry storage, fuel, bait and tackle, and boat rental. *8701 Coconut Palm Dr. (S.W. 248th St.), Naranja, tel. 305/257–5100. No credit cards. Open weekdays 7 AM–sundown, weekends open 6 AM.*

Flamingo Lodge Marina & Outpost Resort. Fifty-slip marina rents 40 canoes, 10 power skiffs, 5 houseboats, and several private boats available for charter. There are two ramps, one for Florida Bay, the other for Whitewater Bay and the back country. The hoist across the plug dam separating Florida Bay from the Buttonwood Canal can take boats up to 26 feet long. A small marina store sells food, camping supplies, bait and tackle, and automobile and boat fuel. *Tel. 305/253–2241 from Miami, 813/*

695–3101 from Gulf Coast. AE, DC, MC, V. Open winter 6 AM–7 PM, summer 7–6.

Homestead Bayfront Park Bait and Tackle. Facilities include dock and wet slips, fuel, bait and tackle, ice, boat hoist, and ramp. The marina is near Homestead Bayfront Park's tidal swimming area and concessions. *North Canal Dr., Homestead, tel. 305/245–2273. AE, MC, V. Open weekdays 7–5, weekends 7–6; in the summer daily until 7.*

Diving
Dive Boats and Instruction

Biscayne National Park Tour Boats. This is the official concessionaire for Biscayne National Park. The center provides equipment for dive trips and sells equipment. Snorkeling and scuba trips include about 2 hours on the reefs. *Reef Rover IV and V*, aluminum dive boats, each carries up to 49 passengers. The resort course and private instruction lead to full certification. *Office and dive boat at Convoy Point. Mailing address: Box 1270, Homestead 33030, tel. 305/247–2400. Cost: $24.50 snorkeling, $34.50 scuba. Reservations required. Children welcome. AE, MC, V. Open daily 8–6. Snorkeling and scuba trips daily 1:30–5 PM; group charters any day.*

Dive Zone. This is the last dive store north of the Keys, and it rents, sells, and repairs diving equipment. Staff teaches all sport-diving classes, including resort course, deep diver, and underwater photography. The center does not have a boat; instead they use dive boats at Homestead Bayfront Park and at other places in the Keys. NAUI and PADI affiliation. *35414 S. Dixie Hwy., Florida City 33034, tel. 305/248–4050. AE, D, DC, MC, V. Open weekdays 10–8, Fri. 10–10; Sat. and Sun. 7–5. Open 24 hours during annual 4-day sport divers' lobster season (in July or Aug.).*

Fishing

The rangers in the two parks enforce all state fishing laws and a few of their own. Ask at each park's visitor centers for that park's specific regulations.

Swimming

Homestead Bayfront Park. This saltwater atoll pool, adjacent to Biscayne Bay, which is flushed by tidal action, is popular with local family groups and teenagers. Highlights include a newly installed tot lot playground, ramps for disabled people including a ramp that leads into the swimming area, and four new barbecues in the picnic pavilion. *N. Canal Dr., Homestead, tel. 305/247–1543. Admission: $3 per car, $5 admission on boat ramp, hoist available for $10. Open daily, 7 AM to sundown.*

Elliott Key. Boaters like to anchor off Elliott Key's 30-foot-wide sandy beach, the only beach in Biscayne National Park. It's about a mile north of the harbor on the west (bay) side of the key.

Bicycling and Hiking

Biscayne National Park. Elliott Key's resident rangers lead informal nature walks on a 1½-mile nature trail. You can also walk the length of the 7-mile key along a rough path that developers bulldozed before the park was created.

Everglades National Park. Shark Valley's concessionaire has rental bicycles. You may ride or hike along the Loop Road, a 15-mile round-trip. Yield right of way to trams. *Shark Valley Tram Tours, Box 1729, Tamiami Station, Miami 33144, tel. 305/221–8455. Cost: $2 per hr. No reservations. No credit cards. Rentals daily 8:30–3, return bicycles by 4.*

Ask the rangers for *Foot and Canoe Trails of the Flamingo Area,* a leaflet that also lists bike trails. Inquire about water

You've Let Your Imagination Go, Now Get Up And Follow Your Dreams.

For The Vacation You're Dreaming Of, Call American Express® Travel Agency At 1-800-YES-AMEX.*

American Express will send more than your imagination soaring. We'll fly you, sail you, drive you to any Fodor's destination and beyond. Because American Express believes the best vacations happen from Europe to the Orient, Walt Disney® World to Hawaii and everywhere in between.

For dependable service, expert advice, and value wherever your dreams take you, call on American Express. After all, the best traveling companion is a trustworthy friend.

AMERICAN EXPRESS **Travel Agency**

It's easy to recognize a good place when you see one.

American Express Cardmembers have been doing it for years.

The secret? Instead of just relying on what they see in the window, they look at the door. If there's an American Express Blue Box on it, they know they've found an establishment that cares about high standards.

Whether it's a place to eat, to sleep, to shop, or simply meet, they know they will be warmly welcomed.

So much so, they're rarely taken in by anything else.

Always a good sign.

levels and insect conditions before you go. Get a free back-country permit if you plan to camp overnight.

Dining

Although the two parks are wilderness areas, there are restaurants within a short drive of all park entrances: between Miami and Shark Valley along the Tamiami Trail (U.S. 41), in the Homestead-Florida City area, in Everglades City, and in the Keys along the Overseas Highway (U.S. 1). The only food service in either park is at Flamingo in the Everglades.

The list below is a selection of independent restaurants on the Tamiami Trail, in the Homestead–Florida City area, and at Flamingo. Many of these establishments will pack picnic fare that you can take to the parks. (You can also find fast-food establishments with carryout service on the Tamiami Trail and in Homestead-Florida City.)

Highly recommended restaurants are indicated by a star ★.

Category	Cost*
Very Expensive	over $60
Expensive	$40–$60
Moderate	$20–$40
Inexpensive	under $20

*per person, excluding drinks, service, and 6% sales tax.

Flamingo
American

Flamingo Restaurant. The view from this three-tier dining room on the second floor of the Flamingo Visitor Center will knock your socks off. Picture windows overlook Florida Bay, giving you a bird's-eye view (almost) of soaring eagles, gulls, pelicans, terns, and vultures. Try to dine at low tide when flocks of birds gather on a sandbar just offshore. Specialties include a flavorful, mildly spiced conch chowder; teriyaki chicken breast; and pork loin roasted Cuban-style with garlic and lime. The tastiest choices, however, are the seafood. If marlin is on the dinner menu, order it fried so that the moisture and flavor of the dark, chewy meat are retained. Picnic baskets available. They will cook the fish you catch if you clean it at the marina. *At Flamingo Visitor Center in Everglades National Park, Flamingo, tel. 305/253–2241 from Miami, 813/695–3101 from Gulf Coast. Reservations advised at dinner. Dress: casual. AE, DC, MC, V. Closed early May–mid-Oct. (The snack bar and Buttonwood Lounge at the marina store stay open all year to serve pizza, sandwiches, and salads.) Moderate.*

Florida City
Italian
★

Richard Accursio's Capri Restaurant and **King Richard's Room.** One of the oldest family-run restaurants in Dade County— since 1958—this is where locals dine out—business groups at lunch, the Rotary Club each Wednesday at noon, and families at night. Specialties include pizza with light, crunchy crusts and ample toppings; mild, meaty conch chowder; mussels in garlic-cream or marinara sauce; Caesar salad with lots of cheese and anchovies; antipasto with a homemade, vinegary Italian dressing; pasta shells stuffed with rigatoni cheese in tomato sauce; yellowtail snapper Française; and Key lime pie with plenty of real Key lime juice. *935 N. Krome Ave., Florida City, tel. 305/*

247–1544. Reservations advised. Dress: casual. AE, D, MC, V. Closed Sun. except Mother's Day. Closed Christmas. Moderate–Inexpensive.

Homestead
American

Potlikker's. This southern country-style restaurant takes its name from the broth—*pot liquor*—left over from the boiling of greens. Live plants dangle from the sides of open rafters in the lofty pinelined dining room. Specialties include a lemon-pepper chicken breast with lemon sauce, fresh-carved roast turkey with homemade dressing, and at least 11 different vegetables to serve with lunch and dinner entrées. For dessert, try Key lime pie—four inches tall and frozen; it tastes great if you dawdle over dessert while it thaws. *591 Washington Ave., tel. 305/248–0835. No reservations. Dress: casual. AE, MC, V. Closed Christmas Day. Inexpensive.*

Tiffany's. This country French cottage with shops and restaurant under a big banyan tree looks like a converted pioneer house with its high-pitched roof and lattice. That's because fourth-generation Miamian Rebecca DeLuria, who built it in 1984 with her husband, Robert, wanted a place that reminded her of the Miami she remembered. Teaberry-colored tables, moiré satin-like floral placemats, marble-effect floor tiles, fresh flowers on each table, and lots of country items lend to the tea-room style found here. Featured entrées include hot crabmeat au gratin, asparagus supreme (rolled in ham with hollandaise sauce), quiche of the day, and fettucini Alfredo. Homemade desserts are to die for: old-fashioned (very tall) carrot cake, strawberry whipped cream cake, and a harvest pie with double crust that layers apples, cranberries, walnuts, raisins, and a caramel topping. Stop in on Sunday for brunch, or any morning Monday–Saturday for breakfast. *22 N.E. 15th St., tel. 305/246–0022. Reservations accepted. Dress: neat but casual. AE, MC, V. No dinner. Closed Memorial Day, Labor Day, Christmas, New Year's Day. Inexpensive.*

Mexican

El Toro Taco. The Hernandez family came to the United States from San Luis Potosí, Mexico, to pick crops. They opened this Homestead-area institution in 1971. They make salt-free tortillas and nacho chips with corn from Texas that they cook and grind themselves. The cilantro-dominated salsa is mild for American tastes; if you like more fire on your tongue, ask for a side dish of minced jalapeño peppers to mix in. Specialties include chile rellenos (green peppers stuffed with meaty chunks of ground beef and topped with three kinds of cheese), and chicken *fajitas* (chunks of chicken marinated in Worcestershire sauce and spices, grilled in butter with onions and peppers, and served with tortillas and salsa). Bring your own beer and wine; the staff will keep it cold for you and supply lemon for your Corona beer. *1 S. Krome Ave., tel. 305/245–8182. No reservations. Dress: casual. No credit cards. Inexpensive.*

Seafood

Mutineer Restaurant. Former Sheraton Hotels builder Allan Bennett built this roadside restaurant with its indoor-outdoor fish and duck pond solid and stylish as a big-city hotel at a time (1980) when Homestead was barely on the map. Bilevel dining rooms (doubled in size in 1990) are up-scale with sea-scene dividers in etched glass, striped velvet chairs, original pirate art, stained glass, and a few portholes, but there's no excess. The Wharf Lounge behind its solid oak doors on ballbearing brass hinges is equally imaginative with magnified aquarium and nautical antiques such as a crow's nest with real stuffed crow, gold parrot, and treasure chest. The big menu features 18 seafood entrées plus another half dozen daily seafood specials, as well as game, ribs, and steaks. Favorites include quail & tail (quail stuffed with blended wild rice and a broiled Florida lobster tail), and snapper Oscar (topped with crabmeat and asparagus). Bathrooms are tiled and mirrored as beautifully as in hotel suites. Enjoy live music Thursday–Saturday evenings. *11 S.E. 1st Ave., tel. 305/245–3377. Reservations accepted. Dress: neat but casual. AE, D, DC, MC, V. Moderate.*

Tamiami Trail
American

The Pit Bar-B-Q. This place will overwork your salivary glands with its intense aroma of barbecue and blackjack oak smoke. You order at the counter, then come when called to pick up your food. Specialties include barbecued chicken and ribs with a tangy sauce, french fries, coleslaw, and a fried biscuit, and catfish, frogs' legs, and shrimp breaded and deep-fried in vegetable oil. *16400 S.W. 8th St., Miami, tel. 305/226–2272. Dress: casual. No reservations. Closed Christmas Day. MC, V. Inexpensive.*

American Indian

Miccosukee Restaurant. Murals with Indian themes depict women cooking and men engaged in a powwow. Specialties include catfish and frogs' legs breaded and deep-fried in peanut oil, Indian fry bread (a flour-and-water dough deep-fried in peanut oil), pumpkin bread, Indian burger (ground beef browned, rolled in fry bread dough, and deep-fried), and Indian taco (fry bread with chili, lettuce, tomato, and shredded cheddar cheese on top). *On Tamiami Trail, near the Shark Valley entrance to Everglades National Park, tel. 305/223–8380, ext. 332. No reservations. Dress: casual. AE, DC, MC, V. Inexpensive.*

Floridian

Coopertown Restaurant. A rustic 30-seat restaurant full of Floridiana, including alligator skulls, stuffed alligator heads, alligator accessories (belts, key chains, and the like). Specialties include alligator and frogs' legs, breaded and deep-fried in vegetable oil, available for breakfast, lunch, or dinner. *22700 S.W. 8th St., Miami, tel. 305/226–6048. Reservations accepted. Dress: casual. No credit cards. Inexpensive.*

Lodging

Many visitors to the two parks stay in the big-city portion of Greater Miami and spend a day visiting one or both of the parks. For serious outdoors people, such a schedule consumes too much time in traffic and leaves too little time for nature-study and recreation.

At Shark Valley, due west of Miami, you have no choice. Only the Miccosukee Indians live there; there is no motel.

Southwest of Miami, Homestead has become a bedroom community for both parks. You'll find well-kept older properties and shiny new ones, chain motels, and independents. Prices tend to be somewhat lower than in the Miami area.

Hotel and motel accommodations are available on the Gulf Coast at Everglades City and Naples.

The list below is a representative selection of hotels and motels in the Homestead area. Also included are the only lodgings inside either park. The rate categories in the list are based on the all-year or peak-season price; off-peak rates may be a category or two lower.

Category	Cost*
Very Expensive	over $120
Expensive	$90–$120
Moderate	$50–$90
Inexpensive	under $50

per room, double occupancy, excluding 6% state sales tax and modest resort tax

Flamingo Lodge Marina & Outpost Resort. This rustic low-rise wilderness resort, the only lodging inside Everglades National Park, is a strip of tentative civilization 300 yards wide and 1½ miles long. Accommodations are basic but attractive and well kept. An amiable staff with a sense of humor helps you become accustomed to alligators bellowing in the sewage-treatment pond down the road, raccoons roaming the pool enclosure at night, and the flock of ibis grazing on the lawn. The rooms have wood-paneled walls, contemporary furniture, floral bedspreads, and art prints of flamingos and egrets on the walls. Most bathrooms are near the door, so you won't track mud all over the room. Television reception has been improved with addition of a satellite dish, but you don't come here to watch TV. All motel rooms face Florida Bay but don't necessarily overlook it. The cottages are in a wooded area on the margin of a coastal prairie. Ask about reserving tours, skiffs, and canoes when you make reservations. Also inquire about the *M/V Bald Eagle*, the new 100-passenger tour boat for day and sunset cruises. *Box 428, Flamingo 33090, tel. 305/253–2241 from Miami, 813/695–3101 from Gulf Coast. 125 units with bath, including 101 motel rooms, one 2-bath suite for up to 8 people, 24 kitchenette cottages (2 for handicapped guests). Facilities: screened outdoor freshwater pool, restaurant, lounge, marina, marina store with snack bar, gift shop, coin laundry. AE, DC, MC, V. Lodge, marina, and marina store open all year; restaurant, lounge, and gift shop closed May 1–Oct. 31. Moderate.*

Holiday Inn. This low-rise motel is situated on a commercial strip. The best rooms look out on the landscaped pool and adjoining Banana Bar. Rooms have contemporary walnut furnishings and firm, bouncy mattresses. A guest laundry and fitness room were added in 1992. *990 N. Homestead Blvd., Homestead 33030, tel. 305/247–7020 or 800/HOLIDAY. 150 rooms with bath. Facilities: outdoor freshwater pool, restaurant and lounge with nightly entertainment, poolside bar, cable TV, massage shower heads. AE, D, DC, MC, V. Moderate.*

Hampton Inn. This two-story, 102-unit motel just off the highway has good clean rooms and some public-friendly policies. There's a free Continental breakfast daily, free local calls, and the TV gets the Disney Channel at no extra charge. All rooms have at least two upholstered chairs, twin reading lamps, and a desk and chair. Units are color-coordinated and carpeted. Baths have tub-showers. *124 E. Palm Dr., Florida City 33034, tel. 800/426–7866, 305/247–8833. Facilities: outdoor pool. AE, D, DC, MC, V. Moderate–Inexpensive.*

Camping
Biscayne National Park

You can camp on designated keys 7 miles offshore at primitive sites or in the backcountry. Carry all your food, water, and supplies onto the keys, and carry all trash off when you leave. Bring plenty of insect repellent. *Free. No reservations. No ferry or marina services. For backcountry camping, obtain a required free permit from rangers at Adams Key, Convoy Point, or Elliott Key.*

Everglades National Park

All campgrounds are primitive, with no water or electricity. Come early to get a good site, especially in winter. Bring plenty of insect repellent. *Admission: $8 per site in winter, free in summer, except for walk-in sites at Flamingo, which are $4. Stay limited to 14 days Nov. 1–Apr. 30. Check-out time 10 AM. Register at campground. Open all year.*

Long Pine Key. 108 campsites, drinking water, sewage dump station.

Flamingo. 235 drive-in sites, 60 walk-in sites, drinking water, cold-water showers, and sewage dump station.

Backcountry. 48 designated sites (2 accessible by land, others only by canoe), 14 with chickees (raised wood platforms with thatch roofs). All have chemical toilets, including the 29 ground sites. Four chickee sites and nine of the ground sites are within an easy day's canoeing of Flamingo; five of the ground sites are within an easy day's canoeing of Everglades City. Call ahead for information on handicap accessibility and updates. Carry all your food, water, and supplies in; carry out all trash. Get free permit from rangers at Everglades City or Flamingo. Permits issued for a specific site. Capacity and length of stay limited. Call for daily updates, but sites available first come, first served. *Flamingo Ranger Stn., Backcountry Reservations Office, Box 279, Homestead 33034, tel. 305/242–7700, 813/695–3101, ext. 182.*

4 Fort Lauderdale

Introduction

*Updated by
Herb Hiller*

If you think of Fort Lauderdale only as a spring-break mecca for collegians seeking sun, suds, and surf, your knowledge is both fragmentary and out of date. The 1960 film *Where the Boys Are* attracted hordes of young people to the city's beaches. And because Fort Lauderdale became a popular place for students on spring break, upscale visitors shunned the city at that time and, unfortunately, year-round as well. City officials intentionally discouraged college revelers after a record number of 350,000 appeared in 1985; by 1991 that number dropped to fewer than 15,000 (most have relocated to Daytona Beach and Panama City), while for the second straight year metropolitan visitorship neared a record five million.

Fort Lauderdale today emphasizes year-round family tourism focused on a wide assortment of sports and recreational activities, an extensive cultural calendar, artistic and historic attractions, and fine shopping and dining opportunities.

Sandwiched between Miami to the south and Palm Beach to the north along southeast Florida's Gold Coast, Fort Lauderdale is the county seat of Broward County. The county encompasses 1,197 square miles—17 square miles less than the state of Rhode Island. Broward County has 23 miles of Atlantic Ocean beach frontage, and it extends 50 miles inland to the west. A coastal ridge rising in places to 25 feet above sea level separates the coastal lowlands from the interior lowlands of the Everglades.

Broward County is named for Napoleon Bonaparte Broward, Florida's governor from 1905 to 1909. His drainage schemes around the turn of the century opened much of the marshy Everglades region for farming, ranching, and settlement. In fact, the first successful efforts at large-scale Everglades drainage took place within Broward County's boundaries.

Fort Lauderdale's first known white settler, Charles Lewis, established a plantation along the New River in 1793. The city is named for a fort that Major William Lauderdale built at the river's mouth in 1838 during the Seminole Indian wars.

The area was still a remote frontier when Frank Stranahan arrived in 1892 to operate an overnight camp on the river. Stranahan began trading with the Indians in 1901 and built a store, which later became his residence. It's now a museum.

Fort Lauderdale incorporated in 1911 with just 175 residents, but it grew rapidly during the Florida boom of the 1920s. Today the city's population of 150,000 remains relatively stable, while suburban areas bulge with growth. Broward County's population is expected to reach 1.4 million in 1995—more than double its 1970 population of 620,000. Most of the recent gains reflect changes in inland Broward's 28 municipalities. Once a home for retirees, Broward County now attracts younger working-age families as well.

New homes, offices, and shopping centers have filled in the gaps between older communities along the coastal ridge. Now they're marching west along I–75, I–595, and the Sawgrass Expressway. There the mammoth new Sawgrass Mills Mall (*see* Shopping, below) is a magnet for further development of the east Everglades. Meanwhile, downtown Fort Lauderdale is building skyscrapers and civic centers downtown to cement its position as the county's financial, commercial, and cultural hub. Chief facilities include the Broward County Main Library; the Broward Center for the Performing Arts, which opened in 1991; the Museum of Art; and the 2-mile Riverwalk (*see* Exploring Fort Lauderdale, below), where construction is complete on the north side of the New River. Distinguished from riverfront development in other Florida cities, the renewal project emphasizes historical, educational, and scenic attractions.

Broward County is developing a concentration of clean high-technology industries, including computer manufacturing, data processing, and electronics. Port Everglades, a major deep-water seaport, handles refined petroleum products and general cargo. A cruise terminal at Port Everglades caters to luxury liners, leaving the mass-market cruise business to the Port of Miami. A new $49-million, tri-level convention center opened in 1991 at Port Everglades, where next to come is a 33-acre, $250-million retail complex with a new hotel, shopping and dining mall, and cruise terminal all tied together with climate-controlled skywalks. A special-events hotline (tel. 305/765–4466), provides information about seasonal events. Information for senior citizens regarding special discounts at area lodgings, restaurants, and attractions is also provided; ask for the "Senior Super Saver" directory.

To accommodate the traffic that comes with all this growth, the Florida Department of Transportation in 1991 completed a major expansion of Broward County's road system (*see* Getting Around By Car, below). Even if you're stuck in traffic, you can still enjoy Broward County's near-ideal weather. The average temperature is about 75 degrees (winter average 66 degrees, summer average 84 degrees). Rainfall averages 65 inches a year, with 60% of the total occurring in afternoon thunderstorms June–October. The warm, relatively dry winters help to give the county about 3,000 hours of sunshine a year.

Essential Information

Arriving and Departing by Plane

Airport **Fort Lauderdale–Hollywood International Airport (FLHIA)**, (tel. 305/357–6100), 4 miles south of downtown Fort Lauderdale, is Broward County's major airline terminal. To get there off I–95, take the I–595 east exit to U.S. 1 and follow the signs to the airport entrance. From the south (Miami), exit on Griffin Road to U.S. 1 and follow the signs to the airport. In 1991 the airport completed the lengthening of its runways to 9,000 feet to accommodate jumbo jets. As a result, international charter service has expanded dramatically from the United Kingdom, Scandinavia, and Germany. Among North American carriers, Continental, Delta, USAir, United, Northwest Airlines, Braniff International, TWA, Air Canada, and American Airlines have all augmented their Fort Lauderdale schedules.

Between the Airport and Center City **Broward Transit**'s bus route No. 1 operates between the airport and its main terminal at N.W. 1st Street and 1st Avenue in the center of Fort Lauderdale. Service north from the airport begins daily at 5:40 AM; the last bus from the downtown terminal to the airport leaves at 9:30 PM. The fare is 85¢. Limousine service is available from **Airport Express** (tel. 305/527–8690) to all parts of Broward County. Fares range from $6 to $13 or more per person, depending on distance. Fares to most Fort Lauderdale beach hotels are in the $6–$8 range. Pickup points are at each of the new terminals.

Arriving and Departing by Car, Train, and Bus

By Car The access highways to Broward County from the north or south are Florida's Turnpike, I–95, U.S. 1, and U.S. 441; for a more scenic—and slower—drive, Rte. A1A, which generally parallels the beach area. The I–75 (Alligator Alley) connects Broward County with the west coast of Florida and recently has been expanded and upgraded to a four-lane interstate highway. The primary access road to Broward County from the west is I–595, paralleled by Rte. 84.

By Train **Amtrak** provides daily service to Broward County, with stops at Hollywood, Fort Lauderdale, and Deerfield Beach. *Fort Lauderdale station, 200 S.W. 21st Terr., tel. 305/463–8251; reservations, tel. 800/872–7245.*

Tri-Rail, which connects Broward, Dade, and Palm Beach counties, has six stations in Broward. All stations are west of I–95. Service operates daily except Sunday. Morning service begins northbound and southbound before 6:00; last trains leave from Miami and West Palm Beach around 7:30 PM. *Tel. 305/728–8445 or 800/TRI–RAIL (in Dade, Broward, and Palm Beach counties).*

By Bus **Greyhound/Trailways** (513 N.E. 3rd St., Ft. Lauderdale, tel. 305/764–6551).

Getting Around

By Car North-south I–95 now ties to east-west I–595, which carries high-speed traffic from westernmost Broward County to Fort Lauderdale–Hollywood International Airport in about 20 minutes. Except during rush hour, Broward County has become easy to get around.

Major bottlenecks in Broward are expected through mid-1994 on the 2-mile stretch of I–95 between S.R. 84 and Sunrise Boulevard, the last section of I–95 in the county to be scheduled for widening.

Car Rentals Rental car stations located directly in FLHIA include **Avis** (tel. 305/359–3255), **Budget** (tel. 305/359–4700), **Dollar** (tel. 305/359–7800), **Hertz** (tel. 305/359–5281), and **National** (tel. 305/359–8303).

By Bus **Broward County Mass Transit** serves the entire county. The fare is 85¢ (senior citizens, handicapped persons, and students 40¢) plus 10¢ for a transfer, with some bus routes starting as early as 5 AM; some continuing to 9 PM. Call for route information (tel. 305/357–8400). There are also special seven-day tourist passes for $8 that are good for unlimited use on all county buses. These are available at some hotels and at Broward County libraries.

By Taxi It's difficult to hail a taxi on the street; sometimes you can pick one up at a major hotel. Otherwise, phone ahead. Fares are not cheap; meters run at the rate of $2.20 for the first mile and

$1.50 for each additional mile, waiting time 25¢/minute. The major company serving the area is **Yellow Cab** (tel. 305/565–5400).

By Water Taxi **Water Taxi** (tel. 305/565–5507) provides service along the Intracoastal Waterway between Port Everglades and Commercial Boulevard 10 AM–1 AM. In 1992 new service began between Atlantic Boulevard and Hillsboro Boulevard in Pompano Beach. Taxis operate between noon and midnight. The boats stop at more than 30 restaurants, hotels, shops, and nightclubs; the fare is $4.50 one way, $9 round-trip, all-day pass $12 (no credit cards, reservations accepted).

Important Addresses and Numbers

Tourist Information The main office of the **Greater Fort Lauderdale Convention & Visitors Bureau** (tel. 305/765–4466) is at 200 E. Las Olas Boulevard, Suite 1500. The office is open weekdays 8:30–5. The Greater Fort Lauderdale Chamber of Commerce (tel. 305/462–6000, 800/22–SUNNY for brochures) is at 512 N.E. 3rd Ave., 33301. Other communities in Broward County also have individual chambers of commerce, including Dania (Box 838, Dania 33004, tel. 305/927–3377), Hollywood (4000 Hollywood Blvd., Ste. 265–South, Hollywood 33021, tel. 305/985–4000), Deerfield Beach (1601 E. Hillsboro Blvd., Deerfield Beach 33441, tel. 305/427–1050), and Pompano Beach (2200 E. Atlantic Blvd., Pompano Beach 33062, tel. 305/941–2940).

Emergencies Dial 911 for **police** and **ambulance** in an emergency.

Poison Control (tel. 800/282–3171).

Hospitals. The following hospitals have a 24-hour emergency room: **Holy Cross Hospital** (4725 N. Federal Hwy., Fort Lauderdale, tel. 305/771–8000; physician referral, tel. 305/776–3223), **Imperial Point Hospital** (6401 N. Federal Hwy., Fort Lauderdale, tel. 305/355–4888; physician referral, tel. 305/776–8500), and **Broward General Medical Center** (1600 S. Andrews Ave., Fort Lauderdale, tel. 305/355–4400; physician referral, tel. 305/355–4888).

24-Hour Pharmacies. Eckerd Drug (1385 S.E. 17th St., Fort Lauderdale, tel. 305/525–8173; and 154 University Dr., Pembroke Pines, tel. 305/432–5510). **Walgreens** (2855 Stirling Rd., Fort Lauderdale, tel. 305/981–1104; 5001 N. Dixie Hwy., Oakland Park, tel. 305/772–4206; and 289 S. Federal Hwy., Deerfield Beach, tel. 305/481–2993).

Special Services **Telecommunications for the Hearing-Impaired.** United Hearing and Deaf Services operates weekdays 8:30 to 5 (4850 W. Oakland Park Blvd., Suite 207, Lauderdale Lakes, tel. 305/731–7208). A telephone relay service operates 24 hours a day, seven days a week (tel. 305/731–7200).

Access for Handicapped Persons. Throughout Broward County, beaches, hotels, cruise ships, cultural centers, and rental cars are equipped with facilities for disabled people. The newest installation is a cedar wheelchair ramp on Fort Lauderdale Beach that leads to the water's edge. Expanded parking offers direct access to the beach. Other wheelchair-accessible facilities include Fisherman's Wharf, Ocean World, Jungle Queen cruise ship, Discovery Center, and Fort Lauderdale Historical Society. For details, contact the Greater Fort Lauderdale Convention & Visitors Bureau (Dept. MS, 200 E. Las Olas, Ste. 1500, Fort Lauderdale 33301, tel. 305/765–4466).

Guided Tours

The *Jungle Queen* operates a 155-passenger single-deck boat, and a 578-passenger double-decker designed to resemble an old-time steamboat. Both travel day and night up the New River through the heart of Fort Lauderdale. Three-hour day cruises depart 10 and 2 (adults $6.95, children 2–12 $4.95); four-hour dinner cruises at 7 ($20.95). The same company sends boats to Miami's Bayside Marketplace. All cruises leave from the Bahia Mar dock on Rte. A1A. *Tel. 305/462–5596 (Broward County), 305/947–6597 (Dade County). No credit cards.*

Las Olas Horse and Carriage operates Tuesday through Sunday evening between 7 and midnight. The New River Tour lasts 20 minutes and goes through the Riverwalk area ($8 per person); the Colee-Hammock Tour is 30 minutes and takes in old Fort Lauderdale ($12 per person). A new Royal Palm Tour through residential neighborhoods, Colee-Hammock, and Las Olas Boulevard takes 1¼ hours ($90 for up to 6 persons). Transportation between Las Olas Boulevard and the Broward County Center for the Performing Arts is available either one-way or round-trip ($45 or $80, for up to 6). *610 E. Las Olas Blvd., tel. 305/763–7393. Reservations advised.*

River/Walking Tours are co-sponsored by the Fort Lauderdale Historical Society. A two-hour tour of the New River and a portion of the Intracoastal Waterway runs Saturday mornings from 10 to noon. The boat leaves from the Chart House Restaurant dock (301 S.W. 3rd Ave.) and the tour costs $13.50. Walking tour schedules vary by season but generally last 2–3 hours with a limit of 20 persons. *219 S.W. 2nd Ave., Fort Lauderdale 33301, tel. 305/463–4431. Reservations required. MC, V.*

South Florida Trolley Tours (tel. 305/522–7701; 305/528–6340 driver's night beeper) offers fully narrated 90-minute tours on *Lolly the Trolley* daily from 9 to 5. The trolley stops at all major hotels from Rte. A1A and Sunrise Boulevard to 17th St. and Eisenhower Boulevard. Pick-ups are generally along Las Olas Boulevard, but with reservations the trolley can also pick up passengers elsewhere nearby. Passengers can board and reboard the trolley all day for $10 per person and thus can sightsee, dine, and shop at their own pace (children 7–12 $5, under 6 free). *MC, V.*

Exploring Fort Lauderdale

Numbers in the margin correspond to points of interest on the Fort Lauderdale Area map.

Central Fort Lauderdale is diverse, picturesque, and surprisingly compact. Within a few blocks you'll find modern high-rise office buildings; a historic district with museums, restaurants, and antiques shops; a scenic riverfront drive; upscale shopping; and the only vehicular tunnel in Florida—all within 2 miles of the beach.

This tour begins on the beach at Las Olas Boulevard and Rte. A1A. Go north on Rte. A1A along **the beach,** with hotels, restaurants, and shops on your left, the ocean on your right.

Through much of this stretch, the beach road (Rte. A1A) and beachfront are being improved with planters, palms, and a beachfront wall of ornamental entrances, whorled and scrolled in European styling. Throughout the beach area, distinctive signage, street furniture, and a central wave theme will unify the area and become the symbol of the beachfront revitalization. The entire project will stretch 2½ miles and cost approximately $26 million. More than ever, the boulevard will be worth promenading. As part of improvements, a new road is being constructed west of present Hwy. A1A which will accommodate southbound traffic. Turn left off A1A at Sunrise Boulevard, then right into **Hugh Taylor Birch State Recreation Area.** Amid the 180-acre park's tropical greenery, you can stroll along a nature trail, visit the Birch House Museum, picnic, play volleyball, pitch horseshoes, ride a rental bike or paddleboats, and canoe. *3109 E. Sunrise Blvd., tel. 305/564-4521; concessions tel. 305/564-4572. Admission: $3.25 per car. Open 8-sundown. Ranger-guided nature walks Fri. 10:30.*

You can visit the **Bonnet House** anytime but winter. To do so, when leaving the park, cross Sunrise Boulevard south. This lyrical house built by artist Frederic Bartlett is on land he was given by his first father-in-law, Hugh Taylor Birch. The house and its subtropical 35-acre estate has since been donated to the Florida Trust for Historic Preservation. From May through November the house is open to visitors with its original works of art, including whimsically carved animals, a swan pond, and, most of all, its tranquility. *900 N. Birch Rd., tel. 305/563-5393. Reservations required. Admission $7.50 adults, $5 senior citizens, students, and military personnel; children under 6 free.*

Leaving Bonnet House, return to A1A, go south to Las Olas Boulevard, turn right, and cross the Intracoastal Waterway. You're now westbound through **The Isles,** Fort Lauderdale's most expensive and prestigious neighborhood, where the homes line a series of canals with large yachts beside the seawalls. When you reach the mainland, Las Olas becomes an upscale shopping street with Spanish-Colonial buildings housing high-fashion boutiques, jewelry shops, and art galleries. The heart of the **Las Olas Shopping District** is from S.E. 11th Avenue to S.E. 6th Avenue.

Turn left on S.E. 6th Avenue, and visit **Stranahan House,** home of pioneer businessman Frank Stranahan, and oldest standing structure in Fort Lauderdale. He arrived in 1892 and began trading with the Seminole Indians. In 1901 he built a store, and later made it his home. Now it's a museum with many of the Stranahans' furnishings on display. Friday evening socials are held September through May from 5:30 to 8 and are a good way to meet local people. For $5 the social includes three drink tickets, food, and house tours. *1 Stranahan Pl. (335 S.E. 6th Ave.), tel. 305/524-4736. Admission: $3, $2 children under 12. Open Wed., Fri., Sat. 10-3:30.*

Return to Las Olas Boulevard, turn right on Andrews Avenue, and park in one of the municipal garages. Visit the **Museum of Art,** which features a major collection of works from the CoBrA (Copenhagen, Brussels, and Amsterdam) movement, plus American Indian, pre-Columbian, West African, and Oceanic ethnographic art. Edward Larabee Barnes designed the museum building, which opened in 1986. In late 1991, the museum opened its exhibit of the $50 million collection of 224 works by

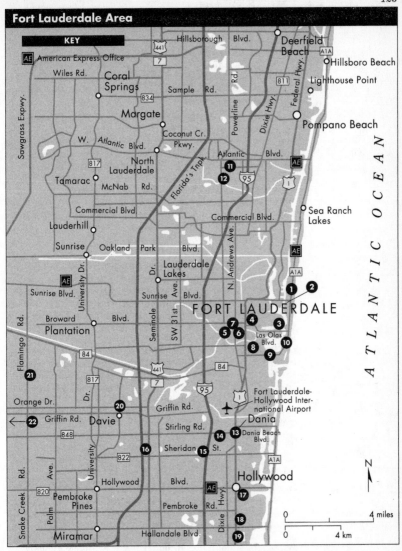

Fort Lauderdale Area

KEY

AE American Express Office

Art and Cultural
Center of Hollywood, **17**

Atlantis the
Water Kingdom, **14**

Bonnet House, **2**

Brooks Memorial
Causeway, **9**

Broward County
Main Library, **6**

Dania Jai-Alai
Palace, **13**

Davie Arena for
Rodeo, **20**

Everglades Holiday
Park and
Campground, **22**

Flamingo Gardens, **21**

Gulfstream Park
Race Track, **19**

Hollywood Greyhound
Track, **18**

Hugh Taylor Birch
State Recreation
Area, **1**

International Swimming
Hall of Fame Museum
and Pool, **10**

The Isles, **3**

Museum of Art, **5**

Ocean World, **8**

Pompano Harness
Track, **11**

Quiet Waters
Park, **12**

Riverwalk, **7**

Seminole Native
Village, **16**

Stranahan House, **4**

Topeekeegee
Yugnee Park, **15**

celebrated Ashcan School artist William Glackens and other early-20th-century American painters. Portions of this largest donation of art on record in Florida were expected to be on view in 1992. *1 E. Las Olas Blvd., tel. 305/525–5500. Admission: $3.25 adults, $2.75 seniors, $1.25 students, free under 12. Free 1-hr highlight tours Tues. 1 and 6:30 PM, Thurs. and Fri. at 1, Sat., Sun. 2 PM. Open Tues. 11–9, Wed.–Sat. 10–5, Sun. noon–5. Parking nearby in municipal garage.*

6 Walk 1 block north to the **Broward County Main Library.** Designed by Marcel Breuer, the library is distinguished by its display of many works from Broward's Art in Public Places program, including a painting by Yaacov Agam, wood construction by Marc Beauregard, an outdoor aluminum-and-steel sculpture by Dale Eldred that responds to the sun and artificial night lights, and ceramic tile by Ivan Chermayeff. Productions from theater to poetry readings are presented in a 300-seat auditorium. *100 S. Andrews Ave., tel. 305/357–7444; 305/357–7457 for self-guided Art in Public Places walking tour brochure. Admission free. Open. Mon.–Thurs. 10–9, Fri.–Sat. 9–5, Sun. 1–5. Closed holidays.*

Go north to Broward Boulevard, turn left between 5th and 6th avenues into the Arts and Science District parking garage. You **7** can now walk to the palm-lined **Riverwalk.** As part of a planned multi-million-dollar revitalization of downtown Fort Lauderdale, the 2-mile, $4.65 million Riverwalk consists of 28.8 open and developed acres that connect the following: the **Arts and Science District,** with the new $52 million Broward Center for the Performing Arts (which opened in 1991); the **Historic District/Entertainment Center** that houses many museums and restaurants, and the historic Stranahan House and Riverside Hotel. **The Broward Center for the Performing Arts** (tel. 305/462–0222) includes the 2,700-seat Au-Rene Theater for major productions, and the 595-seat Amaturo Theater for more intimate performances. More than 550 programs a year are planned. The Arts and Science District features an indoor-outdoor **Esplanade** (opened in 1990), and an education and performance park for children with exhibits that offer informative lessons on south Florida's climate and environment.

Just north of the esplanade is the **Discovery Center,** which includes a science museum in the **New River Inn,** Fort Lauderdale's first hotel, and a pioneer residence museum in the restored **King-Cromartie House.** The museum is a child-oriented place with hands-on exhibits that explore optical illusions and bend rays of light, an insect zoo, a glass-front beehive, a loom, a computer center, and a small planetarium. The center will be replaced by a new $29 million, 300,000-square-foot **Museum of Discovery and Science** by 1993, and will include a 300-seat IMAX theater. *231 S.W. 2nd Ave., tel. 305/462–4115. Admission: $5, $4 children and seniors, children under 3 free. Open Tues.–Fri. and Sun. noon–5; Sat. and school holidays in winter 10–5. Museum closed Mon. in summer.*

East of the Esplanade along the Riverwalk is the **Fort Lauderdale Historical Society Museum,** which surveys the city's history from the Seminole Indian era to World War II. A model in the lobby depicts old Fort Lauderdale. The building also houses a research library and a bookstore. *219 S.W. 2nd Ave., tel. 305/463–4431. Admission $2 adults, $1 children 6–12, children under 6 free. Open Tues.–Sat. 10–4, Sun. 1–4.*

Return to your car; go to Broward Boulevard, turn right and go east to Federal Highway (U.S. 1). Turn right and go south through the **Henry E. Kinney Tunnel,** named for a founder of Fort Lauderdale; Florida's only tunnel dips beneath Las Olas Boulevard and the New River.

⑧ Continue south on Federal Highway to S.E. 17th Street, then turn left. About a mile east is the entrance to **Ocean World,** an intimate marine park. Six shows daily feature trained dolphins and sea lions. Display tanks hold sharks, sea turtles, alligators, and river otters. You can feed and pet a dolphin here. *1701 S.E. 17th St., tel. 305/525–6611. Admission: $9.95 adults, $7.95 children 4–12, under 4 free. Boat tour admission: $6 adults, $5 children 4–12, under 4 free. Tours at 12:30, 2:50, and 5:05 last about an hour. Open 10–6, last show starts 4:15.*

Across 17th Street is the new **Greater Fort Lauderdale/Broward County Convention Center,** home of boat shows, antique shows, and mammoth meetings.

⑨ Go east on S.E. 17th Street across the **Brooks Memorial Causeway** over the Intracoastal Waterway, and bear left onto Seabreeze Boulevard (Rte. A1A). You'll pass through a neighborhood of older homes set in lush vegetation before emerging at the south end of Fort Lauderdale's beachfront strip. On your left at **Bahia Mar Resort & Yachting Center,** novelist John McDonald's fictional hero, Travis McGee, is honored with a plaque at the marina where he docked his houseboat. *801 Seabreeze Blvd., tel. 305/764–2233 or 800/327–8154.*

⑩ Three blocks north, visit the **International Swimming Hall of Fame Museum and Pool,** where in 1991 a new 10-lane, 50-meter pool with locker rooms and weight rooms was completed. Also included is an expanded exhibition building that features photos, medals, and other souvenirs from major swimming events around the world. *1 Hall of Fame Dr., museum tel. 305/462–6536, pool tel. 305/523–0994. Museum admission: $3 adults, $2 children 6–21, senior citizens, and military personnel, $5 family. Pool admission: $3 nonresident adults, $2 nonresident students, $1 resident students, senior citizens, military personnel. Open Mon.–Sat. 10–5, Sun. 11–4.*

This concludes the central Fort Lauderdale tour. To return to the starting point, continue north on Seabreeze Boulevard to Las Olas Boulevard.

Broward

Time Out To start a brief exploration of the North Broward, take I–95 North to Cypress Creek Road. Turn west 2 miles to 21st Avenue, then right on 21st to the first light (McNab Road), right again onto 20th Avenue, and right to the end of the street. On your left in a warehouse district is **Acme Smoked Fish** where, in a scene reminiscent of New York's East Side in its sights and smells, you're among deli mavens relishing the smoked salmon, whitefish, and herrings. Acme also sells deli meats and crackers so you can nosh while soaking up the atmosphere. *6704 N.W. 20th Ave., tel. 305/974–8100. No credit cards. Open Tues.–Sat. 9–4.*

Return to I–95 and go north to the Atlantic Boulevard exit and go west to Power Line Road, which will lead you to the popular

⑪ **Pompano Harness Track** (1800 S.W. 3rd St., Pompano Beach), Florida's only harness track. Early in 1992 the 327-acre facility was put up for sale after six years of unprofitable operations. For now, however, it's business as usual. The Top 'O The Park restaurant overlooks the finish line. Post time: 7:30; call for dates, tel. 305/972-2000.

⑫ A unique water skiing cableway is at **Quiet Waters Park,** just north of the racetrack, on Power Line Road. **Ski Rixen** (tel. 305/429-0215) offers waterskiing lessons for beginners, plus skis and life vests. A cable pulls the skiers. If you're skilled enough, you can try all sorts of variations to the two-hand, two-ski way of skimming across the water. *Tel. 305/360-1315. Admission: weekdays free, weekends and holidays $1 driver, 75¢ per passenger; children under 5 free. Open daily 8–sunset.*

Return to Atlantic Boulevard and turn east to Hwy. A1A. Turn north along scenic route A1A passing Lighthouse Point, the brightest light in the southeast; Hillsboro Beach, with its million-dollar homes along the ocean and the Intracoastal Waterway; and Deerfield Beach, with its popular public facilities.

Southern Broward

In southern Broward County, an exploration can include Native American crafts and lifestyles, high-stakes pari-mutuel wagering, and a unique natural park, all within the same driving loop.

⑬ Start with the **Dania Jai-Alai Palace** (301 E. Dania Beach Blvd., Dania, tel. 305/428-7766), offering one of the fastest games on the planet from early November–April (winter season) and May–November (summer season).

⑭ Follow Dania Beach Boulevard west to U.S. 1, turn left, go south to Stirling Road, turn right, and go west to **Atlantis The Water Kingdom,** one of the world's largest water-theme parks. It has 2 million gallons of water in 45 pools and water slides up to seven stories high, plus children's entertainment. Highlights include a wave pool and an activity pool with trolleys, slides, and rope ladders, and a new attraction known as The Awesome Twosome, a pair of completely enclosed slides that take two at a time. Riders on Thunderball, the steepest water slide, reach speeds near 40 mph. The park sets minimum and maximum height requirements for participants in some activities. *2700 Stirling Rd., Hollywood, tel. 305/926-1000. Admission: $13.95 adults, $6.95 senior citizens over 55, $10.95 children 3–11. Summer hours 10 AM to between 5 and 10 PM; phone for hours at other times of year.*

⑮ Travel on I–95 south to the Sheridan Street exit, then west to **Topeekeegee Yugnee Park.** Rentals include sailboats, sailboards, paddleboats, and canoes. *3300 N. Park Rd., tel. 305/985-1980. Admission weekends and holidays: $1 car and driver, 75¢ each passenger, children under 6 free. Open daily sunrise–sunset.*

⑯ Drive from Sheridan Street west to U.S. 441/Rte. 7, turn right, and go north through the **Seminole Native Village,** a reservation of the never-conquered Seminole Indian tribe. The Indians sell native arts and crafts and run a high-stakes bingo parlor (4150 N. Rte. 7, tel. 305/961-5140, for recorded information or 305/961-3220, for general information). Four bingo games daily; call recording for information. Continue north to **Anhinga Indian Museum and Art Gallery,** where Joe Dan and Virginia Osceola display a collection of artifacts from the Seminoles and other American Indian tribes. They also sell contemporary Indian art and craft objects. *5791 S. Rte. 7, tel. 305/581–8411. Open daily 9–5. MC, V.*

⑰ Newly opened in 1992 was the **Art and Cultural Center of Hollywood,** set in a 1924 Mediterranean-style one-time residence. The community hopes that the Sunday concerts and daily art exhibits will help to revitalize the downtown area. Additional galleries and a museum store are planned for the future. *1650 Harrison St., Hollywood, tel. 305/921–3274. Admission: $2 Wed.–Sat., $3 Sun. concerts, donations accepted Tues. Open Tues.–Sat. 10–4, Sun. 1–4.*

⑱ From U.S. 441/Rte. 7 south to Pembroke Road go east to Federal Highway to the **Hollywood Greyhound Track** (831 N. Federal Highway, Hallandale, tel. 305/454–9400). Open day after Christmas until late April.

⑲ Take Federal Highway south to **Gulfstream Park Race Track** (901 S. Federal Hwy., tel. 305/454–7000), home of the Florida Derby, one of the southeast's foremost horse racing events, and the Breeders Cup. Race dates always during winter.

Inland

Between the coastal cities and the watery wilderness of the Everglades, urban sprawl is rapidly devouring Broward County's citrus groves and cow pastures. If you go inland, you can still find vestiges of the county's agricultural past.

⑳ The **Davie Arena for Rodeo** at Orange Drive and Davie Road holds rodeos throughout the year. *6591 S.W. 45th St. (Orange Dr.), Davie 33314, tel. 305/797–1145. Admission for jackpot events: $4 adults, $2 children; five-star rodeo, $8 adults, $5 children.*

Now, take Davie Road south past Orange Drive, cross the South New River Canal, and turn right on Griffin Road. Go half a mile west to **Spykes Grove & Tropical Gardens,** where the entire family can hop aboard a tractor-pulled tram for a 15-minute tour of working citrus groves, which have been in operation since 1944. A bear born in captivity, gators, prairie dogs, roosters, and peacocks also are on exhibit. *7250 Griffin Rd., tel. 305/583–0426. Admission free. Tours hourly 11–4. Open daily Oct.–June, 9–5:30.*

㉑ Head 7 miles west on Griffin Road and turn right onto Flamingo Road to **Flamingo Gardens.** Flamingo Island offers gators, crocodiles, river otters, birds of prey, a plant house, and Everglades Museum in the pioneer Wray Home. A new, 23,000-square-foot walk-through aviary was added in 1991. Admission includes a 1½-hour guided tram ride through a citrus grove and wetlands area. *3750 Flamingo Rd., tel. 305/473–2955. Admission: $6 adults, $2.50 children 4–12. Senior citizens and AAA members 20% discount. Open daily 9–5.*

㉒ Return to Griffin Road and go almost 8½ miles west until the road ends at the edge of the Everglades. There you'll find **Everglades Holiday Park and Campground,** which offers a 60-minute narrated airboat tour and an alligator-wrestling show featuring Seminole Indians. The park has a 100-space campground that accommodates recreational vehicles and tents. *21940 Griffin Rd., Ft. Lauderdale 33332, tel. 305/434–8111 (Broward County), 305/621–2009 (Miami). Tour: $12 adults, $6 children, under 3 free. MC, V.*

What to See and Do with Children

Butterfly World. This attraction in Tradewinds Park South is a screened-in aviary in a tropical rain forest on 2.8 acres of land, where thousands of caterpillars pupate and emerge as butterflies. Up to 150 species flit through the shrubbery. Many are so tame they will land on you. Best time to go is in the afternoon; school groups fill the place in the mornings. *3600 W. Sample Rd., Coconut Creek, tel. 305/977–4400. Admission: $7.95 adults, $5 children 3–12, $6.95 senior citizens. AE, MC, V. Open Mon.–Sat. 9–5, Sun. 1–5.*

Discovery Center (*see* Exploring Fort Lauderdale, above).

Ocean World (*see* Exploring Fort Lauderdale, above).

Atlantis The Water Kingdom (*see* Exploring Southern Broward, above).

Shopping

Shopping Districts
Major Malls

Broward Mall, the county's largest upscale shopping center, features such stores as Burdines, J.C. Penney, and Sears. *8000 W. Broward Blvd., Plantation, tel. 305/473–8100. Open Mon.–Sat. 10–9, Sun. noon–5:30.*

Fashion Mall features Macy's and Lord and Taylor among 150 shops, boutiques, and restaurants in a three-level, 669,000-square-foot landscaped, glass-enclosed facility. *University Blvd., Plantation, tel. 305/370–1884. Open Mon.–Sat. 10–9:30, Sun. noon–6.*

Galleria Mall on Sunrise Boulevard, just west of the Intracoastal Waterway, occupies more than one million square feet and includes Neiman-Marcus, Lord & Taylor, Saks Fifth Avenue, and Brooks Brothers. *Tel. 305/564–5015. Open 10–9 Mon.–Sat., noon–5:30 Sun.*

Pompano Fashion Square in Pompano Beach has 110 shops with three department stores and food stalls. *2255 N. Federal Hwy., tel. 305/943–4683. Open Mon.–Sat. 10–9, Sun. noon–5:30.*

Sawgrass Mills Mall is a candy-colored Disney-style discount mall—said to be the largest in America—that opened in late 1990 with more than two million square feet of stores, restaurants, and entertainment activities. The mall sprawls at the intersection of Flamingo Road and Sunrise Boulevard in west Broward *Open Mon.–Sat. 10–9:30, Sun. 11–6.*

Antiques
More than 75 dealers line U.S. 1 (Federal Hwy.) in Dania, a half mile south of the Fort Lauderdale International Airport and a half mile north of Hollywood. Open 10–5 every day but Sunday. Exit Griffin Road East off I–95.

Beaches

The Fort Lauderdale area boasts an average temperature of about 75 degrees and 23 miles of oceanfront beach. Parking is readily available, often at parking meters. At the southern end of Broward County, **John U. Lloyd Beach State Recreation Area** (6503 N. Ocean Dr., Dania) offers a beach for swimmers and sunners, but also 251 acres of mangroves, picnic facilities, fishing, and canoeing. *Open 8 AM–sunset. Park tel. 305/923–2833. Admission: $3.25 per car. Call the park number for information about the concession, scheduled to reopen in 1992.*

Throughout Broward County, each municipality along the Atlantic has its own public beach area. Hollywood also has a 2.5-mile Broadwalk, edged with shops and eateries. Pompano Beach and Lauderdale-by-the-Sea have piers you can fish off of in addition to the beaches. The most crowded portion of beach in this area is along the **Fort Lauderdale "Strip,"** which runs from Las Olas Boulevard north to Sunrise Boulevard.

In past years, there have been serious oil spills and dumpings by freighters and tankers at sea, and the gunk has washed ashore in globules and become mixed with the beach sand. The problem has been somewhat eased, but some hotels still include a tar-removal packet with the toilet amenities. If you're concerned, ask at the desk of your hotel or motel.

Participant Sports

Biking   Cycling is popular in Broward County, though statistically this is one of the most dangerous places to ride in Florida. Popular routes are along A1A, especially early in the morning before traffic builds, and many shops along the beach rent bikes. Other popular riding areas are the more rural parts of the county—the **Parkland** area of northwestern Broward and the vast **Weston** community in the southwest. Weston has already installed some 10 miles of the 21 total miles of bike lanes planned for the community. Along the I–595 corridor the Rte. 84 bike path provides 6 miles for off-street cycling from University Drive to Markham Park. However, between Rte. 7 and the Florida Turnpike, Rte. 84 merges with I–595 and is closed to cyclists. Traveling from the east, cyclists along this stretch must use Davie Boulevard; from the west, Peters Road. Both are north of the corridor. South of the corridor, cyclists must use Griffin Road. A new 330-meter velodrome—first in Florida—is scheduled to open by late September 1992 at Brian Piccolo Park in Cooper City, at Sheridan Street and N.W. 101st Avenue. The track will be open to the public most of the time. Visiting cyclists in Broward County can request a new route map scheduled for publication in 1993. For details, contact the **County Bicycle Coordinator** (tel. 305/357–6661).

Diving   Good diving can be enjoyed within 20 minutes of the shore along Broward County's 25-mile coast. Among the most popular of the county's 80 dive sites is the 2-mile-wide, 23-mile-long Fort Lauderdale Reef.

Broward County features Florida's most successful artificial reef-building program, which began in 1984 with the sinking of a 435-foot freighter donated by an Oklahoma marine electronics manufacturer. Since then more than a dozen houseboats, ships, and oil platforms have been sunk to provide habitat for fish and other marine life, as well as to help stabilize beaches. The most famous sunken ship is the 200-foot German freighter *Mercedes*, which was blown ashore in a violent Thanksgiving storm onto Palm Beach socialite Mollie Wilmot's pool terrace in 1984; the ship was purposefully sunk. Today it lies a mile off Fort Lauderdale beach. For more information, contact the Greater Fort Lauderdale Convention & Visitors Bureau (*see* Important Addresses and Numbers, above).

Dive Boats and Instruction All **Force E** stores rent scuba and snorkeling equipment. Instruction is available at all skill levels. Dive boat charters are available. *2700 E. Atlantic Blvd., Pompano Beach, tel. 305/943–3483. Open in winter Mon.–Sat. 8–7, Sun. 8–5; in summer weekdays 8–8:30, Sat. 8–7, Sun. 8–5. 2104 W. Oakland Park Blvd., Oakland Park, tel. 305/735–6227. Open winter weekdays 10–8:30, Sat. 8–7, Sun. 8–4; summer weekdays 8 AM–9 PM, Sat. 8–7, Sun. 8–4. AE, D, MC, V.*

Lauderdale Diver offers packages with the Marriott Hotel & Marina and Fort Lauderdale Oceanside Inn, which include transportation to Tugboat Annie's in Dania, from where its 42-foot fully equipped diveboat departs. Dive trips last approximately three to four hours; nonpackage reef trips are also open to divers for $35, to snorkelers for $25, including snorkel equipment; scuba gear is extra. PADI affiliated. *1334 S.E. 17th St. Causeway, Fort Lauderdale, tel. 305/467–2822 or 800/654–2073. AE, D, DC, MC, V. Open in winter weekdays 10–6, Sat. 8–6, Sun. 8–1; in summer weekdays 9–7, Sat. 8–7, Sun. 8–1.*

Pro Dive, the area's oldest diving operation, offers packages with Bahia Mar Resort & Yachting Center, from where its 60-foot fully equipped boat departs. Nonpackage snorkelers can go out for $25 on the 4-hour dive trip, or for $20 on the 2-hour snorkeling trip, which includes snorkel equipment but not scuba gear. *Bahia Mar Resort & Yachting Center, Rte. A1A, Fort Lauderdale, tel. 305/761–3413 or 800/772–DIVE outside FL. AE, MC, V.*

Fishing Deep-sea and freshwater fishing are year-round pursuits in Broward. Fishing piers draw anglers for pompano, amberjack, bluefish, snapper, blue runners, snook, mackerel, and Florida lobsters. Pompano Beach's **Fisherman's Wharf** extends 1,080 feet into the Atlantic. The cost is $1.95 for adults, 95¢ for children under 10; rod-and-reel rental is $4.75. **Anglin's Fishing Pier** in Lauderdale-by-the-Sea reaches 875 feet and can be fished off 24 hours a day. Fishing is $2.50 for adults and $1.75 for children up to 12, tackle rental $5.

Charters Two primary centers for charter boats are Fort Lauderdale's **Bahia Mar Yachting Center,** and the **Fish City Marina** on Highway A1A and Hillsboro Inlet in Pompano Beach. Half-day charters usually run from $200 to $250 for up to six persons; full days between $400 and $475. Skipper and crew plus bait and tackle are included. Split-parties can be arranged at a cost of about $50 per person. Among marinas catering to freshwater fishing are **Sawgrass Recreation** and **Everglades Holiday Park,** where fisherpeople can rent a 14-foot, flat-bottomed John boat carrying up to four persons for about $30–$32.50 for five hours. Tackle rents for $5–$8; bait is extra. For details contact Greater Fort Lauderdale Convention & Visitors Bureau (*see* Important Addresses and Numbers, above).

Golf More than 50 courses, public and private, green the landscape in metro Fort Lauderdale, including some of the most famous championship links—such as the Eagle Trace, Weston Hills (site of the PGA Honda Classic) and the Bonaventure Country Club.

Spas If you watch "Lifestyles of the Rich and Famous" on TV, you'll recognize the names of Greater Fort Lauderdale's two world-famous spas, the Bonaventure Resort & Spa and Palm-Aire Spa Resort. At each resort, women comprise 75%–80% of the spa clientele. Both resorts offer single-day spa privileges to nonguests. Price and availability of services vary with seasonal demand; resort guests have priority. At each resort, day users may receive a body massage, exercise class, facials, herbal wrap, spa-cuisine lunch, and other spa facilities and services. Bring your own sneakers and socks. The spa provides everything else you'll need. Each spa will help you design a personal exercise-and-diet program tied to your lifestyle at home. If you already have an exercise program, bring it with you. If you have a medical problem, bring a letter from your doctor.

Bonaventure Resort and Spa (250 Racquet Club Rd., Fort Lauderdale, tel. 305/389–3300 or 800/327–8090), which underwent a $1-million face-lift in 1992 offers complimentary caffeine-free herbal teas in the morning, fresh fruit in the afternoon. Staff nutritionist follows American Heart Association and American Cancer Society guidelines, and can accommodate macrobiotic and vegetarian diets. Full-service beauty salon open to the public.

Palm-Aire Spa Resort (2601 Palm-Aire Drive N., Pompano Beach, tel. 305/972–3300 or 800/272–5624) is a 192-room, 750-acre health, fitness and stress-reduction spa offering exercise activities, personal treatments, and calorie-controlled meals. It's 15 minutes from downtown Fort Lauderdale.

Spectator Sports

For tickets to sporting events, call Ticketmaster (tel. 305/523–3309).

Baseball The New York Yankees hold spring training in 7,000-seat Fort Lauderdale Stadium (5301 N.W. 12th Ave., Fort Lauderdale, tel. 305/776–1921). The Fort Lauderdale Yankees compete between April and August in the Florida State League, as do the Pompano Beach Miracles at Pompano Municipal Stadium (1799 N.E. 8th St., tel. 305/783–2111).

Rugby The Fort Lauderdale Knights play rough and ready on the green at Holiday Park. *Off Federal Hwy., 2 blocks south of Sunrise Blvd., Fort Lauderdale, tel. 305/561–5263 for a recorded message. Admission free. Games Sept.–Apr., Sat. 2 PM.*

Dining

The list below is a representative selection of independent restaurants in Fort Lauderdale and Broward County, organized by type of cuisine. Unless otherwise noted, they serve lunch and dinner.

Highly recommended restaurants are indicated by a star ★.

Category	Cost*
Very Expensive	over $55
Expensive	$35–$55
Moderate	$15–$35
Inexpensive	under $15

per person, excluding drinks, service, and 6% sales tax

American **Burt & Jack's.** This restaurant, situated at the far end and most scenic lookout of Port Everglades, has been around in some capacity since the late 1970s. Finally, after three restaurants failed here, in 1984, Burt Reynolds and Jack Jackson hit it right and, despite scarce signage, diners find their way through the port-management maze. Behind the heavy mission doors and bougainvillea guests are rewarded with Maine lobster, steaks, and chops. The two-story gallery of hacienda-like dining rooms surrounded by glass have stunning views of the Intracoastal Waterway and John U. Lloyd State Park. Come to this very romantic spot Saturday or Sunday early evening for cocktails (served from 4:30, dinner from 5) and watch the cruise ships steam out. *Berth 23, Port Everglades, Fort Lauderdale, tel. 305/522–2878. Reservations advised. Jacket required. Dinner only. AE, DC, MC, V. Closed Christmas. Expensive.*

★ **Cafe Max.** As you enter Cafe Max, you're greeted by the aroma of fragrant spices issuing from the open theater kitchen. The decor includes art deco–style black wood chairs, original creations, and cut flowers. Booth seating is best; the tables are quite close together. Owner-chef Oliver Saucy combines the best of new American cuisine with traditional *escoffier* cooking. Specialties include Anaheim chili peppers stuffed with Monterey Jack cheese; mushroom duxelles served with goat cheese sauce; duck and smoked mozzarella ravioli with sun-dried tomatoes and basil butter; soft-shell crab with fresh tomato-jicama relish; and grilled veal chops. Daily chocolate dessert specials include hazelnut chocolate cappuccino torte and white-chocolate mousse pie with fresh raspberries. Other desserts include fresh fruit sorbets and homemade ice cream served with sauce *anglaise* and fresh raspberries. *2601 E. Atlantic Blvd., Pompano Beach, tel. 305/782–0606. Reservations advised. Dress: neat but casual. Dinner only. AE, D, DC, MC, V. Closed July 4, Super Bowl Sun. Expensive.*

Bimini Boatyard. With sky-high sloped roof, loads of windows, and paddlefans, this is a rarity among architecturally distinctive restaurants: inexpensive menu, ambience, and a quality bar. Try the Sam Adams with a loaf of Bimini bread or buffalo chicken wings. Heartier fare? Go for the *fettuccine al salmone affumicato* (smoked salmon, capers, whole-grain mustard, white wine, cream, and leeks). The extensive menu includes salads, burgers, and dishes from the cookbooks of the Bahamas, Jamaica, and Indonesia (grilled chicken breast with peanut sauce). The restaurant is on the 15th Street canal, and there is seating outside where the yachts tie up, or in. On weekends Bimini hosts progressive jazz bands. *1555 S.E. 17th St., tel. 305/525–7400. Reservations accepted for groups. Dress: casual. Limited menu after 11. AE, MC, V. Closed Christmas. Moderate.*

Ernie's Bar-B-Q & Lounge. Soup you can chew, thick barbecue between slabs of Bahama bread, and a wacky wall collection of

Fort Lauderdale Area Dining and Lodging

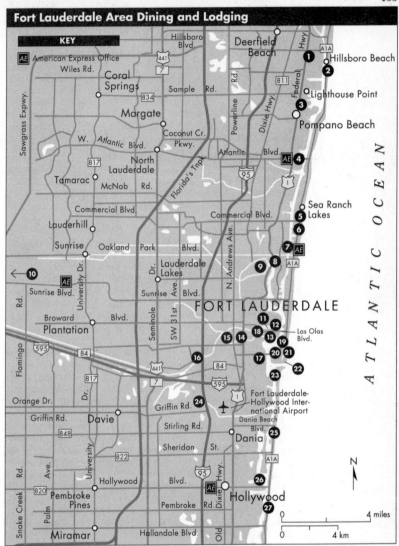

Lodging

Bahia Cabana Beach Resort, **19**

Banyan Marina Apartments, **11**

Carriage House Resort Motel, **2**

Di Vito By the Sea, **26**

Driftwood On the Ocean, **27**

Lago Mar Resort Hotel & Club, **22**

Marriott's Harbor Beach Resort, **21**

Pier 66 Resort and Marina, **20**

Pier Pointe Resort, **6**

Riverside Hotel, **13**

Tropic Seas Resort Motel, **5**

Dining

Bimini Boatyard, **17**

Burt & Jack's, **23**

Cafe Max, **4**

Cap's Place, **3**

Casa Vecchia, **12**

Don Arturo, **24**

Down Under, **7**

Ernie's Bar-B-Q & Lounge, **14**

Grainary Cafe, **1**

Il Tartuffo, **8**

Martha's, **25**

Old Florida Seafood House, **9**

Rennaissance Resturant, **10**

Rustic Inn Crabhouse, **16**

Santa Lucia, **18**

Shirttail Charlie's, **15**

memorabilia from a previous owner make Ernie's a must. Since 1976, Jeff Kirtman (from Brooklyn) has run this two-story eatery, which has an open-deck patio upstairs overlooking six-lane Federal Highway. The downstairs murals tout zany slogans and are adorned with former owner Ernie Siebert's dodo birds. Current owner Kirtman has supplied plenty of new reasons for visiting, including his conch-rich thick chowder, the hot open BBQ pork and beef sandwiches, and the combo ribs and chicken dinner with corn on the cob and baked beans. *1843 S. Federal Hwy., Fort Lauderdale, tel. 305/523–8636. No reservations. Dress: casual. MC, V. Inexpensive.*

Continental **Down Under.** When Al Kocab and Leonce Picot opened Down Under in 1968, the Australian government sent them a boomerang as a gift. The name actually describes the restaurant's location, below a bridge approach at the edge of the Intracoastal Waterway. The two-story structure was built to look old, with walls of antique brick deliberately laid off-plumb. Dishes include a classic cobb salad, Florida seafoods—snapper, crab, lobster—duck, and beef Wellington, all in traditional presentations. Other specialties include fresh Belon oysters and littleneck clams from Maine; Florida blue crab cakes; Brutus salad (Down Under's version of Caesar salad); fresh Idaho trout lightly sautéed and topped with Florida blue crab and hollandaise sauce. Desserts include Key lime pie with meringue, crème brûlée, and pecan squares. *3000 E. Oakland Park Blvd., tel. 305/563–4123. Reservations advised. Dress: neat but casual. AE, MC, V. Expensive.*

Martha's. Situated on the Intracoastal across from a 417-acre mangrove preserve, just downstream of the Dania Boulevard Bridge, the restaurant evokes sheer elegance. The downstairs decor includes tables adorned with orchid buds, fanned napery, etched glass dividers, brass, and rosewood, and the outdoor patio is surrounded by a wildly floral mural. Piano music accompanies happy hour, and at night, a band and dancing set a supper-club mood. The upstairs dining area (reached by elevator) is casual, with a tropical setting of painted orchids, stained glass, and wave-shaped outdoor furniture. The same menu downstairs and up features outstanding seafood preparations: flaky dolphin in a court-bouillon; shrimp dipped in a piña colada batter, rolled in coconut, panfried with orange mustard sauce; and snapper prepared 17 ways. An assortment of rolls and banana bread come with entrées. For dessert, try fresh sorbet and vanilla and chocolate ice cream topped with meringue and hot fudge brandy sauce. *6024 N. Ocean Dr., Hollywood, tel. 305/923–5444. Reservations advised. Dress: neat but casual downstairs; casual upstairs. AE, DC, MC, V. Expensive.*

Cuban **Don Arturo.** Waiters in tuxedos belie the friendly style of this family-run, romantically lit restaurant popular with the courthouse crowd. Avoid the party room that's near a noisy service area. If you're new to Cuban food, try the tri-steak sampler (chicken filet, palomilla steak, and pork filet), or one of the dinners for two, such as the *zarzuela de mariscos* (assorted seafood and fish smothered in tangy Spanish red sauce). Wash it down with the homemade sangria. English is spoken in this restaurant located four stoplights west of I–95, just north of Davie Boulevard. *1998 S.W. 27th Ave., tel. 305/584–7966 (also at 6522 W. Atlantic Blvd., Margate, tel. 305/968–1608). Reservations accepted. Dress: neat but casual. Dinner only Sun.*

AE, D, DC, MC, V. Closed July 4, Thanksgiving, Christmas, New Year's Day. Moderate.

Italian **Casa Vecchia.** This old house (*casa vecchia*) stands beside the
★ Intracoastal Waterway, surrounded by a formal garden where
you can watch boats cruise past. The garden also grows herbs
that flavor the restaurant's fare. Casa Vecchia was built in the
late 1930s, and diners are encouraged to roam through the
building to admire antique furnishings and original statuary
and paintings. Spanish tiles decorate Casa Vecchia's walls and
many tabletops. The menu changes every three months, but
lately it's been leaning toward lighter fare, with specialties
such as cannelloni Casa Vecchia (escarole leaves rolled with
veal, spinach, and Parmesan cheese), *capellini d'Angelo* (angel
hair pasta with sweet peas, prosciutto, and tomato cream
sauce), broiled swordfish with charmoula vinaigrette, and an
ossobucco. Desserts include full-flavored sorbets of fresh seasonal fruit prepared on the premises and *zabaglione freddo alla
frutta* (cold sabayon with Grand Marnier and fresh fruit). *209
N. Birch Rd., tel. 305/463–7575. Reservations advised. Jacket
preferred. AE, MC, V. Dinner only. Expensive.*

Santa Lucia. "You gotta taste the ocean," says owner/chef
Angelo Ciampa, 43 years in restaurants, who now draws
packed houses to his little 12-table storefront restaurant next
to the fashionable Riverside Hotel on Las Olas Boulevard. The
place smells like it ought to at home: pungent with a lot of subtle wafts. Try the *tuna carpaccio* (fresh tuna with capers, olive
oil, parmesan cheese, and fresh Italian parsley) or the *rigatoni
à la Russa* (tomato, garlic, hot pepper, parmesan, and basil
with a splash of vodka). The *zuccotto* (a homemade sponge
cake), is made with whipped cream, liqueurs, roasted
pinenuts, almonds, and walnuts. Ask for the Moretti beer, a
full-bodied Italian gift to the world. Or choose from three dozen
Italian wines. *602 E. Las Olas Blvd., tel. 305/525–9530. Reservations advised. Dress: neat but casual. AE, MC, V. No lunch.
Closed Sun. and Mon. in summer; closed Aug. Expensive.*

Il Tartufo. Only 16 tables are set here in a hint of a Ligurian
garden with a cherub fountain. Specials include fresh truffles
in November and December, but exquisite preparations can be
found year-round in this family-run restaurant. Try an antipasto of portobello mushrooms with white wine, garlic, olive oil,
herbs, and lemon; or a jumbo shrimp on radicchio flavored with
balsamic vinegar, garlic, olive oil, and cilantro. Exceptional
pastas include: cannelloni stuffed with parmesan and ricotta
cheeses and spinach in a béchamel-tomato sauce; a home-made
pappardelle pasta (wide noodles) with pesto sauce; and ravioli
stuffed with veal in a white Genovese sauce. *2980 N. Federal
Hwy., Fort Lauderdale, tel. 305/564–0607. Reservations advised. Dress: casual but neat. AE, MC, V. Dinner only. Closed
Mon. Moderate.*

Natural **Grainary Cafe.** Tucked away in the little Palm Plaza on the west
★ side of Federal Highway, this is the premiere natural food restaurant in the county. Recently it expanded from 50 to 90 seats
in a café setting, offering gourmet vegetarian food priced for
family pocketbooks. Lunch specials include kasha veggie stew,
tofu potato casserole with vegetable, and sweet potato
ratatouille. In the evening entrées come with brown rice; unlimited bread basket (including macrobiotic brown rice bread,
pita, and outstanding sourdough rolls) with miso-tahini spread
and soy margarine; as well as soup or salad. House-filleted

fresh fish is served in a lemon-ginger sauce, broiled, Cajun-blackened, or in a West Indian sauté that's served hot and spicy or mild and plain. You can get a rice burger with marinara or tahini or a bean and veggie burrito in a corn tortilla with salsa. *847 S. Federal Hwy., Deerfield Beach, tel. 305/360–0824. Reservations accepted. Dress: casual. AE, D, MC, V. BYOB. No lunch Sun. Closed Christmas. Inexpensive.*

Seafood
★

Cap's Place. This restaurant, located on an island previously inhabited by a rum runner, boasts having served such celebrities as Winston Churchill, Franklin D. Roosevelt, and John F. Kennedy. "Cap" was Captain Theodore Knight, born in 1871, who floated a derelict barge with partner-in-crime Al Hasis to the area in the 1920s. Today, the rustic restaurant, built atop the site, is run by descendants of Hasis who make freshness and excellence a priority. Baked wahoo steaks are lightly glazed and meaty; the long-cut french fries arouse gluttony; hot and flaky rolls are baked fresh several times a night, and tangy lime pie is the finishing touch. *Cap's Dock, 2765 N.E. 28th Ct., Lighthouse Point, tel. 305/941–0418. Follow the double-line road leading east on N.E. 24th St. off Federal Hwy. 2 blocks north to Pompano Fashion. No reservations. Dress: casual. AE, MC, V. Dinner only. Closed Sun. June–Nov. Expensive–Moderate.*

Old Florida Seafood House. Owner Bob Wickline has run this traditional seafood restaurant since 1978 with a West Virginian's eye toward giving value for money so he keeps his trade: plain on atmosphere, friendly on price. Nothing's frozen, nothing portion-controlled. He'll bring out a whole swordfish to show that it's fresh or take you to the cutting room with him. Best recommendation: Local waiters, waitresses, bartenders, and fellow restaurateurs all patronize the place that's not gourmet, just good. Try the veal Gustav (sautéed veal topped with a lobster tail), and a snapper New Orleans (sautéed with mushrooms and artichokes, laced with a light brown sauce). There's usually a 30-minute wait weekends. *1414 N.E. 26th St., Wilton Manors, tel. 305/566–1044. Also at 4535 Pine Island Rd., Sunrise, tel. 305/572–0444. Dress: neat but casual. AE, MC, V. No Sat. lunch. Closed Thanksgiving. Moderate.*

Rustic Inn Crabhouse. Wayne McDonald started with a cozy one-room roadhouse saloon in 1955 when this was a remote service road just west of the little airport. Now, the plain, rustic place situated around the New River Waterway seats 700. Since its opening, the owners have sold about as many garlic crabs as the other McDonald has sold burgers. Steamed crabs, seasoned with garlic and herbs, spices, and oil, are served with mallets on tables covered with newspapers; peel-and-eat shrimp is served either Key West–style with garlic and butter, or spiced and steamed with Old Bay seasoning. The big menu includes other seafood items as well. Pies and cheesecakes are on offer for dessert. *4331 Ravenswood Rd., Fort Lauderdale, tel. 305/584–1637. No reservations. Dress: casual. AE, D, DC, MC, V. Closed Thanksgiving, Christmas. Moderate.*

Shirttail Charlie's. You can watch the world go by from the outdoor deck or upstairs dining room of Shirttail Charlie's. Boats glide up and down the New River. Sunday–Thursday diners may take a free 30–40 minute after-dinner cruise on the 26-foot, 28-passenger *Shirttail Charlie's Express*, which chugs upriver past an alleged Al Capone speakeasy. Charlie's itself is built to look old, with 1920s tile floor that leans toward the water. Florida-style seafood offerings include an alligator-tail appetizer served with *tortuga* sauce (a béarnaise with turtle broth and sherry); conch served four ways; crab balls; swordfish bites; blackened tuna with Dijon mustard sauce; crunchy coconut shrimp with a not-too-sweet piña colada sauce; and a superbly tart Key lime pie with graham cracker-crust. *400 S.W. 3rd Ave., tel. 305/463–3474. Reservations advised upstairs. Dress: casual but neat. AE, D, MC, V. Moderate.*

Seafood **Renaissance Restaurant.** This gourmet restaurant, in the Bonaventure Resort and Spa, five-star-rated by the Confrérie de la Chaine des Rôtisseurs, features mesquite-grilled seafood and California cuisine with Florida adaptations. You dine in a rain forest setting, with views of a waterfall surrounded by palm and ficus trees, ferns and blooming flowers, and a pond with variegated foot-long carp. Specialties include chilled cream of avocado and cucumber soup; hot cream of poblano pepper soup with chunks of brie; a spinach-and-bean sprout salad with pickled eggs and rosemary vinaigrette dressing; whole wheat fettuccine sautéed with chunks of Maine lobster, scallops, and chives in a lobster sauce; mako shark in a lime-parsley-butter sauce. *250 Racquet Club Rd., tel. 305/389–3300 or 800/327–8090. Reservations required. Jacket preferred. AE, DC, MC, V. Dinner only. Expensive.*

Lodging

In Fort Lauderdale, Pompano Beach, and the Hollywood-Hallandale area, dozens of hotels line the Atlantic Ocean beaches. You can find accommodations ranging from economy motels to opulent luxury hotels with posh, pricey suites. An innovative Superior Small Lodging program, set up by the Greater Fort Lauderdale Convention and Visitors Bureau and administered by the hospitality department of Broward County's Nova University has led to substantial upgrading of many smaller properties. Some are described below. Inland, the major chain hotels along I–95 north and south of the airport cater primarily to business travelers and overnight visitors en route to somewhere else.

Wherever you plan to stay in Broward County, reservations are a good idea throughout the year. Tourists from the northern United States and Canada fill up the hotels from Thanksgiving through Easter. In summer, southerners and Europeans create a second season that's almost as busy. The list below is a representative selection of hotels and motels, organized by price and alphabetically. The rate categories in the list are based on the all-year or peak-season price; off-peak rates may be a category or two lower.

Highly recommended hotels are indicated by a star ★.

Category	Cost*
Very Expensive	over $120
Expensive	$90–$120

Moderate	$50–$90
Inexpensive	under $50

*All prices are for a standard double room, excluding 6% state sales tax and nominal tourist tax.

Lago Mar Resort Hotel & Club. The Banks family has owned this sprawling resort since the early 1950s. Under Walter Banks it draws lots of customers back again because of the easygoing management style that leaves guests feeling they're in a much smaller place. After a half-dozen expansions in different architectural styles, the eclectic look helps make guests feel they're in their own compound. Everyone shares the broad beach in this Harbor Beach section of the city, which is cut off from the rowdiness that sometimes affects the beachfront farther north. If you like a larger room, ask for a newer wing, although you'll pay less for the older. *1700 S. Ocean Lane, 33316, tel. 305/523–6511 or 800/255–5246. On the ocean just south of 17th St. causeway. 180 rooms with bath, including 135 suites. Facilities: 2 outdoor heated pools, 4 tennis courts, 2 volleyball courts, 4 shuffleboard courts, miniature golf, putting green, room service. AE, DC, MC, V. Very Expensive.*

Marriott's Harbor Beach Resort. Fort Lauderdale's only AAA-rated five-diamond hotel is a 14-story tower on 16 acres of oceanfront and has a free-form pool with a cascading waterfall. Built in 1984, its guest rooms were renovated in 1989. Room furnishings are light wood with mauve, pink, blue, and green hues; each room has a balcony facing either the ocean or the Intracoastal Waterway. *3030 Holiday Dr., 33316, tel. 305/525–4000 or 800/228–9290. 624 rooms with bath, including 36 suites, 108 nonsmoker rooms, 7 rooms for handicapped guests. Facilities: 1,100 ft of beach frontage, cabanas, windsurfing, Hobie cats, 65-foot catamaran, parasailing, outdoor heated freshwater pool and whirlpool, 5 tennis courts, fitness center, men's and women's saunas, masseuse, 3 boutiques, 5 restaurants, 3 lounges, in-room minibars, HBO, TV movies, complimentary 1-hr. weekly adult bike tours. AE, DC, MC, V. Very Expensive.*

★ **Pier 66 Resort and Marina.** Phillips Petroleum built Fort Lauderdale's landmark high-rise resort, best known for its revolving rooftop Pier Top Lounge. Its tower and lanai lodgings are "tops" from the ground up. The 17-story tower dominates a 22-acre spread that includes a 142-slip marina. A complete spa was added in 1989 and all rooms were renovated in 1989/90. *2301 S.E. 17th St., 33316, tel. 305/525–6666, 800/432–1956 (FL) 800/327–3796 (rest of US). 388 rooms with bath, including 8 suites. Facilities: 7 restaurants and lounges, water taxi to beach, outdoor freshwater pool, heated Jacuzzi, full-service marina with 142 wet slips for boats up to 200 ft long, scuba diving, snorkling, parasailing, small boat rentals, waterskiing, fishing and sailing yacht charters, 2 clay tennis courts, indoor health club with saunas and exercise equipment, massage therapy. AE, DC, MC, V. Very Expensive.*

Bahia Cabana Beach Resort. *Boating Magazine* ranks this resort's waterfront bar and restaurant among the 10 best. Rooms are spread out in five contiguous buildings furnished in tropical-casual style. Best of the 116 rooms and suites are #129—a two-bedroom suite with private terrace overlooking the tanning garden and pool, and #245—a one-bedroom suite with private deck that overlooks the yacht basin and skyline. Rooms in the 500 Building are more motel-like and overlook the parking lot, but rates here are lowest. The bar-restaurant is far enough from guest rooms so that the nightly entertainment does not disturb anyone. *3001 Harbor Dr., Fort Lauderdale 33316, tel. 305/524–1555, 800/BEACHES (U.S.), 800–3BEACH (Canada), or 800/922–3008 (FL). 116 rooms and suites with bath. Facilities: 3 heated freshwater pools, Jacuzzi, saunas, marina shuffleboard court, general store, restaurant, cafe, pool bar, patio bar. AE, D, DC, MC, V. Expensive.*

Pier Pointe Resort. Built in the 1950s, this oceanfront resort in Lauderdale-by-the-Sea, a block off the main street (Highway A1A), a block from the fishing pier, and backed by the beach, reminds one of the Gold Coast 40 years ago. The newly aqua-colored canopied entry opens onto two- and three-story buildings (most units with kitchens) set among brick pathways on cabbage palm lawns. The attractive wood pool deck is set off by sea grapes and rope-strung bollards. Rooms are plain, comfortable, and have balconies. All linens and drapes were redone in 1991. *4324 E. Mar Dr., Lauderdale-by-the-Sea 33308, tel. 305/776–5121 or 800/331–6384. 106 suites, efficiencies, and apartments with bath. Facilities: beach, 3 heated freshwater pools, gardens, barbecues. AE, DC, MC, V. Expensive.*

★ **Riverside Hotel.** This six-story hotel, on Fort Lauderdale's most fashionable shopping thoroughfare, was built in 1936, and has been steadily upgraded since 1987. In 1991 and 1992 80 rooms received new soft goods; the rest of the units are scheduled for 1992–1993. In-room coffee makers are a new feature, too. The tropical murals are the work of Bob Jenny, who painted a New Orleans–style mural across 725 square feet of the hotel's Las Olas facade, and whose pieces also appear at the President's Camp David retreat. An attentive staff includes many with the hotel for two decades or more. Each room is unique, with antique oak furnishings, framed French prints on the walls, in-room refrigerators, and European-style baths. Best rooms face south, overlooking the New River; worst rooms, where you can hear the elevator, are the 36 series. *620 E. Las Olas Blvd., 33301, tel. 305/467–0671, 800/325–3280. 117 rooms with bath, including 5 suites, 15 nonsmoker rooms. Facilities: heated freshwater pool beside the New River, 540 ft of dock with mooring space available by advance reservation, volleyball court, 2 restaurants, poolside bar. AE, DC, MC. Expensive.*

Tropic Seas Resort Motel. It's only a block off A1A, but it might as well be a mile. A million-dollar location directly on the beach, the motel is 2 blocks from municipal tennis courts. Built in the 1950s, units are plain but clean and comfortable, with tropical rattan furniture and ceiling fans. Managers Linda and Joe Surace maintain the largely repeat family-oriented clientele. Added features include a weekly wiener roast and rum swizzle party—both are good opportunities to mingle with other guests. *4616 El Mar Dr., Lauderdale-by-the-Sea 33308, tel. 305/772–2555. 16 rooms, efficiencies, apartments with bath. Facilities: beach, heated freshwater pool, shuffleboard, barbecue. AE, D, DC, MC, V. Expensive.*

★ **Banyan Marina Apartments.** Outstanding waterfront apartments on a residential island just off Las Olas Boulevard feature imaginative landscaping that includes a walkway through the upper branches of a banyan tree, dockage for eight yachts, and exemplary housekeeping. Luxurious units with leather sofas, springy carpets, real potted plants, sheer curtains and full drapes, and jalousies for sweeping the breeze in make these apartments as comfortable as any first-class hotel—but for half the price. Also included is a full kitchen, dining area, water view, and beautiful gardens. This is Florida the way you want it to be. *111 Isle of Venice, tel. 305/524–4430, fax 305/764–4870. Canalside just east of downtown on the way to the beach. 10 hotel rooms, efficiencies, and 1- and 2-bedroom apartments. Facilities: swimming pool, waterfront deck. MC, V. Expensive–Moderate.*

★ **Carriage House Resort Motel.** Very clean and tidy, this very good 30-unit beachfront motel sits 1 block from the ocean. Run by a French-American couple, the two-story, all white, black-shuttered colonial-style motel is actually two buildings connected by a second-story sun deck. Steady improvements have been made to the facility, including the addition of new furniture and Bahama beds that feel and look like sofas. Kitchenettes are equipped with quality utensils. Rooms are self-contained and quiet. *250. S. Ocean Blvd., Deerfield Beach 33441, tel. 305/427–7670. 30 rooms, efficiencies, apartments with bath. Facilities: heated pool, shuffleboard. AE, MC, V. Moderate.*

Driftwood on the Ocean. This attractive motel, built in 1959, occupies three buildings, and its lawn faces the beach at the secluded south end of Surf Road. Most units have a kitchen, and all are tropical in feel and have balconies. *2101 S. Surf Rd., Hollywood 33019, tel. 305/923–9528. 49 rooms, efficiencies, apartments with bath; 39 with kitchen. Facilities: beach, heated pool, shuffleboard, bicycles, laundry, barbecue. AE, MC, V. Moderate.*

The Arts and Nightlife

For the most complete weekly listing of events, read the "Showtime!" entertainment insert and events calendar in the Friday *Fort Lauderdale News/Sun Sentinel.*

Tickets are sold at individual box offices and through Ticketmaster (tel. 305/523–3309 in Broward County), a computerized statewide sales system.

The Arts **Broward Center for the Performing Arts** (201 S.W. 5th Ave.,
Theater Fort Lauderdale, tel. 305/522–5334) is the waterfront centerpiece of Fort Lauderdale's new outdoor complex. More than 500 cultural and recreational-themed events a year are scheduled at the performing arts center, including Broadway musicals, plays, dance, symphony and opera, rock, film, lectures, comedy, and children's theater. *See* Exploring Fort Lauderdale, above, for details.

Parker Playhouse (808 N.E. 8th St., Holiday Park, Fort Lauderdale, tel. 305/764–0700) features Broadway plays, musicals, drama, and local productions.

Sunrise Musical Theatre (5555 N.W. 95th Ave., Sunrise, tel. 305/741–7300) stages Broadway musicals, a few dramatic plays with name stars, and concerts by well-known singers throughout the year. The theater is 14 miles west of Fort Lauderdale Beach via Commercial Boulevard.

Vinnette Carroll Theatre (503 S.E. 6th St., Fort Lauderdale, tel. 305/462–2424), a multiethnic theater company, housed in a renovated church, is known for such Broadway hits as "Your

Arms Too Short to Box with God," and "Don't Bother Me I Can't Cope."

Concerts **Bailey Concert Hall** is a popular place for classical music concerts, dance, drama, and other performing arts activities, especially October–April. *Central Campus of Broward Community College, 3501 S.W. Davie Rd., tel. 305/475–6884 for reservations.*

The Florida Philharmonic Orchestra, south Florida's only fully professional orchestra, is Broward-based but performs in six locations in Broward, Dade, and Palm Beach counties. It offers a variety of series and individual-performance tickets; write for schedule. *1430 N. Federal Hwy., 33304, tel. 305/561–2997; (Dade County), 305/945–5180 (Boca Raton) 407/392–5443; (Palm Beach) 407/659–0331; 800/226–1812 (Ticketmaster statewide). Office open weekdays 9–5. AE, MC, V.*

The Fort Lauderdale Opera Guild presents the current production of the Greater Miami Opera and of the Palm Beach Opera, as well as productions of the Guild itself, in the Broward Center for the Performing Arts. For tickets, contact the Guild office. *333 S.W. 2nd St., 33312, tel. 305/728–9700. Office open weekdays 9–5. AE, MC, V.*

Nightlife **Cheers.** Lots of parties (Capricorns' night, full-moon night,
Bars and Roseanne Barr sing-alike night) and a "happy birthday club"
Nightclubs when celebrants enjoy bottomless mugs, entice those seeking fun to this woody night spot with two bars and dance floor. Monday is New Orleans jazz; other days mainly rhythm and blues. *941 E. Cypress Creek Rd., tel. 305/771–6337. Bands nightly 10:30–3:30, plus Sun. open mike jam session 7–midnight. Grazing menu served 11:30 AM–4 AM. Cover charge Fri. $3. AE, D, MC, V.*

Confetti. Since the mid-1980s, this has been the high energy "in" spot for 35–50 year olds. A DJ spins top 40 tunes for dancers as they are doused with confetti, and helium balloons bob around the 10 bars. Bartenders blow flames and do tricks, waitresses serve blue vodka-based drinks from racks of vials. The Saturday night motto is "come and party with 6,000 of your closest friends." At 11 PM when the upstairs opens you can walk through the game room to the **Reunion Room** with lots of black light and paintings by Art Institute students. The music is alternative and progressive, but if the disco scene isn't your thing, you can tune in one of the four screens that show wildlife videos. *2660 E. Commercial Blvd., tel. 305/776–4081. $5 cover. Open Wed.–Fri. 8–2, Sat. 8–3. Closed Mon.–Tues. Reunion Room features local and national acts 1st set only Fri. 11:30 PM–12:30 AM. Fri. no cover in Confetti 8–10.*

Crocco's is the action place for singles. Free drinks for women Wed. nights from 8 to 11. *3339 N. Federal Hwy., Oakland Park, tel. 305/566–2406.*

Musician Exchange. This 200-seat club, heading into its 17th year, features an eclectic mix of blues, jazz, and rock-and-roll, with reggae on Sundays. Performers include local bands as well as leading musicians like Donovan, John Lee Hooker, Laura Nyro, Carmen McCrae, and Stan Getz. *729 W. Sunrise Blvd., tel. 305/764–1912. Admission price varies with show. National big-name acts Fri. and Sat. Call for schedule and reservations.*

Shirttail Charlie's Downstairs Bar. A scenic place to have a beer or snack and watch boat traffic on the New River through downtown Fort Lauderdale. Entertainment Wed., Thurs. 5–9,

Fri. 5:30–9:30, Sat. 6–10, Sun. 2–6. Informal. *400 S.W. 3rd Ave., tel. 305/463–3474. Open Mon.–Sat. 11:30–10, Sun. 11:30–9.*

Squeeze. Hard-core new-wavers to yuppie types all fit in here. Fluorescent paints create monstrous wildflower effects, and pterodactyls look very 3-D. A juice bar is offered for designated drivers. The younger crowd goes for the black-and-white Alley with its two bars, dance floor, and the giant green chicken-wire sculpture. The special effects are by Michael Hardwick who hit his stride with sculptures at the late Club Nu in Miami Beach. *2 S. New River Dr., tel. 305/522–2068. Tues.–Sat. 8 PM till early morning. $5 cover; Tues. free. Special parties nightly.*

Sushi Blues. A very small restaurant with great Japanese food also plays good music in the evenings. *1836 Young Circle, Hollywood, tel. 305/929–9560.*

Yesterday's. This upscale disco attracts middle-agers but it's no sleeper. Instead it's more like Saturday Night Fever, with pulsing bass, light show, and confetti. There are four bars, a huge wine cellar, and gourmet menu in the opulent Plum Room (private screens by your banquette on request). Tables and booths overlook the Intracoastal. Special late-night gourmet pizzas are offered. *East Oakland Park Blvd. at the Intracoastal, tel. 305/561–4400. Nightly from 8–2 AM, Sat. to 3. Plum Room 7–11, Fri.–Sat. to midnight. Wed. "ladies night," with complimentary drinks 8–10, $1 drinks for unescorted women after 10 PM.*

Comedy Clubs **The Comic Strip.** Stand-up comedians from New York work among framed old newspaper funnies—Katzenjammer Kids, Superman, Prince Valiant, L'il Orphan Annie, Hubert, etc.— and there's a full restaurant menu (two-drink minimum— alcoholic and nonalcoholic beverages). *1432 N. Federal Hwy., tel. 305/565–8887. Showtime Sun.–Fri. 9:30, Sat. 8:30 and 11. Subject to change on holidays. AE, MC, V.*

Country/Western **Do-Da's Country Music Emporium.** The Frontier Room seats 800 at buckboard tables and has a 2,100-square-foot sunken wood dance floor, popular for square dancing; the smaller pecky-board Tennessee Room seats 100. Glass-and-brick arches enclose the Tex-Mex dining area, Steak House. Do-Da's presents an international buffet during happy hour, weekdays 5–7:30. Otherwise it's ribs, gator, wings, along with the Tex-Mex menu. *700 S. U.S. 441, Plantation, tel. 305/792–6200. Mon.–Tues. 5–2, Wed.–Fri. 5–4, Sat. 6–4. Closed Sun. Live music nightly 9–2. AE, MC, V.*

> This trip
> we found a
> road less
> traveled.
> And the
> perfect way
> to see it.

©1992 Budget Rent a Car Corporation

Vacation Cars. Vacation Prices. Wherever you travel, Budget offers you a wide selection of quality cars – from economy models to roomy minivans and even convertibles. You'll find them all at competitively low rates that include unlimited mileage. At over 1500 locations in the U.S. and Canada. For information and reservations, call your travel consultant or Budget at **800-527-0700**. In Canada, call **800-268-8900**.

THE SMART MONEY IS ON BUDGET.®

We feature Lincoln-Mercury and other fine cars. *A system of corporate and licensee owned locations.*

No matter what your travel style, the best trips start with **Fodor's**

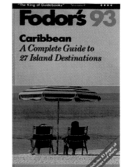

5 Palm Beach and Palm Beach County

Introduction

Updated by Herb Hiller

Wealth has its privileges. That's the continuing reality of Palm Beach. Those privileges include the finest homes, cars, food, wine, furniture, jewelry, art, clothing, and toys that money can buy—and the right to stare back at the tourists who visit this elegant barrier-island enclave 70 miles north of Miami.

Henry Morrison Flagler created Palm Beach in 1894. Earlier he helped John D. Rockefeller establish the Standard Oil Company, then retired and put his money into Florida railroads and real estate. He bought a small railroad between Jacksonville and St. Augustine and extended it southward. Eventually it was called the Florida East Coast Railroad. Along the rail line he built hotels to generate traffic, including a huge wooden structure, the 2,000-room Royal Poinciana, beside a tidal bay called Lake Worth.

Flagler created an international high-society resort at Palm Beach, attracting the affluent for the Season, New Year's Day to Washington's Birthday. Then they departed for Europe, extolling Palm Beach's virtues and collecting great art to ship back to the mansions they were building on the island.

A workman told Flagler that people liked to picnic along the beach "down by the breakers," so he built a second hotel there in 1896. It burned, was rebuilt, and burned again. The third structure to bear the name The Breakers rose in 1926 and stands today as the grande dame of Palm Beach hostelries.

Socialites and celebrities still flock to The Breakers for charity galas. They browse in the stores along Worth Avenue, regarded as one of the world's classiest shopping districts. They swim on secluded beaches that are nominally public but lack convenient parking and access points. They pedal the world's most beautiful bicycle path beside Lake Worth. And what they do, *you* can do—if you can afford it.

Despite its prominence and affluence, the Town of Palm Beach occupies far less than 1% of the land area of Palm Beach County, which is 521 square miles larger than the state of Delaware and is a remarkably diverse political jurisdiction.

West Palm Beach, on the mainland across Lake Worth from Palm Beach, is the city Flagler built to house Palm Beach's servants; today it's the county seat and commercial center of Palm Beach County, with a population of about 80,000. Both the downtown and uptown areas are undergoing immense revitalization. Among the biggest and most immediate changes are the completion of the 2,200-seat Raymond K. Kravis Center for the Performing Arts (scheduled to open in November 1992) and the $2 million restoration of the historic Seaboard Railroad Station which reopened the year before. Other new and welcome additions to the downtown scene are the Palm Beach Opera, which arrived in 1991 and, at its heels, the Florida Ballet, in 1992.

Making it simpler for residents and visitors to get to and around downtown will be the so-called Inter-Modal, a networking transportation facility that should be operating by 1994. The system will link together all sorts of transport including Amtrak, Greyhound/Trailways, TriRail (a commuter line), CoTran (a county bus system), and taxis. Beginning in 1993 will be a free shuttle service—the first stage of the project's development—which will link up with the downtown commercial district, a 15-block area where some 10,000 square feet of retail space was added in 1992. Already half a dozen new restaurants and trendy bars are in full swing along the 5 blocks of Clematis Street alone.

Lantana, to the south of West Palm Beach, has a large Finnish population. Delray Beach began as an artists' retreat and a small settlement of Japanese farmers, including George Morikami, who donated the land for the beautiful Morikami Museum of Japanese Culture (4000 Morikami Park Rd., Delray Beach 33446, tel. 407/495–0233), to the county park system. The museum is open Tuesday–Sunday 10–5; closed Easter, Thanksgiving, Christmas, New Year's Day. Boca Raton, an upscale community developed by pioneer architect Addison Mizner as a showcase for his Spanish Revival style, retains much of its 1920s ambience through strict zoning. The newest apparition of the Mizner style is the $75 million Mizner Park, a de rigueur–pink civic cultural center and shopping mall with outdoor amenities that opened in 1991.

To the north, Palm Beach Gardens is a golf center, home of the Professional Golfer's Association. Jupiter boasts the Jupiter Theater and a dune-fringed beach that remains largely free of intrusive development.

Many visitors to Palm Beach County don't realize that the borders extend 50 miles inland to encompass the southeastern quadrant of 448,000-acre Lake Okeechobee, the fourth-largest natural lake in the United States. Its bass and perch attract fisherfolk; catfish devotees prize the hearty flavor of succulent Okeechobee "sharpies."

Marinas at Pahokee and Belle Glade provide lake access. In Lake Harbor, about as far west as you can go in Palm Beach County, the state is restoring a lock built early in the 20th century on the Miami Canal.

Palm Beach County is also the main gateway to the Treasure Coast, consisting of Martin, St. Lucie, and Indian River counties along the Atlantic Coast to the north.

Essential Information

Arriving and Departing by Plane

Airport **Palm Beach International Airport (PBIA)** (Congress Ave. and Belvedere Rd., West Palm Beach, tel. 407/471–7400) is equipped with a 25-gate terminal to handle five million passengers a year, and will add up to 24 more gates by 1995.

Between the Airport and City Center Route No. 10 of **Tri-Rail Commuter Bus Service** joins PBIA and Tri-Rail's Palm Beach Airport station during weekday rush hours only. For schedule, call 800/TRI–RAIL. For connections with CoTran (Palm Beach County Transportation Authority) routes, call 407/686–4560 or 407/686–4555 in Palm Beach, 407/272–6350 in Boca Raton–Delray Beach. Route 4–S operates from PBIA to downtown West Palm Beach every two hours on the half hour starting at 7:30 AM until 5:30 PM. Fare is 90¢. Rental car companies that operate directly within PBIA include **Alamo** (tel. 407/684–6806), **Avis** (tel. 407/233–6400), **Budget** (tel. 407/

683–2401), **Dollar** (tel. 407/686–3300), **Hertz** (tel. 407/684–4300), and **National** (tel. 407/233–7350).

Palm Beach Transportation (tel. 407/689–4222) provides taxi and limousine service from PBIA. Reserve at least a day in advance for a limousine. Lowest fares are $1.50 per mile, with the meter starting at $1.25. Depending on your destination, a flat rate may save money. Inquire about minimum fares required for use of credit cards. *MC, V.*

Arriving and Departing by Train and Car

By Train **Amtrak** (201 S. Tamarind Ave., West Palm Beach, tel. 800/872–7245 or 407/832–6169) connects West Palm Beach with cities along Florida's east coast and the northeast daily.

Tri-Rail has six stations in Palm Beach County. For details, call 800/TRI–RAIL or 305/728–8445.

By Car Most visitors explore Palm Beach County by car. I–95 runs north-south, to link West Palm Beach with Miami and Fort Lauderdale to the south. To get to central Palm Beach, exit at Belvedere Road or Okeechobee Boulevard. Southern Boulevard (U.S. 98) runs east-west. From West Palm Beach, take I–95 south to Delray Beach and Boca Raton, north to Palm Beach Gardens and Jupiter.

Getting Around

By Bus CoTran buses require exact change (90¢, 45¢ for seniors and handicapped persons, plus 25¢ for a transfer). Service is provided from 5 AM to 8:30 PM, with individual route variations. For details, call 407/686–4560 or 407/686–4555 (Palm Beach), 407/272–6350 (Boca Raton-Delray Beach).

By Taxi **Palm Beach Transportation** (tel. 407/689–4222). Cab meters start at $1.25. Each mile within West Palm Beach city limits is $1.25; if the trip at any point leaves the city limits, $1.50. Some cabs may charge more. Waiting time is 25¢ per 75 seconds.

Important Addresses and Numbers

Tourist Information **Palm Beach County Convention & Visitors Bureau** (1555 Palm Beach Lakes Blvd., Suite 204, West Palm Beach 33401, tel. 407/471–3995) is open weekdays 8:30–5.

Chamber of Commerce of the Palm Beaches (401 N. Flagler Dr., West Palm Beach 33401, tel. 407/833–3711) is open weekdays 8:30–5.

Palm Beach Chamber of Commerce (45 Cocoanut Row, Palm Beach 33480, tel. 407/655–3282) is open weekdays 9–5.

Deaf Service Center of Palm Beach County (5730 Corporate Way, Suite 230, West Palm Beach 33407, TDD tel. 407/478–3904; toll-free from south Palm Beach County tel. 407/392–6444, voice tel. 407/478–3903) is open weekdays 8–4:30; closed Thanksgiving, Christmas, December 26, and New Year's Day. Relay operates until 9 PM, Saturday 9–noon.

Emergencies Dial 911 for **police** and **ambulance** in an emergency.

Hospitals Three hospitals in West Palm Beach with 24-hour emergency rooms are **Good Samaritan Hospital** (Flagler Dr. and Palm Beach Lakes Blvd., tel. 407/655–5511; doctor-referral, tel. 407/650–6240); **Palm Beach Regional Hospital** (2028 10th Ave., tel. 407/967–7800; doctor-referral, tel. 800/237–6644); and **St. Mary's Hospital** (901 45th St., tel. 407/844–6300; doctor-referral, tel. 407/881–2929).

24-Hour Pharmacies **Eckerd Drugs** (3343 S. Congress Ave., Palm Springs, southwest of West Palm Beach, tel. 407/965–3367; and 7016 Bera Casa Way, Boca Raton, tel. 407/391–8770). **Walgreen Drugs** (1688 Congress Ave., Palm Springs, tel. 407/968–8211; and 7561 N. Federal Hwy., Boca Raton, tel. 407/241–9802).

Guided Tours

Boat Tours **Star of Palm Beach** (900 E. Blue Heron Blvd., Riviera Beach, tel. 407/842–0882) offers sightseeing as well as dinner-dance tours that cruise the Intracoastal Waterway past millionaire row. Two vessels, which depart from Phil Foster Park, include the 250-passenger *Star of Palm Beach*, a replica of a Mississippi paddlewheeler; and a steamboat. *MC, V. Tours operate daily year-round.*

Since 1988, the *Manatee Queen* (1000 U.S. Hwy. 1, Jupiter, tel. 407/744–2191) a 40-foot, 49-passenger Caribbean catamaran, has offered afternoon, sunset, and evening wine-and-cheese cruises on the Intracoastal Waterway between November and May. Cruises include tours up the Loxahatchee River into cypress swamps of the Jonathan Dickinson State Park and depart from Charlie's Crab at Jupiter Harbor.

Wildlife Tour **Tropical Wildlife Tours** (1001 S. Federal Hwy., Lake Worth, tel. 407/582–5947) offers year-round guided tours of Palm Beach and the Everglades that include hotel pick-up and return in a luxurious van. Prices range from $29 to $69. *MC, V.*

Exploring Palm Beach and Palm Beach County

Numbers in the margin correspond to points of interest on the Palm Beach and Palm Beach County map.

Palm Beach is an island community 12 miles long and no more than a ¼-mile across at its widest point. Three bridges connect Palm Beach to West Palm Beach and the rest of the world. This tour takes you through both communities.

Begin at Royal Palm Way and County Road in the center of Palm Beach. Go north on County Road past the Episcopal ❶ church, **Bethesda-by-the-Sea**, built in 1927 by the first Protestant congregation in southeast Florida. Inspiring stained-glass windows and a lofty, vaulted sanctuary grace its Spanish-Gothic design. A stone bridge with an ornamental tile border spans the pond; bubbling fountains feed it. *141 South County Rd., Palm Beach, tel. 407/655–4554. Gardens open 8–5. Services Sun. 8, 9, and 11 AM in winter, 8 and 10 June–Aug.; phone for weekday schedule.*

❷ Continue north on County Road past **The Breakers** (1 S. County Rd., Palm Beach), an ornate Italian renaissance hotel (*see*

Palm Beach and Palm Beach County

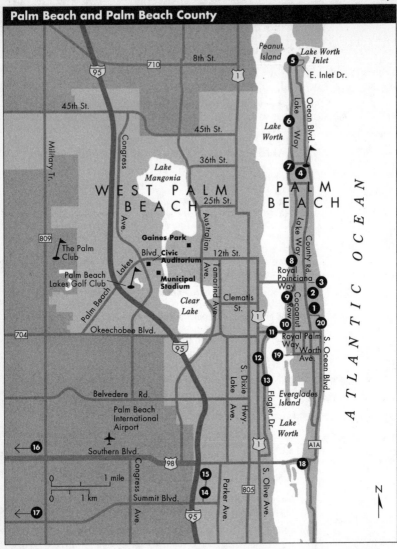

Ann Norton Sculpture
Gardens, **13**
Bethesda-by-
the-Sea, **1**
The Breakers, **2**
Canyon of Palm
Beach, **7**

Dreher Park Zoo, **14**
E. Inlet Drive, **5**
Lion Country
Safari, **16**
Mar-A-Lago, **18**
Norton Gallery of
Art, **12**
Palm Beach Bicycle
Trail, **6**

Palm Beach Biltmore
Hotel, **8**
Palm Beach Country
Club, **4**
Palm Beach Post
Office, **3**
Pine Jog Environmental
Sciences Center, **17**

Public Beach, **20**
Royal Palm Bridge, **11**
Society of the Four
Arts, **10**
South Florida Science
Museum, **15**
Whitehall, **9**
Worth Ave., **19**

Lodging, below) built in 1926 by railroad magnate Henry M. Flagler's widow to replace an earlier hotel, which had burned, twice. Explore the elegant public spaces—especially on a Sunday morning, when you can enjoy the largest champagne brunch in Florida at The Beach Club.

3 Continue north on County Road to Royal Poinciana Way. Go inside the **Palm Beach Post Office** to see the murals depicting Seminole Indians in the Everglades and royal and coconut palms. *95 N. County Rd., Palm Beach, tel. 407/832–0633 or 407/832–1867. Open weekdays 8:30–5.*

4 Continue 3.9 miles north on County Road to the north end of the island, past the very-private **Palm Beach Country Club** and a neighborhood of expansive (and expensive) estates. From the coastal road you can catch glimpses of Singer Island, with its Oz-like scenery.

5 You must turn around at **E. Inlet Drive,** the northern tip of the island, where a dock offers a view of Lake Worth Inlet, the U.S. Coast Guard Reservation on Peanut Island, and the Port of Palm Beach across Lake Worth on the mainland. Observe the no-parking signs; Palm Beach police will issue tickets.

6 Turn south and make the first right onto Indian Road, then the first left onto Lake Way. You'll return to the center of town through an area of newer mansions, past the posh, private Sailfish Club. Lake Way parallels the **Palm Beach Bicycle Trail** along the shoreline of Lake Worth, a palm-fringed path through the backyards of some of the world's priciest homes. Watch on your right for metal posts topped with a swatch of white paint, marking narrow public-access walkways between houses from the street to the bike path.

7 Lake Way runs into Country Club Road, which takes you through the **Canyon of Palm Beach,** a road cut about 25 feet deep through a ridge of sandstone and oolite limestone.

8 As you emerge from the canyon, turn right onto Lake Way and continue south. Lake Way becomes Bradley Place. You'll pass the **Palm Beach Biltmore Hotel,** now a condominium. Another flamboyant landmark of the Florida boom, it cost $7 million to build and opened in 1927 with 543 rooms.

9 As you cross Royal Poinciana Way, Bradley Place becomes Cocoanut Row. Stop at **Whitehall,** the palatial 73-room mansion that Henry M. Flagler built in 1901 for his third wife, Mary Lily Kenan. After the couple died, the mansion was turned into a hotel. In 1960, Flagler's granddaughter, Jean Flagler Matthews, bought the building. She turned it into a museum, with many of the original furnishings on display. The art collection includes a Gainsborough portrait of a girl with a pink sash, displayed in the music room near a 1,200-pipe organ. Exhibits also depict the history of the Florida East Coast Railroad. Flagler's personal railroad car, "The Rambler," is parked behind the building. A tour by well-informed guides takes about an hour; afterwards, you may browse on your own. *Cocoanut Row at Whitehall Way, Palm Beach, tel. 407/655–2833. Admission: $5 adults, $2 children 6–12. Open Tues.–Sat. 10–5, Sun. noon–5. Closed Mon.*

10 Continue south on Cocoanut Row to Royal Palm Way. Turn right and then right again onto the grounds of the **Society of the Four Arts.** This 56-year-old cultural and educational institution is privately endowed and incorporates an exhibition hall for art, concerts, films, and lectures; a library open without charge; 13 distinct gardens, and the Philip Hulitar Sculpture Garden. *Four Arts Plaza, tel. 407/655–7226. Admission: $20 concerts, $15 lectures, $2.50 Friday films, $1 young people's programs; exhibitions: suggested donation $3; Sun. art films and gallery talks, free. Concert and lecture tickets for non-members may be purchased one week in advance. Tickets for Fri. films available at time of showing. Exhibitions and programs, Dec.–mid-Apr., Mon.–Sat. 10–5, Sun. 2–5. Library open Nov.–Apr., Mon.–Sat. 10–5; May–Oct., weekdays 10–5. Gardens open Nov.–Apr., Mon.–Sat. 10–5; Jan.–Apr. 15, Sun. 2:30–5; May–Oct., weekdays 10–5.*

Continue west on Royal Palm Way across the Royal Park Bridge into West Palm Beach. On the mainland side, turn left onto Flagler Drive, which runs along the west shore of Lake **11** Worth. A half-mile south of the **Royal Palm Bridge,** turn right onto Actaeon Street, which is the north edge of a sloping mall **12** leading up to the **Norton Gallery of Art.**

Founded in 1941 by steel magnate Ralph H. Norton, the Norton Gallery boasts an extensive permanent collection of 19th- and 20th-century American and European paintings with emphasis on 19th-century French Impressionists, Chinese bronze and jade sculptures, a sublime outdoor patio with sculptures on display in a tropical garden, and a library housing more than 3,000 art books and periodicals. The Norton also secures many of the best traveling exhibits to reach south Florida. *1451 S. Olive Ave., West Palm Beach, tel. 407/832–5194. Admission free; $5 donation requested. Open Tues.–Sat. 10–5, Sun. 1–5.*

Return to Flagler Drive, go a ½-mile south to Barcelona Road, **13** and turn right again. You're at the entrance to the **Ann Norton Sculpture Gardens,** a monument to the late American sculptor Ann Weaver Norton, second wife of Norton Gallery founder Ralph H. Norton. In three distinct areas of the 3-acre grounds, the art park displays seven granite figures and six brick megaliths. Plantings were designed by Norton, an environmentalist, to attract native birdlife. Native plants include 150 different kinds of palms. Other sculptures in bronze, marble, and wood are on display in Norton's studio. *253 Barcelona Rd., West Palm Beach, tel. 407/832–5328. Admission: $2 adults, children under 12 free. Open Tues.–Sat. noon–4 or by appointment.*

Return again to Flagler Drive and continue south to Southern Boulevard (U.S. 98). Turn right and go west almost a mile, turn left onto Parker Avenue, and go south about a mile. Turn right onto Summit Boulevard, and right again at the next stoplight **14** into the parking lot at the **Dreher Park Zoo.** The 29-acre zoo has more than 400 animals representing more than 100 different species, including an endangered Florida panther. Of special interest are the reptile collection and the petting zoo. *1301 Summit Blvd., West Palm Beach, tel. 407/547–WILD (recording) or 407/533–0887. Admission: $5 adults, $4.50 senior citizens over 60, $3.50 children 3–12. Open daily 9–5.*

15 About a ¼-mile from the zoo is the **South Florida Science Museum.** Here you'll find hands-on exhibits, aquarium displays with touch-tank demonstrations, planetarium shows, and a chance to observe the heavens Friday nights through the most powerful telescope in south Florida (weather permitting). *4801 Dreher Trail N, West Palm Beach, tel. 407/832–1988. Admission: $5 adults, $4.50 senior citizens over 62, $3 students 13– 21, $1.50 children 4–12; laser show $2 extra. Planetarium admission: $1.75 extra. Open daily 10–5, Fri. 10–10.*

Leaving the science museum, retrace your path on Summit Boulevard and Parker Avenue to Southern Boulevard (Rte. **16** 80), turn left, and go about 16 miles west to **Lion Country Safari,** where you drive (with car windows closed) on 8 miles of paved roads through a 500-acre cageless zoo where 1,000 wild animals roam free. Lions, elephants, white rhinoceroses, giraffes, zebras, antelopes, chimpanzees, and ostriches are among the species in residence. Try to go early in the day, before the park gets crowded. If you have a convertible or a new car on which you don't want animals to climb, the park will rent you a zebra-stripe, air-conditioned sedan. An adjacent KOA campground offers campers a park discount. *Box 16066, West Palm Beach 33416, tel. 407/793–1084. Admission: $11.95 adults, $9.95 children 3–16, $8.55 senior citizens over 65, under 3 free; car rental $5 per hour. Open daily 9:30–5:30.*

Returning to town on Southern Boulevard, turn right onto Jog **17** Road, left onto Summit Boulevard to the **Pine Jog Environmental Sciences Center.** After 30 years as a limited-admission nature center, in 1991 Pine Jog was opened by Florida Atlantic University to the public. The 150-acre site is mostly undisturbed Florida pine flatwoods. There's a self-guided ½-mile trail, and formal landscaping around the five one-story buildings features an array of native plants. Dioramas and displays show native ecosystems, and environmental education programs are offered. *6301 Summit Blvd., West Palm Beach, tel. 407/686–6600. Admission free. Open weekdays 9–5, weekends 1–4. Closed major holidays.*

Return to Southern Boulevard, turn right, look for the Italianate **18** ate towers of **Mar-A-Lago** (1100 S. Ocean Blvd.) silhouetted against the sky as you cross the bridge to Palm Beach. Mar-A-Lago, the former estate of breakfast-food heiress Marjorie Meriweather Post, has lately been owned by real estate magnate Donald Trump, who is trying to subdivide it.

Turn north on Ocean Boulevard, one of Florida's most scenic drives. The road follows the dune top, with the beach falling away to surging surf on your right, and some of Palm Beach's most opulent mansions on your left. You will pass the east end **19** of **Worth Avenue** (*see* Shopping, below), regarded by many as the world's classiest shopping street.

20 As you approach Worth Avenue, the **public beach** begins. Parking meters along Ocean Drive between Worth Avenue and Royal Palm Way signify the only stretch of beach in Palm Beach with convenient public access.

This concludes the tour. To return to its starting point, turn left on Royal Palm Way and go 1 block west to County Road.

What to See and Do with Children

Burt Reynolds Ranch and Mini Petting Farm. Farm and exotic animals can be petted on this 160-acre working horse ranch and feed store complex owned by the famous actor. *16133 Jupiter Farms Rd., Jupiter (2 mi west of I–95 off exit 59-B), tel. 407/*

747–5390. Open daily 10–4:30. Closed major holidays. Admission free.

Children's Museum of Boca Raton at Singing Pines. This learning center for children features hands-on exhibits, workshops, and special programs. *498 Crawford Blvd., Boca Raton, tel. 407/368–6875. Admission: $1. Open Tues.–Sat. noon–4.*

Children's Science Explorium. This museum features 40 hands-on exhibits as well as ongoing special events. On Saturdays there's a science cinema and Wizard's Workshop that features crafts for young children. *Royal Palm Plaza, Suite 15, 131 Mizner Blvd., Boca Raton, tel. 407/395–8401. Admission: $3.50 adults, $3 senior citizens and children over 3. Open Mon.–Sat. 10–5, Sun. noon–5.*

Gumbo Limbo Nature Center. At this unusual nature center, you can stroll a 1,628-foot boardwalk through a dense tropical forest and climb a 50-foot tower to overlook the tree canopy. The forest is a coastal hammock, with tropical species growing north of the tropics. One tree species you're sure to see—the gumbo-limbo, with its red peeling bark—is often called "the tourist tree." A guide to dune plants was published in 1991 in the same format and at the same price as the *Coastal Park Plant Guide* ($4) for Gumbo Limbo, James Rutherford, Red Reef, and Spanish River parks. The guide details the parks' flora, with photos and brief text keyed to numbered posts along the trails. In the nature center building, a diorama depicts the nest of a loggerhead sea turtle along the nearby beach. The center's staff leads guided turtle walks to the beach to see nesting mothers come ashore and lay their eggs. *1801 N. Ocean Blvd., Boca Raton, tel. 407/338–1473. Admission: $3. Ticket must be purchased in advance for the night tour. Open Mon.–Sat. 9–4. Admission free. Turtle walks late May–late July Mon.–Thurs. 9 PM–midnight.*

Off the Beaten Track

Arthur R. Marshall Loxahatchee National Wildlife Refuge Loxahatchee Refuge is 221 square miles of saw grass marshes, wet prairies, sloughs, and tree islands. You go there to stroll the nature trails, see alligators and birds (including the rare snail kite). You can also fish for bass and panfish, ride an airboat, or paddle your own canoe through this watery wilderness. Loxahatchee refuge was renamed in memory of Art Marshall, a Florida environmental scientist instrumental in Everglades preservation efforts. *Open ½ hr before sunrise–½ hr after sunset. Refuge entrance fee: $3 per car, $1 per pedestrian.*

The refuge has three access points, but only the headquarters has its own facilities and services:

Headquarters The ranger at the visitor center will show a seven-minute slide presentation on request. Walk both nature trails—a boardwalk through a dense cypress swamp, and a marsh nature trail to a 20-foot-tall observation tower overlooking a pond. A 7-mile canoe trail starts at the boat-launching ramp here. *Entrance off U.S. 441 between Boynton Blvd. (Rte. 804) and Atlantic Ave. (Rte. 806), west of Boynton Beach. Mailing address: Rte. 1, Box 278, Boynton Beach 33437–9741, tel. 407/732–3684 or 407/734–8303.*

Hillsboro Recreation Area At press time the contract for the concession was in the process of changing hands, but it is expected that the new concessionaire will probably provide the same services as the former. The last concessionaire offered airboat rides, boat rentals, guide services, and a store with snacks, fishing tackle, and bait. The airboat ride lasts ½ hour, in a 20-passenger craft with a Cadillac engine; the driver took passengers into the middle of the Everglades, then shut off the engine and explained the unique ecosystem. The following information applies to the former concessionaire, and services, prices, and hours may change. *Entrance off U.S. 441 on Lox Rd. (Rte. 827), 12 mi south of Headquarters and west of Boca Raton.*

20-Mile Bend Recreation Area Boat ramp and fishing area at north end of refuge. *Entrance off U.S. 98/441, due west of West Palm Beach.*

Shopping

Worth Avenue One of the world's strongholds for quality shopping, Worth Avenue runs a ¼ mile east–west across Palm Beach, from the beach to Lake Worth.

The street has more than 250 shops: The 300 block, with a maze of Italianate villas designed by Addison Mizner, retains a quaint charm; the 100 and 200 blocks are more overtly commercial. Most merchants open at 9:30 or 10 AM, and close at 5:30 or 6 PM.

Parking on and around Worth Avenue is quite limited. On-street parking has a strictly enforced one- or two-hour limit. An alternative is Apollo Valet Parking at Hibiscus and Peruvian avenues, a block off Worth Avenue. Merchants will stamp your parking ticket if you buy something (or if you look like a prospective customer); each stamp is good for an hour of free parking.

Apollo's parking deal is just one reason to look presentable when you tour Worth Avenue. Come dressed to feel comfortable, blend in, and indulge your fantasies.

The Worth Avenue Association has strict rules to keep the street chic; no renovations are allowed from December to May, and special sales are limited to 21 consecutive days anytime between April and October.

Many "name" stores associated with fine shopping have a presence on Worth Avenue, including Brooks Brothers, Cartier, F.A.O. Schwarz, Gucci, Hermès, Pierre Deux, Saks Fifth Avenue, Tiffany's, and Van Cleef & Arpels. No other street in the world has such a concentration of these upscale firms—and they tend to send their best merchandise to Worth Avenue to appeal to the discerning tastes of their Palm Beach clientele.

Also appealing to shoppers are the 6 blocks of South County Road, north of Worth Avenue.

Beaches

The widest beaches in Palm Beach County are in the Jupiter area, on Singer Island, and in Boca Raton; many of the beaches in Palm Beach County have begun to erode. Surfing isn't a major draw for this portion of the Atlantic although locals do come out for strong winds and high tides at Palm Beach and Highland

Beach. Clarity of the water, especially in Palm Beach—where the northernmost tropical reef extension runs closest to the shore—affords excellent snorkeling and diving opportunities.

Participant Sports

Biking Bicycle with caution while on city and county roads, especially when there's a lot of traffic. A safe ride, because there are no cross-streets, is the **10-mile path** that borders Lake Worth in Palm Beach, from the Flagler Bridge to the Lake Worth Inlet. For on-the-road rides, group rides, and schedules of longer rides and general cycling savvy, contact the **West Palm Beach Bicycle Club** (Tracy Chambers, Public Affairs Director, tel. 407/659–7644 day, 407/832–9945 evening). Other contacts: **Palm Beach County Bicycle Coordinator** (Wendell Phillips, tel. 407/684–4170); **Boca Raton Bicycle Club** (Jay Lentz, tel. 407/784–7000 day, 407/998–9150 evenings). Rentals, as well as mopeds and rollerblades, are available at **Palm Beach Bicycle Trail Shop**, *223 Sunrise Ave., Palm Beach, tel. 407/659–4583. Open daily 9–5:30. Closed Christmas. AE, MC, V.*

Diving You can drift-dive or anchor-dive along Palm Beach County's 47-mile Atlantic Coast. Drift divers take advantage of the Gulf Stream's strong currents and proximity to shore—sometimes less than a mile. A group of divers joined by nylon line may drift across coral reefs with the current; one member of the group carries a large, orange float that the charter-boat captain can follow. Drift diving works best from Boynton Beach north. South of Boynton Beach, where the Gulf Stream is farther from shore, diving from an anchored boat is more popular. Among the more intriguing artificial reefs in the area is a 1967 Rolls-Royce Silver Shadow in 80 feet of water off Palm Beach.

Dive Boats and Instruction The following **Force E** stores rent scuba and snorkeling equipment and have PADI affiliation and instruction available at all skill levels; dive-boat charters are also available. All shops are closed Thanksgiving, Christmas, and New Year's Day and accept AE, D, MC, V.

1399 N. Military Trail, West Palm Beach, tel. 407/471–2676. Open weekdays 9–8:30, Sat. 8–7, Sun. 8–4.

155 E. Blue Heron Blvd., Riviera Beach, tel. 407/845–2333. Open weekdays year-round. 8–6:30, Sat. 6:30–6:30, Sun. 6:30–4:30.

11911 U.S. 1, Suite 111, N. Palm Beach, tel. 407/624–7136. Open year-round weekdays 10–7, Sat. 8–6, Sun. 8–4.

877 E. Palmetto Park Rd., Boca Raton, tel. 407/368–0555. Open winter, Mon.–Sat. 8–7, Sun. 8–5; summer, weekdays 8 AM–9 PM, weekends same as in winter.

7166 Beracasa Way, Boca Raton, tel. 407/395–4407. Open weekdays 10–9:30 (summer 9–8:30), Sat. 8–7, Sun. 8–4.

Fishing Palm Beach County is fisherfolks' heaven, from deep-sea strikes of fighting sailfish and wahoo to the bass, speckled perch, and bluegill of Lake Okeechobee. In between there are numerous fishing piers, bridges, and waterways where pompano, sheepshead, snapper, and grouper are likely catches. Representative of the fleets and marinas are:

Deep-Sea Fishing **B-Love Fleet.** *314 E. Ocean Ave., Lantana, tel. 407/588–7612. Mornings at 8; afternoons at 1; evenings at 7. $19 per person includes rod, reel, bait.*

Lake Fishing **Slim's Fish Camp.** *Drawer 250, Belle Glade 33430, tel. 407/996–3844. Guided tour 1 or 2 people $185 per day. Boat rental $35 per day. License required: non-Florida resident 7-day permit $16.50, 1-year permit $31.50; Florida resident 1-year permit $13.50.*
J-Mark Fish Camp. *Box 2225, Belle Glade 33430, tel. 407/996–5357. Guided tour 1 or 2 people $200 per day. Boat rental $35 per day (sunrise–sunset). License required.*

Gliding **Glider Rides of America** offers two-passenger rides manned by experienced pilots. Flights last approximately 15–30 minutes. *2633 Lantana Rd., Suite 4, Lantana, tel. 407/965–9101. Open Jan.–Apr., Thurs.–Mon. Reservation required. From 3,000 feet, $39.95 per person; from 4,000, $59.95; from 5,000, $79.95. AE, D, MC, V.*

Golf There are 145 public, private, and semiprivate golf courses in the Palm Beach County area. A **Golf-A-Round** program lets guests at any of 92 hotels in the county golf at one of 10 courses each day, without greens fees, between April and December. For details and for a complete list of courses, contact the Palm Beach County Convention & Visitors Bureau (*see* Important Addresses and Numbers, above).

Spas **Hippocrates Health Institute** was founded in Boston in 1963 by Ann Wigmore and moved to its present 10-acre site in 1987. Guests receive complete examinations by traditional and alternative health-care professionals. Personalized programs include juice fasts and the eating of raw foods. *1443 Palmdale Ct., West Palm Beach, tel. 407/471–8876 or 407/471–8868. AE, MC, V.*

The Spa at PGA National Resort. Styled after a Mediterranean fishing village, the new 17,800-square-foot spa building features six outdoor therapy pools. The facility encompasses 22 rooms for private treatments, including Swedish and shiatsu massage, hydrotherapy and mud treatments, men's and women's Jacuzzis and saunas, and a selection of salon treatments. Also available in a 26,000-square-foot Health & Racquet Center are five racquetball courts, complete Nautilus center, aerobics and dance studios, men's and women's locker rooms, and a fitness-oriented Health Bar. *400 Ave. of the Champions, Palm Beach Gardens 33418–3698; tel. 800/633–9150; 407/627–2000. AE, DC, MC, V.*

Spectator Sports

The *Palm Beach Post's* weekly "TGIF" section on Friday carries information on sports activities. For tickets to Sporting events call **Ticketmaster** (tel. 407/839–3900).

Auto Racing Drag racing, stock car racing, and other two-axle racing takes place at the **Moroso Motorsports Park** (17047 Beeline Hwy., Palm Beach Gardens, tel. 407/622–1400; for information: Box 31907, Palm Beach Gardens 33410, tel. 407/622–1400).

Baseball The **Atlanta Braves** and the **Montreal Expos** both conduct spring training in West Palm Beach's Municipal Stadium, which is also home to the Palm Beach Expos, a Class-A team in the Florida State League. *1610 Palm Beach Lakes Blvd., Box 3087, West Palm Beach 33402, stadium tel. 407/683–6012. Expos tickets: Box 3566, West Palm Beach 33402, tel. 407/689–9121, AE, MC, V. Braves tickets: Box 2619, West Palm Beach 33402, tel. 407/683–6100. No credit cards.*

Greyhound Racing **Palm Beach Kennel Club** opened in 1932 and has 3,000 free seats. Dine in the Paddock Dining Room or watch and eat on the Terrace. Call for schedule. *1111 N. Congress Ave., Palm Beach 33409, tel. 407/683–2222. Admission: 50¢ general admission, $2 dining rooms. Matinees free. Free parking. Wed., Thurs., Sat. 12:30 and 7:30; Tues. and Fri. 7:30; Sun. 1.*

Jai Alai **Palm Beach Jai Alai.** This jai-alai fronton is the site of two world records: for the largest payoff ever, $988,325; and for the fastest ball ever thrown, 188 mph. *1415 45th St., West Palm Beach, ¼ mi east of I–95 off exit 54, tel. 407/844–2444 or 407/427–0009 (toll-free south to Pompano Beach). Admission: 50¢ to $3.50. Senior citizens free Wed., Fri., Sat. matinees. Tues., "ladies' night," women are admitted free. Children 39½" or taller ½-price. Free parking. Sala Del Toro Restaurant. Game time is 7 PM. Schedule changes seasonally. No cameras. Open Sept. to July.*

Equestrian Sports and Polo Palm Beach county is the home of three major polo organizations. Seventy miles north in Vero Beach, the **Windsor Polo and Beach Club** held its first polo match in February 1989. Although only the affluent can support a four-member polo team, admission is free for some games and priced reasonably for others. If you like horses and want to rub elbows with the rich and famous, dress like the locals in tweeds or a good golf shirt and khakis and spend an afternoon watching some of the world's best professional polo players.

Polo teams play under a handicap system in which the U.S. Polo Association ranks each player's skills; a team's total handicap reflects its members' individual handicaps. The best players have a 10-goal handicap. The average polo game lasts about 90 minutes. Each game consists of six periods or chukkers of 7½ minutes each.

Gulf Stream Polo Club, the oldest club in Palm Beach, began in the 1920s and plays medium-goal polo (for teams with handicaps of 8–16 goals). It has six polo fields. *4550 Polo Rd., Lake Worth 33467, tel. 407/965–2057. Play Dec.–April. Games Fri. 3 PM and Sun. 1 PM. Admission free.*

Royal Palm Polo, founded in 1959 by Oklahoma oilman John T. Oxley, has seven polo fields with two stadiums and Oxley's Restaurant. The complex is home to the $100,000 International Gold Cup Tournament. *6300 Old Clint Moore Rd., Boca Raton 33496, tel. 407/994–1876. General admission $5, box seats $15, $3 children and students. High-goal winter season Jan.–Apr. Low-goal summer season June–Oct. Games Sun. 1 and 3 PM.*

Palm Beach Polo and Country Club (*see* Lodging, below). Started in 1979, this is the site each April of the $100,000 Regina World Cup competition. *Stadium address: 13198 Forest Hill, West Palm Beach, 33414, tel. 407/798–7605. General admission $6, reserve $10, lower level $14, upper level $17. AE, MC, V. Games Sun. 3 PM.*

Rugby **Boca Raton Rugby Club** practices on Tuesday and Thursday nights. Home games are played Saturday 2 PM at Boca Raton's

Lake Wyman Park. *For information, contact Allerton "Bing"*
Towne, president, Florida Rugby Football Clubs, 1580 S.W.
6th Ave., Boca Raton 33486, tel. 407/998–9700 weekdays or 407/
395–4259 weekends and nights.

Dining

The list below is a representative selection of independent restaurants in Palm Beach County, organized geographically, and
by type of cuisine within each region of the county. Unless otherwise noted, they serve lunch and dinner.

Highly recommended restaurants are indicated by a star ★.

Category	Cost*
Very Expensive	over $55
Expensive	$35–$55
Moderate	$15–$35
Inexpensive	under $15

per person, excluding drinks, service, and 6% sales tax

Boca Raton
Continental

Gazebo Cafe. The locals who patronize this popular restaurant
know where it is, even though there is no sign and it's difficult
to find: Look for the Barnett Bank Pantry Pride Plaza, a block
north of Spanish River Boulevard. Once you find the place,
await your table in the open kitchen where chef Paul Sellas (co-
owner with his mother Kathleen) and his staff perform a gas-
tronomic ballet. The high noise level of the main dining room
has been reduced with an acoustical ceiling but you may still be
happier in the smaller back dining room. Specialties include
lump crabmeat with an excellent glaze of Mornay sauce on a
marinated artichoke bottom; spinach salad with heart of palm,
egg white, bacon, croutons, mushrooms, fruit garnish, and a
dressing of olive oil and Dijon mustard; Paul Sellas's "classic"
bouillabaisse with Maine lobster, shrimp, scallops, clams, and
mussels topped with julienne vegetables in a robust broth flavored with garlic, saffron, and tomatoes; and raspberries with
a Grand Marnier–Sabayon sauce. The staff can accommodate
travelers in seven languages. *4199 N. Federal Hwy., Boca*
Raton, tel. 407/395–6033. Reservations advised. Jacket pre-
ferred. AE, D, DC, MC, V. Closed Sun. except New Year's Eve
through Mother's Day. Expensive.

French
★

La Vieille Maison. This elegant French restaurant occupies a
two-story dwelling that dates from the 1920s (hence the name,
meaning "old house"). The structure, believed to be an Addison
Mizner creation, has been renovated repeatedly, but still retains details which typify the architect's style. Among the
unique features of this restaurant is the use of space. Closets
and cubbyholes have been transformed into intimate private
dining rooms. You may order from a fixed-price or an à la carte
menu throughout the year; in summer, a separate fixed-price
menu available Sunday through Thursday offers a sampling of
the other two at a more modest price. Specialties include *pom-*
pano aux pecans (pompano filets sautéed in butter strewn with
pecans under a creamy chardonnay sauce) and *le saumon fumé*
aux endives (smoked salmon, onions, and Belgian endive with

light vinaigrette). Dessert specialties include *crêpe soufflé au citron* and a chocolate tart. *770 E. Palmetto Park Rd., tel. 407/ 391–6701 in Boca Raton, 407/737–5677 in Delray Beach and Palm Beach, 305/421–7370 in Ft. Lauderdale. Reservations suggested. Jacket preferred. AE, D, MC, V. Closed Memorial Day, Labor Day, July 4th. Expensive.*

Soul Food **Tom's Place.** "This place is a blessing from God," says the sign over the fireplace, to which, when you're finally in and seated (this place draws long lines) you'll add, "Amen!" That's in between mouthfuls of sauce-slathered ribs and chicken cooked in a peppery mustard sauce over hickory and oak. Tom Wright purely brings it on—pork chop sandwich to sweet potato pie. You'll want to leave with a bottle or two of Tom's BBQ sauce: $2.25/pint. You'll return, though, just as Mr. T, Sugar Ray Leonard, Joe Frazier, and a rush of NFL pro players do. You can bet the place is family run. *7251 N. Federal Hwy., tel. 407/ 997–0920. No reservations. Dress: neat but casual. No credit cards. Open Mon. at 4 PM. Closed all holidays, including Mother's and Father's Day, and for a month around Sept. Inexpensive.*

Jupiter **Log Cabin Restaurant.** "Too much!" exclaim first-timers, re-
American sponding to the decor and whopping portions. Everybody takes home a doggie bag, except for the all-you-can-eat meals when the policy is suspended. This rustic roadhouse (very easy to drive past)—with a new porch dining area—has old bikes, sleds, clocks, and quilts hanging from the rafters. For $3.25 you get eggs, French toast, home fries or grits, biscuits and gravy, and coffee. All-you-can-eat specials are featured nightly. *631 N. A1A, tel. 407/746–6877. No reservations. Dress: casual. AE, D, DC, MC, V. Closed Christmas. Inexpensive–Moderate.*

Lighthouse Restaurant. Another family eatery thrives on the Gold Coast and has been for more than 60 years. You'll see the same familiar faces at the counter drinking coffee at 6 AM and midnight. House specialties include roast turkey with giblet gravy, leg of lamb with mint jelly, fresh ham with applesauce, Yankee pot roast, deep-fried Okeechobee catfish, prime rib. "They love my meat loaf and biscuits," manager Renée Jordan says. "But I keep 'em in suspense. They never know when I'm gonna have it." You can get breakfast 24 hours a day, Sunday dinner at noon. *1510 U.S. 1, tel. 407/746–4811. No reservations. Dress: casual. MC, V. Closed Christmas Eve and 1 Sun. night a month (call ahead). Inexpensive.*

Lake Worth **John G's.** About the only time the line lets up here is when the
American restaurant closes. Otherwise, there's little to complain about:
★ certainly not the service, the price, or the noise. The menu is as big as the crowd: eggs every which way, including a UN of ethnic omelets; big fruit platters; sandwich board superstars; grilled burgers and seafood. The Greek shrimp (seven at recent count) come on fresh linguine topped by feta. Decor is not the thing: a big, open room with tables and counter seats under nautical bric-a-brac. *On the beach, Lake Worth Casino, tel. 407/ 585–9860. No reservations. Dress: casual. No credit cards. No dinner. Closed Christmas, New Year's Day. Inexpensive.*

Lantana **Old House.** Line ahead of you? Wait a minute, they'll hammer on
Seafood a few more seats. Partners Wayne Cordero and Captain Bob Hoddinott are ever expanding this unpretentious seafood house on the Intracoastal Waterway. The premises—the Lyman House—is the oldest house in town, dating to 1889. Out

back, a patchwork of shed-like spaces has a seating capacity that now totals 225. Baltimore steamed crab is a specialty, though most of the seafood's from Florida. All dinners come with unlimited salad, fresh baked bread, fries, and parsley potatoes or rice. *300 E. Ocean Ave., tel. 407/533-5220. No reservations. Dress: casual. AE, MC, V. Moderate.*

Palm Beach
American

Chuck & Harold's. Boxer Larry Holmes and thespians Brooke Shields and Burt Reynolds are among the celebrities who frequent this combination power-lunch bar, celebrity sidewalk cafe, and nocturnal big-band/jazz garden restaurant. A blue-and-yellow tent on pulleys rolls back in good weather to expose the garden to the elements. Local businesspeople wheel and deal at lunch in the bar area while quaffing Bass ale on tap. Locals who want to be part of the scenery frequent the front-porch area, next to pots of red and white begonias mounted along the sidewalk rail. Specialties include a mildly spiced conch chowder with a rich flavor and a liberal supply of conch; an onion-crunchy gazpacho with croutons, a cucumber spear, and a dollop of sour cream; a *frittata* (an omelet of bacon, spinach, pepperohcini, potatoes, smoked mozzarella, and fresh tomato salsa); and a tangy Key lime pie with a graham cracker crust and a squeezeable lime slice for even more tartness. *207 Royal Poinciana Way, tel. 407/659-1440. Reservations advised. Dress: neat but casual. AE, DC, MC, V. Moderate.*

Dempsey's. A New York–style Irish pub under the palms: green baize, plaid café curtains, brass rods, burgundy banquettes, *Ring Magazine* covers, open beams, paddlefans, sculpted horse heads, mounted hat racks, horse prints, and antique coach lanterns. George Dempsey was a Florida horse rancher until he entered the restaurant business 13 years ago. This place is packed, noisy, and as electric as Black Friday at the stock exchange when major sports events are on the big TV. Along with much socializing, people put away plates of chicken hash Dempsey (with a dash of Scotch), shad roe, prime rib, and hot apple pie. You go for the scene. Dempsey's is knock-out champ at making it. *50 Cocoanut Row, tel. 407/835-0400. Reservations advised for 6 or more. Dress: neat but casual. AE, MC, V. Closed Thanksgiving, Christmas. Moderate.*

Continental

The Breakers. The main hotel dining area at The Breakers consists of the elegant Florentine Dining Room, decorated with fine 15th-century Flemish tapestries; the adjoining Celebrity Aisle where the maître d' seats his most honored guests; and the Circle Dining Room, with a huge circular skylight framing a bronze-and-crystal Venetian chandelier. Specialties include rack of lamb Dijonnaise; salmon *en croûte* with spinach, herbs and sauce Véronique (a grape sauce); *vacherin glacé* (praline-flavored ice cream encased in fresh whipped cream and frozen in a baked meringue base); and Key lime pie. The Breakers also serves less formally at its Beach Club, where locals flock for the most sumptuous Sunday champagne brunch in Florida, and at the Fairway Cafe in the golf-course clubhouse. *1 S. County Rd., tel. 407/655-6611 or 800/833-3141. Reservations required. Jacket and tie required winter. AE, DC, MC, V. Expensive.*

Ta-boo. Real estate investor Franklyn P. deMarco, Jr. has teamed up with Maryland restaurateur Nancy Sharigan to successfully re-create the legendary Worth Avenue bistro that debuted in 1941. Decorated in gorgeous pinks, greens, and florals, the space is divided into discrete salons: one resembles a courtyard; another, an elegant living room with a fireplace; a third, a gazebo under a skylight. The Tiki Tiki bar is frequented by regulars. The round-the-clock menu includes chicken and arugula from the grill, prime ribs and steaks, gourmet pizzas, and main course salads (a tangy warm steak salad, for instance, comes with grilled strips of marinated filet mignon tossed with greens, mushrooms, tomato, and red onion). *221 Worth Ave., tel. 407/835-3500. Reservations advised. Jacket preferred. AE, MC, V. Closed Christmas. Moderate.*

Deli **TooJay's.** Jewish deli food with California accents best describes this restaurant's menu, with daily specials that may include matzoh ball soup, corned beef on homemade, hand-sliced rye, killer cake with five chocolates, and homemade whipped cream. Naturally, Hebrew National kosher salami layered with onions, muenster cheese, cole slaw, and Russian dressing on rye or pumpernickel is a house favorite. There's also dill-chicken; seafood with crabmeat, shrimp, and sour cream; and for the vegetarians, hummus, tabouleh, and a wheatberry salad. On the high holy days look for carrot *tzimmes* (a sweet compote), beef brisket with gravy, potato pancakes, and roast chicken. Wise-cracking waitresses set the fast pace of this bright restaurant with a high, open packing-crate board ceiling, and windows overlooking the gardens. In addition to this location, Palm Beach County has seven other TooJay's restaurants. *313 Royal Poinciana Plaza, tel. 407/659-7232. No reservations. Dress: casual. AE, MC, V. Beer and wine only. Closed Yom Kippur, Thanksgiving, Christmas. Inexpensive.*

French **Jo's.** This is an intimate, candlelit bistro with flowers on pink
★ cloths, greenery against lattice backdrops, and, after nine years, a well-rehearsed menu. The three-soup sampler is tried and true: buttery lobster bisque, potage St. Germain (green pea soup), and beef consommé. Osso buco, always on the chalkboard, is served with rice and vegetables. Chef Richard Kline, Jo's son, faithfully prepares a moist (but never rare) half roast duckling (boned) with orange demiglaze. For dessert try the fresh apple *tarte tatin* or fresh raspberries Josephine. Jo's is tucked off County Road behind the Church Mouse Thrift Shop. *200 Chilian Ave., tel. 407/659-6776. Reservations advised. Jacket preferred. Dinner only. MC, V. Closed Aug. and Christmas. Expensive.*

Italian **Bice Ristorante.** "Bice" is short for Beatrice, mother of Robert Ruggeri, who founded the Milanese original in 1926. Now in Palm Beach other locations include Paris, New York, Chicago, Washington, Atlanta, and Beverly Hills. Brilliant flower arrangements and Italian stylings—brass, greens, and a dark beige and yellow color scheme—are matched by exquisite aromas of *antipasti* and *pratti del giorni* laced with basil, chive, mint, and oregano. Divine home-baked *focaccia*—a Tuscany-style bread topped with red onion rings—accompanies house favorites such as *robespierre alla moda della bice* (sliced steak topped with arugala salad); *costoletta di vitello impanata alla milanese* (breaded veal cutlet with a tomato shallot salad); and *trancio di spada alla mediterranea* (grilled swordfish with black olives, capers and plum tomatoes). Leave room for *frutta, dolci,* and *gelati*—not an Italian law firm! *313½ Worth Ave., tel. 407/835-1600. Reservations advised. Dress: neat but casual. AE, DC, MC, V. Closed Christmas, New Year's Day. Expensive.*

Seafood **Charley's Crab.** Audubon bird prints, fresh flowers, and French posters accent the walls of this restaurant that sits across the street from the beach. During the season, the dinner line forms early. The raw bar, dropped for the delectable dessert bar a year ago, is back, making meals sumptuous start to finish—even by Palm Beach standards. Dressier than most seafood houses, Charley's offers rooms toward the back of this 315-seater that are particularly fancy and most appropriate for special occassions. Menus change daily. Specialties include 8–10 daily fresh fish specials. *456 S. Ocean Blvd., tel. 407/659–1500. Reservations advised. Dress: casual. AE, D, DC, MC, V. Moderate–Expensive.*

Palm Beach **The Explorers.** You sit in red leather hobnail chairs at tables lit
Gardens with small brass and glass lanterns. Above you hovers a ceiling
Continental mural of stars and the Milky Way; about the room are memora-
★ bilia of famous explorers: Daniel Boone, John Glenn, Sir Edmund Hillary, Tenzing Norkay. The à la carte menu includes a variety of international and American regional preparations, including specialties such as a fresh sushi appetizer with soy, wasabi, and pickled ginger; a crab-topped 9-oz. snapper filet; loin of deer with lingonberry conserve; and almond snow eggs, an egg-shaped meringue poached in almond cream, plated between three-fruit coulis (boysenberry, mango, and tamarillo) and garnished with a nest of butter caramel. The Explorers Wine Club meets fortnightly for wine and food tastings and is open to the public for a one-time $5 membership. Contact the club for a schedule of events. *400 Ave. of the Champions, tel. 407/627–2000. Reservations advised. Jacket required. Dinner only. AE, MC, V. Closed Sun.–Mon. May–Sept. Expensive.*

Lodging

The list below is a representative selection of hotels and motels in Palm Beach County. The rate categories in the list are based on the all-year or peak-season price; off-peak rates may be a category or two lower.

Highly recommended hotels are indicated by a star ★.

Category	Cost*
Very Expensive	over $120
Expensive	$90–$120
Moderate	$50–$90
Inexpensive	under $50

*All prices are for a standard double room, excluding 6% state sales tax and nominal tourist tax.

Very Expensive **Boca Raton Resort & Club.** Architect and socialite Addison
★ Mizner designed and built the original; the tower was added in 1961, the ultramodern Boca Beach Club, in 1981. In 1991 an eight-year, $55 million renovation was completed that includes, among other revitalizations, the upgrade of 300 accommodations in the tower, soundproofing, a new fitness center, the redesigned Cloister lobby and adjacent golf course, and a new 180-seat restaurant, Nick's Fishmarket, at the Beach Club. In 1992 the 27-story-high Top of the Tower Italian Res-

taurant opened. Room rates during the winter season are based on the modified American plan (including breakfast and dinner). The rooms in the older buildings tend to be smaller and cozily traditional; those in the newer buildings are light, airy and contemporary in color schemes and furnishings. *501 E. Camino Real, Boca Raton 33431–0825, tel. 407/395–3000 or 800/327–0101. 963 rooms: 100 in the original 1926 Cloister Inn, 333 in the 1931 addition, 242 in the 27-story Tower Building, 214 in the Boca Beach Club, plus the Golf Villas. Facilities: 1½ mi of beach, 4 outdoor freshwater pools, two 18-hole golf courses, 22 tennis courts (2 lighted), health spa, 23-slip marina, fishing and sailing charters, 7 restaurants, 3 lounges, in-room safes. AE, DC, MC, V.*

★ **Brazilian Court.** The color palette at the Brazilian Court captures the magic of the bright Florida sun indoors and out. After a year of management turmoil, the BC, with its 128 courtyard rooms and suites, is again the pick of Palm Beach without snoot. Spread out over half a block, the yellow-stucco facade with gardens and a red tile roof helps you imagine what the place must have been like 67 years ago, at BC's birth. Rooms are brilliantly floral—yellows, blues, greens, with theatrical bed canopies, big white-lattice patterns on carpets, and sunshiny paned windows. Shelf space is small in the bathrooms, but closets will remind you that people once came with trunks enough for the entire season. French doors, bay windows, rattan loggias, cherub fountains, chintz garden umbrellas beneath royal palms are just some of the elements that compose the lyrical style. *301 Australian Ave., Palm Beach 33480, tel. 407/655–7740 or 800/552–0335, 800/228–6852 in Canada. 128 guest rooms and 6 suites. Facilities: swimming pool, 2 restaurants, bar. AE, D, DC, MC, V.*

★ **The Breakers.** This historic seven-story oceanfront resort hotel, built in 1926, enlarged in 1969, and sprawling over 140 acres of splendor in the heart of some of the most expensive real estate in the world, is currently undergoing a five-year, $50-million renovation. In an overall brightening and lightening, more than 400 of its 526 guest rooms have been made over, and its North Loggia has been enlivened with new yellow drapes, yellow sofa cushions, and great pots of yellow mums. At this palatial Italian Renaissance structure, cupids wrestle alligators in the Florentine fountain in front of the main entrance. Inside the lofty lobby, your eyes lift to majestic ceiling vaults and frescoes. The hotel's proud tradition of blending formality with a tropical resort ambiance remains. After 7 PM, men and boys must wear jackets and ties in the public areas. (Ties are optional in summer.) The new room decor follows two color schemes: cool greens and soft pinks in an orchid-patterned English cotton chintz fabric; and shades of blue, with a floral and ribbon chintz. Both designs include white plantation shutters and wall coverings, Chinese porcelain table lamps, and original 1920s furniture restored to its period appearance. The original building has 15 different room sizes and shapes. If you prefer more space, ask to be placed in the newer addition. *1 S. County Rd., Palm Beach 33480, tel. 407/655–6611 or 800/833–3141. 526 rooms with bath, including 42 suites. Facilities: ½ mi of beachfront, outdoor heated freshwater pool, 20 tennis courts, 2 golf courses, health club with Keiser and Nautilus equipment, men's and women's saunas, lawn bowling, croquet, shuffleboard, shopping arcade with upscale boutiques, 4 restaurants, lounge. AE, DC, MC, V.*

★ **The Chesterfield Hotel Deluxe.** You'll be met at the airport in the house Rolls-Royce, whereupon you'll be conveyed to the finest European hotel in Florida. A little pretense, a lot of style, and a super abundance of service marks this 58-room property located a block from Worth Avenue. The Chesterfield may be a Mizner copy, but it's an original achievement in *luxe*. Dating from 1926 when it opened as the Royal Palm, this accommodation has gone through changes, but none have been more enhancing than this current rendition, which used rich chintz, mahogany, leather, and brass. The lobby boasts chintz and plaid with flowered dust ruffles and frou-frou drapes; the Game Room has baize tables so red they could only be a dare; the Library has an aura of brandy in the air after the hunt, with the important newspapers racked and waiting; the Key West-styled pool patio has pink keystone. The dining room is luxuriously adorned in pink and green. No two of the English-country-style bedrooms are alike, but expect lots of wood and brass, with beds recessed into stagey nooks. Details on the upholstery, quilts, ruffles, and drapes keep rooms unique. Baths are travertine with full amenities. *363 Cocoanut Row, Palm Beach 33480, tel. 407/659–5800. 58 rooms and suites with bath. Facilities: heated freshwater pool, restaurant, lounge. AE, D, DC, MC, V.*

The Colony. Still a block from Worth Avenue, The Colony has been a Palm Beach legend since its completion in 1947. But big change in 1990 transformed the lobby into a Park Avenue salon of plush white silks, chandeliers, scenic oils, and a baby grand piano. All of the 119 rooms and suites have also metamorphosed from tropical pastels to cool neutrals. New features include a tiki bar and outdoor grill for casual outdoor dining. Low-rise maisonettes built in the mid-1950s, and apartments from the 1960s, are across the street, as well as seven new villas added in a recently acquired neighborhood house. *155 Hammon Ave., Palm Beach 33480, tel. 407/655–5430, fax 407/832–7318. 106 rooms, including 36 suites and apartments and 7 villas. Facilities: outdoor heated freshwater pool, restaurant serves 3 meals daily, dancing nightly with live band, beauty parlor. AE, D, DC, MC, V.*

The Ocean Grand. This new property at the south end of Palm Beach is cooly elegant, but warm in detail and generous in amenity. Marble, art, fanlight windows through which the sun pours, swagged drapes, chintz, and palms create an ambience of Grecian serenity. In the Restaurant and the Ocean Bistro you'll be serenaded with piano, harp, and guitar music that accompanies the skilled cuisine. In the Living Room cocktails are served daily. Although the hotel's name suggests grandeur, it's more like a small jewel, with only four stories and a long beach. All rooms are spacious—equivalent to some suites in other hotels—and are furnished in finery typical of Palm Beach. Muted natural tones prevail in guest rooms, with teal, mauve, and salmon accents. Each room has a loveseat, upholstered chairs, desk, TV, armoire, and large closet. *2800 S. Ocean Blvd., Palm Beach 33480, tel. 407/582–2800, fax 407/ 547–1557. 212 rooms, including suites. Facilities: 2 restaurants, lounge, beachfront, heated outdoor freshwater pool, 3 tennis courts, health club, saunas, shops. AE, MC, V.*

PGA National Resort & Spa. The $10 million spa that opened in 1992 is to rave about, as are the limitless sports facilities and The Explorers restaurant (*see* Dining, below). This sprawling resort is the focus of the 2,340-acre PGA National community of 39 neighborhoods and 4,250 residences and is home to the Professional Golfers Association of America and the United States Croquet Association. Its championship golf courses and croquet courts are adorned with 25,000 flowering plants and situated amidst a 240-acre nature preserve. *400 Ave. of the Champions, Palm Beach Gardens 33418 tel. 407/627–2000 or 800/633–9150. 335 rooms and 92 suites, with bath. 36 nonsmoker rooms, 14 rooms for handicapped guests, 80 2-bedroom, 2-bath cottages with fully equipped kitchen. Facilities: 5 golf courses, 19 tennis courts (12 lighted), 5 croquet courts, 5 indoor racquetball courts, outdoor freshwater pool, sand beach on 26-acre lake, sailboats and aquacycles for rent, spa, sauna, whirlpool, aerobic dance studio, 7 restaurants, 2 lounges, in-room minibars and safes. AE, DC, MC, V.*

Palm Beach Polo and Country Club. Individual villas and condominiums are available in this exclusive 2,200-acre resort where Britain's Prince Charles comes to play polo. A polo school is conducted during the sport's season (February–April), and there's a seven-week equestrian festival. Arrange to rent a dwelling closest to the sports activity that interests you: polo, tennis, or golf. Each residence is uniquely designed and furnished by its owner according to standards of quality set by the resort. *13198 Forest Hill Blvd., West Palm Beach 33414, tel. 407/798–7000 or 800/327–4204. 140 privately owned studios, one- and two-bedroom villas, and condominiums available for rental when the owners are away. Facilities: 10 outdoor freshwater pools, 24 grass, clay, and hard-surface tennis courts (20 lighted), two 18-hole golf courses and one 9-hole course, men's and women's saunas, 10 polo fields, and 9 polo barns, equestrian club and trails through a nature preserve, 7 stable barns, 2 lighted croquet lawns, squash and racquetball courts, sculling equipment and instruction, 5 dining rooms. AE, DC, MC, V.*

★ **The Seagate Hotel & Beach Club.** One of the best garden hotels in Palm Beach County if you're looking for value, comfort, style, and personal attention. You can dress up and dine in a smart little mahogany- and lattice-trimmed beachfront salon or have the same Continental fare in casual attire in the equally stylish bar. Lodgings are on the west side of the two-lane road, and it still feels like the country here. The deluxe one-bedroom suite looks sharp in chintz and rattan, with plenty of upholstered pieces. Kitchens in the least expensive studio suites are compact but complete behind foldaway doors. The standard one-bedroom suite has its own touches: make-up lights, double doors between bedroom and living room, and access to bathroom from both. The beachfront facility is actually a private club in which overnight guests can gain membership. Winter rates are high, but after May 1st until mid-November they drop substantially. *400 S. Ocean Blvd., Delray Beach 33483, tel. 407/276–2421, 800/233–3581 (U.S. & Canada). 70 1- and 2-bedroom suites, including 2 penthouses. Facilities: beach, freshwater pool, heated saltwater pool, Jacuzzi, beach cabanas ($10/day), restaurant, lounge. AE, DC, MC, V.*

Expensive–Moderate **Sea Lord Hotel.** If you don't need glamor or brand names, and you're not the bed-and-breakfast type, this is for you. Choose from a room that overlooks Lake Worth, the pool, or the ocean while you vacation in this personally run garden-style hideaway. The reasonably priced 20-seat cafe, which attracts repeat clientele, adds to the at-home, comfy feeling you'll get from this place. Rooms are plain but not cheap, and come with carpet, at least one comfortable chair, small or large fridge, and tropical print fabrics. Most were refurbished in 1991. *2315 S. Ocean Blvd., Palm Beach 33480, tel. 407/582–1461. 40 units, including 15 efficiencies and suites all with bath. Facilities: beach, freshwater pool, restaurant. No credit cards.*

Bed-and-Breakfast Rated *Expensive–Moderate* here, the bed-and-breakfast has become a popular alternative to pricey Palm Beach County accommodations. The stand-out is seven-room **Hibiscus House** (501 30th St., West Palm Beach 33407, tel. 407/863–5633). For the entire county, contact **Open House Bed & Breakfast,** *Box 3025, Palm Beach 33480, tel. 407/842–5190.*

The Arts and Nightlife

The *Palm Beach Post*, in its "TGIF" entertainment insert on Friday lists all events for the weekend, including concerts. Admission to some cultural events is free or by donation. Call **Ticketmaster** (407/839–3900) for tickets for performing arts events.

Nightclub **Wildflower Waterway Cafe.** Nightly DJs spin the top of the pops for a mostly young crowd that adores this luxuriantly tropical Boca bistro by the bridge over the Intracoastal Waterway. *551 E. Palmetto Park Rd., Boca Raton, tel. 407/391–0000. Open to 2 AM. Dress: casual but neat. Reservations not accepted except for groups. AE, MC, V.*

Performing Arts **Raymond F. Kravis Center for the Performing Arts.** This new
Center $53 million 2,200-seat showcase, scheduled to open by early 1993, will feature high-quality seating, acoustics, and architecture in downtown West Palm Beach. The performance schedule will include about 300 events a year. *701 Okeechobee Blvd., West Palm Beach, tel. 407/833–8300.*

Theater **Caldwell Theatre Company.** In addition to hosting the annual multimedia Mizner Festival each April–May, this professional Equity regional theater, part of the Florida State Theater system, presents four shows in winter. *7783 N. Federal Hwy., Boca Raton 33429, tel. 407/241–7432 (Boca Raton), 407/832–2989 (Palm Beach), 305/462–5433 (Broward County).*

Royal Palm Dinner Theater. The Equity cast performs five or six contemporary musicals each year. *303 S.E. Mizner Blvd., Royal Palm Plaza, Boca Raton 33432, tel. 407/392–3755 or 800/ 841–6765 in Florida. AE, MC, V. Tues.–Sat. 8 PM, Sun. 6 PM, Wed. and Sat. matinees 2 PM.*

Royal Poinciana Playhouse. The Equity cast performs six productions each year between December and April. *70 Royal Poinciana Plaza, Palm Beach 33480, tel. 407/659–3310.*

Excursion to Treasure Coast

Numbers in the margin correspond to points of interest on the Treasure Coast map.

This excursion north from **Palm Beach** through the Treasure Coast counties of Martin, St. Lucie, and Indian River traverses an area that was remote and sparsely populated as recently as the late-1970s. Resort and leisure-oriented residential development has swollen its population. If you plan to stay overnight or dine at a good restaurant, reservations are a must.

The interior of all three counties is largely devoted to citrus production, and also cattle ranching in rangelands of pine-and-palmetto scrub. St. Lucie and Indian River counties also contain the upper reaches of the vast St. Johns Marsh, headwaters of the largest northward-flowing river in the United States. If you take Florida's Turnpike from Palm Beach north to the Orlando–Disney World area, you will dip into the edge of St. Johns Marsh about 8 miles north of the Fort Pierce exit. Along the coast, the broad expanse of the Indian River (actually a tidal lagoon) separates the barrier islands from the mainland. It's a sheltered route for boaters on the Intracoastal Waterway, a nursery for the young of many saltwater game fish species, and a natural radiator keeping frost away from the tender orange and grapefruit trees that grow near its banks.

Completion of I–95's missing link from Palm Beach Gardens to Fort Pierce in 1987 eliminated the Treasure Coast's last vestiges of relative seclusion. Hotels, restaurants, and shopping malls crowd the corridor from I–95 to the beach throughout the 70-mile stretch from Palm Beach north to Vero Beach. The Treasure Coast has become another link in the chain of municipalities that some Floridians call "the city of U.S. 1."

Of special interest in this area are the sea turtles that come ashore at night from April to August to lay their eggs on the beaches. Conservation groups, chambers of commerce, and resorts organize turtle-watches, which you may join.

Exploring Treasure Coast

1 This tour takes you north from **Palm Beach** along the coast as far as Sebastian Inlet, but you can break away at any intermediate point and return to Palm Beach on I–95.

2 From downtown **West Palm Beach,** take U.S. 1 about 5 miles north to Blue Heron Boulevard (Rte. A1A) in Riviera Beach, turn right, and cross the **Jerry Thomas Bridge** onto Singer Island. Sightseeing boats depart from **Phil Foster Park** on the island side of the bridge.

Continue on Rte. A1A as it turns north onto Ocean Boulevard, past hotels and high-rise condominiums to **Ocean Reef Park** (3860 N. Ocean Dr., Riviera Beach, tel. 407/966–6655), a snorkeling spot where the reefs are close to shore in shallow water. You may see angelfish, sergeant-majors, rays, robin fish, and occasionally a Florida lobster (actually a species of saltwater crayfish). Wear canvas sneakers and cloth gloves.

Go north on Rte. A1A to **John D. MacArthur State Park** (10900 Rte. A1A, North Palm Beach, tel. 407/624–6952), which offers more good snorkeling along almost 2 miles of beach, and interpretive walks to the mangrove estuary in the upper reaches of Lake Worth. In 1990 a 4,000-square-foot nature center with a 15-minute video on the natural habitat and two large aquariums was installed. Turtle nesting site walks take place nights during late June and early July.

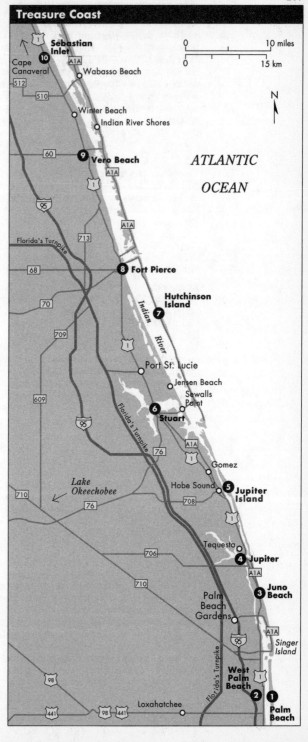

North of MacArthur State Park, Rte. A1A rejoins U.S. 1, then
③ veers east again 1½ miles north at **Juno Beach.** Take Rte. A1A
north to the **Loggerhead Park Marine Life Center of Juno
Beach,** established by Eleanor N. Fletcher, "the turtle lady of
Juno Beach." Museum displays interpret the sea turtles' natural history; hatchlings are raised in saltwater tanks, tagged
and released into the surf. The museum conducts guided turtle
watches June 1–July 15, at the height of the nesting season.
Also on view are displays of coastal natural history, sharks,
whales, and shells, and there are saltwater aquariums. *1111
Ocean Dr., but enter at 1200 U.S. 1, on the west side of the park,
Juno Beach, tel. 407/627–8280. Admission free. Open Tues.–
Sat. 10–3, Sun. 12–3.*

④ From Juno Beach north to **Jupiter,** Rte. A1A runs for almost 4
miles atop the beachfront dunes. West of the road, about half
the land is undeveloped, with endangered native plant communities. The road veers away from the dunes at **Carlin Park** (400
Rte. A1A, Jupiter, tel. 407/964–4420), which provides beach
frontage, covered picnic pavilions, hiking trails, a baseball dia-
mond, tot-lot, six tennis courts, and fishing sites. The Park
Galley, serving snacks and burgers, is usually open daily sunrise to sunset (closed Christmas Eve and Christmas Day).

At the northwest corner of Indiantown Road and Rte. A1A is
The Jupiter Theater (formerly the Burt Reynolds Jupiter Theater). Reynolds grew up in Jupiter; his father was a Palm Beach
County sheriff. More than 150 Broadway and Hollywood stars
have performed here since the theater opened in 1979. In 1989
Richard Akins acquired it and quickly established a reputation
for quality productions. In addition to mainstage attractions, a
murder mystery series with audience participation has been
added, and on some Saturday mornings there is a children's
theater presentation. *1001 E. Indiantown Rd., Jupiter, tel.
407/747–5566.*

Leave the theater grounds on Indiantown Road, go west to
U.S. 1, and turn right. About a mile north on Jupiter Island,
turn right into Burt Reynolds Park to visit the **Loxahatchee
Historical Society Museum.** Permanent exhibits completed in
1990 emphasize Seminole Indians, the steamboat era, pioneer
life on the Loxahatchee River, shipwrecks, railroads and modern-day development. A pioneer dwelling at the mouth of the
river, the Dubois Home, is open Sunday 1–3:30; ask for directions at the museum. *805 N. U.S. 1, Box 1506, Jupiter, tel. 407/
747–6639. $3 adults, $2 senior citizens, $1 children 6–18. Open
Tues.–Fri. 10–3, weekends 1–4. Closed Mon.*

Continue north on U.S. 1 across the Loxahatchee River and
⑤ pick up Rte. 707 north from the lighthouse onto **Jupiter Island.**
Just north of the Martin County line, stop at the Nature
Conservancy's 73-acre **Blowing Rocks Preserve,** where a new
information kiosk opened late in 1991. Within the preserve you
find plant communities native to beachfront dune, strand (the
landward side of the dunes), marsh, and hammock (tropical
hardwood forest). Sea grape, cabbage palms, saw palmetto,
and sea oats help to anchor the dunes. The floral beauty of Indian blanket, dune sunflower, and goldenrod carpets the ground.
A 2.5-acre native-plant nursery opened in 1992, and within the
grounds live pelicans, seagulls, ospreys, redbellied and pile-
ated woodpeckers, and a profusion of warblers in spring and
fall. A trail takes you over the dune to the beach. Best time to

go is early morning, before the crowds. The parking lot holds just 18 cars, with room for three cars to wait; Jupiter Island police will ticket cars parked along the road shoulder. *Box 3795, Tequesta, tel. 407/575–2297. No food, drinks, ice chests, pets, or spearfishing allowed. No rest rooms. Donation. Open 6–5.*

Continue north through the town of Jupiter Island, a posh community where President Bush's mother and many other notables dwell in estates screened from the road by dense vegetation. Some of the best surfing in Florida is found off Hobe Sound Beach Park, open to the public. At the north end of Jupiter Island, **Hobe Sound National Wildlife Refuge** has a 3½-mile beach where turtles nest and shells wash ashore in abundance. However, high tides and strong winds late in 1991 severely eroded the beach back to the dune. Only at low tide is there beach to walk on (admission: $3 per vehicle). On the mainland at refuge headquarters, visit the **Elizabeth W. Kirby Interpretive Center.** Take Rte. 707 and County Road 708 through the town of Hobe Sound to U.S. 1, then turn left and go about 2 miles south. The center is on the left (east) side of the highway. An adjacent ½-mile trail winds through a forest of sand pine and scrub oak—one of Florida's most unusual and endangered plant communities. *13640 S.E. Federal Hwy., Hobe Sound 33455, refuge tel. 407/546–2067. Trail open sunrise to sunset. Nature center open weekdays 9–11 and 1–3, group tours by appointment.*

From the interpretive center, go south 2½ miles to the entrance to **Jonathan Dickinson State Park.** Follow signs to Hobe Mountain, an ancient dune topped with a tower where you'll have a panoramic view across the park's 10,284 acres of varied terrain. It encompasses sand pine, slash pine, and palmetto flatwoods, mangrove river swamp, and the winding upper northwest fork of the Loxahatchee River, which is part of the federal government's wild and scenic rivers program and populated by manatees in winter and alligators all year. *14800 S.E. Federal Hwy., Hobe Sound, tel. 407/546–2771. Admission: $3.25 per car up to 8 persons, $1 per additional person. Facilities: bicycle and hiking trails, campground, snack bar. Contact State Vending Corp., 16450 S.E. Federal Hwy., Hobe Sound 33455, tel. 407/746–1466 for information and reservations on cabins, rental canoes. 2-hr narrated river cruise: $9 adults, $4 children under 12. Open daily 8–sundown.*

6 Return to U.S. 1 and proceed north. Quality-of-life values are most apparent in **Stuart**—the county seat—where downtown revival is making this one-time fishing village of fewer than 15,000 residents a magnet for people who want to live and work in a small-town atmosphere. Strict architectural and zoning standards guide civic renewal projects in the older section of Stuart. Recent completions include a 200-seat amphitheater at the foot of St. Lucie Street as centerpiece to the first mile of a 2-mile riverwalk scheduled for completion sometime in 1993. Meanwhile, the old courthouse has been opened for cultural exhibits, and a newly built gazebo features free music performances at noon about once a month. The Lyric Theater has been revived for performing and community events.

7 Continue north on Rte. A1A to **Hutchinson Island.** At Indian River Plantation, turn right onto MacArthur Boulevard 1.4 miles to the **House of Refuge Museum,** built in 1875 and now restored to its original appearance. It's one of 10 such structures that were erected by the U.S. Life Saving Service (an ancestor of the Coast Guard) to aid stranded sailors along Florida's then-remote Atlantic Coast. The keeper here patrolled the beach looking for shipwreck victims whose vessels foundered on Gilbert's Bar, an offshore reef. Exhibits include antique life-saving equipment, maps, ships' logs, artifacts from nearby wrecks, boatmaking tools, and six tanks of local fish from the ocean and the Indian River. The 35-foot watch-tower in the front yard was used during World War II by submarine spotters. *301 S.E. MacArthur Blvd., Stuart, tel. 407/225–1875. Admission: $1 adults, 50¢ children 6–13, under 6 free. Open Tues.–Sun. 1–4. Closed Mon. and holidays.*

Just south of the House of Refuge Museum, at the southern tip of Hutchinson Island, is **Bathtub Beach,** a public facility ideal for visitors with children because the waters are shallow for about 300 feet offshore and usually calm. At low tides bathers can walk to the reef. Facilities include rest rooms and showers.

Return to Rte. A1A and go ³⁄₁₀ mile north to the expanding **Coastal Science Center** (890 N.E. Ocean Blvd., Stuart 34996, tel. 407/225–0505) of the Florida Oceanographic Society. Its nearly 40-acre site combines a coastal hardwood hammock and mangrove forest. So far, resources include temporary displays about coastal ecology, a library program, and an interpretive nature trail. A visitor center is expected to be completed by early 1993.

Continue up Rte. A1A as far as the Jensen Beach Bridge. Cut back to the mainland and turn right on Indian River Drive, Rte. 707. This scenic road full of curves and dips follows the route of early-20th-century pineapple plantations. In **Fort Pierce,** turn right over the South Beach Causeway Bridge. On the east side, take the first road left onto the grounds of the **St. Lucie County Historical Museum,** where a memorial garden was added in 1991. Enter through a replica of the old **Fort Pierce FEC Railroad Station.** Among exhibits and early-20th-century memorabilia are photos and murals of Indian River Drive, along which you've just driven. A model of downtown Fort Pierce (ca. 1914) is under construction, but may be viewed before its completion, which is set for 1993–1994. Other displays include vintage farm tools, a newly restored 1919 fire engine, replica of a general store, and the restored 1905 Gardner House. *414 Seaway Dr., Fort Pierce, tel. 407/468–1795. Admission: $2 adults, $1 children 6–11, under 6 free. Open Tues.–Sat. 10–4, Sun. noon–4.*

From here, backtrack to the mainland, head north (right), and then turn east across North Beach Causeway. About a mile east, as you approach the ocean, Rte. A1A turns left. Go right instead to visit **Fort Pierce Inlet State Recreation Area,** where a sand bottom creates the Treasure Coast's safest surfing conditions and a nature trail winds through a coastal hammock.

North on Rte. A1A at Pepper Park is the **UDT-Seal Museum,** beside the beach where more than 3,000 Navy frogmen trained during World War II. The museum traces the exploits of Navy divers from the 1944 Normandy invasion through Korea, Vietnam, and astronaut landings at sea. *3300 N. AIA, Ft. Pierce, tel. 407/595–1570. Admission: $1 adults, 50¢ children 6–11, under 6 free. Open Tues.–Sat., 10–4, Sun. noon–4.*

Within a mile north of Pepper Beach, turn left to the parking lot for the 958-acre **Jack Island wildlife refuge,** accessible only by footbridge. The 1.4-mile Marsh Rabbit Trail across the island traverses a mangrove swamp to a 30-foot observation tower overlooking the Indian River. You'll see ospreys, brown pelicans, great blue herons, ibis, and other water birds. Trails cover 4.3 miles altogether.

9 Return to Rte. A1A and go north to **Vero Beach,** an affluent city of about 30,000; retirees comprise half the winter population. In the exclusive Riomar Bay section, north of the 17th Street Bridge, "canopy roads" shaded by massive live oaks cross the barrier island between Rte. A1A and Ocean Drive. **Painted Bunting Lane,** a typical canopy road, is lined with elegant homes—many dating from the 1920s.

The city provides beach-access parks (open daily 7 AM–10 PM, admission free) with boardwalks and steps bridging the foredune. From shore, snorkelers and divers can swim out to explore reefs 100–300 feet off the beach. Summer offers the best diving conditions. At low tide you can see the boiler and other remains of an iron-screw steamer, *Breconshire,* which foundered in 1894 on a reef just south of Beachland Boulevard.

Along Ocean Drive near Beachland Boulevard, a specialty shopping area includes art galleries, antique stores, and upscale clothing stores. Also in this area is **The Driftwood Inn Resort** (3150 Ocean Dr., Vero Beach, tel. 407/231–0550), a unique beachfront hotel (a time-share) and restaurant built in the 1930s by Waldo Sexton, an eccentric plow salesman from Indiana. He used driftwood and other scavenged lumber as well as art treasures salvaged from Palm Beach mansions torn down during the Depression.

Well endowed cultural life in Vero Beach centers around the twin arts facilities in Riverside Park. In the 633-seat **Riverside Theatre** (3250 Riverside Park Dr., Vero Beach, 32963, tel. 407/231–6990), the resident Equity troupe performs six shows a season and hosts road shows and visiting performers. The new $700,000 **Agnes Wahlstrom Youth Playhouse** opened in 1991 and is the home of the Riverside Childrens Theatre. **The Center for the Arts** (3001 Riverside Park Dr., tel. 407/231–0707), opened in 1986, operates the largest museum art school in Florida and houses a collection of 20th-century American art and contemporary Florida sculpture, and presents films, concerts, humanities lectures, seminars, and a year-round program of local and visiting exhibitions.

Continue north on Rte. A1A past the John's Island development. Turn left onto Old Winter Beach Road: The pavement turns to hard-packed dirt as the road curves north, indicating the old **Jungle Trail.** Portions of the trail along the Indian River are still undeveloped, with palms and moss-covered oaks abounding, and provide a glimpse of yesteryear Florida. Continue across paved Wabasso Beach Road (Rte. 510). Although the end of the trail is unmarked, the route is completed at Hwy. A1A, less than a half mile south of **McLarty Museum and Visitor's Center** (13180 N. Hwy. A1A, tel. 407/589–2147, Sebastian; open daily 10–5). Displays here are dedicated to the 1715 hurricane that sank a fleet of Spanish treasure ships. Turn left and

10 proceed 7 miles to **Sebastian Inlet.** The high bridge offers spectacular views as it connects the two sides of the 576-acre **State Recreation Area.** A vast stacking of fisherfolk clambers on jetties, walls, and piers. Sebastian offers the best inlet fishing in

Florida: catch depending on season includes bluefish, flounder, jack, redfish, sea trout, snapper, snook, or Spanish mackerel. Swimming and driftwood collecting are also popular. A concession on the north side of the inlet is open daily from 8–6 in summer and 8–8 in winter, selling fast food, apparel, and souvenirs. The bait shop is open 7–6 year-round. A party boat is available for offshore fishing. Two smaller concessions that serve hot dogs, burgers, and daily specials are also nearby: **Hobo 1** (on the north side) opens when the main concession closes and does not close as long as fisherfolk are around; **Hobo Too** (on the south side), is open from around 11 AM until dark.

Return via Rte. A1A to the Wabasso Beach Road, turn right, and continue via Rtes. 510 and 512 to I–95, turning south to complete the tour.

Spectator Sports

Baseball The **Los Angeles Dodgers** train each March in the 6,500-seat Holman Stadium at Dodgertown 4101 26th St., near the Municipal Airport. *Box 2887, Vero Beach 32961, tel. 407/569–4900.*

The **New York Mets** hold spring training in the 7,300-seat St. Lucie County Sport Complex, home stadium for the Florida League's St. Lucie Mets. A new exit—Exit 63C, St. Lucie West Blvd., off I–95—was opened in 1989. Take it east to Peacock Boulevard, where the stadium is located. *525 N.W. Peacock Blvd., Port St. Lucie 34986, tel. 407/871–2115.*

Polo **Windsor.** Geoffrey and Jorie Kent's polo club featured England's Prince Charles in a special charity game, the Prince of Wales Cup, when it opened in February of 1989. The season usually runs from mid-January to early April. Charity events benefit the international Friends of Conservation, of which Prince Charles is a patron. *3125 Windsor Blvd., Vero Beach 32963, tel. 407/388–5050 or 800/233–POLO.*

Dining

The list below is a representative selection of restaurants on the Treasure Coast, organized geographically, and by type of cuisine within each community. Unless otherwise noted, they serve lunch and dinner.

Highly recommended restaurants are indicated by a star ★.

Category	Cost*
Very Expensive	over $55
Expensive	$35–$55
Moderate	$15–$35
Inexpensive	under $15

average cost of a 3-course dinner, per person, excluding drinks, service, and 6% sales tax

The following credit card abbreviations are used: AE, American Express; D, Discover; DC, Diners Club; MC, MasterCard; and V, Visa.

Fort Pierce
Seafood

Mangrove Mattie's. Since its opening five years ago, this upscale rustic spot on Fort Pierce Inlet has provided dazzling views and imaginative decor with food to match. Try the shrimp brochette Key Largo, sizzled with garlic and butter; or on Thursday evenings, build your own roast beef sandwich for $1; and Friday evenings you can get ¼-lb. shrimp for $1. *1640 Seaway Dr., tel. 407/466–1044. Reservations advised. Dress: neat but casual. MC, V. Closed Christmas. Moderate.*

Theo Thudpucker's Raw Bar. Businesspeople dressed for work mingle here with people who come in off the beach wearing shorts. On squally days everyone piles in off the jetty. Specialties include oyster stew, smoked fish spread, conch salad and fritters, fresh catfish, and alligator tail. *2025 Seaway Dr. (South Jetty), tel. 407/465–1078. No reservations. Dress: informal. No credit cards. Closed Christmas, Thanksgiving. Inexpensive.*

Jensen Beach
Continental

11 Maple Street. This 13-table cracker-quaint restaurant sits 2 blocks off the railroad tracks and offers gourmet specialties made from scratch, including a walnut bread with melted fontina cheese appetizer; and shrimp pasta with sun-dried tomatoes, vermouth, and herbs fresh from the garden. While you wait for dinner, prepared to order, you can indulge with beer and wine on the tropical porch or in the flower garden. *3224 Maple Ave., tel. 407/334–7714. Reservations required. Dress: neat but casual. MC, V. Closed Mon.; Mon.–Wed. June–Aug.; no weekend lunches. Moderate.*

Seafood
★

Conchy Joe's. This classic Florida stilt-house full of antique fish mounts, gator hides, and snakeskins dates from the late 1920s, though Conchy Joe's, like a hermit crab sidling into a new shell, only sidled up in '83 from West Palm Beach for the relaxed atmosphere of Jensen Beach. It still feels utterly island where, under a huge Seminole-built *chickee* with a palm through the roof, you get the freshest Florida seafoods from a menu that changes daily—though some things never change: grouper marsala, the house specialty; broiled sea scallops; fried cracked conch. Try the rum drinks with names like Goombay Smash, Bahama Mama, and Jamaica Wind, while you listen to steel band calypsos Thursday through Sunday nights. *3945 N. Indian River Dr., tel. 407/334–1131. No reservations. Dress: casual. AE, MC, V. Closed Thanksgiving, Christmas Eve, Christmas, New Year's Day, Superbowl Sun. Moderate.*

Rio
Continental

The Country Place. Superb dinners are served at this little English country-style restaurant rich in lace, burgundy, and paisley. A pleasant stop on the winding road between Stuart and Jensen Beach, the Country Place exudes coziness. Family culinary tradition stems from Bournemouth brothers Barry (chef) and John (maître d') whose father was a chef on the original *Queen Elizabeth.* Nightly specials may include jumbo scallops in black bean sauce; raspberry duck; or a seafood Wellington: salmon, scallops, shrimp, and crabmeat beautifully layered in a puff pastry on bed of spinach, with plenty fresh basil from Lucky, the Thai waitress and gardener. Save room for the homemade whisky pie, the crème brûlée, or strawberries Grand Marnier. *1205 N.E. Dixie Hwy. (S.R. 707), tel. 407/334–4563. Reservations advised. Dress: casual but neat. Beer and wine only. Dinner only. AE, MC, V. Closed Sun. and Mon. June–Dec; New Year's Day, Super Bowl Sun., Thanksgiving, Christmas. Moderate.*

Stuart *American*	**The Emporium.** Indian River Plantation's coffee shop is an old-fashioned soda fountain and grill that also serves hearty breakfasts. Specialties include eggs Benedict, omelets, and fresh-baked pastries. *555 N.E. Ocean Blvd., Hutchinson Island, tel. 407/225–3700. No reservations. Dress: informal. AE, DC, MC, V. Inexpensive.*

The Porch. This casual indoor/outdoor restaurant overlooks the tennis courts at Indian River Plantation. Specialties include hearty clam chowder, a daily quiche, fried calamari, and two daily selections of fresh fish. *555 N.E. Ocean Blvd., Hutchinson Island, tel. 407/225–3700. No reservations. Dress: informal. AE, DC, MC, V. Inexpensive.*

Continental

★ **The Inlet.** This intimate 60-seat restaurant in the heart of Indian River Plantation features fine dining on gold-rimmed plates in a setting of ethereal pinks and earth tones. Specialties include oysters Rockefeller, creamy lobster bisque with cognac, steak Diane, and fresh snapper. *555 N.E. Ocean Blvd., Hutchinson Island, tel. 407/225–3700. Reservations required. Jacket required. AE, DC, MC, V. No lunch. Closed Sun. and Mon. Expensive.*

★ **Scalawags.** Part of Indian River Plantation's new hotel complex, Scalawags can seat you on a terrace overlooking the marina, in a dining room decorated with original paintings of Florida birds, or in a private 20-seat wine room. Specialties include Caribbean conch soup, sea scallops with fresh dill sauce, seafood ravioli, and rack of lamb. The Sunday champagne brunch is superb. *555 N.E. Ocean Blvd., Hutchinson Island, tel. 407/225–3700. Reservations suggested. Dress: casual but neat. AE, DC, MC, V. Dinner only. Expensive.*

The Ashley. Opened in 1990 this art- and plant-filled 84-seater is on the site of an early Stuart bank that was robbed three times by the Ashley gang. The bank impression has been revived with an old cashier's cage, original tile floor, open-beam ceiling, and brick columns. Breakfast is offered Saturdays and Sundays; lunch and dinner are served daily. The menu appeals with the freshest foods, and features lots of salads, fresh fish, and pastas. *61 S.W. Osceola St., tel. 407/221–9476. Dress: casual but neat. AE, MC, V. Closed major holidays. Moderate.*

Seafood

★ **Mahony's Oyster Bar.** Mike Mahony ensures the personal scale by limiting what he buys to what he can carry on his bike. Well, the beer's trucked in—real stuff like Guinness and Harp, and Molson on draft. Choose from 12 tables and booths, or sit at the 14-stool bar, where Mike's got 13 hot sauces lined up to go with the oysters, clams, and shrimp stew. A chalkboard lists items such as sardines and greens on toast, with green onions, red pepper ring, and parsley and a basic pub salad. Decor consists of wind socks, oars, fish traps and nets, charts, and a couple worshipful paintings of Mike and his bar, and another of Chief Osceola. *201 St. Lucie Ave., tel. 407/286–9757. No reservations. Dress: casual. Beer and wine only. No credit cards. Closed Sun. and dinner Mon.–Wed., major holidays (except St. Patrick's Day), and Aug.–Sept. Inexpensive.*

Vero Beach
American **The Patio.** What immediately catches your eye is the tile bar from Spain, the Druze-tribe wood panels from Lebanon, and rafter ceilings and lighting fixtures from the Dodge, Mizner, Rockefeller, and Stotesbury estates. Young professionals to retirees pack the place evenings by 5 when hot hors d'oeuvres—ample as a meal—are served in the happy hour bar. Open 365 days a year, The Patio features big weekly events such as the Friday and Saturday night video sing-alongs and the Sunday all-you-can-eat champagne brunch at $11.95 (60-plus items with endless bubbly and mimosas). Otherwise it's all-American fare, with steaks, prime ribs, chicken, and seafood. *1103 Miracle Mile, Vero Beach, tel. 407/567–7215. Dress: casual but neat. AE, MC, V. Moderate.*

Continental **The Black Pearl.** This intimate restaurant (19 tables) with pink
★ and green art deco furnishings offers entrées that combine fresh local ingredients with the best of the Continental tradition. Specialties include chilled leek-and-watercress soup, local fish in parchment paper, feta cheese and spinach fritters, mesquite-grilled swordfish, and pan-fried veal with crab meat with hollandaise and asparagus. *1409 Rte. A1A, tel. 407/234–4426. Reservations advised. AE, MC, V. Dinner only. Closed major holidays and Super Bowl Sun. Moderate.*

Seafood **Ocean Grill.** Opened by Waldo Sexton as a hamburger shack in 1938, the Ocean Grill has since been refurbished and outfitted with antiques—Tiffany lamps, wrought-iron chandeliers, and Beanie Backus paintings of pirates and Seminole Indians. The menu has also changed with the times and now includes black bean soup, crisp onion rings, jumbo lump crabmeat salad, at least three kinds of fish every day, prime rib, and a tart Key lime pie. *Sexton Plaza (Beachland Blvd. east of Ocean Dr.), tel. 407/231–5409. Reservations accepted for parties of 5 or more. AE, MC, V. Closed weekend lunch, Thanksgiving, Super Bowl Sun., 2 weeks following Labor Day. Moderate.*

Lodging

The list below is a representative selection of hotels and guest houses on the Treasure Coast. The rate categories in the list are based on the all-year or peak-season price; off-peak rates may be a category or two lower.

Highly recommended lodgings are indicated by a star ★.

Category	Cost*
Very Expensive	over $120
Expensive	$90–$120
Moderate	$50–$90
Inexpensive	under $50

*All prices are for a standard double room, excluding 6% state sales tax and nominal tourist tax.

Stuart **Indian River Plantation.** Situated on a 192-acre tract of land on
★ Hutchinson Island, this resort includes a three-story luxury hotel that is an architectural gem in the Victorian Beach Revival style, with tin roofs, shaded verandas, pink stucco, and much latticework. Seventy new oceanfront rooms and suites with microwave and range-top kitchens opened in 1992. *555 N.E. Ocean Blvd., Hutchinson Island, 34996, tel. 407/225–3700 or 800/444–3389. 200 hotel rooms with bath, including 10 rooms for handicapped guests; 54 1- and 2-bedroom oceanfront condominium apartments with full kitchens. Facilities: 3 pools, outdoor spa, 13 tennis courts (7 lighted), golf course, 77-*

slip marina, power boat and jet-ski rentals, beach club with
tiki bar and grill, 5 restaurants. AE, DC, MC, V. Very Expensive.

Guest House   **The Homeplace.** The house was built in 1913 by pioneer Sam
Matthews who contracted much of the early town construction
for railroad developer Henry Flagler. To preserve the structure, present-day developer Jim Smith moved it from Frazier
Creek to Creekside Common. The new riverwalk will wrap
around the property. Smith's wife Jean Bell has restored the
house to its early look, from hardwood floors to fluffy pillows.
Fern-filled dining and sun rooms, full of chintz-covered cush-
ioned wicker, overlook a pool and patio. Three guest rooms are
Captain's Quarters, Opal's Room, and Prissy's Place. *501 Ak-
ron Ave., 34994, tel. 407/220–9148. 3 rooms with bath. Facilities: pool, spa. MC, V. Expensive–Moderate.*

Vero Beach   **Guest Quarters Suite Hotel.** Built in 1986, this five-story rose-
color stucco hotel on Ocean Drive provides easy access to Vero
Beach's specialty shops and boutiques. First-floor rooms have
patios opening onto the pool. *3500 Ocean Dr., 32963, tel. 407/
231–5666 or 800/742–5388. 55 1- and 2-bedroom suites with
bath. Facilities: pool, outdoor pool bar/restaurant, TV, movie
rentals. All suites with balconies and ocean views, in-room
refrigerators stocked with candy bars, snacks, sodas; coffee-
makers; VCRs. AE, D, DC, MC, V. Very Expensive.*

6 The Florida Keys

Introduction

By George and
Rosalie Leposky

Updated by Herb
Hiller

The Florida Keys are a wilderness of flowering jungles and
shimmering seas, a jade pendant of mangrove-fringed islands
dangling toward the tropics. The Florida Keys are also a 110-
mile traffic jam lined with garish billboards, hamburger
stands, shopping centers, motels, and trailer courts. Unfortunately, you can't have one without the other. A river of tourist
dollars gushes southward along the only highway—U.S. 1—to
Key West. Many residents of Monroe County live by diverting
some of that river's green flow to their own pockets, in ways
that have in spots blighted the Keys' fragile beauty—at least
on the 34 islands linked to the mainland by the 42 bridges of the
Overseas Highway. In effect, the Keys' natural resources have
paid the price. However, new protective national and state leg-
islation has begun to challenge local landowners, and soon visitors may be asked to share in the cost. In 1990 President Bush
approved a new 200-mile-long Florida Keys National Marine
Sanctuary (the largest in the nation), for which the National
Oceanic and Atmospheric Administration intends to develop a
management strategy for the Keys by 1993. The Monroe County Commission in 1991 went on record favoring a five-year mor-
atorium on almost all new development beginning the end of
1992. The State of Florida seems more likely than ever to coop-
erate.

For now, however, take pleasure as you drive down U.S. 1
through the islands. The silvery blue and green Atlantic, with
its great living reef, is on your left, and Florida Bay, the Gulf of
Mexico and the back country are on your right. At points the
ocean and the gulf are 10 miles apart; on the narrowest landfill
islands, they are separated only by the road.

The Overseas Highway varies from a frustrating traffic-
clogged trap to a mystical pathway skimming across the sea.
There are more islands than you will be able to remember. Follow the little green mile markers by the side of U.S. 1, and even
if you lose track of the names of the islands, you won't get lost.

There are many things to do along the way, but first you have to
remind yourself to get off the highway, which—lined with
junk—still has the seductive power of keeping you to itself.
Once you leave this road, you can rent a boat and find a secluded
anchorage at which to fish, swim, and marvel at the sun, sea,
and sky. To the south in the Atlantic, you can dive to spectacular coral reefs or pursue dolphin, blue marlin, and other deep-
water game fish. Along the Florida Bay coastline you can seek
out the bonefish, snapper, snook, and tarpon that lurk in the
grass flats and in the shallow, winding channels of the back
country.

Along the reefs and among the islands are more than 600 kinds
of fish. Diminutive deer and pale raccoons, related to but distinct from their mainland cousins, inhabit the Lower Keys. And
throughout the islands you'll find such exotic West Indian
plants as Jamaica dogwood, pigeon plum, poisonwood, satinwood, and silver and thatch palms, as well as tropical birds like
the great white heron, mangrove cuckoo, roseate spoonbill,
and white-crowned pigeon.

Another Keys attraction is the weather: in the winter it's typically 10 degrees warmer in the Keys than on the mainland; in

the summer it's usually 10 degrees cooler. The Keys also get substantially less rain, around 30 inches annually compared to 55–60 inches in Miami and the Everglades. Most of the rain falls in brief, vigorous thunderstorms on summer afternoons. In winter, continental cold fronts occasionally stall over the Keys, dragging temperatures down to the 40s.

The Keys were only sparsely populated until the early 20th century. In 1905, however, railroad magnate Henry Flagler began building the overseas extension of his east coast Florida railroad south from Homestead to Key West. His goal was to establish a rail link to the steamships that sailed between Key West and Havana, just 90 miles away across the Straits of Florida. The railroad arrived at Key West in 1912 and remained a lifeline of commerce until the Labor Day hurricane of 1935 washed out much of its roadbed. For three years thereafter, the only way in and out of Key West was by boat. The Overseas Highway, built over the railroad's old roadbeds and bridges, was completed in 1938.

Although on the surface the Keys seem homogenous to most mainlanders, they are actually quite varied in terms of population and ambience. Most of the residents of the Upper Keys, which extend from Key Largo to Long Key Channel, moved to Florida from the Northeast and Midwest; many are retirees. Most of the work force is employed by the tourism and service industries. Key Largo, the largest of the keys and the one closest to the mainland, is becoming a bedroom community for Homestead, South Dade, and even the southern reaches of Miami. In the Middle Keys, from Long Key Channel through Marathon to Seven Mile Bridge, fishing and related services dominate the economy. Most residents are the children and grandchildren of migrants from other southern states. The Lower Keys from Seven Mile Bridge down to Key West have a diverse population: native "Conchs" (white Key Westers, many of whom trace their ancestry to the Bahamas), freshwater Conchs (longtime residents who migrated from somewhere else years ago), gays (who now make up at least 20% of Key West's citizenry), Bahamians, Hispanics (primarily Cubans), recent refugees from the urban sprawl of Miami and Fort Lauderdale, transient Navy and Air Force personnel, students waiting tables, and a miscellaneous assortment of vagabonds, drifters, and dropouts in search of refuge at the end of the road.

Essential Information

Arriving and Departing

By Plane Shuttle and connecting flights go to **Key West International Airport** (S. Roosevelt Blvd., tel. 305/296–5439) from the Miami and Orlando International airports. From Miami, you can fly direct to Key West on American Eagle and USAir. From Fort Lauderdale-Hollywood you can fly direct on Delta ComAir. From Orlando you must change planes in Miami unless you fly with Delta ComAir, which has limited nonstop service to Key West as well as connecting service through Fort Lauderdale–Hollywood.

Chalk's (1000 MacArthur Cswy., tel. 305/371–8628 or 800/424–2557), the venerable seaplane service operating out of Miami, flies 17-passenger seaplanes five days a week to Key West: two flights Friday and Sunday (9:15 AM and 2:40 PM), and one flight Monday, Wednesday, and Saturday at 1:05. Depending on how far in advance you buy your ticket, round-trip fare ranges between $124 and $256. Flights land and take off from Key West International Airport while Chalk's continues to look for a suitable marine ramp.

Carriers that provide direct service between Miami and **Marathon Airport** (MM 52, BS, 9000 Overseas Hwy., tel. 305/743–2155) include Airways International (tel. 305/743–0500), and American Eagle (tel. 800/433–7300). **Air Sunshine** (tel. 305/434–8900 in Fort Lauderdale; 800/432–1744 elsewhere in FL) provides direct service between Fort Lauderdale and Marathon.

Between Miami and the Keys   **The Airporter.** Scheduled van and bus service is available from the lower level of MIA's Concourse E to major hotels in Key Largo ($25 per person) and Islamorada ($28 per person). *88890 Overseas Hwy., Tavernier 33070, MM 88.8, tel. 305/852–3413, 305/852–3306 (Tavernier), 305/247–8874 (Miami). Reservations required.*
Island Taxi. Meets arriving flights at MIA. Reservations are required 24 hours in advance for arrivals, one hour for departures. Accompanied children under 12 ride free. *Tel. 305/664–8181 (Upper Keys), 305/743–0077 (Middle Keys), 305/745–2200 (Lower Keys). Fare from airport to destination for 1 or 2 persons: $80 Key Largo, $100 Islamorada, $175 Marathon, $200 Key West; each additional person $5, except to Key West $10. Inquire for arrangements north of Miami and for van rates.*

By Car   If you want to avoid Miami traffic on the way to the Keys, take the Homestead Extension of Florida's Turnpike; although it's a toll road that carries a lot of commuter traffic, it's still the fastest way to go. From MIA, take LeJeune Road (SW 42nd Ave.) south, turn west on the Dolphin Expressway (Rte. 836) to the turnpike, then go south to the turnpike's southern end. If you prefer traffic to tolls, take LeJeune Road south to U.S. 1 and turn right.

Just south of Florida City, the turnpike joins U.S. 1 and the Overseas Highway begins. Once you cross the Jewfish Creek bridge at the north end of Key Largo, you're officially in the Keys.

From Florida City, you can also reach Key Largo on Card South Road. Go 13 miles south to the Card Sound Bridge (toll: $1), which offers a spectacular view of blue water and mangrove-fringed bays (and of Florida Power & Light Company's hulking Turkey Point nuclear power plant in the distance to your left). At low tide, flocks of herons, ibis, and other birds frequent the mud flats on the margin of the sound. Beyond the bridge, on north Key Largo, the road traverses a mangrove swamp with ponds and inlets harboring the exceedingly rare Florida crocodile. At the only stop sign, turn right onto Route 905, which cuts through some of the Keys' few remaining large tracts of tropical hardwood jungle. You'll rejoin U.S. 1 in north Key Largo 31 miles from Florida City.

Car Rentals   All six of the rental-car firms with booths inside Miami International Airport also have outlets in Key West, which means you can drive into the Keys and fly out. Don't fly into Key West and drive out; the rental firms have substantial drop charges to leave a Key West car in Miami. Some rental car locations other than the airport include **Hertz** (3840 N. Roosevelt Blvd., tel. 305/294–1039 or 800/654–3131); **Keys Jeep Eagle** (1111 Eaton St., tel. 305/294–2883); **National** (2826 N. Roosevelt Blvd., tel. 305/296–7760 or 800/CAR–RENT); and **Tropical Rent A-Car** (1300 Duval St., tel. 305/294–8136). Avis and Hertz also serve Marathon Airport.

Enterprise Rent-A-Car has offices at MIA, several Keys locations, and participating hotels in the Keys where you can pick up and drop off cars when the offices are closed. You can rent a car from Enterprise at MIA and return it there, or leave it in the Keys for a drop charge. *Tel. 305/876–9749 or 800/325–8007 (Miami); 305/451–3998 (Key Largo); tel. 305/292–0220 (Key West). AE, D, DC, MC, V. Open weekdays 8–6, Sat. 9–noon.*

By Bus **Greyhound/Trailways.** Buses traveling between Miami and Key West make 8 scheduled stops, but you can flag down a bus anywhere along the route. *Tel. 305/374–7222 (Miami) for schedule; 24-hr Miami Greyhound Station, Miami Airport, 4111 N.W. 27th St., tel. 305/871–1810; Downtown Miami, 700 Biscayne Blvd., tel. 305/379–7403; Tavernier, tel. 305/852–4666; Big Pine Key, tel. 305/872–4022; Key West, 615½ Duval St., tel. 305/296–9072. No reservations.*

By Boat Boaters can travel to Key West either along the Intracoastal Waterway through Florida Bay, or along the Atlantic Coast. The Keys are full of marinas that welcome transient visitors, but they don't have enough slips for everyone who wants to visit the area. Make reservations in advance, and ask about channel and dockage depth—many Key marinas are quite shallow.

Florida Marine Patrol (MM 49, OS, 2835 Overseas Hwy., Marathon, tel. 305/289–2320).

Coast Guard Group Key West provides 24-hour monitoring of VHF-FM Channel 16. Safety and weather information is broadcast at 7 AM and 5 PM Eastern Standard time on VHF-FM Channel 16 and 22A. *Key West 33040, tel. 305/292–8727. 3 stations in the Keys: Islamorada, tel. 305/664–4404; Marathon, tel. 305/743–6778; Key West, tel. 305/292–8856.*

Getting Around

The only address many people have is a mile marker (MM) number. The markers themselves are small green rectangular signs along the side of the Overseas Highway (U.S. 1). They begin with MM 126 a mile south of Florida City and end with MM 0 on the corner of Fleming and Whitehead streets in Key West. Keys residents also use the abbreviation BS for the Bay Side of U.S. 1, and OS for the Atlantic Ocean Side of the highway.

Florida Visitor Centers and the Florida Department of Commerce distribute *Florida's Official Transportation Map* free. Write to Florida Department of Commerce (Collins Bldg., Tallahassee 32304).

The best road map for the Florida Keys is published by the Homestead/Florida City Chamber of Commerce. You can obtain a copy at the Tropical Everglades Visitor Center in Florida

City, or by mail. *160 U.S. Hwy. 1, Florida City 33034, tel. 305/ 245–9180. Open daily 8–6. Map costs $2.*

Throughout the Keys, the local chambers of commerce, marinas, and dive shops will offer you the local **Teall's Guide**—a land and nautical map—for $1, which goes to build mooring buoys to protect living coral reefs from boat anchors. The separate guides that used to cover Miami to Key Largo, John Pennekamp Coral Reef State Park and Key Largo National Marine Sanctuary, the Middle Keys, and Marathon-Key West are now in a 12″×18″ complete Florida packet that costs $14.95, postage included. The packet for only the Florida Keys and the Everglades is $5.95. Order from Teall's Florida Guides (111 Saguaro Ln., Marathon 33050, tel. 305/743–3942).

By Car   The 18-mile stretch of U.S. 1 from Florida City to Key Largo is a hazardous two-lane road with heavy traffic (especially on weekends) and only two passing zones. Try to drive it in daylight, and be patient day or night. The Overseas Highway is four lanes wide in Key Largo, Marathon, and Stock Island (just north of Key West), but narrow and crowded elsewhere. Expect delays behind large tractor-trailer trucks, cars towing boats, and rubbernecking tourists. Allow at least five hours from Florida City to Key West on a good day. After midnight, you can make the trip in three hours—but then you miss the scenery.

In Key West's Old Town, parking is scarce and costly ($1.50 per hour at Mallory Square, however the first 10 minutes are free). Use a taxicab, bicycle, moped, or your feet to get around. Elsewhere in the Keys, however, having a car is crucial. Gas prices are higher in the Keys than on the mainland. Fill your tank in Miami and top it off in Florida City.

By Bus   The **City of Key West Port and Transit Authority** operates two bus lines: Mallory Square (counterclockwise around the island) and Old Town (clockwise around the island). A free Shopping Center Shuttle (Key Plaza to Searstown), which runs Tuesday and Thursday afternoon only, has been resumed. *Tel. 305/292– 8165. Exact fare: 75¢, senior citizens and students with ID, children under 5 and handicapped riders 35¢; monthly pass, $20, senior citizens and students $12.*

By Taxi   **Island Taxi** offers 24-hour service from Key Largo to Boca Chica Key. Accompanied children ride free. There is service to downtown Key West but no pick-up there. *Tel. 305/664–8181 (Upper Keys), 305/743–0077 (Middle Keys), 305/745–2200 (Lower Keys). Fare: $4 for first 2 mi, then $1.50 per mi.*

Maxi-Taxi Sun Cab System (tel. 305/294–2222 or 305/296–7777) provides 24-hour service in Key West.

By Limousine   **Carriage Trade Limousine Service** (tel. 305/296–0000) provides airport van service: $5 per person; cab service: $6 per person. Local metered service, $1.40 first ⅕-mi, 35¢ each additional ⅕-mi. Inquire for group and zone rates.

Important Addresses and Numbers

Tourist Information   **Florida Keys & Key West Visitors Bureau** (Box 1147, Key West 33041, tel. 800/FLA–KEYS). Ask for their free accommodations guide.

Local chambers of commerce in Key Largo, Islamorada, Marathon, the Lower Keys, and Key West have visitor centers with information on accommodations, recreation, restaurants, and special events:

Key Largo Chamber of Commerce (MM 106, BS, 105950 Overseas Hwy., Key Largo 33037, tel. 305/451–1414 or 800/822–1088).
Islamorada Chamber of Commerce (MM 82.5, BS, Box 915, Islamorada 33036, tel. 305/664–4503 or 800/FAB–KEYS).
Greater Marathon Chamber of Commerce (MM 48.7, BS, 3330 Overseas Hwy., Marathon 33050, tel. 305/743–5417 or 800/842–9580).
Lower Keys Chamber of Commerce (MM 31, OS, Box 511, Big Pine Key 33043, tel. 305/872–2411 or 800/872–3722).
Greater Key West Chamber of Commerce (402 Wall St., Key West 33040, tel. 305/294–2587 or 800/648–6269).

Emergencies   Dial 911 for **ambulance** and **police.**

Hospitals   The following hospitals have 24-hour emergency rooms: **Mariners Hospital** (MM 88.5, BS, 50 High Point Rd., Tavernier, Plantation Key 33070; physician-referral service, tel. 305/852–9222), **Fishermen's Hospital** (MM 48.7, OS, 3301 Overseas Hwy., Marathon, tel. 305/743–5533), and **Florida Keys Memorial Hospital** (MM5, BS, 5900 Junior College Rd., Stock Island, tel. 305/294–5531).

Late-Night   The Keys have no 24-hour pharmacies. Hospital pharmacists
Pharmacies   will help with emergencies after regular retail business hours.

Guided Tours

Orientation Tours   **The Conch Tour Train.** This 90-minute narrated tour of Key West travels 14 miles through Old Town and around the island. The driver pauses frequently to discuss points of historical interest and to chat with friends. *Boarding Locations: Mallory Sq. Depot every half hour, Roosevelt Blvd. Depot just north of the Quality Inn every hour on the half hour; tel. 305/294–5161. Fare: $11 adults, $5 children. No credit cards. Runs daily 9–4:30.*

Old Town Trolley. Key West has 11 trackless trolley-style buses that run every 30 minutes. The trolleys are smaller than the Conch Tour Train and go places the train won't fit. The narrated trolley tour lasts 90 minutes, passes more than 100 points of interest, and makes 14 stops all around the island. You may disembark at any stop and reboard a later trolley. *1910 N. Roosevelt Blvd., Key West 33040, tel. 305/296–6688. Admission: $12 adults, $5 children. D, MC, V. Runs 9 AM–4:30 PM.*

Special-Interest   **Island Aeroplane Tours.** Tours in this open cockpit biplane oper-
Tours   ate out of Key West International Airport, and up to two people
Air Tours   can fly for a quick overview of Key West ($50 for two), to up to 50 minutes for a long look at the offshore reefs ($200 for two, other tours priced in between). Flights operate between 9 AM and sunset. *3469 S. Roosevelt Blvd. (Key West International Airport), tel. 305/294–TOUR. Reservations advised. AE, MC, V.*

Key West Seaplane Service. Enjoy either half-day or full-day trips to the Dry Tortugas in single-engine seaplanes, with flights operating every day, weather permitting. All tours depart Stock Island (last island before Key West). Half-day tours run 8 AM and 12 noon, with two hours on the island; full-day tours leave 8 AM, with six hours on the island. Camping trips from over-night for up to two weeks (you supply all your own gear, including water) also available. Capacity is five passengers per plane. *5603 Junior College Rd., Key West 33040, tel. 305/294–6978. Half-day tours $139 per person, full-day $239; camping trips $259. Reservations required. AE, MC, V.*

Canoe Tours **Canoeing Nature Tours.** Stan Becker leads a full-day 5-mile ca-noe and hiking trip in the Key Deer National Wildlife Refuge. The trip includes three hours in canoes and four hours explor-ing Watson Hammock on Big Pine Key. *MM 28, BS, Box 62, Big Pine Key 33043, tel. 305/872–2620. Reservations required. Children welcome; no pets. Box lunch provided. Fee: $65 per person. 9 AM–4 PM.*

Kayak Tours **Mosquito Coast Island Outfitters & Kayak Guides.** Half-day guided sea kayak tours explore the lush backcountry marsh just east of Key West. Two-person kayaks allow a parent to ac-company a child. Only bad weather cancels daily year-round departures. *1107 Duval St., Key West. tel. 305/294–7178. Reservations required. Mineral water, granola bars, cap, and snorkel gear provided. Cost: $45 per person. AE, MC, V. 8:45 AM departure, 3 PM return.*

Sunset and Harbor Boat Tours Residents and tourists alike flock to west-facing restaurants, hotel docks, and bars to watch the glowing orb sink into the sea. Hundreds of people gather on Key West's Mallory Square Dock, where street performers and food vendors vie with the sunset for your attention. Throughout the keys, many motor yacht and sailboat captains take paying passengers on sunset cruises. Contact local chambers of commerce and hotels for in-formation.

M/V *Miss Key West* offers a one-hour narrated cruise that ex-plores Key West's harbor up to a half-mile from shore. The 45-passenger, 45-foot motor yacht passes Trumbo Point Navy Base, home of all six of the Navy's hydrofoil guided-missile de-stroyers. The sundown cruise includes live music. Call for de-parture times and for additional snorkel trips (all equipment and lessons provided). *Zero Duval St. (booth in front of Ocean Key House), tel. 305/296–8865, in FL 800/238–9815. Admis-sion: harbor and sunset cruise $8 adults, children under 12 free. AE, MC, V. Open 8 AM–11 PM.*

Walking Tours **Pelican Path** is a free walking guide to Key West published by the **Old Island Restoration Foundation.** The tour discusses the history and architecture of 43 structures along 25 blocks of 12 Old town streets. Pick up a copy at the Key West Chamber of Commerce.

Solares Hill's Walking and Biking Guide to Old Key West, by lo-cal historian Sharon Wells, contains at least six walking tours of the city and a short tour of the Key West cemetery. Free cop-ies are available from Key West Chamber of Commerce, many hotels and stores.

Water Wildlife Tours, run by native-born Capt. Vicki Impal-lomeni, an authority on the ecology of Florida Bay and activist for its preservation, features half-day and full-day charters in her 22-ft. Aquasport open fisherman, *The Imp II.* Families es-pecially like exploring with Capt. Vicki because of her ability to teach youngsters. *23 Key Haven Terr., Key West 33040, tel.*

305/294–9731. Tours depart Paradise Marina on Stock Island typically 8:30 and 12:30 for half-day ($250), as early as 7 for full-day ($350), for up to 5 passengers. Reservations necessary, at least a month ahead in winter. AE, MC, V.

Exploring the Florida Keys

Numbers in the margin correspond to points of interest on the Florida Keys map.

The Upper Keys

This tour begins on Key Largo, the northeasternmost of the Florida Keys accessible by road. The tour assumes that you have come south from Florida City on **Card Sound Road** (Rte. 5). If you take the Overseas Highway (U.S. 1) south from Florida City, you can begin the tour with Key Largo Underseas Park. Attractions are listed by island or by mile marker (MM) number.

Cross the **Card Sound Bridge** onto **North Key Largo,** where Card Sound Road forms the eastern boundary of **Crocodile Lakes National Wildlife Refuge.** In the refuge dwell some 300 to 500 crocodiles, the largest single concentration of these shy, elusive reptiles in North America. There's no visitor center here—just 6,800 acres of mangrove swamp and adjoining upland jungle. For your best chance to see a crocodile, park on the shoulder of Card Sound Road and scan the ponds along the road with binoculars. In winter, crocodiles often haul out and sun themselves on the banks farthest from the road. Don't leave the road shoulder; you could disturb tern nests on the nearby spoil banks or aggravate the rattlesnakes.

Take Card Sound Road to Route 905, turn right, and drive for 10 miles through **Key Largo Hammock,** the largest remaining stand of the vast West Indian tropical hardwood forest that once covered most of the upland areas in the Florida Keys. The state and federal governments are busy acquiring as much of the hammock as they can to protect it from further development, and they hope to establish visitor centers and nature trails. For now, it's best to admire this wilderness from the road. According to law-enforcement officials, this may be the most dangerous place in the United States, a haven for modern-day pirates and witches. The "pirates" are drug smugglers who land their cargo along the ocean shore or drop it into the forest from low-flying planes. The "witches" are practitioners of voodoo, *santeria*, and other occult rituals. What's more, this jungle is full of poisonous plants. The most dangerous, the manchineel or "devil tree," has a toxin so potent that rainwater falling on its leaves and then onto a person's skin can cause sores that resist healing. Florida's first tourist, explorer Juan Ponce de León, died in 1521 from a superficial wound inflicted by an Indian arrowhead dipped in manchineel sap.

❶ Continue on U.S. 1 to Transylvania Avenue (MM 103.2) and turn left to visit the **Key Largo Undersea Park.** The family attractions include an underwater museum that you have to snorkel or dive to, underwater music, and an air-conditioned grotto theater with a 13-minute multimedia slide show devoted to the history of man and sea. *Key Largo Undersea Park, 51 Shoreland Dr., Box 3330, Key Largo, tel. 305/451–2353. Aquarium*

The Florida Keys

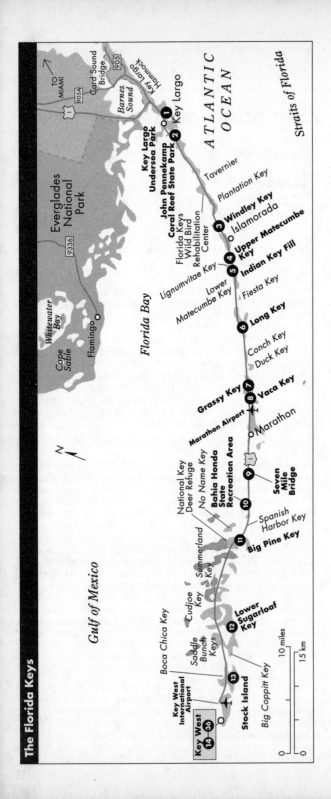

TO MIAMI

Card Sound Bridge

905

905A

Barnes Sound

Key Largo Hammock

1

ATLANTIC OCEAN

Straits of Florida

❶ Key Largo

❷

Key Largo Undersea Park

John Pennekamp Coral Reef State Park

Tavernier

Plantation Key

Florida Keys Wild Bird Rehabilitation Center

❸ **Windley Key**

Islamorada

❹ **Upper Matecumbe Key**

❺ **Indian Key Fill**

Lignumvitae Key

Lower Matecumbe Key

Fiesta Key

❻ **Long Key**

Conch Key

Duck Key

❼ **Vaca Key**

❽

Grassy Key

Marathon Airport

Marathon

1

❾

Seven Mile Bridge

❿

Spanish Harbor Key

National Key Deer Refuge

No Name Key

Bahia Honda State Recreation Area

⓫ **Big Pine Key**

Summerland Key

Cudjoe Key

Boca Chica Key

⓬ **Lower Sugarloaf Key**

Saddle Bunch Keys

⓭

Big Coppitt Key

Stock Island

Key West International Airport

⓮ 86 **Key West**

Everglades National Park

9336

Whitewater Bay

Cape Sable

Flamingo

Florida Bay

Gulf of Mexico

N

10 miles

15 km

0

0

theater admission free; scuba fee, including tanks and gear: $20–$30; snorkel fee, including gear: $10, $35 for family of 4. Open daily 9–5.

② Return to U.S. 1, turn left, and left again into **John Pennekamp Coral Reef State Park.** The primary attraction here is diving on the offshore coral reefs (*see* Participant Sports, below), but even a landlubber can appreciate the superb interpretive aquarium in the park's visitor center. A concessionaire rents canoes and sailboats and offers boat trips to the reef. The park also includes a nature trail through a mangrove forest, a swimming beach, picnic shelters, a snack bar, a gift shop, and a campground. *MM 102.5, OS, Key Largo, tel. 305/451–1202. Admission: $3.25 per vehicle for up to 8 persons plus $1 each additional, and 50¢ per person county surcharge. Open daily 8 AM–sunset.*

Return to U.S. 1 and turn left. At MM 100, turn left again into the parking lot of the Holiday Inn Key Largo Resort. In the adjoining Key Largo Harbor Marina you'll find the *African Queen,* the steam-powered workboat on which Katharine Hepburn and Humphrey Bogart rode in their movie of the same name. Also displayed at the resort is the *Thayer IV,* a 22-foot mahogany Chris Craft built in 1951 and used by Ms. Hepburn and Henry Fonda in Fonda's last film, *On Golden Pond.*

Continuing south on U.S. 1 you'll cross **Plantation Key** (MM 93–87), named for the plantings of limes, pineapples, and tomatoes cultivated here at the turn of the century. In 1991, woodcarver and teacher Laura Quinn moved her **Florida Keys Wild Bird Rehabilitation Center** here. Nowhere else in the Keys can you see birdlife so close up. Many are kept for life because of injuries that can't be healed. Others are brought for rehabilitation and then set free. At any time there's likely to be lots of pelicans, cormorants, terns, and herons of various types. *93600 Overseas Hwy., MM 93.6 BS, Tavernier 33070, tel. 305/852–4486. Admission free, donations accepted. Open daily sunrise–sunset.*

③ Next comes **Windley Key,** notable for **Theater of the Sea,** where nine dolphins, two sea lions, and an extensive collection of tropical fish swim in the pits of a 1907 railroad quarry. Allow at least two hours to attend the dolphin and sea lion shows and visit all the exhibits, which include an injured birds of prey exhibit, a "bottomless" boat ride, touch tank, shark-feeding pool, and a 300-gallon "living reef" aquarium with invertebrates and small reef fishes. At the entrance is a feeding station for abandoned cats. *MM 84.5, OS, Box 407, Islamorada, tel. 305/664–2431. Admission: $11.75 adults, $6 children 3–12. Swim with dolphins (30-min orientation and 30 min in the water): $65. Reservations required with 50% deposit, minimum age 13, mask and swim fins recommended, life vests optional. Video or still photos $65 (inquire at concession). AE, MC, V. Open daily 9:30 AM–4 PM.*

Watch for the **Hurricane Memorial** (MM 82) beside the highway. It marks the mass grave of 423 victims of the 1935 Labor Day hurricane. Many of those who perished were veterans who had been working on the Overseas Highway; they died when a tidal surge overturned a train sent to evacuate them. The art deco-style monument depicts wind-driven waves and palms bowing before the storm's fury.

❹ At the lower tip of **Upper Matecumbe Key,** stop at the **International Fishing Museum** in Bud n' Mary's Marina. The museum contains a collection of antique fishing tackle and a video library with information on fishing activities, fishery conservation, and the natural history of various species of local fishes. The videos don't circulate, but you can watch them in the museum. The museum staff can also help you find a charter captain for deep-sea or back-country fishing. *MM 79.5, OS. For information, contact Bob Epstein, 124 Gardenia St., Tavernier 33070, tel. 305/664-2767 (office), 305/852-8813 (home). Open Mon.-Sat. 9-5, Sun. 9-noon. Admission free.*

❺ The dock on **Indian Key Fill** at MM 78, BS, is the closest point on the Overseas Highway to three unusual state parks accessible only by water. The newest of these parks, dedicated in 1989, is **San Pedro Underwater Archaeological Preserve** (*see* Participant Sports, below). State-operated boat tours aboard the M. V. *Monroe* will take you to the other two, **Indian Key State Historic Site** (OS) and **Lignumvitae Key State Botanical Site** (BS). Indian Key was a county seat town and shipwrecker's station until an Indian attack wiped out the settlement in 1840. Dr. Henry Perrine, a noted botanist, was killed in the raid. Today you'll see his plants overgrowing the town's ruins. A virgin hardwood forest still cloaks Lignumvitae Key (where the dock was repaired early in 1991), punctuated only by the home and gardens that chemical magnate William Matheson built as a private retreat in 1919. *MM 78. For information and tour boat reservations, contact Long Key State Recreation Area, Box 776, Long Key, tel. 305/664-4815. Indian Key open daily 8 AM-sunset; Lignumvitae Key open Thurs.-Mon. with 1-hr guided tour (admission: $1 adults, children under 6 free) at 10:30 AM, 1 and 2:30 PM for visitors from private boats. State tour boat admission: $7 adults, $3 children under 12, for 3-hr tours Thurs.-Mon. to Indian Key, 8:30 AM, to Lignumvitae Key, 1:30 PM.*

❻ Return to U.S. 1 and turn right. Continue down to **Long Key** (MM 69), where you'll pass a tract of undisturbed forest on the right (BS) just below MM 67. Watch for a historical marker partially obscured by foliage. Pull off the road here and explore **Layton Trail,** named after Del Layton, who incorporated the city of Layton in 1963 and served as its mayor until his death in 1987. The marker relates the history of the Long Key Viaduct, the first major bridge on the rail line, and the Long Key Fishing Club that Henry Flagler established nearby in 1906. Zane Grey, the noted western novelist, was president of the club. It consisted of a lodge, guest cottages, and storehouses—all obliterated by the 1935 hurricane. The clearly marked trail leads through the tropical hardwood forest to a rocky Florida Bay shoreline overlooking shallow grass flats offshore.

Less than a mile below Layton Trail, turn left into **Long Key State Recreation Area,** then left again to the parking area for the **Golden Orb Trail.** This trail leads onto a boardwalk through a mangrove swamp alongside a lagoon where many herons and other water birds congregate in winter. The park also has a campground, a picnic area, a canoe trail through a tidal lagoon, and a not-very-sandy beach fronting on a broad expanse of shallow grass flats. Instead of a pail and shovel, bring a mask and snorkel here to observe the marine life in this rich nursery area. *Box 776, Long Key, MM 67.5 OS, tel. 305/664-4815. Admission: $3.25 per car for up to 8 persons, $1 per additional*

*person, plus 50¢ per person county surcharge. Bike rental $10
deposit and $2.14 per hour (includes tax). Open daily 8 AM–
sunset.*

The Middle Keys

Below Long Key, the Overseas Highway crosses Long Key
Channel on a new highway bridge beside the railroad's **Long
Key Viaduct.** The second-longest bridge on the rail line, this 2-
mile-long structure has 222 reinforced-concrete arches. It ends
at **Conch Key** (MM 63), a tiny fishing and retirement community. Below Conch Key, the causeway on your left at MM 61 leads
to **Duck Key,** an upscale residential community and the **Hawk's
Cay Resort** (*see* Lodging, below).

⑦ Next comes **Grassy Key** (MM 59). Watch on the right for the
Dolphin Research Center and the 35-foot-long concrete sculpture of the dolphin Theresa and her offspring Nat outside the
former home of Milton Santini, creator of the original *Flipper*
movie. The 14 dolphins here today are free to leave and return
to the fenced area that protects them from boaters and preda-
tors. *MM 59, BS, Box Dolphin, Marathon Shores, tel. 305/289–
0002. Admission: $7.50 adults, $5 donation children 4–12.
Walking tours at 10 AM, 12:30, 2 and 3:30 PM. Swim with dolphins (20 min., part of 2½-hr instruction/education program)
$65. Children 5–12 swim with an accompanying, paying adult
(also $65). Reserve for dolphin swim on the first day of the month
for the following month. Visitor center open Wed.–Sun. 9 AM–4
PM, closed Christmas, New Year's Day, Thanksgiving.*

Continuing down U.S. 1, you'll pass the road to **Key Colony
Beach** (MM 54, OS), an incorporated city developed in the 1950s
as a retirement community. It has a golf course and boating fa-
⑧ cilities. Soon after, you'll cross a bridge onto **Vaca Key** and enter **Marathon** (MM 53–47), the commercial hub of the Middle
Keys.

On your right (BS) at 55th Street is **Crane Point Hammock,** a
63-acre tract that includes the last known undisturbed thatch-
palm hammock. The Florida Keys Land Trust, a private, nonprofit conservation group, paid $1.2 million to acquire the
property in 1988. Early in 1990, behind a stunning bronze-and-
copper door crafted by Roy Butler of Plantation, Florida, the
Trust opened **The Museum of Natural History of the Florida
Keys** as the first phase of educational facilities planned for the
hammock. A children's museum opened early in 1991. The tract
also includes an exotic plant arboretum, several archaeological
sites, and the remnants of a Bahamian village with the oldest
surviving example of Conch-style architecture outside Key
West. Special weekly Hammock tours are offered as part of
your admission from November to Easter; bring good walking
shoes and bug repellent. *MM 50, BS, 5550 Overseas Hwy., Box
536, Marathon 33050, tel. 305/743–9100. Admission: $4.50
adults, $2.50 senior citizens, $1 children 12–17 and students.
Open Mon.–Sat. 9–5, Sun. noon–5.*

⑨ As you approach the new **Seven Mile Bridge,** turn right at MM
47 to the entrance to the **Old Seven Mile Bridge.** An engineering
marvel in its day, the bridge rested on 546 concrete piers spanning the broad expanse of water that separates the Middle and
Lower Keys. Monroe County maintains a 2-mile stretch of the
old bridge to provide access to **Pigeon Key** (MM 45), where the

county's public schools and community college run marine-science classes in a railroad work camp built around 1908. In 1990 Pigeon Key was placed on the National Register of Historic Places, a status the Old Seven Mile Bridge already enjoyed. *For information, contact James Lewis, Chairman, Pigeon Key Advisory Authority, 2945 Overseas Hwy., Marathon 33050, tel. 305/743-6040.*

Return to U.S. 1 and proceed across the new **Seven Mile Bridge** (actually only 6.79 miles long!). Built between 1980 and 1982 at a cost of $45 million, the new Seven Mile Bridge is the world's longest segmental bridge, with 39 expansion joints separating its cement sections. Each April runners gather in Marathon for the annual Seven Mile Bridge Run.

The Lower Keys

⑩ At **Bahia Honda State Recreation Area** (MM 36.5) on Bahia Honda Key, you'll find a sandy beach most of the time. Lateral drift builds up the beach in summer; winter storms whisk away much of the sand. The park's Silver Palm Trail leads you through a dense tropical forest where you can see rare West Indian plants, including the Geiger tree, sea lavendar, Key spider lily, bay cedar, thatch and silver palms, and several species found nowhere else in the Florida Keys: the West Indies yellow satinwood, Catesbaea, Jamaica morning glory, and wild dilly. The park also includes a campground, cabins, gift shop, snack bar, marina, and dive shop offering snorkel trips to offshore reefs. *MM 36.5, OS, Rte. 1, Box 782, Big Pine Key, tel. 305/ 872-2353. Admission: $3.25 per vehicle for up to 8 passengers plus $1 per additional person and 50¢ per person county surcharge. Open daily 8 AM–sunset.*

Cross the Bahia Honda Bridge and continue past Spanish Harbor Key and Spanish Harbor Channel onto **Big Pine Key** (MM 32–30), where prominent signs warn drivers to be on the lookout for Key deer. Every year cars kill 50 to 60 of the delicate creatures. A subspecies of the Virginia white-tailed deer, Key deer once ranged throughout the Lower and Middle Keys, but hunting and habitat destruction reduced the population to fewer than 50 in 1947. Under protection in the **National Key Deer Refuge** since 1954, the deer herd grew to about 750 by the early 1970s. The government owns only about a third of Big Pine Key, however, and as the human population on the remaining land grew during the 1980s, the deer herd declined again until today only 250 to 300 remain. Plans for a new road that may have threatened the remaining deer were canceled in 1991.

To visit the refuge, turn right at the stoplight, then bear left at the fork onto Key Deer Boulevard (Rte. 940). Pass Road Prison No. 426 and a fire tower on the way to Watson Boulevard, then turn left and go about a mile to the **Refuge Headquarters** to see interpretive displays and obtain brochures.

The best place to see Key deer is on **No Name Key,** a sparsely populated island just east of Big Pine Key. To get there, take Watson Boulevard east to Wilder Road, and turn left. You'll go 2 miles from Key Deer Boulevard to the middle of the Bogie Channel Bridge, which links Big Pine and No Name Keys, and 1½ miles from there across No Name Key. If you get out of your car at the end of the road to walk around, close all doors and windows to keep raccoons from wandering in. Deer may turn up along this road at any time of day—especially in early morning and late afternoon. Admire their beauty, but don't try to feed them—it's against the law. To resume your journey, take Wilder Road back to Key Deer Boulevard at the fork just before the stoplight on U.S. 1. Turn right at the stoplight, and continue on down the Keys across **Big Torch, Middle Torch,** and **Little Torch Keys** (named for the torchwood tree, which settlers used for kindling because it burns easily even when green). Next comes **Ramrod Key** (MM 27.5), a base for divers in **Looe Key National Marine Sanctuary** 5 miles offshore (*see* Participant Sports, below).

Time Out Find top dining at **Mangrove Mama's,** a lattice-fronted conch house, remnant from a time when trains outnumbered cars in the Keys *ca.* 1919. Fresh fish, seafoods, some decent beers, and rave-worthy Key lime pie are served. Concrete floors, Keys art on the walls, Tennessee oak bar, and lights twinkling at night in the banana trees are just a few details that contribute to the ambience here. It gets awfully romantic for just down home. *MM 20, BS, tel. 305/745–3030. Reservations accepted. Casual. MC, V. Moderate.*

⓬ On **Lower Sugarloaf Key,** you'll find the Sugar Loaf Lodge (MM 17, BS), an attractive motel known for its performing dolphin named Sugar, who lives in a lagoon behind the restaurant (*see* Lodging, below). Follow the paved road northwest from the motel for a ½ mile past an airstrip, and keep going on an unpaved spur. There, in bleak, gravel-strewn surroundings, you'll find a reconstruction of R. C. Perky's **bat tower.** Perky, an early real estate promoter, built the tower in 1929 to attract mosquito-eating bats, but no bats ever roosted in it.

Continue on through the Saddlebunch Keys and Big Coppitt Key to **Boca Chica Key** (MM 10), site of the Key West Naval Air Station. You may hear the roar of jet fighter planes in this vicinity. ⓭ At last you reach **Stock Island** (MM 5), the gateway to Key West. Pass the 18-hole **Key West Resort Golf Course,** then turn right onto Junior College Road and pause at the **Key West Botanical Garden,** where the Key West Garden Club has labeled an extensive assortment of native and exotic tropical trees.

Key West

Numbers in the margin correspond to points of interest on the Key West map.

In April 1982, the U.S. Border Patrol threw a roadblock across the Overseas Highway just south of Florida City to catch drug runners and illegal aliens. Traffic backed up for miles as Border Patrol agents searched vehicles and demanded that the occupants prove U.S. citizenship. City officials in Key West, outraged at being treated like foreigners by the federal government, staged a mock secession and formed their own "nation," the so-called Conch Republic. They hoisted a flag and distributed mock border passes, visas, and Conch currency. The embarrassed Border Patrol dismantled its roadblock, and now an annual festival recalls the secessionists' victorious exploits.

The episode exemplifies Key West's odd station in life. Situated 150 miles from Miami and just 90 miles from Havana, this tropi-

cal island city has always maintained its strong sense of detachment, even after it was connected to the rest of the United States—by the railroad in 1912 and by the Overseas Highway
⓮ in 1938. The U.S. government acquired **Key West** from Spain in 1819 along with the rest of Florida. The Spanish had named the island Cayo Hueso (Bone Key) in honor of Indian skeletons they found on its shores. In 1822, Uncle Sam sent Commodore David S. Porter to the Keys to chase pirates away.

For three decades, the primary industry in Key West was "wrecking"—rescuing people and salvaging cargo from ships that foundered on the nearby reefs. According to some reports, when business was slow, the wreckers hung out lights to lure ships aground. Their business declined after 1852, when the federal government began building lighthouses along the reefs.

In 1845 the Army started to construct Fort Taylor, which held Key West for the Union during the Civil War. After the war, an influx of Cuban dissidents unhappy with Spain's rule brought the cigar industry to Key West. Fishing, shrimping, and sponge-gathering became important industries, and a pineapple-canning factory opened. Major military installations were established during the Spanish-American War and World War I. Through much of the 19th century and into the second decade of the 20th, Key West was Florida's wealthiest city in per-capita terms.

In the 1920s the local economy began to unravel. Modern ships no longer needed to stop in Key West for provisions, the cigar industry moved to Tampa, Hawaii dominated the pineapple industry, and the sponges succumbed to a blight. Then the Depression hit, and even the military moved out. By 1934 half the population was on relief. The city defaulted on its bond payments, and the Federal Emergency Relief Administration took over the city and county governments.

Federal officials began promoting Key West as a tourist destination. They attracted 40,000 visitors during the 1934–35 winter season. Then the 1935 Labor Day hurricane struck the Middle Keys, sparing Key West but wiping out the railroad and the tourist trade. For three years, until the Overseas Highway opened, the only way in and out of town was by boat.

Ever since, Key West's fortunes have waxed and waned with the vagaries of world affairs. An important naval center during World War II and the Korean conflict, the island remains a strategic listening post on the doorstep of Fidel Castro's Cuba. Although the Navy shut down its submarine base at Truman Annex and sold the property to a real-estate developer, the nearby Boca Chica Naval Air Station and other military installations remain active.

As the military scaled back, city officials looked to tourism again to take up the slack. Even before it tried, Key West had much to sell—superb frost-free weather with an average temperature of 79°F, quaint 19th-century architecture, and a laid-back lifestyle. Promoters have fostered fine restaurants, galleries and shops, and new museums to interpret the city's intriguing past. There's also a growing calendar of artistic and cultural events and a lengthening list of annual festivals—including the Conch Republic celebration in April, Hemingway Days in July, and a Halloween Fantasy Fest rivaling the New Orleans Mardi Gras.

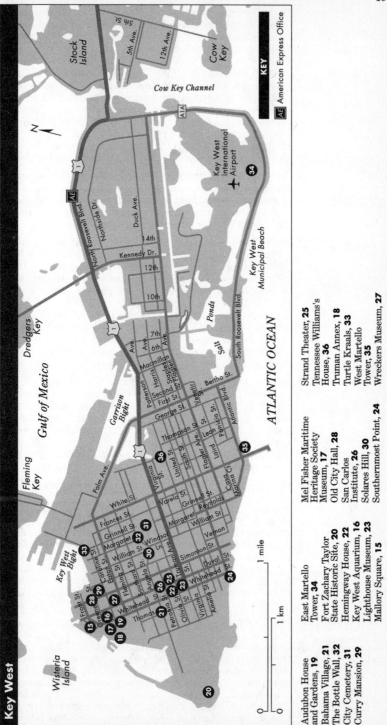

Key West

Gulf of Mexico

Fleming Key

Dredgers Key

Garrison Bight

Wisteria Island

Key West Bight

Stock Island

Cow Key Channel

Cow Key

5th St.
5th Ave.
12th Ave.

N

Northside Dr.
Duck Ave.
14th
Kennedy Dr.
12th
10th
Ave.
7th
6th
Macmillan
Harris
Second St.
First St.
Patterson
George St.

Key West International Airport

Salt Ponds

Key West Municipal Beach

South Roosevelt Blvd.

North Roosevelt Blvd.

AE

Thompson St.
United St.
South St.
Virginia
Flagler Ave.
Leon
Patricia St.
Bertha St.
Atlantic Blvd.
Casa Marina

White St.
Varela St.
Grinnell St.
Margaret
Reynolds
William St.
Vernon
Simonton St.
Duval St.
Whitehead St.
Amelia St.
Virginia St.
Thomas St.
Olivia St.
Petronia St.
Angela St.
Southard St.
Fleming St.
Eaton St.
Caroline St.
Baton St.
Windsor Ln.
Truman Ave.
Palm Ave.

Frances St.
Grinnell St.
Margaret
William St.

Front St.
Greene St.

ATLANTIC OCEAN

ATLANTIC OCEAN

15
18
17
16
19
28
29
27
33
31
32
30
21
26
25
22
23
24
20
36
35
34

KEY

AE American Express Office

0   1 km
0   1 mile

Audubon House
and Gardens, **19**
Bahama Village, **21**
The Bottle Wall, **32**
City Cemetery, **31**
Curry Mansion, **29**

East Martello
Tower, **34**
Fort Zachary Taylor
State Historic Site, **20**
Hemingway House, **22**
Key West Aquarium, **16**
Lighthouse Museum, **23**
Mallory Square, **15**

Mel Fisher Maritime
Heritage Society
Museum, **17**
Old City Hall, **28**
San Carlos
Institute, **26**
Solares Hill, **30**
Southernmost Point, **24**

Strand Theater, **25**
Tennessee Williams's
House, **36**
Truman Annex, **18**
Turtle Kraals, **33**
West Martello
Tower, **35**
Wreckers Museum, **27**

Gentrification is in the breeze. New city rules say no to retail T-shirt displays on sidewalks, and to amplified sound spilling out of open-air bars. Sundown revelry at Mallory Square has been uneasily reconciled with use of the Mallory Docks by a growing fleet of cruise ships calling at Key West. The rule since 1991 has been that the ships, if staying overnight, have to go offshore for an hour or so at sunset and leave the spectacle unblocked for celebrants. No question—reform is in the air. But the bans on bad taste and loud noise should be seen as part of an overall environmental regard, although it seems the changes more often occur to benefit commercial tourism than the environment. While the wheel turns, begin this tour at Front and Duval streets, near the Pier House hotel and Ocean Key House.

15 Start by going west on Front Street to **Mallory Square,** named for Stephen Mallory, secretary of the Confederate Navy, who later owned the Mallory Steamship Line. On the nearby **Mallory Dock,** a nightly sunset celebration draws street performers, food vendors, and thousands of onlookers.

16 Facing Mallory Square is the **Key West Aquarium,** which features hundreds of brightly colored tropical fish and other fascinating sea creatures from the waters around Key West. A touch tank enables visitors to handle starfish, sea cucumbers, horseshoe and hermit crabs, even horse and queen conchs—living totems of the Conch Republic. Built in 1934 by the Works Progress Administration as the world's first open-air aquarium, the building has been enclosed for all-weather viewing. *1 Whitehead St., tel. 305/296–2051. Guided tours 11 AM, 1, 3, 4:30; shark feeding on every tour. Admission: $5.50 adults, $2.75 children 8–15. Open daily, 10–6 (10–7 in winter).*

Return to Front Street and turn right to **Clinton Place,** where a Civil War memorial to Union soldiers stands in a triangle formed by the intersection of Front, Greene, and Whitehead streets. On your right is the **U.S. Post Office and Customs House,** a Romanesque Revival structure designed by prominent local architect William Kerr and completed in 1891. Tour guides claim that federal bureaucrats required the roof to have a steep pitch so it wouldn't collect snow.

17 On your left is the **Mel Fisher Maritime Heritage Society Museum,** which displays gold and silver bars, coins, jewelry, and other artifacts recovered in 1985 from the Spanish treasure ships *Nuestra Señora de Atocha* and *Santa Margarita.* The two galleons foundered in a hurricane in 1622 near the Marquesas Keys, 40 miles west of Key West. In the museum you can lift a gold bar weighing 6.3 Troy pounds and see a 77.76-carat natural emerald crystal worth almost $250,000. *200 Greene St., tel. 305/294–2633. Museum admission: $5 adults; $4 military, Conch Train and trolley passengers with ticket stub, and AAA members; $1.50 children 6–12. Open daily 10–5; last video showing 4:30.*

18 Mel Fisher's museum occupies a former navy storehouse that he bought from Pritam Singh, the developer of **Truman Annex** (Key West 33040, tel. 305/296–5601). After a $17.25 million fast-start investment followed by a quick stall because of recession, Pritam Singh, the Key West hippie-turned-millionaire, is successfully transforming the 103-acre Truman Annex into a suburban community of pastel, picket, and lattice charm. The parade grounds and barracks that during World War II housed some 18,000 military and civilian employees now house singles and retirees in affordable condominiums, and families in grassy-yard homes surrounded by colorful bougainvillea and allamanda vines. The whole community is set behind high black wrought iron gates and architecturally designed in the Victorian style that knits Old Town together. Also on the grounds is the **Harry S. Truman Little White House Museum.** Pedestrians and cyclists are welcome on the complex daily between 8 AM and sunset. They'll find a dream community that, though less than full blown, considering the abominations that other developers have dumped on Key West in recent years, is a model of urban good taste. *Museum tel. 305/294–9911. Admission: $6 adults, $3 children 12 and under. Open daily 9–5.*

⑲ From Mel Fisher's museum, cross Whitehead Street to visit the **Audubon House and Gardens.** A museum in this three-story dwelling built in the mid-1840s commemorates ornithologist John James Audubon's 1832 visit to Key West. On display are several rooms of period antiques and a large collection of Audubon engravings. There is a self-guided walking tour of the tropical gardens, keyed to an eight-page brochure, and an exquisite collection of porcelains of American birds and foliage by Dorothy Doughty is one in a series of rotating exhibits. In 1989 a children's room was opened, furnished in 18th- and 19th-century antiques. *205 Whitehead St., tel. 305/294–2116. Admission: $5 adults, $1 children 6–12. Open daily 9:30–5.*

Continue up Whitehead Street past **Pigeonhouse Patio Restaurant & Bar** (301 Whitehead St., tel. 305/296–9600). This building was the first headquarters of Pan American World Airways, the first U.S. airline to operate scheduled international air service. The inaugural flight took off from Key West International Airport on October 28, 1927: Passengers paid $9.95 for the 90-mile, 80-minute flight from Key West to Havana aboard *The General Machado*, a Fokker F–7 trimotor.

⑳ Turn right onto Southard Street and follow the signs to the **Fort Zachary Taylor State Historic Site.** Built between 1845 and 1866, the fort served as a base for the Union blockade of Confederate shipping during the Civil War. More than 1,500 Confederate vessels captured while trying to run the blockade were brought to Key West's harbor and detained under the fort's guns. What you will see at Fort Taylor today is a fort within a fort. In 1989 a moat was dug to suggest how the fort originally looked when it was surrounded by water. Snorkeling is excellent here because of an artificial reef, except when the wind blows south-southwest and muddies the water. Look for a new concession stand on the beach this winter. *Box 289, tel. 305/292–6713. Free 90-min tour daily at 2 PM. Admission: $3.25 per car for up to 8 passengers, $1 per additional passenger, plus 50¢ county surcharge per person. Park open daily 8–sunset, fort open 8–5.*

Time Out   Pause for a libation at the open-air **Green Parrot Bar.** Built in 1890, the bar is said to be Key West's oldest, a sometimes-rowdy saloon where locals outnumber the tourists, especially on weekends when bands play. *601 Whitehead St. (corner of Southard St.), tel. 305/294–6133. No credit cards. Open daily noon–4 AM.*

Return to Thomas Street, turn right 2 blocks to the corner of Petronia Street, and you're at **Blue Heaven,** (729 Thomas St., tel. 305/296–8666), an old blue-on-blue clapboard, peach-and-yellow-trimmed Greek Revival Bahamian house, in the heart of **㉑ Bahama Village,** where Bahamians settled Key West a century and a half ago. Blue Heaven is an up-by-the-bootstraps little conch- and Caribbean-food restaurant popular for its take-out. Not too long ago it was a bordello where Ernest Hemingway refereed boxing matches and where Captain Tony in his premayoral days took in the cockfights. There's still a rooster graveyard out back, as well as a water tower hauled here from Little Torch Key in the 1920s.

Time Out Up to your ears in margaritas? Stop by **Casablanca at Bogarts** for an ice-cold pint of Guinness or any of the other imported beers that are on tap. This lively Irish-owned and -run pub is attached to a restaurant (that serves both Irish and Caribbean cuisine) and a guest house. *900 Duval St. (corner of Olivia St.), tel. 305/296–0637. MC, V. Open daily noon–4 AM.*

Return to Whitehead Street east on Petronia Street, turn right **㉒** 1 block to the **Hemingway House,** now a museum dedicated to the novelist's life and work. Built in 1851, this two-story Spanish Colonial dwelling was the first house in Key West to have running water and a fireplace. Hemingway bought the house in 1931 and wrote about 70% of his life's work here, including *A Farewell to Arms* and *For Whom the Bell Tolls*. Three months after Hemingway died in 1961, local jeweler Bernice Dickson bought the house and its contents from Hemingway's estate and two years later opened it as a museum. Of special interest are the huge bed with a headboard made from a 17th-century Spanish monastery gate, a ceramic cat by Pablo Picasso (a gift to Hemingway from the artist), the handblown Venetian glass chandelier in the dining room, and the swimming pool. The museum staff gives guided tours rich with anecdotes about Hemingway and his family and feeds the 42 feline habitants (for the 42 bridges in the Keys), descendants of Hemingway's own 50 cats. Kitten adoptions are possible (for a fee), but there's a five-year waiting list. Tours begin every 10 minutes and take 25–30 minutes; then you're free to explore on your own. *907 Whitehead St., tel. 305/294–1575. Admission: $6 adults, $1.50 children 6–12. Open daily 9–5.*

Down the block and across the street from Hemingway House **㉓** (behind spic-and-span white picket fence) is the **Lighthouse Museum,** a 92-foot lighthouse built in 1847 and an adjacent 1887 clapboard house where the keeper lived. Both underwent extensive restoration in 1989, and the museum was largely rearranged a year later. You can climb 98 steps to the top of the lighthouse for a spectacular view of the island town, as well as of the first order (biggest) Fresnel lens, installed at a cost of $1 million in the 1860s. On display in the keeper's quarters are vintage photographs, ship models, nautical charts, and lighthouse artifacts from all along the Key reefs. *938 Whitehead St., tel. 305/294–0012. Admission: $3 adults, $1 children 6–12. Open daily 9:30–5.*

Continue to the foot of Whitehead Street, where a huge concrete marker proclaims this spot to be the **Southernmost Point** **㉔** in the United States. Most tourists snapping pictures of each other in front of the marker are oblivious to Key West's real southernmost point, on a nearby navy base off limits to civilians but visible through the fence to your right. Bahamian vendors of shells and straw hats line the sidewalk and blow a conch horn at passing Conch Tour Trains and Old Town Trolleys.

Turn left on South Street. To your right are two dwellings that both claim to be the **Southernmost House**—the Spanish-style home built in the 1940s at 400 South Street by Thelma Strabel, author of *Reap the Wild Wind,* a novel about the wreckers who salvaged ships aground on the reef in Key West's early days, and the adjoining cream-brick Queen Anne mansion at 1400 Duval Street. Neither is open to the public. Take the next right onto Duval Street, which ends at the Atlantic Ocean and the **Southernmost Beach.** *Admission free. Open daily 7 AM–11 PM.*

Now go north on Duval Street towards downtown Key West. Pause at the **Cuban Club** (1108 Duval St., tel. 305/296–8997). The original building—a social club for the Cuban community—burned in 1983 and has been replaced by shops and luxury condominiums; some of the original facade was retained. Continuing on Duval Street, you'll pass several art galleries from the 1100 block through the 800 block.

㉕ Pause to admire the colorful marquee and ornamental facade of the **Strand Theater,** built in 1918 by Cuban craftsmen. After a period as a movie theater, it now offers a variety of live entertainment under the auspices of Clubland at the Strand. *527 Duval St., tel. 305/293–0116.*

㉖ Continue on to the **San Carlos Institute,** a Cuban-American heritage center, which houses a museum and research library focusing on the history of Key West and of 19th- and 20th-century Cuban exiles. The San Carlos Institute was founded in 1871 by Cuban immigrants who wanted to preserve their language, customs, and heritage while organizing the struggle for Cuba's independence from Spain. Cuban patriot Jose Martí delivered many famous speeches in Key West from the balcony of the auditorium. Opera star Enrico Caruso sang in the 400-seat hall of the Opera House, which reportedly has the best acoustics of any concert hall in the South. The current building was completed in 1924, replacing the original built in 1871 that burned in the Key West fire of 1886, in which two-thirds of the city was destroyed. A second building succumbed to the hurricane of 1919. After Cuba and the United States broke off diplomatic relations in 1961, the building deteriorated. It was saved from demolition when Miami attorney Rafael A. Peñalver, Jr., secured a $3 million state grant for its restoration. The building reopened January 3, 1992, exactly 100 years after Martí founded the Cuban Revolutionary Party here. Activities include film presentations on the history of Key West and of the Cuban community in the United States, as well as nightly performing arts presentations. *516 Duval St., tel. 305/294–3887. Guided tour, concluding with 30-min film. Admission: $2 adults, $1.50 children. Open daily 9–5.*

㉗ Continue north on Duval Street to the **Wreckers Museum,** which is alleged to be the oldest house in Key West. It was built in 1829 as the home of Francis Watlington, a sea captain and wrecker. He was also a Florida state senator, but resigned to serve in the Confederate Navy during the Civil War. Six of the home's eight rooms are now a museum furnished with 18th- and 19th-century antiques. In an upstairs bedroom is an eight-room miniature dollhouse of Conch architectural design, outfitted with tiny Victorian furniture. *322 Duval St., tel. 305/294–9502. Open daily 10–4; closed Christmas. Admission: $2 adults, 50¢ children 3–12.*

(28) Take Duval Street to Front Street, turn right, go two blocks to Simonton Street, turn right again and go 1 block to Greene Street to see the **Old City Hall,** returned to use after a $1 million restoration. In 1990 the City Commission began meeting here again for the first time since the early 1960s. There is a permanent exhibition of old Key West photographs, including an 1845 Daguerreotype, the oldest known photographic image of Key West. Designed by William Kerr, the architect also responsible for the Customs House, the Old City Hall opened in 1891. It has a rectangular tower with four clock faces and a fire bell. The ground floor, used as a city market for many years, now houses the **Historic Key West Shipwreck Museum.** Among the displays are relics from the *Isaac Allerton*, built at Portsmouth, New Hampshire, in 1838 and sunk off Key West in 1856. The second floor houses the city commission's meeting room and offices of the city government and the Historic Florida Keys Preservation Board (tel. 305/292–6718). *510 Greene St., tel. 305/292–9740. Open daily 10–5. Museum admission: $4 adults, $2 students and children 10–16.*

Time Out Stop next door to the **Cuban Coffee Queen Cafe** (512 Greene St., tel. 305/296–2711), run by a mother/daughter team from Central Chaparra, in Cuba's Oriente Province. Locals love the hot bollos, conch fritters, pigs feet, ham and eggs, sangría, and Cuban coffee.

(29) Return to Simonton Street, go 1 block south to Caroline Street, and turn right to the **Curry Mansion** (*see* Lodging, below). Built in 1899 for Milton Curry, the son of Florida's first millionaire, this 22-room Victorian mansion is an adaptation of a Parisian town house. It has the only widow's walk open to the public in Key West. The owners have restored and redecorated most of the house. Take an unhurried self-guided tour with a comprehensive brochure, which includes floor plans, full of detailed information about the history and contents of the house. *511 Caroline St., tel. 305/294–5349. Admission: $5 adults, $1 children under 12. Open daily 10–5.*

(30) Return to Simonton Street, go south to Angela Street, and turn left. Before you rises **Solares Hill,** the steepest natural grade in Key West. Its summit, the island's loftiest elevation, is 18 feet above sea level.

(31) Now cross Elizabeth Street and bear right onto Windsor Lane to the **City Cemetery.** Turn left onto Passover Lane to the entrance at Margaret Street. Clustered near a flagpole resembling a ship's mast are the graves of 22 sailors killed in the sinking of the battleship U.S.S. *Maine. Guided tours weekends by appointment; call Susan Olsen, tel. 305/296–3913. Admission free. Tour donation: $5. Open sunrise–sunset.*

(32) At the corner of Margaret and Angela streets, pause at **The Bottle Wall.** Hundreds of bottles from vintage champagne to ketchup have been mortared into a homespun work of art that's equally practical. Carolyn Gorton Fuller says she's done it so the dazzle keeps vehicles from missing the curve and crashing into her house. The first wall built 17 years ago went down in a firetruck crash. Note one of the doorsteps of Ms. Fuller's Conch house: the headstone for a grave—in place, she says, when she bought the house.

33 Go up Margaret Street to the harbor docks and visit the **Turtle Kraals,** where the Florida Marine Conservancy runs a hospital for sea creatures. Biologist Linda Bohl maintains a touch tank with horseshoe crabs, sea anemones, sea urchins, and other benign beasts you can fondle—but keep your fingers away from Hawkeye and Gonzo, a churlish pair of 150-pound, 32-year-old hawksbill turtles. A fish pond on the premises gives you a good look at live denizens of local waters, including barracuda, bluefish, lemon and nurse sharks, and yellowtail snapper. *231 Margaret St., tel. 305/294–2640. Admission free; donation accepted. Open 11 AM–1 AM Mon.–Sat., Sun. noon–1 AM.*

Return to Margaret Street and go a block south to Eaton Street, turn left and continue east past White Street, where Eaton Street doglegs to the right into Palm Avenue. You'll cross a causeway and bridge to the corner of **Garrison Bight Yacht Basin,** where many charter-fishing boats dock.

Turn left onto North Roosevelt Boulevard (U.S. 1) and go east. Past the turnoff to Stock Island at the east end of Key West, North Roosevelt Boulevard becomes South Roosevelt Boulevard and turns west. On your left is a small community of houseboats. On your right, just past the entrance to Key West **34** International Airport, stands **East Martello Tower,** one of two Civil War forts of similar design overlooking the Atlantic Ocean. Housed in a portion of this tower are military uniforms and relics of the battleship U.S.S. *Maine,* which was blown up in Havana Harbor in 1898. Also, the **Key West Art and Historical Society** operates a museum in East Martello's vaulted casemates. The collection includes Stanley Papio's "junk art" sculptures, Cuban primitive artist Mario Sanchez's chiseled and painted wood carvings of historic Key West street scenes, memorabilia from movies shot on location in the Keys, and a display of books by many of the 55 famous writers (including seven Pulitzer Prize winners) who live in Key West. Historical exhibits have been developed to present a chronological history of the Florida Keys and are on display. A circular 48-step staircase in the central tower leads to a platform overlooking the airport and surrounding waters. *3501 S. Roosevelt Blvd., tel. 305/ 296–6206 or 305/296–3913. Admission: $3 adults, $1 children. Open daily 9:30–5.*

Continue west on South Roosevelt Boulevard past Smathers Beach on your left. To your right are the **salt ponds,** where early residents evaporated seawater to collect salt. This area, a vestige of the old Key West, and for years a wildlife sanctuary, in 1991 was saved from intensive development when conservation-minded groups joined forces to acquire the remaining acreage. Today, instead of more condominiums, there's Little Hamaca Park, with a boardwalk leading into the natural area. Where South Roosevelt Boulevard ends at Bertha Street, turn right, then make the first left onto Atlantic Avenue. Near White Street are **Higgs Memorial Beach** (a Monroe County **35** park) and **West Martello Tower,** a fort built in 1861 and used as a lookout post during the Spanish-American War. Within its walls the Key West Garden Club maintains an art gallery and tropical garden. *Tel. 305/294–3210. Donations accepted. Open Wed.–Sun. 10–11:30 AM and 1–3:30 PM.*

36 Take White Street 9 blocks north to Duncan Street, turn right, and go 3 blocks to **Tennessee Williams's House** (1431 Duncan St., at the corner of Duncan and Leon Sts.), a modest Bahamian-style cottage where the playwright lived from 1949 until his death in 1983.

Shopping

Throughout the Keys many shopping centers cater to the basic needs of locals and visitors alike. In season, supermarkets and roadside stands sell tropical fruits. Look for Key limes (April to January), guavas (August to October), lychee nuts (June), and sapodillas (February to March).

Key West In Key West's Old Town, you'll find specialty shops with international reputations:

Fast Buck Freddie's. Imaginative items you'd never dream of are sold here, including battery-operated alligators that eat Muenster cheese, banana leaf–shaped furniture, fish-shaped flatwear, and every flamingo item anyone's ever come up with. The 100 feet of Duval Street windows change every three weeks and always pick up on holiday themes (witches on broomsticks hang from the ceiling for Fantasy Fest, red carpet is rolled out for Christmas and tree lights are in tropical fish shapes). This is not only a unique place to shop, but it's also a great spot to retreat to when you've had enough sun. *500 Duval St., tel. 305/294–2007. AE, D, MC, V. Open daily 10–6. Closed Thanksgiving, Christmas, Easter.*

Greenpeace. This store, opened in 1983, is operated by Greenpeace, an international conservation organization known for its efforts to prevent the killing of whales and seals. Conservation-oriented educational materials, gift items, and T-shirts are sold here. *719 Duval St., tel. 305/296–4442. AE, MC, V. Open Mon.–Sat. 10–10, Sun. 10–6.*

Key West Aloe. A company founded in a garage in 1971, Key West Aloe today produces some 300 perfume, sunscreen, and skin-care products for men and women. When you visit the factory store, you can watch the staff measure and blend ingredients, then fill and seal the containers. *Main store: 524 Front St., tel. 305/294–5592, 800/445–2563 (US). Open daily 9–8. Factory store: Greene and Simonton Sts. AE, D, DC, MC, V. Open 9–5, production weekdays 9–5. Free self-guided tour.*

Key West Hand Print Fabrics. In the 1960s, Lilly Pulitzer's designs made Key West Hand Print Fabrics famous. Shoppers can watch workers making handprinted fabric on five 50-yard-long tables in the Curry Warehouse, a brick building erected in 1878 to store tobacco. *201 Simonton St., tel. 305/294–9535. AE, MC, V. Open daily 10–6.*

Tikal Trading Co. Since 1975, owners George and Barbara Webb have designed, produced, and sold double-stitched women's clothing of hand-woven Guatemalan cotton. *129 Duval St., tel. 305/296–4463. AE, MC, V. Open daily 10–10.*

Just east of Key West Seaport is Key West Bight. Popular storefronts there include the following:

Old Town Fish Market (513 Green St., tel. 305/294–8046) is one place to go for good daily catches.

Waterfront Baits & Tackle. (201 William St., tel. 305/292–1961). This store sells bait and fishing gear.

Waterfront Fish Market, Inc. (201 William St., tel. 305/294–8046). Fresh seafood is the draw here.

Waterfront Market. (201 William St., tel. 305/294–8418 or 305/296–0778). Health and gourmet foods, deli items, fresh produce, and salads are featured.

Ever since John James Audubon came to Key West in 1832, artists have flocked to the Florida Keys. Today's flourishing art community provides a rich array of merchandise for galleries throughout the Keys.

The Rain Barrel on Islamorada represents 450 local and national artists and has eight resident artists in a 3-acre crafts village attended by free-running cats. The third weekend of March each year the largest arts show of the Keys takes place here, when some 20,000 visitors view the work of 100 artists. *MM 86.7, BS, 86700 Overseas Hwy., Islamorada, tel. 305/852–3084. AE, MC, V. Open daily 9–5; closed Thanksgiving and Christmas.*

Lane Gallery specializes in Key West artists. *1000 Duval St., Key West, tel. 305/294–0067. AE, MC, V. Open daily 11–6; closed Sept.*

Gingerbread Square Gallery, the oldest gallery in Key West, owned by former two-time Key West Mayor Richard Heyman, mainly represents Keys artists who have attained national prominence. *1200 Duval St., Key West, tel. 305/296–8900. AE, MC, V. Open winter, daily 11–6; summer, Thurs.–Mon.*

Haitian Art Co. sells the works of 200-plus Haitian artists. *600 Frances St., Key West, tel. 305/296–8932. AE, D, DC, MC, V. Open daily 10–6.*

Participant Sports

Biking   A bike path parallels the Overseas Highway from Key Largo through Tavernier and onto Plantation Key, from MM 106 (at the Route 905 junction) to MM 86 (near the Monroe County Sheriff's Substation). The **Marathon** area is popular with bikers. Some of the best areas include the paths along Aviation Boulevard on the bay side of Marathon Airport; the new four-lane section of the Overseas Highway through Marathon; Sadowski Causeway to Key Colony Beach; Sombrero Beach Road from the Overseas Highway to the Marathon public beach; the roads on Boot Key (across a bridge from Vaca Key on 20th Street, OS); and a 2-mile section of the old Seven Mile Bridge that remains open to Pigeon Key, where locals like to ride to watch the sunset.

Key West is a cycling town, but many tourists aren't accustomed to driving with so many bikes around, so ride carefully. Some hotels rent bikes to their guests; others will refer you to a nearby bike shop and reserve a bike for you.

Key Largo Bikes stocks adult, children's, and tandem bikes, all single-speed with coaster brakes, and multispeed mountain bikes. *MM 99.4, 99275 Overseas Hwy., Key Largo, tel. 305/451–1910. MC, V. Open Tues.–Sat. 9:30–6.*

KCB Bike Shop rents single-speed adult and children's bikes. *MM 53 (11518 Overseas Hwy.), Marathon, tel. 305/289–1670. MC, V. Open weekdays 8:30–5, Sat. 8:30–2. Closed Sun.*

Keys Moped & Scooter rents beach cruisers with large baskets as well as mopeds and scooters. *523 Truman Ave., Key West, tel. 305/294–0399. AE, D, DC, MC, V. Open daily 9–6. Closed Thanksgiving, Christmas, New Year's Day.*

Camping   The State of Florida operates recreational-vehicle and tent campgrounds in **John Pennekamp Coral Reef State Park,** MM 102.5 (Box 487, Key Largo 33037, tel. 305/451–1202); **Long Key State Recreation Area,** MM 67.5 (Box 776, Long Key 33001, tel. 305/664–4815); and **Bahia Honda State Recreation Area,** MM 36.5 (Rte. 1, Box 782, Big Pine Key 33043, tel. 305/872–2353). Bahia Honda also has rental cabins. Best bet to reserve one is to call 8 AM 60 calendar days before your planned visit.

The **Florida Campground Association** (1638 N. Plaza Dr., Tallahassee 32308, tel. 904/656–8878) publishes a free annual directory of over 200 member campgrounds in 11 regions. The Keys are in Region L, which lists 12 commercial campgrounds from Key Largo to Key West. The guide is available at Florida Welcome Centers or by mail.

Diving   Although there are reefs and wrecks all along the east coast of Florida, the state's most extensive diving grounds are in the Keys. Divers come for the quantity and quality of living coral reefs within 6 or 7 miles of shore, the kaleidoscopic beauty of 650 species of tropical fish, and the adventure of probing wrecked ships that foundered in these seemingly tranquil seas during almost four centuries of exploration and commerce. A popular dive destination is the 9-foot **Christ of the Deep** statue, a gift to the Underwater Society of America from an Italian dive equipment manufacturer. The statue is about 6 miles eastnortheast of Key Largo's South Cut in about 25 feet of water. It's a smaller copy of the 50-foot Christ of the Abysses off Genoa, Italy.

Much of the Keys' expanse of coral reefs is protected in federal, state, and county parks and sanctuaries. From Key Biscayne south almost to Key Largo, **Biscayne National Park** (*see* Chapter 5) encompasses most of Biscayne Bay, its barrier islands, and the patch reefs eastward to a depth of 60 feet. Biscayne National Park's southern boundary is the northern boundary of John Pennekamp Coral Reef State Park and Key Largo National Marine Sanctuary.

John Pennekamp Coral Reef State Park encompasses 78 square miles of coral reefs, sea grass beds, and mangrove swamps on the Atlantic Ocean side of Key Largo. The park is 21 miles long and extends to the seaward limit of state jurisdiction 3 miles offshore. Its reefs contain 40 of the 52 species of coral in the Atlantic Reef System. *MM 102.5, OS, tel. 305/451–1201. Park admission: $3.25 per car for up to 8 persons, plus $1 per additional person, and 50¢ per person county surcharge. Park open daily 8 AM–sunset. Coral Reef Park Co., a concessionaire, offers glass-bottom boat, scuba, sailing, and snorkeling tours: Box 1560, Key Largo 33037, tel. 305/451–1621. AE, MC, V. Concession open daily 8–5:30.*

The **Key Largo National Marine Sanctuary** (Box 1083, Key Largo 33037, tel. 305/451–1644) protects 103 square miles of coral reefs from the eastern boundary of John Pennekamp Coral Reef State Park, 3 miles off Key Largo, to a depth of 300 feet some 8 miles offshore. Managed by the National Oceanic and Atmospheric Administration (NOAA), the sanctuary includes Elbow,

French, and Molasses reefs; the 1852 Carysfort Lighthouse and its surrounding reefs; Christ of the Deep; Grecian Rocks, Key Largo Rocks, and the torpedoed WW II freighter *Benwood*.

San Pedro Underwater Archaeological Preserve. The state recently established this underwater park in 18 feet of water about a mile off the western tip of Indian Key. The *San Pedro* was part of a Spanish treasure fleet wrecked by a hurricane in 1733. You can get there on the *Coral Sea*, a 40-passenger glass-bottom dive and snorkel boat, from the dive shop at Bud 'n' Mary's Fishing Marina. *MM 79.5 OS, Box 1126, Islamorada, tel. 305/664–2211. 3-hr trips at 9 AM and 1:30 PM. Call for reservations. Cost: $15 adults, $7.50 children under 12. AE, D, MC, V.*

Marathon Marine Sanctuary. Monroe County recently established its first underwater park off the Middle Keys in Hawk Channel opposite MM 50, OS. It runs from Washerwoman Shoal on the west to navigation marker 48 on the east. The 2-square-mile park contains a dozen patch reefs ranging from the size of a house to about an acre. *Greater Marathon Chamber of Commerce, MM 49, BS, 330 Overseas Hwy., Marathon, tel. 305/743–5417 or 800/842–9580.*

National Key Deer Refuge (Box 510, Big Pine Key 33043, tel. 305/872–2239) and **Great White Heron National Wildlife Refuge.** Reefs where the Keys' northern margin drops off into the Gulf of Mexico attract fewer divers than the better-known Atlantic Ocean reefs. A favorite Gulf spot for local divers is the Content Keys, 5 miles off Big Pine Key (MM 30).

Looe Key National Marine Sanctuary (Rte. 1, Box 782, Big Pine Key 33043, tel. 305/872–4039). Many divers say Looe Key Reef, 5 miles off Ramrod Key (MM 27.5), is the most beautiful and diverse coral community in the entire region. It has large stands of elkhorn coral on its eastern margin, large purple sea fans, and ample populations of sponges and sea urchins. On its seaward side, it has an almost-vertical dropoff to a depth of 50–90 feet. The reef is named for H.M.S. *Looe*, a British warship wrecked there in 1744.

From shore or from a boat, snorkelers can easily explore grass flats, mangrove roots, and rocks in shallow water almost anywhere in the Keys. You may see occasional small clusters of coral and fish, mollusks, and other sea creatures. Ask dive shops for snorkeling information and directions. Diving and snorkeling are prohibited around bridges and near certain keys.

Dive shops all over the state organize Keys dives and offer diving instruction. South Florida residents fill dive boats on weekends, so plan to dive Monday through Thursday, when the boats and reefs are less crowded.

Jules Undersea Lodge, the world's first underwater hotel, takes reservations 30 days in advance from divers who want to stay in its two-room lodge in 30 feet of water. A resort course for new divers is offered. PADI and NAUI affiliations. *MM 103.2, OS, Box 3330, Key Largo 33037, tel. 305/451–2353. AE, D, MC, V.*

Dive Shops All of the dive shops listed below organize dives, fill air tanks, and sell or rent all necessary diving equipment. All have NAUI and/or PADI affiliation.

Quiescence Diving Service, Inc. Six people per boat. *MM 103.5, BS, 103680 Overseas Hwy., Key Largo, tel. 305/451–2440. AE, MC, V. Open daily 8–6. Closed Thanksgiving, Christmas.*

Capt. Corky's Diver's World of Key Largo. A reef and wreck diving package is available. Reservations accepted for wreck diving of the *Benwood*, Coast Guard cutters *Bibb* and *Duane*, and French and Molasses reefs. *MM 99.5, OS, Box 1663, Key Largo 33037, tel. 305/451–3200, outside FL 800/445–8231. MC, V. Open daily 8–5. Closed Thanksgiving, Christmas.*

Florida Keys Dive Center organizes dives from John Pennekamp Coral Reef State Park to Alligator Light. This center has two Coast Guard–approved dive boats and offers training from introductory scuba through instructor course. *MM 90.5, OS, 90500 Overseas Hwy., Box 391, Tavernier, tel. 305/852–4599 or 800/433–8946. AE, MC, V. Open daily 8–5.*

Treasure Divers, Inc., tucked just across Snake Creek Bridge on Windley Key, is a full-service dive shop with instructors, that arranges dives to reefs, Spanish galleons, and other wrecks. *MM 85.5, BS, 85500 Overseas Hwy., Islamorada, tel. 305/664–5111 or 800/356–9887. AE, MC, V. Open daily 8–5.*

Hall's Dive Center and Career Institute offers trips to Looe Key, Sombrero Reef, Delta Shoal, Content Key, and Coffins Patch. *MM 48.5, BS, 1994 Overseas Hwy., Marathon, tel. 305/743–5929 or 800/331–4255. AE, D, MC, V. Open daily 9–6.*

Looe Key Dive Center. This is the dive shop closest to Looe Key National Marine Sanctuary, a 5-star PADI facility in the lower Keys. In connection with its resort, the center offers overnight dive packages. *MM 27.5, OS, Box 509, Ramrod Key, tel. 305/872–2215 or 800/942–5397. MC, V. Open daily 7:30–6.*

Captain's Corner. Seven full-time instructors provide dive classes in English, French, German, Italian, and Japanese. All captains are licensed dive masters. Reservations are accepted for regular reef and wreck diving, spear and lobster fishing, and archaeological and treasure hunting. The shop also runs fishing charters and a 60-foot dive boat—*Sea Eagle*—which departs daily. *Store at 513 Greene St., Key West, tel. 305/296–8918. Open 9–5. Booth at Zero Duval St., Key West, tel. 305/296–8865. Dive boat departs 9:30 and 1:30. Cost: $20 snorkeling, children half price; $30 scuba. AE, MC, V. Booth open daily 8 AM–11 PM.*

Fishing and Boating

Fishing is popular throughout the Keys. You have a choice of deep-sea fishing on the ocean or the gulf or flat-water fishing in the mangrove-fringed shallows of the backcountry. Each of the areas protected by the state or federal government has its own set of rigorously enforced regulations. Check with your hotel or a local chamber of commerce office to find out what the rules are in the area where you're staying. The same sources can refer you to a reliable charter-boat or party-boat captain who will take you where the right kind of fish are biting.

Glass-bottom boats, which depart daily (weather permitting) from docks throughout the Keys, are popular with visitors who want to admire the reefs without getting wet. If you're prone to seasickness, don't try to look through the glass bottom in rough seas.

Motor yachts, sailboats, Hobie Cats, Windsurfers, canoes, and other water-sports equipment are all available for rent by the day or on a long-term basis. Some hotels have their own rental services; others will refer you to a separate vendor.

Treasure Harbor Marine on Plantation Key rents bare sail-boats, from a 19-foot Cape Dory to 65-foot custom-built ketch; and powerboats, from a 32-foot Bayliner to a 42-foot Grand Banks. Captains and provisions available. In 1990 Treasure Harbor combined with Florida-Bahamas Sailing Charters and now offers American Sailing Association courses. Inquire for times and charges. No pets are allowed. *MM 86.5, OS, 200 Treasure Harbor Dr., Islamorada, tel. 305/852–2458 or 800/ FLA–BOATS, fax 305/852–5743. Reservations and advance deposit required; $100 per day captain fee. AE, MC, V. Open 9–6.*

Golf Two of the five golf courses in the Keys are open to the public:

Key Colony Beach Par 3. Nine-hole course near Marathon. *MM 53.5, 8th St., Key Colony Beach, tel. 305/289–1533. Fees: $8 for 9 holes. Open 7:30 AM–7 PM.*

Key West Resort Golf Course. Eighteen-hole course on the bay side of Stock Island. *6450 E. Junior College Rd., Key West, tel. 305/294–5232. Fees: $37.45 18 holes with cart; $27.82 9 holes with cart.*

Beaches

Keys shorelines are either mangrove-fringed marshes or rock outcrops that fall away to mucky grass flats. Most pleasure beaches in the Keys are manmade, with sand imported from the U.S. mainland or the Bahamas. There are public beaches in **John Pennekamp Coral Reef State Park** (MM 102.5), **Long Key State Recreation Area** (MM 67.5), **Sombrero Beach** in Marathon (MM 50), **Bahia Honda State Recreation Area** (MM 36.5), and at many roadside turnouts along the Overseas Highway. Many hotels and motels also have their own small shallow-water beach areas.

When you swim in the Keys, wear an old pair of tennis shoes to protect your feet from rocks, sea-urchin spines, and other potential hazards.

Key West **Smathers Beach.** This beach features almost 2 miles of sand beside South Roosevelt Boulevard. Trucks along the road will rent you rafts, Windsurfers, and other beach "toys."

Higgs Memorial Beach. Near the end of White Street, this is a popular sunbathing spot. A nearby grove of Australian pines provides shade and the **West Martello Tower** provides shelter should a storm suddenly sweep in.

Dog Beach. At Vernon and Waddell streets, this is the only beach in Key West where dogs are allowed.

Southernmost Beach. On the Atlantic Ocean at the foot of Duval Street, this spot is popular with tourists at nearby motels. It has limited parking and a nearby buffet-type restaurant.

Fort Zachary Taylor State Historic Site. The beach here, several hundred yards of shoreline near the western end of Key West, adjoins a picnic area with barbecue grills in a stand of Australian pines. The restoration project begun in 1989 has leveled the beach after much sand erosion. Snorkeling is good except when winds blow from the south-southwest. This beach is relatively uncrowded and attracts more locals than tourists.

Simonton Street Beach. At the north end of Simonton Street, facing the Gulf of Mexico, this is a great place to watch boat traffic in the harbor, but parking here is difficult.

Two hotels in Key West have notable beaches:

Pier House (1 Duval St.) A beach club for locals and patrons of certain nearby guest houses is available here.

Several hotels allow varying degrees of undress on their beaches. Pier House permits female guests on its beach to go topless, and topless bathing is acceptable at the **Atlantic Shores Motel** (510 South St.). Contrary to popular belief, the rangers at Fort Taylor beach do *not* allow nude bathing.

Dining

By Rosalie Leposky

Don't be misled by the expression *Key-easy*. Denizens of the Florida Keys may be relaxed and wear tropical-casual clothes, but these folks take food seriously. A number of young, talented chefs have settled here in the last few years to enjoy the climate and contribute to the Keys' growing image as a fine-dining center. Best-known among them is Doug Shook, who made his reputation at Louie's Backyard, along with lately departed (for Miami Beach's Art Deco District) Norman Van Aken, whose book, *Feast of the Sunlight* (Random House, 1988) describes the delights of Key West's "fusion cuisine," a blend of Florida citrus, seafood, and tropical fruits with Southwestern chilis, herbs, and spices.

The restaurant menus, the rum-based fruit beverages, and even the music reflect the Keys' tropical climate and their proximity to Cuba and other Caribbean islands. The better American and Cuban restaurants serve imaginative and tantalizing dishes that incorporate tropical fruits and vegetables, including avocado, carambola (star fruit), mango, and papaya.

Freshly caught local fish have been on every Keys menu in the past, but that is starting to change. The Keys' growing population has degraded the environment, disrupting fisheries and pricing fishermen out of the local housing market. Because many venerable commercial fish houses have abandoned the business in the past decade, there's a good chance the fish you order in a Keys restaurant may have been caught somewhere else. Since 1985, the U.S. government has protected the queen conch as an endangered species, so any conch you order in the Keys has come fresh-frozen from the Bahamas, Belize, or the Caribbean. Florida lobster and stone crab should be local and fresh from August through March.

Purists will find few examples of authentic Key lime pie: a yellow lime custard in a Graham-cracker crust with a meringue top. Many restaurants now serve a version made with white-pastry crust and whipped cream, which is easy to prepare and hold for sale. For the real thing, try **Papa Joe's** (MM 79.7 BS, Islamorada on Upper Matecumbe Key) or **Mangrove Mama's** (MM 20 BS, Sugarloaf Key).

The list below is a representative selection of independent restaurants in the Keys, organized by mile marker (MM) number in descending order, as you would encounter them when driving down from the mainland. Small restaurants may not follow the hours listed here. Sometimes they close for a day or a week, or cancel lunch for a month or two, just by posting a note on the door.

Highly recommended restaurants are indicated by a star ★.

Category	Cost*
Very Expensive	over $55
Expensive	$35–$55
Moderate	$15–$35
Inexpensive	under $15

per person, excluding drinks, service, 6% state sales tax, and local tourist tax

Florida City **Alabama Jack's.** In 1953 Alabama Jack Stratham opened his restaurant on two barges at the end of Card Sound Road, 13 miles south of Homestead in an old fishing community between Card and Barnes sounds. The spot, something of a no-man's-land, belongs to the Keys in spirit thanks to the Card Sound toll bridge, which joined the mainland to upper Key Largo in 1969. Regular customers include Keys fixtures such as balladeer Jimmy Buffett, Sunday cyclists, local retirees, boaters who tie up at the restaurant's dock, and anyone else fond of dancing to country-western music and clapping for cloggers. You can also admire the tropical birds cavorting in the nearby mangroves and the occasional crocodile swimming up the canal. Though Jack's been gone since the early 1980s, owner Phyllis Sague has kept the favorites, including peppery homemade crab cakes; crispy-chewy conch fritters; crunchy breaded shrimp; homemade tartar sauce; and a tangy cocktail sauce with horseradish. Ask about availability of a 6-passenger dive boat. *58000 Card Sound Rd., tel. 305/248–8741. No reservations. Dress: casual. No credit cards. Open 8:30–7. Live band Sat.–Sun. 2–7. Moderate.*

Key Largo **Crack'd Conch.** Behind the white clapboard lattice exterior and the green and violet trim, foreign money and patrons' business cards festoon the main dining room, where vertical bamboo stakes support the bar. There's also a screened outdoor porch. Specialties include conch (cracked and in chowder, fritters, and salad), fried alligator, smoked chicken, and 89 kinds of beer. *MM 105, OS, Rte. 1, 105045 Overseas Hwy., tel. 305/451–0732. No reservations. Dress: casual. AE. Open Thurs.–Tues. noon–10. Closed Wed.; Tues. from Easter through Memorial Day, and Sept. through Christmas. Moderate.*

Harriette's Retreat. Typical of one of those roadside places where the Coca-Cola sign appears larger than the restaurant's, and where tidying is always in order—although recently Harriette's has seen some refurbishments—this place hangs thick with down-home personality. Owner Harriette Mattson makes it her business to know many of her guests by name, and even takes the trouble to remember what they eat. Wise-cracking waitresses, perfectly styled for this joint, will tell you that the three-egg omelet is usually a six-egg omelet because Harriette has a heavy hand. Light on prices, though, this 48-seater that Harriette calls "a hash house, not a gourmet house" is famous for its breakfasts: featuring steak and eggs with hash browns or grits and toast and jelly for $5.95; or old-fashioned hot cakes with whipped butter and syrup and sausage or bacon for $3.25. Count on a strictly homey, tacky atmosphere with crafts and photos on consignment. *MM 95.7, 95710 Overseas Hwy., BS, Key Largo, tel. 305/852–8689. No reservations. Dress: casual. Open 6–2. No credit cards. Closed Thanksgiving, Christmas. Inexpensive.*

★ **Mrs. Mac's Kitchen.** Hundreds of beer cans, beer bottles, and expired auto license plates from all over the world decorate the walls of this wood-paneled, open-air restaurant. At lunchtime, the counter and booths fill up early with locals. Regular nightly specials are worth the stop: meatloaf on Monday, Mexican on Tuesday, Italian on Wednesday, and seafood Thursday through Saturday. The chili is always good, and the imported beer of the month is $1.50 a bottle or can. Open 7 AM–9:30 PM. *MM 99.4, Rte. 1, tel. 305/451–3722. No reservations. Dress: casual. No credit cards. Closed Sun. and major holidays. Inexpensive.*

Islamorada **Green Turtle Inn.** Photographs of locals and famous visitors dating from 1947 line the walls and stuffed turtle dolls dangle from the ceiling over the bar. Henry Rosenthal, the restaurant's third owner, retains the original menu cover and some of the original dishes. Specialties include a turtle chowder; conch fritters, nicely browned outside, light and fluffy inside; conch salad with vinegar, lime juice, pimiento, and pepper; alligator steak (tail meat) sautéed in an egg batter; and Key lime pie. Whole pies are available for carryout. *MM 81.5, OS, tel. 305/664–9031. No reservations. Dress: casual. AE, D, DC, MC, V. Closed Mon. and Thanksgiving Day. Moderate.*

★ **Marker 88.** The best seats in chef/owner Andre Mueller's main dining room catch the last glimmers of sunset. Hostesses recite a lengthy list of daily specials and offer you a wine list with more than 200 entries. You can get a good steak or veal chop here, but 75% of the food served is seafood. Specialties include a robust conch chowder; banana blueberry bisque; salad Trevisana, made with radicchio, leaf lettuce, Belgium endive, watercress, and sweet-and-sour dill dressing (President Bush's favorite); sautéed conch or alligator steak meunière; grouper Rangoon, served with chunks of papaya, banana, and pineapple in a cinnamon and currant jelly sauce; and Key lime pie. *MM 88 Overseas Hwy., BS, Plantation Key, tel. 305/852–9315. Reservations advised. Dress: casual. AE, DC, MC, V. Dinner only. Closed Mon. Moderate.*

Papa Joe's Landmark Restaurant. Never mind the heavily chlorinated water and the pasty white bread when you can savor succulent dolphin and fresh green beans and carrots al dente. Here, they will still clean and cook your own catch: $8.95 up to 1 pound per person fried, broiled, sautéed; $10.95 any other style, which includes meunière, blackened, coconut-dipped, Cajun, amandine, or Oscar (sautéed, topped with béarnaise sauce, crabmeat, and asparagus). Joe's—which first opened under another name in 1937—reopened in 1991 after an 18-month remodeling project which includes an upper-level, over-the-water tiki bar with 25 seats. "Early American dump," is how owner Frank Curtis describes the look: captain's chairs, mounted fish, hanging baskets, fish buoys, and driftwood strung year-round with Christmas lights. The decor never gets ahead of the food, which is first rate. An early bird menu from 4 to 6 PM is priced $7.95–$8.95. For dessert dive into the Grand Marnier cheesecake, the mud pie, or the rum chocolate cake. *MM 79.7 Overseas Hwy., BS, tel. 305/664–8756. No reservations. Dress: casual. AE, MC, V. Open daily 11–10. Closed Thanksgiving, Christmas. Moderate.*

Whale Harbor Inn. This coral rock building has oyster shells cemented onto the walls, an old Florida Keys bottle collection, and a water mark at the 7-foot mark as a reminder of Hurricane

Donna's fury in 1960. Several restaurant employees rode out the storm in the building's lighthouse tower. The main attraction is a 50-foot-long all-you-can-eat buffet, which includes a stir-fry area for wok cookery and a plentiful supply of shrimp, mussels, crayfish, and snow crab legs. In 1991 seating was expanded from 300 to 400 places in the main Grotto Dining Room, a second buffet set up, and a second lounge opened. The adjoining Dockside Restaurant and Lounge are open for breakfast. The raw bar and grill are open to midnight. *MM 83.5, OS, Upper Matecumbe Key, tel. 305/664–4959. No reservations. Dress: casual. AE, DC, MC, V. Moderate.*

Marathon **Kelsey's.** The walls in this restaurant at the Faro Blanco Marine Resort are hung with boat paddles inscribed by the regulars and celebrities such as Joe Namath and Ted Turner. All entrées here are served with fresh-made yeast rolls brushed with drawn butter and Florida orange honey. You can bring your own cleaned and filleted catch for the chef to prepare. Dessert offerings change nightly and may include Mrs. Kelsey's original macadamia pie (even though she's sold out and gone to the old Riverview Hotel in New Smyrna Beach) and Key lime cheesecake. *MM 48, BS, 1996 Overseas Hwy., tel. 305/743–9018. Reservations necessary. Dress: casual. Dinner only. AE, MC, V. Closed Mon. Moderate.*

Ship's Pub and Galley. The collection of historic photos on the restaurant walls depict the railroad era in the Keys, the development of Duck Key, and many of the notables who have visited here. Dinners include soup and a 40-item salad bar with all the steamed shrimp you can eat. Specialties include homemade garlic bread, Swiss onion soup, certified New York Angus beef, at least two fish specials, Florida stone crab claws (in season), and mile-high shoofly mud pie, a 6-inch-high coffee ice-cream pie with a whipped cream topping. The adjoining lounge has live entertainment and a dance floor. *MM 61, OS, tel. 305/743–7000, ext. 3627. Reservations accepted. Dress: casual. Early bird specials. AE, DC, MC, V. Moderate.*

Herbie's Bar. A local favorite for lunch and dinner since the 1940s, Herbie's has three small rooms with two bars. Indoor diners sit at wood picnic tables or the bar; those in the screened outdoor room use concrete tables. Specialties include spicy conch chowder with chunks of tomato and crisp conch fritters with homemade horseradish sauce. Nightly specials. *MM 50.5, BS, 6350 Overseas Hwy., tel. 305/743–6373. No reservations. Dress: casual. No credit cards. Closed Sun. and Easter–Nov. Inexpensive.*

★ **Mile 7 Grill.** This open-air diner built in 1954 at the Marathon end of Seven Mile Bridge has walls festooned with beer cans, mounted fish, sponges, and signs describing individual menu items. Specialties include conch chowder, fresh fish sandwich of the day, and a foot-long chili dog on a toasted sesame roll. Even if you're not a dessert eater, don't pass up the peanut butter pie, served near frozen, in a chocolate-flavored shell. Made with cream cheese, it's a cross between pudding and ice cream. *MM 47.5, BS, 1240 Overseas Hwy., tel. 305/743–4481. No credit cards. Open daily for lunch and dinner. Closed Wed.–Thurs., Christmas Eve–first Fri. after New Year's, and when they want to in Aug.–Sept. Inexpensive.*

Key West **Louie's Backyard.** Abstract art and old Key West paintings *American* adorn the interior of this Key West institution, while outside ★ you dine under the mahoe tree and feel the cool breeze coming off the sea. The ambience, however, takes second place to chef Doug Shook's culinary expertise. The loosely Spanish-Caribbean menu changes twice yearly, but might include such house specials as pan-cooked quail stuffed with lobster and wild mushrooms in Madeira sauce or grilled sirloin steak with a rum-tamarind-chili glaze and roasted vegetables. Top off the meal with Louie's lime tart or an irresistible chocolate brownie brulée. *700 Waddell Ave., tel. 305/294–1061. Reservations advised. Dress: casual. AE, DC, MC, V. Very Expensive.*

★ **Pier House Restaurant.** Steamships from Havana once docked at this pier jutting out into the Gulf of Mexico. Now it's an elegant place to dine, indoors or out, and to watch boats gliding by in the harbor. At night the restaurant shines lights into the water, attracting schools of brightly colored parrot fish. The menu emphasizes tropical fruits, spices, and fish and includes grilled sea scallops with black bean cake and *pico de gallo* (tomato, shallots, cilantro, chopped chayote); lobster ravioli in a creamy pesto sauce and salmon caviar; and a seafood catch prepared with tomatillo vinaigrette and saffron aioli. Ordered specially, a poached yellowtail is served with broccoli flowerets and red peppers triangulated on alternate rounds of yellow and green squash. Even simple food becomes art. *1 Duval St., tel. 305/296–4600, ext. 555. Reservations advised. Dress: neat but casual. AE, DC, MC, V. Very Expensive.*

Cafe Marquesa. Only 15 tables and banquettes, the secret of the cafe's success is its openness in all respects. It is open to innovative cuisine, it has a friendly staff, an open kitchen through a *trompe l'oeil* pantry mural—nothing's snooty about this place. Owners of the hotel now attract locals and visitors alike with affordable meals that include arugula salad with sun-dried tomatoes, fresh mushrooms, corn kernels, and bacon; a delicate, generously served blue corn pasta layered with spinach, mushrooms, red bell peppers, ricotta and parmesan cheeses, with a vegetarian béchamel on a bed of zucchini coulis; grilled shrimp with *piripiri* sauce (a salsa of tomatoes, chilis, garlic, cilantro, and shallots). Limitless helpings of the excellent sesame flatbread with black pepper accompany all meals. For dessert try the fruit tart with kiwi, strawberries, and crème fraîche. *600 Fleming St., tel. 305/292–1244. Reservations accepted. Dress: neat but casual. AE, MC, V. Closed lunch and Tues. in summer. Moderate.*

Pepe's Cafe and Steak House. Judges, police officers, carpenters, and fisherpeople rub elbows every morning in their habitual breakfast seats, at three tables and four pine booths under a huge paddlefan. Outdoors are more tables and an open-air bar under a canvas tarp. Pepe's was established downtown in 1909 and moved to the current site in 1962. The specials change nightly: barbecued chicken, pork tenderloin, ribs, potato salad, red or black beans, and corn bread on Sunday; meatloaf on Monday; seafood Tuesday and Wednesday; a full traditional Thanksgiving dinner every Thursday; filet mignon on Friday; and prime rib on Saturday. *806 Caroline St., tel. 305/294–7192. No reservations. Dress: casual. D, MC, V. Moderate.*

Cuban **El Siboney.** This family-style restaurant serves traditional Cuban food. Specials include chicken and rice every Friday, oxtail stew with rice and beans on Saturday. Always available are roast pork with *morros* (black beans and white rice) and cassava, paella, and *palomilla* steak. *900 Catherine St., tel. 305/296–4184. No reservations. Dress: casual. No credit cards. Closed*

Thanksgiving, Christmas, New Year's Day, 2 wks in June. Inexpensive.

Delicatessen **Market Bistro.** The Pier House's deli and fine-dining snack
shop, which recently added an espresso bar, sells the hotel's
classic Key lime pie by the slice, as well as a chocolate deca-
dence: a triple chocolate flourless torte with raspberry sauce
and rose petals. A cooler holds tropical fruit juices, beer, and
mineral water. Other specialties include sandwiches, salads,
gourmet cheeses, pâtés, and homemade pastries. *1 Duval St. in
the Pier House, tel. 305/296–4600. No reservations. Dress: casual. AE, DC, MC, V. Moderate.*

French **Cafe des Artistes.** This intimate 75-seat restaurant occupies
part of a hotel building constructed in 1935 by C. E. Alfeld, Al
Capone's bookkeeper. Haitian paintings and Keys scenes by local artists decorate the walls. Dining is in two indoor rooms or
on a roof-top open deck beneath a big sapodilla tree. Executive
chef Andrew Berman presents a French interpretation of tropical cuisine, using fresh local seafood and produce and light,
flour-free sauces. Specialties include the restaurant's award-
winning lobster with Cognac, served with shrimp in a mango-
saffron beurre blanc, the half roast duckling with raspberry
sauce, and the *minute de snapper:* paper-thin slices of snapper
flash-broiled and served with a tomato and basil sauce. *1007 Simonton St., tel. 305/294–7100. Reservations advised. Dress:
neat but casual. AE, MC, V. No lunch. Expensive–Moderate.*

Italian **Antonia's.** Since 1979 co-chefs Antonia Berto and Phillip Smith
have turned out fluent northern Italian renditions of Keys' seafood with homemade pastas in this 1861 building, formerly the
site of the Blue Boar Bar and the hippie coffeehouse Crazy
Ophelia's. Behind the stained-glass "615" transom and bay
windows is dining at its finest, including such dishes as homemade mozzarella appetizers, whole oven-roasted yellowtail
snapper, and the generous dolphin fillet with subtle caper
sauce. All pastas and breads are home baked. Many Italian
wines are offered by the glass, but consider having a Peroni
beer before dinner at the striped canvas–canopied bar over-
looked by the bust of Caesar. Room for dessert? Try the
tiramisù, cannoli, or Amaretto pie in coconut cream sauce. The
ice creams and sorbets are made in house. *615 Duval St., tel.
305/294–6565. Reservations advised. Dress: neat but casual.
MC, V. No lunch; Closed 1 month in summer. Moderate.*

Seafood **The Buttery.** The Buttery's waiters have come to be known as
★ "buttercups," a nickname they share with the house's special
drink, a blended frozen concoction of vodka, Kahlúa, Amaretto, coconut milk, and cream. Each of the restaurant's six
rooms has its own character. The back room with the bar has
wood paneling, skylights, and lots of greenery; a small private
dining room in front has green-painted woodwork, a crystal
chandelier, and floral wallpaper. Another is eclectically tropical with bamboo chairs, dark louvered shutters, cut-tin lamps,
and ceiling fans under the tall eave. All tables have hurricane
lamps and fresh flowers. In its 14th year, The Buttery experi-
ments with specials that find their way onto the seasonally
changing menu. Lately rave-worthy were the scallops *Tova*
(wrapped in salmon atop a spinach hollandaise sauce); steak
"Ricardo" (fillets of tenderloin sautéed with mushrooms in Madeira wine sauce); and chilled Senegalese cream of celery soup
made with curry, heavy cream, and mango chutney. *1208*

Simonton St., tel. 305/294–0717. Reservations advised. Dress: neat but casual. AE, D, DC, MC, V. Closed 2–3 wks in Sept. No lunch. Moderate.

Half Shell Raw Bar. "Eat It Raw" is the motto, and even off-season the oyster bar keeps shucking. You eat at shellacked picnic tables and benches in a shed, with ship models, life buoys, mounted dolphin, and old license plates hanging overhead. Classic signs offer homage to Keys' passions. Reads one: "Fishing is not a matter of life and death. It's more important than that." Once a fish market, the Half Shell looks out onto the deep-sea fishing fleet. Eat indoors or out. Specials, chalked on the blackboard, may include broiled dolphin sandwich or linguine seafood marinara. The same owners operate The Turtle Kraals Restaurant & Bar on the other side of Land's End Village. *Land's End Marina, tel. 305/294–7496. No reservations. Dress: casual. No credit cards. Moderate–Inexpensive.*

Dockside Bar and Raw Bar. When the crowds get too thick on the Mallory Dock at sunset, you can come up here, have a piña colada and a snack, and watch the action from afar. This establishment, on a 200-foot dock behind Ocean Key House, has a limited but flavorful menu: freshly smoked fish, crunchy conch salad, crispy conch fritters, steamed lobster (in season), potato salad, and shrimp. Live island music is featured nightly. *Ocean Key House, Zero Duval St., tel. 305/296–7701. No reservations. Dress: casual. AE, D, DC, MC, V. Inexpensive.*

Lodging

Some hotels in the Keys are historic structures with a charming patina of age; others are just plain old. Salty winds and soil play havoc with anything manmade in the Keys. Constant maintenance is a must, and some hotels and motels don't get it. Inspect your accommodations before checking in. The best rooms in the Keys have a clear bay or ocean view and a deep setback from the Overseas Highway.

The city of Key West offers the greatest variety of lodgings, from large resorts to bed-and-breakfast rooms in private homes. Altogether there are about 4,000 units (including about 1,500 rooms in close to 60 guest houses) as well as approximately 1,800 condominium apartments that are available for daily or weekly rental through their homeowners associations.

Accommodations in the Keys are more expensive than elsewhere in south Florida. In part this is due to the Keys' popularity and ability to command top dollar, but primarily it's because everything used to build and operate a hotel costs more in the Keys. All materials and supplies must be trucked in, and electric and water rates are among the steepest in the nation.

The Florida Keys and Key West Visitors Bureau provides a free accommodations guide (*see* Important Addresses and Numbers, above). The list below is a representative selection of hotels, motels, resorts, and guest houses. In the Upper, Middle, and Lower Keys outside Key West, we've listed hotels, motels, and resorts by mile marker (MM) number in descending order, as you would encounter them when driving down from the mainland.

Highly recommended hotels are indicated by a star ★.

Category	Cost*
Very Expensive	over $175
Expensive	$110–$175
Moderate	$75–$110
Inexpensive	under $75

All prices are for a standard double room, excluding 7% state sales tax and local tourist tax.

Key Largo   **Holiday Inn Key Largo Resort & Marina.** James W. Hendricks, the Kentucky attorney who restored the *African Queen*, completed renovations and new landscaping at this resort at the Key Largo Harbor Marina in 1989. The hotel was built in 1971, and a new wing was added in 1981. Decor includes blond wood furniture and a pink-and-green color scheme. *MM 100, OS, 99701 Overseas Hwy., 33037, tel. 305/451–2121, 800/HOLIDAY, or 800/THE KEYS. 132 rooms with bath, including nonsmoker rooms and rooms for handicapped guests. Facilities: 2 pools (1 with waterfall), Jacuzzi, marina with 35 transient spaces, gift shop, dive and glass-bottom tour boats, boat rentals. AE, MC, V. Expensive.*

Marina Del Mar Resort and Marina. This resort beside the Key Largo Harbor Canal caters to sailors and divers. All rooms contain original watercolors by Keys artist Mary Boggs and the best rooms are suites 502, 503 and 504, each of which has a full kitchen and plenty of room for large families or dive groups. The fourth-floor observation deck offers spectacular sunrise and sunset views. Advance reservations are suggested for boat slips. *MM 100, OS, Box 1050, 33037, tel. 305/451–4107, 800/451–3483 or 305/451–4107. 76 rooms with bath, including 8 nonsmoker suites, 16 studios with full kitchens, 16 nonsmoker rooms, and 3 rooms for handicapped guests. Facilities: in-room refrigerators, 40-slip full-service marina, showers and washing machines for marina guests, pool, 2 lighted tennis courts, weight room, washers and dryers on all floors, picnic tables, free Continental breakfast in lobby, restaurant and bar with live nightly entertainment, dive packages, diving and snorkeling charters, fishing charters. No pets. AE, DC, MC, V. Expensive.*

Sheraton Key Largo Resort. This is first of the large, amenity-filled, enclave resorts on the way south. Service can be impersonal, as happens at chain resorts, but day by day, one staff person or another wins you over (typically the chambermaids). The look of this four-story hotel, with hanging gardens, fits well in its surroundings. The three-story atrium with its windowpane and coral-rock walls, Mexican tile floor, and rattan furniture strikes the mood. Least desirable rooms are the 230, 330, and 430 series that overlook the parking lot, but all are spacious and comfortable. Mulched nature trails and boardwalks lead through hammocks to mangrove overlooks by the shore. (Bring bug spray for your walk.) Both Cafe Key Largo, for three meals a day, and Christina's, the gourmet dinner-only room, guarantee grand views three stories above the bay. *MM 97, BS, 97000 Overseas Hwy., 33037, tel. 305/852–5553, 800/325–3535 (US), 800/268–9393 (eastern Canada), or 800/268–9330 (western Canada). 200 rooms with bath, including 10 suites. Facilities: 2 heated pools, 2 lighted tennis courts, 2,000-foot labeled nature trail, sailboat and Windsurfer rental, fish-*

ing and dive charters, 21-slip dock for hotel guests, minibars, 2 restaurants, 3 lounges, beauty shop. AE, DC, MC, V. Expensive.

Largo Lodge. No two rooms are the same in this vintage 1950s resort. A dense palm alley sets the mood. Tropical gardens with more palms, sea grapes, and orchids surround the guest cottages. Late in the day, wild ducks, pelicans, herons, and other birds come looking for a handout from long-time owner Harriet "Hat" Stokes. *MM 101.5, BS, 101740 Overseas Hwy., 33037, tel. 305/451–0424 or 800/IN-THE-SUN. 6 apartments with kitchen, 1 efficiency. Facilities: 200 feet of bay frontage, public phone, boat ramp and 3 slips. Call for restrictions. AE, MC, V. Moderate.*

Sunset Cove Motel. Statues of lions, tigers, and dinosaurs seem to be attracting waterbirds that fly in each morning and afternoon, while an orphaned manatee swims by for a daily visit. The 10 guest units all have kitchens and original hand-painted murals. Special discounts are offered to senior citizens and members of conservation groups. *MM 99.5, BS, Box 99, 33037, tel. 305/451–0705. 10 units with bath and a dormitory group house with kitchen for up to 15 people. Facilities: free watersports equipment (canoes, glass-bottom and regular paddleboat, sailboats, trimaran, and Windsurfers), 115-foot fishing pier, boat ramp. MC, V. Moderate.*

Bay Harbor Lodge. Owner Laszlo Simoga speaks German, Hungarian, and Russian and caters to an international clientele. Situated on two heavily landscaped acres, this resort with a rustic wood lodge and several concrete-block structures had all its kitchens and bathrooms retiled in 1990. All cottages got individual barbecues in 1990, and several tiki huts were put up in 1991. Unit 14, a large efficiency apartment with a deck, has a wood ceiling, original oil paintings, and a dining table made from the hatch cover of a World War II Liberty Ship. *MM 97.5, BS, 97702 Overseas Hwy., 33037, tel. 305/852–5695. 16 rooms with bath. Facilities: Jacuzzi, saltwater shower, Olympic weightlifting equipment, individual outdoor barbecues, paddleboat, rowboats, canoes, 2 docks, cable TV, boat-trailer parking. No pets. D, MC, V. Moderate–Inexpensive.*

Islamorada
★ **Cheeca Lodge.** Winner in 1990 of the hotel industry's top environmental award, and host of an annual fund-raising dinner that benefits The Cousteau Society, this 27-acre low-rise resort on Upper Matecumbe Key satisfies both the leisure needs and environmental ethic of affluent travelers. Guests benefit from an underwater snorkel trail that explains marine ecology; Camp Cheeca employs marine science counselors to make learning about the fragile Keys environment fun for children aged 6–12. Biodegradable products are used, most everything is recycled, and the quiet setting is vouchsafed for guests by the resort's ban on motorized watersports that also reduces oily discharges into the water. Preserved at Cheeca is the beachfront pioneer burial ground of the Matecumbe United Methodist Church, and tranquil fish-filled lagoons and gardens surround. Guest rooms and suites feature periwinkle blue/strawberry, and green/hot orange color schemes; all have British Colonial-style furniture of tightly woven wicker, cane, and bamboo. Touches include intriguing hand-painted mirror frames, faintly surreal art prints and romantic waterscapes, and natural shell soapdishes. Ocean Suite 102 has a cathedral ceiling and a screened porch; fourth-floor rooms in the main

lodge open onto a terrace with either ocean or bay views. The dining room features a carpet in light blue and ivory that resembles the beautiful, rippled pattern of sand that waves create. *MM 82, Upper Matecumbe Key, Box 527, 33036, tel. 305/ 664–4651 (Islamorada), or 305/245–3755 (Miami), or 800/327– 2888 (US and FL). 203 rooms, including 64 suites, 60 non-smoker rooms, and 5 rooms for handicapped guests. Facilities: in-room minibar, free golf-cart shuttle service around the resort, 9-hole par-3 executive golf course designed by Jack Nicklaus, 6 lighted tennis courts, 2 heated pools and one saltwater tidal pool, 525-foot fishing pier, 2 restaurants, lounge. Sun. brunch served in the Atlantic's Edge Dining Room. Beach Hut rents Hobie Cats, rafts, snorkeling and fishing gear, parasailing trips, and non-motorized boats. All-year children's program. AE, D, DC, MC, V. Very Expensive.*

Long Key **Lime Tree Bay Resort.** Vic Bubnow and Phil DeMontmollin (retired from *The Miami Herald*), new owners since 1990, plan changes at this steadily improving 2.5-acre resort built in 1972. Each room is decorated differently. A palm tree grows through the floor of "The Treehouse," a two-bedroom unit with kitchen that is popular with larger families. You can swim and snorkel in the shallow grass flats just offshore. *MM 68.5, BS, Box 839, Layton, 33001, tel. 305/664–4740. 29 rooms with bath. Facilities: outdoor pool and Jacuzzi, tennis court, power and sailboat rentals, dive boats and charter boats, restaurant. No pets. AE, D, MC, V. Moderate–Inexpensive.*

Marathon **Hawk's Cay Resort.** Morris Lapidus, architect of the Fontaine-
★ bleau Hilton hotel in Miami Beach, designed this rambling West Indies-style resort, which opened in 1959 as the Indies Inn and Marina. Over the years it has entertained a steady stream of politicians (including Harry Truman, Dwight Eisenhower, and Lyndon Johnson) and film stars who come to relax and be pampered by a friendly, low-key staff. Hawk's Cay retains the comfortable ambience it has always had, even after an $8-million renovation of rooms, public areas, meeting space, and landscaping designed by architect Bill Cox and completed in 1989. The new decor features wickerwork rattan, a sea-green-and-salmon color scheme, and original contemporary artwork in guest rooms and public areas. Most rooms face the water. Twenty-two two-bedroom marina villas are available to hotel guests. *MM 61, OS, 33050, tel. 305/743–7000, 800/432– 2242 (FL), 800/327–7775 (US). 177 rooms with bath, including 16 suites, 15 rooms for handicapped guests. Facilities: heated pool, 2 whirlpool spas, 1-mi fitness trail, 8 tennis courts, Tim Farwell's Tennis School, use of Sombrero Golf Course in Marathon, 70-slip full-service marina, PADI-certified and handicap diving certified dive boats, Club Nautico boat rentals, fishing and sailing charter boats, 4 restaurants, complimentary full-breakfast buffet, nightclub, 3 boutique and specialty shops, billiard room, video game room. $18-per-child daily summer and holidays program. AE, D, DC, MC, V. Very Expensive.*

Rainbow Bend Fishing Resort. First you notice the shocking-pink exterior, then the well-kept appearance of this 2.7-acre resort built in the late 1950s as a lumberyard and CIA base. Each guest room is uniquely decorated. A restaurant offering complimentary breakfast overlooks an ample manmade beach and barbecue area, good bonefish flats just a few yards offshore, and a dock with boats available free to guests, except for minimum $5 fuel charge. *MM 58, OS, Grassy Key, Route 1, Box 159, 33050, tel. 305/289–1505. 23 rooms with bath, including 19 suites, and efficiencies. Facilities: heated pool and Jacuzzi, small fishing pier, 4 hrs free use of 15-foot Boston Whaler, free use of sailboats and canoe, complete bait and tackle shop, restaurant. Free full breakfast. AE, MC, V. Expensive.*

Little Torch Key
★

Little Palm Island. The lobby is located off the Overseas Highway on Little Torch Key, but the resort itself is a 3-mile boat ride away on a palm-fringed island at the western end of the Newfound Harbor Keys. There you'll find 14 thatch-roof villas, each with two suites. An additional suite is located in the Great House, a cypress fishing lodge built in 1928. Each suite has a Mexican-tile bath and dressing area, Jacuzzi, beds draped with mosquito netting, and Mexican and Guatemalan wicker and rattan furniture, and a second, outdoor shower. Built on stilts 9 feet above mean high tide, all villas are 20 feet from the water. A 53-ft. motor yacht contains another suite called **The Sweet One.** The island is in the middle of Coupon Bight State Aquatic Preserve and is the closest point of land to the Looe Key National Marine Sanctuary. *MM 28.5, Overseas Highway, Route 4, Box 1036, 33042, tel. 305/872–2524 or 800/343–8567. 30 suites, 1 for handicapped guests. Facilities: air conditioners, wet bars and stocked refrigerators, room safes, heated lagoon-style pool, sauna, tiki bar, gift shop, exercise room, restaurant, 12-slip marina for hotel and restaurant guests, and for visiting yachters. Free on-the-hour launch service 7 AM–11 PM. Pickup from Marathon Airport and Key West International Airport, $80 per couple round-trip. Guided tours and excursions. Restaurant reservations: 305/872–2551. Very Expensive.*

Ramrod Key

Looe Key Reef Resort and Dive Center. The rooms in this two-story motel, which attracts divers because of its scuba facilities, were refurnished in 1987. In the tiny lobby, the front desk doubles as a package liquor store. Rooms are spartan but comfortable, with firm mattresses and ocean-blue bedspreads and carpets. The least desirable rooms are the three singles without a canal view. Guests can make an appointment for free pickup from the private airstrip on Summerland Key. *MM 27.5, US 1, OS, Box 509, 33042, tel. 305/872–2215 or 800/942–5397 (outside 305 area, and continental U.S.). 23 rooms with bath, 1 for handicapped guests. Facilities: air conditioners, cable TV, outdoor pool, PADI-rated 5-star dive shop, 400 feet of boat dockage, 3 Coast Guard–certified dive boats, restaurant, poolside tiki bar and raw bar. Dive and snorkel package rates available; discounts for groups. MC, V. Moderate–Inexpensive.*

Lower Sugarloaf Key

Sugar Loaf Lodge. This well-landscaped older motel overlooking mangrove islands and Upper Sugarloaf Sound has one building with soft beds and an eclectic assortment of furniture and another with high ceilings, wall murals, and balconies on the second floor. A friendly dolphin named Sugar inhabits a lagoon just outside the restaurant; diners can watch her perform through a picture window. *MM 17, BS, Box 148, 33044, tel. 305/ 745–3211. 55 rooms with bath. Facilities: pool, tennis court, 18-hole miniature golf course, restaurant, lounge, free dolphin performances at 9 AM, 1 PM, and 5 PM. AE, D, DC, MC, V. Moderate–Inexpensive.*

Key West House and Condominium Rentals

Key West Reservation Service makes hotel reservations and helps visitors locate rental properties (hotels, motels, bed-and-breakfasts, oceanfront condominiums, luxury vacation homes). *628 Fleming St., Drawer 1689, 33040, tel. 305/294–7713, 800/356–3567 (FL), 800/327–4831 (US); fax 305/296–6291. AE, MC, V.*

Property Management of Key West, Inc., offers lease and rental service for condominiums, town houses, and private homes, including renovated Conch homes. *1213 Truman Ave., 33040, tel. 305/296–7744. AE, MC, V.*

Hotels and Motels

The Banyan Resort. A time-share resort across the street from the Truman Annex, the Banyan Resort includes five Victorian houses, a former cigar factory listed on the National Registry of Historic Places, and three modern buildings in the Victorian style. The award-winning gardens are a tropical cornucopia of avocado, Barbados cherry, eggfruit, papaya, Persian lime, and sapodilla. The rooms have a gray, maroon, and mauve color scheme and rattan and wicker furniture. *323 Whitehead St., 33040, tel. 305/296–7786 or 800/225–0639. 38 suites with bath. Facilities: 2 pools (1 heated), Jacuzzi, bar. Call for restrictions. AE, D, MC, V. Very Expensive.*

Hyatt Key West. A first for Hyatt, this "baby grand" resort consists of three four-story buildings surrounding a tropical piazza. The lobby features a Mexican terra-cotta tile floor and cherry wood fixtures; the room decor employs mint, lilac, peach, and teal blue hues with light-wood dressers and wicker chairs. *601 Front St., 33040, tel. 305/296–9900, 800/233–1234, 800/228–9005 (HI, AK), or 800/233–1234. 120 rooms with bath, including 4 suites, 16 nonsmoker rooms, and 6 rooms for handicapped guests. Facilities: pool, Jacuzzi, hot tub, fitness room, massage studio, small private manmade beach, bicycle and motor scooter rental, 6-slip marina, 60-ft rental ketch. AE, DC, MC, V. Very Expensive.*

★ **The Marquesa Hotel.** Key West architect Thomas Pope supervised the restoration of this four-story 1884 home and added onto it in a compatible style. The lobby resembles a Victorian parlor, with antique furniture, Audubon prints, fresh flowers, wonderful photos of early Key West, including one of Harry Truman driving by in an open convertible, and a bowl of apples for nibbles. Rooms have Queen Anne and eclectic antique and reproduction furnishings and dotted Swiss curtains. There are marble vanities in some baths, marble floors in others. Continental breakfast is served poolside ($6 extra). *600 Fleming St., 33040, tel. 305/292–1919 or 800/869–4631. 15 rooms with bath. Facilities: heated pool, room service, 24-hr staff, in-room safe, free off-street parking. AE, MC, V. Very Expensive.*

Marriott's Casa Marina Resort. Henry Morrison Flagler's heirs built La Casa Marina in 1921 at the end of the Florida East Coast Railroad line. The entire 13-acre resort revolves around an outdoor patio and lawn facing the ocean. The lobby, with beamed ceiling, polished Dade County pine floor, and wicker furniture and rooms decorated in mauve and green pastels and Key West scenes exude elegance. Among the best rooms are the two-bedroom loft suites with balconies facing the ocean, and the lanai rooms on the ground floor of the main building with French doors opening directly onto the lawn. In 1990 the grand ballroom was opulently restored, and Flagler's (formerly Henry's), the showplace dining room, was made less formal to keep pace with its lighter cuisine that emphasizes pasta and seafood. *1500 Reynolds St., 33040, tel. 305/296–3535, 800/235–4837 (FL), 800/228–9290 (US). 314 rooms with bath, including 63 suites, 16 nonsmoker rooms, 4 rooms for handicapped guests. Facilities: heated pool, whirlpool, 600-ft fishing pier, health club, massage studio and sauna, 3 tennis courts, 2 gift shops, activity center for children, game room, restaurant, poolside bar. Key West Water Sports, a concessionaire, offers deep-sea charter boats, light-tackle fishing, party-boat fishing, Hobie Cats, Sunfish, jet skis, scuba and snorkel trips, bicycle and moped rentals. AE, DC, MC, V. Very Expensive.*

La Concha Holiday Inn. This seven-story Art Deco hotel in the heart of downtown Key West is the city's tallest building and dates to 1926. The lobby's polished floor of pink, mauve, and green marble and a conversation pit with comfortable chairs are among the details beloved by la Concha's guests. Large rooms are furnished with 1920s-era antiques, lace curtains, and big closets. The restorers kept the old building's original louvered room doors, light globes, and floral trim on the archways. You can enjoy the sunset from "The Top," a restaurant and lounge that overlooks the entire island and features Coconuts Comedy Club at the Top on Tuesday and Sunday nights. From Wednesday through Saturday enjoy cocktails at the Palm Court Piano Bar. *430 Duval St., 33040, tel. 305/296–2991, 800/745–2191, 800/HOLIDAY (US). 160 rooms with bath, including 2 suites, 18 nonsmoker rooms, and 8 rooms for handicapped guests. Facilities: pool and sun deck, whirlpool, fitness room, restaurant, 3 bars, bicycle and motor scooter rentals. AE, D, DC, MC, V. Very Expensive–Expensive.*

★ **Pier House.** This is the catbird seat for touring Key West—just off the intersection of Duval and Front streets and within an easy walk of Mallory Square and downtown. Yet inside the hotel grounds you feel the tranquility of a remote tropical island. New since 1990 is the Caribbean Spa: 22 rooms and suites with hardwood floors and two-poster plantation beds. Eleven of the baths convert to steam rooms; the others have whirlpool tubs. In the new rooms (615 and 619 are 1-bedroom suites) you'll be spoiled by the VCRs and a library of movies and CD players with compact discs. You can also avail yourself of a loofa rub, massages, aromatherapy, or facial in the new fitness center. Weathered-gray buildings flank a courtyard filled with tall coconut palms and hibiscus blossoms. Locals gather around the thatch-roof tiki bar at the Beach Club. The complex's eclectic architecture includes an original Conch house. *1 Duval St., 33040, tel. 305/296–4600, 800/327–8340 (US). 142 rooms with bath, including 13 suites in 5 separate low-rise buildings. Facilities: heated pool, 5 bars, 5 restaurants. AE, MC, V. Very Expensive–Expensive.*

Best Western Key Ambassador Inn. If you want to stay in a hotel near the airport, this is the place to visit. Even though the 100 rooms are typical motel style—functional and unluxurious—and the Ambassador was built in 1952, the surroundings are well cared for and the property offers lots of resort features. Each room has a balcony and most offer ocean and pool views. The mood at the pool bar is upbeat and often swings to a reggae sound. A mangrove-lined stream runs through some of the seven acres and connects the salt ponds in the back with the ocean in front across the road. *375 S. Roosevelt Blvd., Key West 33040, tel. 305/296–3500 or 800/432–4315; fax 305/296–9961. 100 rooms. Facilities: outdoor heated pool, outdoor fitness* *course, snack bar and bar, shuffleboard. AE, D, DC, MC, V. Moderate.*

Guest Houses

★ **The Curry Mansion Inn.** Careful dedication to detail by Key West architect Thomas Pope and owners Al and Edith Amsterdam have produced a near-perfect match between the Victorian Curry Mansion (1899) and its modern bed-and-breakfast addition. Each room has a different color scheme using tropical pastels; all rooms have carpeted floors, wicker headboards and furnishings, and quilts from the Cotton Gin Store at MM 94.5 in Tavernier. Rooms 1 and 8, honeymoon suites, feature canopy beds and balconies. Guests are welcome to a complimentary Continental breakfast and happy hour with an open bar and live piano music. *511 Caroline St., 33040, tel. 305/294–5349. 15 rooms with bath, 2 rooms for handicapped guests. Facilities: pool, fridge, wet bars, wheelchair lift. Guests have privileges at Pier House Beach Club. AE, DC, MC, V. Very Expensive–Expensive.*

Island City House. This guest house is actually three separate buildings: the vintage-1880s Island City House and Arch House (a former carriage house) and a 1970s reconstruction of an old cigar factory that once stood on the site. Arch House features a dramatic high carriage entry from the street to the lush courtyard beneath its second story. Floors throughout are pine, and each of the 24 suites is furnished with antiques. Guests share a private tropical garden and are given free Continental breakfasts. *411 William St., 33040, tel. 305/294–5702, 800/621–9405, or 800/634–8230. 24 parlor suites with bath and kitchen. Facilities: pool, Jacuzzi, bike rental. MC, V. Very Expensive–Expensive.*

★ **The Watson House.** Small in number of rooms but big in amenities, this guest house provides utmost privacy with Duval Street convenience: It's a block from the bustle but light years from the hassle. Ed Czaplicki with partner Joe Beres has restored the house to its 1860s Bahamian look that guests find caressingly soothing. The three units are the deco Cabana Suite by the two-tier pool gardens, the William Suite on the second floor of the house with its new wainscoting and wallpapers, and the connecting or private Susan Room, also with new wallpapers. French doors and gingerbread trim dress up the pristine yellow-and-white exterior. *525 Simonton St., 30040, tel. 305/294–6712 or 800/621–9405. 2 suites with bath and full kitchen, one room with bath. Facilities: heated pool, whirlpool, off-street parking. AE, MC, V. Very Expensive–Expensive.*

Artist House. Dressed in French Empire and Victorian style, with lavender shutters on white clapboard, latticework, wrought-iron spear fencing, and a grand tin-shingled turret, this guest home is a real show stopper. All rooms are antique filled and have Dade County pine floors. Among the rooms you'll find a mix-and-match of brocade sofas, Japanese screens, pull-latch doors, clawfoot tubs, four-poster beds, and elaborate moldings. The little garden out back has a Jacuzzi with a stone lion's head, surrounded by a brick deck, and there's a pond. Rates include full breakfast in winter, Continental breakfast in summer. *534 Eaton St., Key West 30040, tel. 305/296–3977 or 800/582–7882; fax 305/296–3210. 5 rooms and suites. Facilities: Jacuzzi, garden. AE, D, DC, MC, V. Very Expensive–Moderate.*

The Arts and Nightlife

The Arts
The Keys are more than warm weather and luminous scenery—a vigorous and sophisticated artistic community flourishes here. Key West alone currently claims among its residents 55 full-time writers and 500 painters and craftsmen. Arts organizations in the Keys sponsor many special events, some lasting only a weekend, others spanning an entire season.

The monthly *Island Navigator,* Monroe County's only countywide general-interest newspaper, is free at banks, campgrounds, and convenience stores, and other high-traffic businesses. Its monthly community calendar lists cultural and sports events.

Three free publications covering Key West arts, music, and literature are available at hotels and other high-traffic areas:

The weekly *Island Life,* the most current and complete, is published by JBM Publications. *517 Duval St., Suite 200, Key West 33040, tel. 305/294–1616. Subscription by mail: $30/year.* *Solares Hill,* a monthly community newspaper, is published by Key West Publications, Inc. (1217 White St., Key West 33040, tel. 305/294–3602). In the Upper and Middle Keys, the weekly *Free Press* is available at hotels, motels, and retail outlets. *Box 469, Islamorada 33036, tel. 305/664–2266. Subscription by mail: $3/month.*

Theater
Red Barn Theater. This professional, 94-seat theater in its 13th year performs dramas, comedies, and musicals, including plays by new playwrights. *319 Duval St. (rear), Key West, tel. 305/ 296–9911. MC, V. Closed some Mons.*
Waterfront Playhouse. This mid-1850s wrecker's warehouse was converted into an 185-seat non-Equity community theater that specializes in comedy and drama. *Mallory Sq., Key West, tel. 305/294–5015. No credit cards. Open Nov.–May.*
Tennessee Williams Fine Arts Center. A 490-seat theater built in 1980 on Stock Island, BS, the center presents chamber music, dance, jazz concerts, plays (dramatic and musical) with national and international stars, and other performing-arts events. *Florida Keys Community College, 5901 W. Junior College Rd., Key West, tel. 305/296–9081, ext. 326. MC, V. Open Nov.–Apr.*

Nightlife
Key Largo
Coconuts Restaurant and Bar. The soft island music during dinner changes to top 40 after 10 PM. *MM 100, OS, in the Marina Del Mar Resort and Marina, tel. 305/451–4107. AE, DC, MC, V. Open weekdays 11 AM–2 AM, weekends 11–4 AM.*

Key West
Capt. Tony's Saloon. Arson struck this landmark bar in 1990, but this has only added to its legend. In the aftermath of the deliberately set Fantasy Fest blaze, owners turned up a $12.66 check made out to Tennessee Williams, endorsed to Captain Tony Tarracino from the playwright's publisher in the early 1960s. Captain Tony is the former bootlegger, smuggler, mercenary, gunrunner, gambler, raconteur/owner of the bar that was the original Sloppy Joe's (from 1933 to 1937), even though another more touristy bar a block away now uses the name. The building dates from 1851 when it was first used as a morgue and ice house; later it was Key West's first telegraph station. As for Captain Tony, in 1989—a year after he sold the bar—he was elected Mayor of Key West (unseated two years later after a col-

orful term), but his trace—his image on memorabilia that adorns the walls—can still be found in the saloon that reopened two months after the fire. Hemingway was a regular here, and Jimmy Buffet got his start at Capt. Tony's. Live country and rhythm-and-blues makes the scene nowadays, and the house drink, the Pirates' Punch, contains a secret rum-based formula. *428 Greene St., tel. 305/294–1838. No credit cards. Open 10 AM–4 AM.*

Havana Docks Lounge. A high-energy disco club popular with young locals and visitors, this lounge is in the old William R. Porter Docks Shipping Office, now part of the Pier House hotel. The Havana Docks deck is a good place to watch the sun set when Mallory Square gets too crowded. *1 Duval St., tel. 305/296–4600. AE, MC, V. Open Sun.–Thurs. 4 PM–2 AM, Fri.–Sat. 4 PM–4 AM, though sometimes closing at 2 AM.*

Margaritaville Cafe. This place is owned by Key West resident and MCA recording star Jimmy Buffett, who performs here several times a year. The menu, which changes often, serves an entree they call "cheeseburger in paradise." The house special drink is, of course, a margarita. *500 Duval St., tel. 305/292–1435. Live music nightly. Cover charge for special events. AE, MC, V. Open 11 AM–2 AM.*

Sloppy Joe's. Named for its founder, Captain Joe Russell, Sloppy Joe's started as a speakeasy. Ernest Hemingway liked to gamble in a partitioned club room in back. After Hemingway's death, the original manuscript of *To Have and Have Not*, sections of *Death in the Afternoon*, *The Fifth Column*, and notes for *A Farewell to Arms* were found among personal papers he had stored at the bar. Decorated with Hemingway memorabilia and marine flags, the bar is popular with tourists and is full and noisy all the time. There is live entertainment from noon to 2 AM by local and touring groups. *201 Duval St., Key West, tel. 305/294–5717. No reservations. Dress: shoes and shirt required. All customers must show proof of age at night. Usually a $1 cover charge after 8 PM. No credit cards at the bar; major cards accepted to purchase T-shirts. Open 9 AM–4 AM.*

The Top Lounge. Located on the seventh floor of the La Concha Holiday Inn, Key West's tallest building, this is one of the best places from which to view the sunset. The Top features Coconuts Comedy Club Wednesday through Sunday. Also at La Concha, on the ground floor, is Craizy Daizy's. *430 Duval St., tel. 305/296–2991, 800/227–6151 (FL) or 800/745–2191 (US). AE, D, DC, MC, V. Open 11 AM–2 AM. Craizy Daizy's open 11–1 AM serving deli food and presenting weekend entertainment.*

Index

Acapulco
(restaurant), 77
Acme Acting
Company, 91
Acme Smoked Fish
(deli), 125
Actor's Playhouse,
91
Adams Key, 104
Addison Mizner
Festival, 6
Addresses, important
in Florida Keys,
182–183
in Fort Lauderdale,
120–121
in Greater Miami,
31–33
in national parks area,
103–104
in Palm Beach,
103–104
African Queen (boat),
187
Agnes Wahlstrom
Youth Playhouse,
171
Air tours, 33, 101,
183–184
Air travel
from Britain, 4
children and, 10
to the Everglades, 99
to Florida Keys,
179–180
to Fort Lauderdale,
118
to Palm Beach, 145
to Miami, 14–15, 28
Airboat rides, 101
Alabama Jack's
(restaurant), 207
Alexander Hotel, 87
Alliance Film/Video
Project, 91
Alligators, 107, 113,
127–128, 152, 169
A Mano (restaurant),
70
American Indian
(restaurant), 113
American Police Hall
of Fame and
Museum, 59
American

restaurants, 67,
70–71, 111, 112, 113,
132, 134, 158, 159,
174–175, 209–210
Amusement park, 126
Ancient Spanish
Monastery, 59–60
Anhinga Indian
Museum & Art
Gallery, 127
Ann Norton
Sculpture Gardens,
150
Antiques, shopping
for, 17, 128
Antonia's
(restaurant), 211
Aquariums, 55, 125,
150–151, 185, 188
Aragon Cafe, 73
Area Stage, 91
Art and Cultural
Center of
Hollywood, 127
Art Deco District,
Miami, 6, 34, 42, 43,
88
Art festivals, 6–7
Art galleries, 38, 51,
90–91, 127, 201
Arthur R. Marshall
Loxahatchee
National Wildlife
Refuge, 152–153
Artist House (guest
house), 219
Art museums, 35, 43,
44, 45, 50, 53–54,
90, 122, 124,
149–150, 171, 195,
199
Arts, the, 89–93,
140–141, 165, 220
Ashley, The
(restaurant), 174
Atlantic Shores
Motel, 206
Atlantis, The
(condominium), 39
Atlantis (theme
park), 126
Audubon House and
Gardens, 195
Auto racing, 65, 155
Aviaries, 50–51, 53

Bacardi Art Gallery,
90–91
Backcountry
camping, 115
Bahama Village, 196
Bahia Cabana Beach
Resort (hotel),
138–139
Bahia Honda State
Recreation Area,
190, 205
Bahia Mar Resort &
Yachting Center,
125, 130
Bailey Concert Hall,
141
Baja Beach Club, 95
Bakehouse Art
Complex, 91
Bakeries, 43, 57
Bakery Centre, The,
50
Bal Harbour, 17
Ballet, 38, 91
Banks, 7–8
Banyan Marina
Apartments,
139–140
Banyon Resort, The,
(hotel), 217
Baptiste Bakery,
57
Barnacle, The
(historic site), 52
Bars, 37, 93–94,
141–142
Baseball, 65, 131,
155–156, 172
Basketball, 65
Bass Museum of Art,
44
Bathtub Beach, 170
Bat Tower, 191
Bayfront Park, 38
Bay Harbor Inn, 87
Bay Harbor Lodge
(hotel), 214
Bayside Marketplace,
17, 38
Beaches
on Bahia Honda Key,
190
in Biscayne National
Park, 110
in Florida Keys,

17–18, 205–206
in Fort Lauderdale,
18, 121–122, 129
in Key West, 17, 199,
205–206
in Miami area, 61–62
in Palm Beach area,
151, 153–154
of Treasure Coast,
17–18, 168, 170
Virginia Key, 55
Bear Cut, 55
Bed & Breakfast
Accommodations,
24, 165
Belle Glade, 145
Best Western Key
Ambassador Inn,
218–219
Best Western Marina
Park Hotel, 85
Bethesda-by-the-Sea
Church, 147
Bice Ristorante, 160
Bicycling, 18, 21, 62,
110–111, 129, 149,
154, 201–202
Big Cypress National
Preserve, 21,
100–101
Big Pine Key, 190
Bill Baggs Cape
Florida State
Recreation Area, 56
Biltmore Country
Club, 50
Biltmore Hotel, 49,
81
Bimini Boatyard
(restaurant), 132
Birds, 50–51, 55, 101,
127, 152–153,
168–169, 178
Biscayne Kennel
Club, 65
Biscayne National
Park, 98–99, 104,
106, 107, 109,
110–111, 202
camping in, 115
emergencies in, 103
telephone number of,
104
tours of, 101–102
Biscayne Wine

Merchants and Bistro, 74
Black Heritage Museum, 90
Black Pearl, The (restaurant), 175
Black Point Marina, 109
Blowing Rocks Preserve, 168–169
Blue Heaven, 196
Boating, 108
Boat rentals, 110, 130, 154
Boat tours, 33–34, 101–102, 108–109, 147, 184
Boat travel, 100, 120, 181
Boca Chica Key, 191
Boca Chita Key, 104
Boca Festival Days, 6
Boca Raton, 6, 153, 157–158, 161–162
Boca Raton Resort & Club, 161–162
Boca Raton Rugby Club, 156–157
Bonaventure, restaurants in, 137
Bonaventure Resort & Spa, 131, 137
Bonnet House, 122
Books, 13, 42, 61
Botanica La Caridad (shop), 42
Bottle Wall, The, 198–199
Boutiques, 17, 43
Boynton Beach, 154
Brazilian Court (hotel), 162
Breakers, The (hotel and restaurant), 147, 149, 159, 162
Brickell Avenue, 39
Brigade 2506 Memorial, 45
British travelers, 2, 3–4
Broward, Napoleon Bonaparte, 117
Broward Center for the Performing Arts, 124, 140
Broward County, 117–118, 125–126
Broward County Main Library, 124
Burt & Jack's

(restaurant), 132
Burt Reynolds Ranch and Mini Petting Farm, 151–152
Bus travel, 16, 28–29, 100, 119, 145, 146, 180–181, 182
Butterfly World, 128
Buttery, The (restaurant), 211–212

Cactus Cantina (bar), 93–94
Cafe Chauveron (restaurant), 75
Cafe Des Artistes (restaurant), 211
Cafe Des Arts (restaurant), 75
Cafe Marquesa, 210
Cafe Max (restaurant), 132
Cafe Tu Tu Tango (restaurant), 76–77
Calder Race Course, 66
Calder Theatre Company, 165
Calle Ocho, 45
Calusa Indians, 27
Camping, 24, 115, 127–128, 202
Canoeing, 18–19, 21, 108–109, 122, 152, 184, 204
Canyon of Palm Beach, 149
Cape Florida Lighthouse, 56
Captain Tony's Saloon, 220–221
Cap's Place (restaurant), 136
Car rental, 8–9, 29, 99, 119, 145–146, 180–181
in Britain, 4
in Homestead, 99
Caribbean Marketplace, 17, 57
Carlin Park, 168
Carnaval Miami, 6
Carriage House Resort Motel, 140
Cartagena Plaza, 51
Casablanca at Bogarts (pub), 196
Casa Juancho (restaurant), 79

Casa Rolandi (restaurant), 76
Casa Vecchia (restaurant), 135
Cash machines, 7–8
Cauley Square, 60–61
Center for the Arts, 171
Center for the Fine Arts, 35
Challenger memorial, 38
Chamber music, 91
Chambers of commerce, 146, 183
Charley's Crab (restaurants), 161
Cheeca Lodge (hotel), 214–215
Cheers (bar), 141
Chef Allen's (restaurant), 71
Chesterfield Hotel Deluxe, 163
Chez Moy (restaurant), 75–76
Children
books and toys for, 61
clothing for, 60
tennis tournament for, 64
traveling with, 9–10
what to see and do with, 59–60, 124, 128, 151–152, 171
Children's Museum of Boca Raton, 152
Children's Science Explorium, 152
Chinese restaurants, 72
Christ of the Deep (statue), 202
Chuck & Harold's (restaurant), 159
Churches, 51, 53, 147
Churchill's Hideaway (bar), 94
Citrus fruits, 16–17
City Cemetery (Key West), 198
Claude and Mildred Pepper Bayfront Park, 38
Clay Hotel & International Youth Hostel, 42
Climate, 4–5, 106, 118

Clinton Place, 194
Clothing
to bring, 7
Latin, 60
shopping for, 17, 60–61, 128
Club Tropigala at La Ronde, 96
Coastal Science Center, 170
Coast Guard, U.S., 104, 149
Coconut Grove, 6, 7, 17, 51–54
hotels in, 80–81
nightlife in, 94–95
restaurants in, 52, 72–73, 76–77
Coconut Grove Art Festival, 6
Coconut Grove Chamber of Commerce, 32
Coconut Grove Convention Center, 53
Coconut Grove Farmers Market, 52
Coconut Grove King Mango Strut (parade), 7
Coconut Grove Playhouse, 52, 92
Coconuts Comedy Club, 94
Coconuts Restaurant and Bar, 220
Cocowalk, 17, 52
Colonnade Hotel, 81, 84
Colonnade Building, 49
Colony (hotel), 163
Colony House Theater, 43
Comedy clubs, 94–95, 142
Comic Strip, The (comedy club), 142
Concert Association of Florida, 91
Concerts, 43, 55, 58, 91, 92, 141
Conch Key, 189
Conch Republic Celebration, 6
Conchs, 179
Conchy Joe's (restaurant), 173
Condominiums, 10, 217

Confetti (bar), *141*
Continental restaurants, *72–74, 134, 157, 159–160, 173, 174, 175*
Convoy Point, *104, 106*
Coopertown Restaurant, *113*
Coot Bay Pond, *100*
Copacabana Supper Club, *95*
Coral Castle, *59*
Coral Gables, *7, 45, 48–51*
bar in, *94*
hotels in, *81, 84*
restaurants in, *73, 74–75, 76*
street numbering in, *31*
Coral Gables Chamber of Commerce, *32*
Coral Gables City Hall, *49*
Coral Gables Merrick House and Gardens, *49*
Coral Gables Waterway, *50*
Coral reefs, *104, 130*
Coral Way, *48*
Country music, *142*
Country Place, The (restaurant), *173*
Crack'd Conch (restaurant), *207*
Crandon Park, *55, 62*
Crane Point Hammock, *189*
Credit cards, *7–8, 25*
Crime, *27–28*
Crocco's (bar), *141*
Crocodile Lakes National Wildlife Refuge, *185*
Cuban Club, *197*
Cuban Coffee Queen Cafe, *198*
Cuban Museum of Art and Culture, *45*
Cuban refugees, *39, 44–45*
Cuban restaurants, *45, 74, 134–135, 198, 210–211*
Curry Mansion, *198*
Curry Mansion Inn

(guest house), *219*
Customs and duties, *3*

Dade County Auditorium (theater), *92*
Dade County Courthouse, *35*
Dance, *43*
Dania, *129*
Dania Jai-Alai Palace, *126*
Davie Arena for Rodeo, *127*
Daytona Beach, *117*
Delano (hotel), *43–44*
Deli, *160, 211*
Delray Affair (festival), *6*
Delray Beach, *145*
Dempsey's (restaurant), *159*
Dentists, *33*
Depot, The (restaurant), *71*
De Soto Plaza, *49*
Dinner Key Marina, *53, 63*
Disabled travelers, *11–12, 120–121*
Disco/rock clubs, *95*
Discovery Center, *124*
Diving, *20, 63–64, 110, 129–130, 154, 185, 202–204*
Dockside Bar and Raw Bar (restaurant), *212*
Do-Da's Country Music Emporium, *142*
Dog Beach, *205*
Dog racing, *65, 127, 156*
Dolphin Research Center, *189*
Dominique's (restaurant), *75*
Don Arturo (restaurant), *134–135*
Don Shula's Hotel and Golf Inn, *88–89*
Doral Resort & Country Club, *89*
Doral Saturnia International Spa Resort, *62*
Doubletree Hotel at

Coconut Grove, *81*
Down Under (restaurant), *134*
Downtown Miami, *34–35, 37–39*
bar in, *37, 95–96*
emergencies in, *32–33*
hotels in, *84–85*
restaurants in, *37, 67, 70, 77, 78, 79*
Dreher Park Zoo, *150*
Drift diving, *154*
Driftwood Inn Resort, The (hotel and restaurant), *171*
Driftwood on the Ocean, (motel), *140*
Dubois Home, *168*
Duck Key, *189*

East Coast Fisheries (restaurant), *78*
East Martellow Tower, *199*
Eating Place, The (restaurant), *37*
11 Maple Street, (restaurant), *173*
Elizabeth W. Kirby Interpretive Center, *169*
Elliott Key, *106, 110*
El Siboney (restaurant), *210–211*
El Toro Taco (restaurant), *112*
Emerald Reef, *63*
Emergencies
in the Florida Keys, *183*
in Fort Lauderdale, *120*
in Miami Beach, *32–33*
in National Parks, *103*
in Palm Beach, *146–147*
Emporium (restaurant), *174*
Ermita de la Caridad (church and shrine), *53*
Ernie's Bar-B-Q & Lounge (restaurant), *132, 134*
Espanola Way, *42*
Essex House (hotel), *87–88*
Everglades City, *108,*

111, 113
Everglades Holiday Park & Campground, *127–128, 130*
Everglades National Park, *21, 98–115*
camping in, *115*
emergencies, *103*
tours of, *101–103, 109*
Everglades Safari Park, *107*
Explorers, The (restaurant), *161*

Fairchild Tropical Garden, *51*
Family-style restaurant, *74*
Fantasy Fest, *7*
Festival Miami, *7*
Festivals, *5–7*
Fishing
deep-sea, *19, 130, 154–155, 204*
festival, *6*
freshwater, *19, 110, 130, 154–155, 204*
from piers, *19*
from seawall, *56*
Fish Market (restaurant), *78*
Five Points, *48*
Flagler Dog Track, *65*
Flagler Memorial Monument, *40, 42*
Flagler Street, *17, 37*
Flamingo, *100, 106, 111*
camping at, *115*
Flamingo Gardens, *127*
Flamingo Lake, *51*
Flamingo Lodge Marina & Outpost Resort, *107, 109–110, 114*
Flamingo Restaurant, *111*
Flamingo Tennis Center, *64*
Florida Bay, *102*
Florida Bay Coastline, *178*
Florida City, *108*
lodging in, *114*
restaurants in, *111–112, 207*
Florida Keys,

177–221
arts, *220*
car travel to, *180–181*
emergencies in, *183*
hotels in, *212–219*
nightlife in, *220–221*
population of, *179*
restaurants in, *191,
196, 198, 206–212*
transportation in and
to, *179–182*
Florida Keys Wild
Bird Rehabilitation
Center, *187*
Florida Marlins
(baseball team),
65
Florida
Philharmonic
Orchestra, *141*
Florida Pioneer
Museum, *103*
Floridian restaurant,
113
Folk music, *95, 97*
Fontainbleau Hilton
Resort and Spa, *44,
86*
Football, *65–66*
Forge, The
(restaurant), *73*
Fort Lauderdale, *17,
117–142*
emergencies in, *120*
entertainment in,
140–142
hotels in, *137–140*
restaurants in,
131–132, 134–137
Fort Lauderdale
Historical Society
Museum, *124*
Fort Lauderdale
Opera Guild, *141*
Fort Pierce, *170*
restaurant in, *173*
Fort Pierce Inlet
State Recreation
Area, *170*
Fort Zachary Taylor
State Historic Site,
195, 205
Fowey Reef, *63*
Freedom Tower,
38–39
French restaurants,
*52, 74–75, 157–158,
160, 211*
Friends of Chamber
Music, *91*

Garrison Bight Yacht
Station, *199*
Gazebo Cafe
(restaurant), *157*
Gingerbread Square
Gallery, *201*
Glass-bottomed
boats, *204*
Gliding, *155*
Gold Coast Chamber
of Commerce, *32*
Golden Orb Trail,
188–189
Golf, *19, 49, 55, 62,
131, 155, 191, 205*
Gondola ride, *38*
Grainary Cafe
(restaurant),
135–136
Granada Golf
Course, *49*
Grand Bay Hotel, *80*
Grand Cafe
(restaurant), *72–73*
Grand Prix of
Miami, *65*
Granny Feelgood's
(restaurant), *77*
Grassy Key, *189*
Greater Miami
Opera, *92*
Great White Heron
National Wildlife
Refuge, *203*
Greek restaurants, *75*
Green Parrot Bar,
195
Greenpeace (store),
200
Green Streets Cafe,
52
Green Turtle Inn
(restaurant), *208*
Greyhound racing,
65, 127, 156
Grove Isle (hotel),
80–81
Guest houses and
inns, *24, 219*
Guest Quarters Suite
Hotel, *176*
Gulf Coast Ranger
Station, *106–107*
Gulf Stream, *154*
Gulfstream Park
Racetrack, *127*
Gumbo Limbo
Nature Center, *152*
Gusman Center for
the Performing

Arts, *38, 92*
Gusman Concert
Hall, *92*

Haitran Art Co.
(gallery), *201*
Haitian Refugee
Center, *57*
Haitian restaurants,
75–76
Haitians, *56–57*
Half Shell Raw Bar,
212
Hampton Inn, *114*
Harriette's Retreat
(restaurant), *207*
Harry S Truman
Little White House
Museum, *195*
Haulover Park
Marina, *63*
Havana Docks
Lounge (disco), *221*
Hawk's Cay Resort
(hotel), *189, 215*
Hearing-impaired
people, *32, 120, 146*
Hemingway Days
Festival, *6*
Hemingway House,
196
Herbie's Bar
(restaurant), *209*
Hialeah Park, *66*
Hialeah Speedway, *65*
Hibiscus Island, *40*
Higgs Memorial
Beach, *199, 205*
Hiking, *21, 110–111*
Hillsboro Recreation
Area, *153*
Hippocrates Health
Institute, *155*
Hispanic art, *45*
Hispanic clothing, *60*
Hispanic population,
27
Historic Key West
Shipwreck Museum,
198
Historical Museum
of Southern Florida,
37
Historical museums,
*37, 43, 59, 103, 124,
168, 169–170, 171,
188, 189, 194, 195,
196, 197–198, 199*
History tours, *34*
Hobe Sound National

Wildlife Refuge, *169*
Hobie Island, *54*
Holiday Inns, *114,
213*
Hollywood, *140*
Hollywood
Greyhound Track,
127
Holocaust Memorial,
43
Holsum Bakery, *48*
Home exchange, *10*
Homeplace, The
(guesthouse), *176*
Homestead, *108*
lodging in, *114*
restaurants in,
112–113
Homestead Bayfront
Park, *110*
Horseback Riding,
19–20, 21
Horse racing, *66,
126, 127*
Hospitals, *32–33,
103, 120, 147, 183*
Hotel Cardoza, *88*
Hotel Carlyle, *88*
Hotel Cavalier, *88*
Hotel Inter-
Continental
Miami, *38, 84*
Hotel Leslie, *88*
Hotel National, *43*
Hotel Place St.
Michel, *84*
Hotels, *23–25*
Art Deco, *43–44, 88*
children and, *10*
in Fort Lauderdale
area, *137–140*
in Greater Miami
area, *80–81, 84–89*
in Key West, *212–219*
in national parks
areas, *113–114*
in Palm Beach, *161–165*
on Treasure Coast,
175–176
House of India
(restaurant), *76*
House of Refuge
Museum, *169–170*
Houses, historic, *49,
53–54, 122, 124, 149,
195, 196, 197–198*
Hugh Taylor Birch
State Park, *122*
Hungry Sailor (bar),
94

Hunting, 20
Hurricane Memorial, 187
Hutchinson Island, 169–170
Hyatt Key West (hotel), 217
Hyatt Regency Coral Gables, 84
Hyatt Regency Miami (hotel), 84–85
Hy-Vong Vietnamese Cuisine, 79

Ice Skating, 60
Il Tartuffo (restaurant), 135
Imperial, The (condominium), 39
Improv (comedy club), 94–95
Indian Key, 188
Indian restaurants, 76
Indian River County, 165
Indian River Plantation (resort), 175–176
Indians, 16, 27, 56, 117, 126–127. See also Calusa, Miccosukee, Seminole Indians
Inlet, The (restaurant), 174
Insect zoo, 124
International Fishing Museum, 188
International Place, 37
International Swimming Hall of Fame Museum and Pool, 125
International Tennis Center, 55
Islamorada hotels in, 214–215 restaurants in, 208–209
Islamorada Sportfishing Festival, 6
Island City House (guest house), 219
Islas Canarias (restaurant), 74
Italian restaurants,

76, 111–112, 135, 160, 211

Jackie Gleason Theater of the Performing Arts, 43, 92
Jack Island wildlife refuge, 170–171
Jai alai, 66–67, 126, 156
Jamaican restaurant, 37
James L. Knight International Center, 37
Japanese cultural museum, 145
Japanese Garden, 40
Jan McArt's International Room (theater), 92
Jazz, 95
Jensen Beach, restaurants in, 173
Jewish religious stores, 42
Joe Robbie Stadium, 65–66
Joe Stone's Crab Restaurant, 78–79
Jogging, 20, 21
John D. MacArthur State Park, 166
John G's (restaurant), 158
John Pennekamp Coral Reef State Park, 187, 202, 205
John U. Lloyd Beach State Recreation Area, 129
Jonathon Dickinson State Park, 169
Jo's (restaurant), 160
Jules Undersea Lodge, 203
Jungle Trail, 171
Juno Beach, 168
Jupiter, 153, 158, 168
Jupiter Island, 168–169
Jupiter Theater, 168

Kayaking, 21, 184
Kelsey's (restaurant), 209
Kendall, 70
Kennedy Park, 53

Key Biscayne, 6, 54–56 hotels in, 85–86 nightlife in, 95 restaurants in, 72, 78
Key Biscayne Art Festival, 6
Key Biscayne Chamber of Commerce, 32
Key Biscayne Golf Course, 55
Key Colony Beach, 189
Key Colony Beach Par 3 (golf course), 205
Key East (restaurant), 70
Key Largo, 185, 187 hotels in, 213–214 restaurants in, 207–208
Key Largo Hammock, 185
Key Largo National Marine Sanctuary, 202–203
Key Largo Ranger Station, 107
Key Largo Undersea Park, 185, 187
Key-lime pie, 23, 206
Key West, 5, 6, 7, 17, 191–192, 194–200 guest houses in, 219 hotels in, 217–219 restaurants in, 196, 198, 206–212
Key West Aquarium, 194
Key West Art and Historical Society, 199
Key West Botanical Garden, 191
Key West Historical Society (museum), 202
Key West Resort Golf Course, 191, 205
King-Cromartie House, 124
King Orange Jamboree Parade, 64–65
Kosher bakery, 43

La Concha Holiday Inn, 218

Lago Mar Resort Hotel & Club, 138
La Gorce Country Club, 44
Lake Harbor, 144
Lake Okeechobee, 144
Lake Worth, 158
Lane Gallery, 201
Lantana, 158–159
La Paloma (restaurant), 73–74
Largo Lodge (hotel), 214
Las Olas Shopping District, 17, 122
Las Tapas (restaurant), 79
Latin restaurant, 76–77
Lauderdale, William, 117
La Vieille Maison (restaurant), 157–158
Layton Trail, 188
LB's Eatery (restaurant), 74
Le Festival (restaurant), 74–75
Les Violins Supper Club, 96
Libraries, 37, 124, 197
Lighthouse Museum, 196
Lighthouse Restaurant, 158
Lighthouses, 56, 196
Ligumnivitae Key, 188
Lime Tree Bay Resort (hotel), 215
Lincoln Road Arts District, 43
Lincoln Road Mall, 42–43
Lion Country Safari, 151
Lipton International Players Championship (LIPC), 67
Little Haiti, 56–57 bar in, 94 restaurants in, 57, 75–76
Little Havana, 44–45 restaurants in, 45, 74,

77, *79*
theater in, *93*
Little Managua,
    restaurants in,
    77–78
Little Palm Island
    (hotel), *216*
Little Torch Key
    (hotel in), *216*
Log Cabin
    Restaurant, *158*
Loggerhead Park
    Marine Life Center,
    168
Long Key, *188–189*
hotel in, *215*
Long Key State
    Recreation Area,
    205
Long Key Viaduct,
    189
Long Pine Key, *115*
Looe Key National
    Marine Sanctuary,
    191, 203
Looe Key Reef
    Resort and Dive
    Center (hotel), *216*
Los Ranchos
    (restaurant), *77–78*
Louie's Backyard
    (restaurant),
    209–210
Lowe Art Museum,
    50
Lower Keys, The,
    190–191
Lower Sugarloaf
    Key, *191*
hotel in, *216*
Loxahatchee
    Historical Society
    Museum, *168*
Loxahatchee refuge,
    152–153
Lummus Park, *42, 61*

Mac's Club Deuce
    (bar), *94*
Mahoney's Oyster
    Bar, *174*
Mako's Bay Club
    (nightclub), *95–96*
Mallory Square, *194*
Manatees, *99, 169*
Mangrove Mattie's
    (restaurant), *173*
Mangrove Mama's
    (restaurant), *191,*
    206

Mar-A-Lago (estate),
    151
Marathon (Florida
    Keys), *189*
hotels in, *215–216*
restaurants in, *209*
Marathon Marine
    Sanctuary, *203*
Margaritaville Cafe,
    221
Marina del Mar
    Resort and Marina
    (hotel), *213*
Marinas
of Fort Lauderdale,
    125, 130
in Greater Miami, *42,*
    53, 55, 62–63
at Lake Okeechobee,
    145
in national parks,
    103–104, 109–110
in Palm Beach, *145*
Marine Management
    (marina), *109*
Marine science
    museum, *55, 168*
Marker 88
    (restaurant), *208*
Market Bistro
    (restaurant), *211*
Markets, *52, 57*
Mark's Place
    (restaurant), *71*
Marquesa Hotel, *217*
Marriott's Casa
    Marina Resort
    (hotel), *217–218*
Marriott's Harbor
    Beach Resort, *138*
Martha's
    (restaurant), *134*
Martin County, *167*
Martin Luther King
    Jr. Festivals, *6*
Matheson Hammock
    Park, *51*
Mayfair (mall), *52*
Mayfair House
    (hotel), *81*
McLarty Museum
    and Visitor's
    Center, *171*
Mel Fisher Maritime
    Heritage Society
    Museum, *194*
Mental Floss
    (comedy club), *95*
Metro-Dade Center,
    35

Metro-Dade Cultural
    Center, *35*
Metro Zoo, *58*
Mexican restaurants,
    77, 112
Mezzanotte
    (restaurant), *76*
Miamarina, *38*
Miami Arena, *39*
Miami Arts Asylum
    (Performance Art
    Club), *96*
Miami-Bahamas
    Goombay Festival, *6*
Miami Beach, *17–18,*
    39–40, 42–44, 61, 64
emergencies in, *32–33*
hotels in, *86–88*
nightlife in, *93–94,*
    95, 96
restaurants in, *42,*
    70–71, 73, 75, 76,
    77, 78–79
Miami Beach
    Chamber of
    Commerce, *32*
Miami Beach City
    Hall, *43*
Miami Beach
    Convention Center,
    43
Miami Beach
    Marina, *63*
Miami Canal, *143*
Miami City Ballet,
    38, 92
Miami City Hall, *53*
Miami-Dade
    Community College,
    38, 92
Miami Design
    District, *56*
Miami Dolphins,
    65–66
Miami Fashion
    District, *60*
Miami Film Festival,
    89
Miami Freedom
    (soccer team), *67*
Miami Free Zone
    (MFZ), *60*
Miami Heat
    (basketball team),
    65
Miami International
    Airport, *28, 99*
Miami Jai-Alai
    Fronton, *66–67*
Miami Jewelry

Institute (art
    gallery), *91*
Miami Marine
    Stadium, *55*
Miami Museum of
    Science and Space
    Transit
    Planetarium, *53*
Miami River, *6, 37,*
    39
Miami River Inn, *85*
Miami Rivers Blues
    Festival, *6*
Miami Seaquarium,
    55
Miami Youth
    Museum, *50*
Miccosukee Indians,
    17, 107
Miccosukee
    Restaurant, *113*
Middle Keys, The,
    189–190
Mile 7 Grill
    (restaurant), *209*
Minorca Playhouse,
    92
Miracle Mile, *48–49*
Monkey Jungle, *58*
Morikami Museum of
    Japanese Culture,
    145
Motels, *23–24, 138,*
    140, 217–219
Movie festival, *6, 91*
Mrazek Pond, *100*
Mrs. Mac's Kitchen
    (restaurant), *208*
Muffin Man
    (bakery), *42*
Murals, *39, 49, 50,*
    118, 149
Museum of Art, *122,*
    124
Museum of Discovery
    and Science, *124*
Museum of Natural
    History of the
    Florida Keys, *189*
Music, *38, 43, 52, 55,*
    59, 92
Musician Exchange
    (nightclub), *141*
Mutineer Restaurant,
    112–113
Mykonos
    (restaurant), *75*

Naples, *113*
National Key Deer

Refuge, *22, 190, 203*
Natural restaurants, *77*
Nature preserves, *21–22*
Nature trails, *56, 107, 151, 152–153, 188*
New Chinatown (restaurant), *72*
New River Inn, *124*
News Cafe, *70–71*
New Theatre, *92*
New World Symphony, *43, 92*
Nicaraguan restaurant, *77–78*
Nightclubs, *95–96, 141–142, 165*
Nightlife, *93–96, 141–142, 165, 220–221*
Nixon, Richard, *55–56*
No Name Key, *190–191*
North Dade Hotel, *88*
North Miami Beach restaurants in, *71, 73–74, 77*
North Miami Center of Contemporary Art, *90*
Norton Gallery of Art, *150*

Ocean Grill (restaurant), *175*
Ocean Grand (hotel), *163*
Ocean Reef Park, *166*
Ocean World, *125*
Oil spills, *129*
Old City Hall (Key West), *198*
Old Florida Seafood House (restaurant), *136*
Old House (restaurant), *158–159*
Old Rickenbacker Causeway Bridge, *54–55*
Old Seven Mile Bridge, *189–190*
Omni International Hotel, *85*

Opera, *92, 141*
Orange Bowl, *64–65*
Orchid Jungle, *58–59*
Overseas Highway, *177*

PACE (Performing Arts for Community and Education), *59*
Package tours, *2–3*
Packing, *7*
Pahokee, *145*
Palace, The (condominium), *39*
Palm Beach, *17, 143–165*
Palm Beach Biltmore Hotel (condominium), *149*
Palm Beach Bicycle Trail, *149*
Palm Beach Country Club, *149*
Palm Beach County, *146–147*
emergencies in, *146–147*
hotels in, *161–165*
restaurants in, *157–161*
Palm Beach Gardens, *145, 161*
Palm Beach Polo and Country Club, *5, 156, 164*
Palm Beach Post Office, *149*
Palm Island, *40*
Palm-Aire Resort & Spa, *131*
Pan American Ocean Hotel, A Radisson Resort, *86–87*
Papa Joe's Landmark Restaurant, *206, 208*
Parades, *7*
Paragon (nightclub), *95*
Park Central (hotel), *87*
Parker Playhouse (theater), *140*
Parks
local, *38, 42, 51, 54, 61–62, 166, 199*
national, *21–22, 98–115, 202*
state, *22, 56, 122, 126, 166, 169, 170, 171–172, 187, 202*

Parrot Jungle, *50–51*
Passports, *3*
Patio, The (restaurant), *174–175*
Pavillon Grill, The (restaurant), *67, 70*
Pei, I.M., *37*
Penrod's Beach Club and South Beach Raw Bar, *42*
Pepes Cafe and Steak House (restaurant), *210*
Pepper, Claude and Mildred, *38*
Performing arts, *43, 96, 165*
Personal guides in Everglades, *103*
PGA National Resort & Spa, *155, 163–164*
Pharmacies, 24-hour, *33, 120, 147, 183*
Phil Foster Park, *166*
Philharmonic Orchestra of Florida, *141*
Photography, *8*
Physicians, *33, 120*
Pier House (beach), *206*
Pier House (hotel), *218*
Pier House Restaurant, *210*
Pier Pointe Resort (hotel), *139*
Pier 66 Resort and Marina, *138*
Pigeonhouse Patio Restaurant & Bar, *195*
Pigeon Key, *189–190*
Pine Jog Environmental Center, *151*
Pineapples (restaurant), *77*
Pioneer Florida Day, *6*
Pirate's Spa Marina, *109*
Pit Bar-B-Q, The (restaurant), *113*
Planetariums, *53, 124, 154*
Plantation Key, *187*
Plaza de la Cubanidad, *45*

Plymouth Congregational Church, *51*
Poetry readings, *61*
Poison control, *120*
Polo, *5, 156, 172*
Pompano Beach, *126, 129, 132*
Pompano Harness Track, *126*
Porch, The (restaurant), *174*
Porpoises, *55*
Port Everglades, *117*
Post Office and Customs House (Key West), *194*
Potlikker's (restaurant), *112*
Prometeo (Spanish Theater), *93*
Public library, *37*
Publications, *9–10, 11–12, 13–14*

Quiet Waters Park, *126*

Rail travel, *16, 30, 119, 146*
between Miami and West Palm Beach, *119*
Rain Barrel (art gallery), *201*
Rainbow Bend Fishing Resort (hotel), *215–216*
Ramrod Key, *191*
hotel in, *276*
Raymond Kravis Center for the Performing Arts, *165*
Red Barn Theater, *220*
Redland Fruit & Spice Park, *58*
Reggae, *141*
Renaissance Seafood Grill, *137*
Rental cars. *See* Car rental
Restaurants, *22–23*
in Fort Lauderdale area, *131–132, 134–137*
in Greater Miami area, *67, 70–79*

in Key West, *206–212*
in national parks area,
111–113
in Palm Beach area,
157–161
in Treasure Coast,
172–175
Retired travelers,
12–13
Richard Accursio's
Capri Restaurant,
111–112
Rickshaw tours, *34*
Ring Theater, *92*
Rio, *173*
Ritz Plaza (hotel),
44
River Cities Festival,
6
RiverWalk, *124*
Riverside Hotel, *124,*
139
Riverside Theatre,
171
Rock music, *95, 141*
Rockefeller, John D.,
143
Rodeos, *127*
Royal Palm Dinner
Theater, *165*
Royal Palm Visitor
Center, *107*
Royal Poinciana
Playhouse, *165*
Rugby, *64, 131,*
156–157
Rustic Inn
Crabhouse
(restaurant), *136*

Sailing, *63, 204*
St. Johns Marsh, *166*
St. Lucie County,
166
St. Lucie County
Historical Museum,
170
Sales tax, *60*
Salt Ponds, *199*
San Carlos Institute,
197
San Pedro
Underwater
Archaeological
Preserve, *188, 203*
Santa Lucia
(restaurant), *135*
Scalawags
(restaurant), *174*
Scenic drives,

100–101, 151
Scenic views, *54*
Science museums, *53,*
57, 124, 150–151,
152, 168
Scottish Festival and
Games, *6*
Sculpture, *38, 43,*
149–150
Seafood festivals, *6*
Seafood restaurants,
78–79, 112–113,
136–137, 158–159,
161, 173, 174, 175,
211–212
Seagate Hotel &
Beach Club, *164*
Sea Lord Hotel,
164–165
Seal Museum, *170*
Seaplanes, *40*
Seashells, shopping
for, *16*
Seasonal events,
5–7
Sebastian Inlet,
171–172
Seminole Indians, *16,*
37, 56, 117, 126–127,
128
Seminole Native
Village, *126–127*
Senior citizens,
12–13
Seven Mile Bridge,
189–190
Shark River Slough,
107
Shark Valley,
101–102, 107, 113
Sheraton Key Largo
Resort (hotel),
213–214
Sheraton Royal
Biscayne Beach
Resort and Racquet
Club (hotel), *85–86*
Ship's Pub and
Galley (restaurant),
209
Shipwreck museums,
169–170, 197–198
Shirttail Charlie's
(restaurant),
136–137
Shirttail Charlie's
Downstairs Bar,
141–142
Shopping, *16–17*
in Bal Harbour, *17*

in Coconut Grove, *17,*
48–49, 52
in Fort Lauderdale,
128
in Key West, *200–201*
in Miami, *16–17,*
42–43, 60–61
in national parks,
107–108
in Palm Beach, *153*
Shorty's Bar-B-Q
(restaurant), *70*
Shula's (restaurant),
72
Simonton Street
Beach, *205*
Simpson Park, *54*
Singer Island, *153*
Ski Rixen, *126*
Sloppy Joe's (bar and
nightclub), *221*
Smathers Beach, *205*
Snake Bight, *102*
Snorkeling, *20, 110,*
171, 203–204
Soccer, *67*
Society of the Four
Arts, *149–150*
Solares Hill, *198*
Sombrero Beach, *205*
Sonesta Beach Hotel
& Tennis Club, *86*
Soul food, *158*
South Dade, *57–59*
Southernmost Beach,
205
Southernmost House,
197
Southernmost Point,
196–197
South Florida Art
Center, *90*
South Florida Fair
and Exposition, *6*
South Florida
Science Museum,
150–151
South Miami, *33, 45,*
48
restaurants in, *71, 72*
South Pointe Park,
42
Southeast Financial
Center, *38*
Southwest Miami, *75*
Spanish restaurants,
79
Spas, *62, 131, 155*
Speed limits, *16*
Sports

in Fort Lauderdale,
129–131
in Greater Miami,
18–21, 62–67
in Key West, *201–205*
in national parks,
108–111
in Palm Beach area,
154–157
on Treasare Coast,
172
Spykes Grove &
Tropical Gardens,
127
Squeeze (nightclub),
142
Star Island, *40*
Stefano's of Key
Biscayne (disco/rock
club), *95*
Stock Island, *191*
Stranahan, Frank,
122
Stranahan House,
122, 124
Strand Theater, *197*
Street numbering, *31*
Stringfellows
(restaurant/nightclub),
95
Stuart, *169*
hotels in, *175–176*
restaurants in, *174*
Stuart's Bar-Lounge,
94
Sugarloaf Lodge
(hotel), *216*
Sundays on the Bay
(restaurant), *78*
Sundial, *59*
Sunfest, *6*
Sunken ship, *129–130*
Sunrise Musical
Theater, *140*
Sunset Cove Motel,
214
Sunset Drive, *50*
Surfside, *61*
Sushi Blues
(restaurant/club),
142
Swimming, *49, 110,*
125
Symphony
orchestras, *38, 92,*
141

Ta-boo (restaurant),
159–160
Tall ships, *33–34*

Tamiami Trail, *16,*
100–101, 113–114
Tank Island, *194–195*
Taste of the Grove
Food and Music
Festival, *6*
Taurus Steak House
(bar and restaurant),
94
Taxicabs, *29, 31, 100,*
119–120, 146, 182
Teatro Avante, *93*
Teatro de Bellas
Artes, *93*
Telephone, for
hearing impaired, *32*
Telephone numbers
in the Florida Keys,
182–183
in Fort Lauderdale,
120–121
in Greater Miami,
31–33
in national parks area,
103–104
in Palm Beach,
146–147
Tennessee Williams
Fine Arts Center,
220
Tennessee Williams'
house, *200*
Tennis, *21, 55, 64, 67*
Tequesta Indians, *37*
Thai Restaurant, *79*
Thai Toni
(restaurant), *79*
Theater, *43, 52, 89,*
91–92, 124, 140–141,
165, 168, 171, 197,
220
Hispanic, *93*
Theater of the Sea,
187
Theo Thudpuckers
Raw Bar
(restaurant), *173*
Threshold Gallery of
Art, *91*

Tiffany's
(restaurant), *112*
Tobacco Road (bar),
37, 94
Tom's Place
(restaurant), *158*
TooJay's (restaurant),
160
Top Lounge, The
(restaurant/night-
club), *221*
Topeekeegee Yugnee
Park, *126*
Torch Keys, *191*
Tourist information,
2, 3, 16, 31–32, 103,
104, 106, 120, 146,
182–183
Tours
of Florida Keys,
183–185
in Fort Lauderdale,
121
to Miami, *2–3*
in Miami, *33–34*
of national parks,
101–103, 109
of Palm Beach, *147*
Tram tours, *102–103*
Treasure Coast,
165–166, 168–176
hotels on, *175–176*
restaurants on,
172–175
Tropic Seas Resort
Motel, *139*
Tropics International
Restaurant, *94*
Truman Annex,
194–195
Turnberry Isle Yacht
and Country Club,
(hotel), *88*
Turtle Kraals, *199*
Turtles, *152–153,*
166, 168
20-mile Bend
Recreation Area,
153

Two Dragons
(restaurant), *72*
UDT Seal Museum,
170
Uncle Funny's
Comedy Clubs, *95*
Unicorn Village
Restaurant and
Marketplace, *77*
U.S. Courthouse, *39*
University of Miami,
7, 50, 59
Upper Keys, The,
185, 187–189
Upper Matecumbe
Key, *188*

Vaca Key, *189*
Vacation Ownership
Resorts, *24–25*
Van Dome
(nightclub), *95*
Vegetarian
restaurants, *79*
Venetian Pool, *49*
Vero Beach, *171*
hotel in, *176*
restaurants in,
174–175
Versailles
(restaurant), *45*
Victor Hotel, *88*
Vietnamese
restaurant, *79*
Villa Regina
(condominium), *39*
Vinnette Carroll
Theatre, *140–141*
Virginia Key, *54–56*
Virginia Key Critical
Wildlife Area, *55*
Visas, *3*
Vistor Center, *107*
Vizcaya Museum and
Gardens, *53–54*

Walk of the Stars, *43*
Warhol, Andy, *86*
Waterfront

Playhouse, *220*
Watson House (guest
house), *219*
Watson Island, *40*
Watson Island
Marina, *63*
Weather, *4–6, 106, 118*
West Dade
hotel in, *88–89*
restaurant in, *72*
West Martello Tower,
199, 205
West Palm Beach, *6,*
144, 150
Whale Harbor Inn
(restaurant), *208–209*
Whiskey, The
(nightclub), *95*
Whitehall (museum),
149
Wildflower Waterway
Cafe (nightclub), *165*
Wildlife refuges, *169,*
170–171, 185, 190,
203
Wildlife tours, *147*
William M. Powell
Bridge, *55*
Windley Key, *187*
Windsor Polo and
Beach Club, *156, 172*
Windsurfing, *54, 63,*
204
Winter Equestrian
Festival, *6*
World War II
submarine spotters,
169–170
Worth Avenue, *17,*
151, 153
Wreckers Museum,
197–198

Yesterday's (disco),
142
Youth hostel, *42*
Yuca (restaurant), *74*

Zoos, *58, 150*

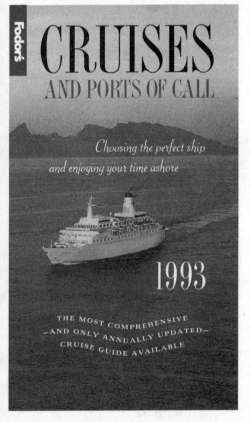

Personal Itinerary

Departure *Date*

Time

Transportation

Arrival *Date*   *Time*

Departure *Date*   *Time*

Transportation

Accommodations

Arrival *Date*   *Time*

Departure *Date*   *Time*

Transportation

Accommodations

Arrival *Date*   *Time*

Departure *Date*   *Time*

Transportation

Accommodations

Personal Itinerary

Arrival *Date*   *Time*

Departure *Date*   *Time*

Transportation

Accommodations

Arrival *Date*   *Time*

Departure *Date*   *Time*

Transportation

Accommodations

Arrival *Date*   *Time*

Departure *Date*   *Time*

Transportation

Accommodations

Arrival *Date*   *Time*

Departure *Date*   *Time*

Transportation

Accommodations

Personal Itinerary

Arrival	*Date*	*Time*
Departure	*Date*	*Time*
Transportation		
Accommodations		

Arrival	*Date*	*Time*
Departure	*Date*	*Time*
Transportation		
Accommodations		

Arrival	*Date*	*Time*
Departure	*Date*	*Time*
Transportation		
Accommodations		

Arrival	*Date*	*Time*
Departure	*Date*	*Time*
Transportation		
Accommodations		

Addresses

Name	*Name*
Address	*Address*
Telephone	*Telephone*
Name	*Name*
Address	*Address*
Telephone	*Telephone*
Name	*Name*
Address	*Address*
Telephone	*Telephone*
Name	*Name*
Address	*Address*
Telephone	*Telephone*
Name	*Name*
Address	*Address*
Telephone	*Telephone*
Name	*Name*
Address	*Address*
Telephone	*Telephone*
Name	*Name*
Address	*Address*
Telephone	*Telephone*
Name	*Name*
Address	*Address*
Telephone	*Telephone*

Fodor's Travel Guides

U.S. Guides

Alaska

Arizona

Boston

California

Cape Cod, Martha's Vineyard, Nantucket

The Carolinas & the Georgia Coast

Chicago

Disney World & the Orlando Area

Florida

Hawaii

Las Vegas, Reno, Tahoe

Los Angeles

Maine, Vermont, New Hampshire

Maui

Miami & the Keys

New England

New Orleans

New York City

Pacific North Coast

Philadelphia & the Pennsylvania Dutch Country

San Diego

San Francisco

Santa Fe, Taos, Albuquerque

Seattle & Vancouver

The South

The U.S. & British Virgin Islands

The Upper Great Lakes Region

USA

Vacations in New York State

Vacations on the Jersey Shore

Virginia & Maryland

Waikiki

Washington, D.C.

Foreign Guides

Acapulco, Ixtapa, Zihuatanejo

Australia & New Zealand

Austria

The Bahamas

Baja & Mexico's Pacific Coast Resorts

Barbados

Berlin

Bermuda

Brazil

Budapest

Budget Europe

Canada

Cancun, Cozumel, Yucatan Penisula

Caribbean

Central America

China

Costa Rica, Belize, Guatemala

Czechoslovakia

Eastern Europe

Egypt

Euro Disney

Europe

Europe's Great Cities

France

Germany

Great Britain

Greece

The Himalayan Countries

Hong Kong

India

Ireland

Israel

Italy

Italy's Great Cities

Japan

Kenya & Tanzania

Korea

London

Madrid & Barcelona

Mexico

Montreal & Quebec City

Morocco

The Netherlands Belgium & Luxembourg

New Zealand

Norway

Nova Scotia, Prince Edward Island & New Brunswick

Paris

Portugal

Rome

Russia & the Baltic Countries

Scandinavia

Scotland

Singapore

South America

Southeast Asia

South Pacific

Spain

Sweden

Switzerland

Thailand

Tokyo

Toronto

Turkey

Vienna & the Danube Valley

Yugoslavia

Fodor's Travel Guides

Special Series

Fodor's Affordables

Affordable Europe

Affordable France

Affordable Germany

Affordable Great
Britain

Affordable Italy

**Fodor's Bed &
Breakfast and
Country Inns Guides**

California

Mid-Atlantic Region

New England

The Pacific Northwest

The South

The West Coast

The Upper Great
Lakes Region

Canada's Great
Country Inns

Cottages, B&Bs and
Country Inns of
England and Wales

The Berkeley Guides

On the Loose in
California

On the Loose in
Eastern Europe

On the Loose in
Mexico

On the Loose in the
Pacific Northwest &
Alaska

**Fodor's Exploring
Guides**

Exploring California

Exploring Florida

Exploring France

Exploring Germany

Exploring Paris

Exploring Rome

Exploring Spain

Exploring Thailand

Fodor's Flashmaps

New York

Washington, D.C.

Fodor's Pocket Guides

Pocket Bahamas

Pocket Jamaica

Pocket London

Pocket New York
City

Pocket Paris

Pocket Puerto Rico

Pocket San Francisco

Pocket Washington,
D.C.

Fodor's Sports

Cycling

Hiking

Running

Sailing

The Insider's Guide
to the Best Canadian
Skiing

**Fodor's Three-In-Ones
(guidebook, language
cassette, and phrase
book)**

France

Germany

Italy

Mexico

Spain

**Fodor's
Special-Interest
Guides**

Cruises and Ports
of Call

Disney World & the
Orlando Area

Euro Disney

Healthy Escapes

London Companion

Skiing in the USA
& Canada

Sunday in New York

**Fodor's Touring
Guides**

Touring Europe

Touring USA:
Eastern Edition

Touring USA:
Western Edition

**Fodor's Vacation
Planners**

Great American
Vacations

National Parks of the
West

**The Wall Street
Journal Guides to
Business Travel**

Europe

International Cities

Pacific Rim

USA & Canada

WHEREVER YOU TRAVEL, *H*ELP IS NEVER FAR AWAY.

From planning your trip to replacing lost Cards, American Express® Travel Service Offices* are always there to help.

9700 Collins Ave.
Bal Harbour
305-865-5959

Adventure Travels
30 SE 7th St.
Boca Raton
407-395-5722

32 Miracle Mile
Coral Gables
305-446-3381

3312-14 NE 32nd St.
Fort Lauderdale
305-565-9481

12231 S. Dixie Hwy.
Kendall
305-221-7454

Boulevard Travel
811 Peacock Plaza
Key West
305-294-3711

330 Biscayne Blvd.
Miami
305-358-7350

Travelwise
100 Westward Dr.
Miami Springs
305-999-1601

Adventure Travels
630 U.S. Highway #1
North Palm Beach
407-845-8701

Jacaranda Travel
8275 Sunrise Blvd.
Plantation
305-473-6611

Adventure Travels
2451 E. Atlantic Blvd.
Pompano Beach
305-942-2300

American Express Travel Service Offices are found in central locations throughout Florida.